P9-DBO-507

family handyman

BEST TIPS & PROJECTS

SPEEDHIDE

family handyman

BEST TIPS & PROJECTS

by The Editors of *Family Handyman* magazine

FAMILY HANDYMAN BEST TIPS & PROJECTS 2020
(See page 288 for complete staff listing.)
Editor-in-Chief: Gary Wentz
Project Editor: Mary Flanagan
Contributing Designers: Andrea Sorensen, Mariah Cates
Contributing Copy Editors: Donna Bierbach, Peggy Parker
Indexing: Lisa Himes

Vice President, Integrated Sales: John Dyckman

Trusted Media Brands, Inc.
President & Chief Executive Officer: Bonnie Kintzer

Warning: All do-it-yourself activities involve a degree of risk. Skills, materials, tools, and site conditions vary widely. Although the editors have made every effort to ensure accuracy, the reader remains responsible for the selection and use of tools, materials, and methods. Always obey local codes and laws, follow manufacturers' operating instructions, and observe safety precautions.

ISBN 978-1-62145-498-4 (dated), 978-1-62145-499-1 (undated)

Address any comments about *Family Handyman Best Tips & Projects 2020* to:
Editor, Best Tips & Projects
2915 Commers Drive, Suite 700
Eagan, MN 55121

To order additional copies of *Family Handyman Best Tips & Projects 2020,* call 1-800-344-2560.

For more Trusted Media Brands products and information, visit our Web site at tmbi.com.
For more about Family Handyman magazine, visit familyhandyman.com.

Printed in the United States of America.
1 3 5 7 9 10 8 6 4 2

SAFETY FIRST–ALWAYS!

Tackling home improvement projects and repairs can be endlessly rewarding. But as most of us know, with the rewards come risks. DIYers use chain saws, climb ladders and tear into walls that can contain big and hazardous surprises.

The good news is, armed with the right knowledge, tools and procedures, homeowners can minimize risk. As you go about your projects and repairs, stay alert for these hazards:

Aluminum wiring

Aluminum wiring, installed in about 7 million homes between 1965 and 1973, requires special techniques and materials to make safe connections. This wiring is dull gray, not the dull orange characteristic of copper. Hire a licensed electrician certified to work with it. For more information go to cpsc.gov and search for "aluminum wiring."

Spontaneous combustion

Rags saturated with oil finishes like Danish oil and linseed oil, and oil-based paints and stains can spontaneously combust if left bunched up. Always dry them outdoors, spread out loosely. When the oil has thoroughly dried, you can safely throw them in the trash.

Vision and hearing protection

Safety glasses or goggles should be worn whenever you're working on DIY projects that involve chemicals, dust and anything that could shatter or chip off and hit your eye. Sounds louder than 80 decibels (dB) are considered potentially dangerous. Sound levels from a lawn mower can be 90 dB, and shop tools and chain saws can be 90 to 100 dB.

Lead paint

If your home was built before 1979, it may contain lead paint, which is a serious health hazard, especially for children six and under. Take precautions when you scrape or remove it. Contact your public health department for detailed safety information or call (800) 424-LEAD (5323) to receive an information pamphlet. Or visit epa.gov/lead.

Buried utilities

A few days before you dig in your yard, have your underground water, gas and electrical lines marked. Just call 811 or go to call811.com.

Smoke and carbon monoxide (CO) alarms

The risk of dying in reported home structure fires is cut in half in homes with working smoke alarms. Test your smoke alarms every month, replace batteries as necessary and replace units that are more than 10 years old.

As you make your home more energy-efficient and airtight, existing ducts and chimneys can't always successfully vent combustion gases, including potentially deadly carbon monoxide (CO). Install a UL-listed CO detector, and test your CO and smoke alarms at the same time.

Five-gallon buckets and window covering cords

Anywhere from 10 to 40 children a year drown in 5-gallon buckets, according to the U.S. Consumer Products Safety Commission. Always store them upside down and store ones containing liquid with the covers securely snapped.

According to Parents for Window Blind Safety, hundreds of children in the United States are injured every year after becoming entangled in looped window treatment cords. For more information, visit pfwbs.org or cpsc.gov.

Working up high

If you have to get up on your roof to do a repair or installation, always install roof brackets and wear a roof harness.

Asbestos

Texture sprayed on ceilings before 1978, adhesives and tiles for vinyl and asphalt floors before 1980, and vermiculite insulation (with gray granules) all may contain asbestos. Other building materials, made between 1940 and 1980, could also contain asbestos. If you suspect that materials you're removing or working around contain asbestos, contact your health department or visit epa.gov/asbestos for information.

For additional information about home safety, visit mysafehomecouncil.org. This site offers helpful information about dozens of home safety issues.

Contents

1. INTERIOR PROJECTS, REPAIRS & REMODELING

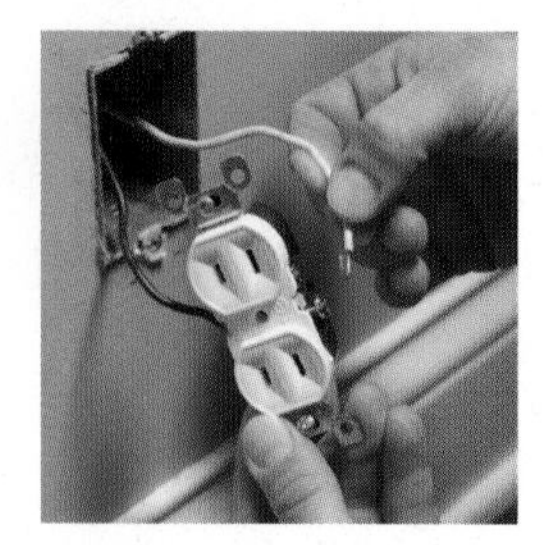

2. ELECTRICAL & HIGH-TECH

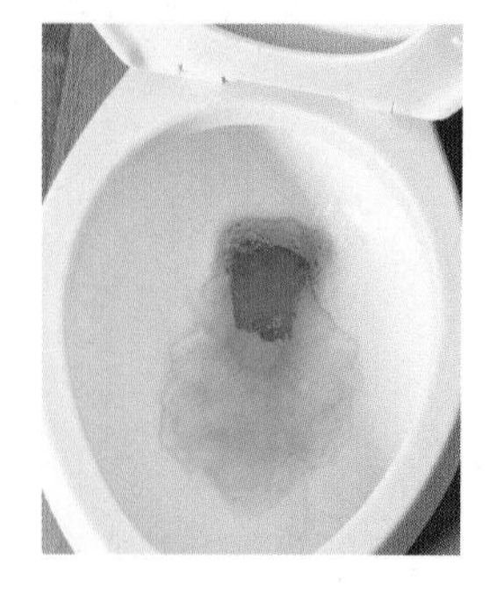

3. PLUMBING, HVAC & APPLIANCES

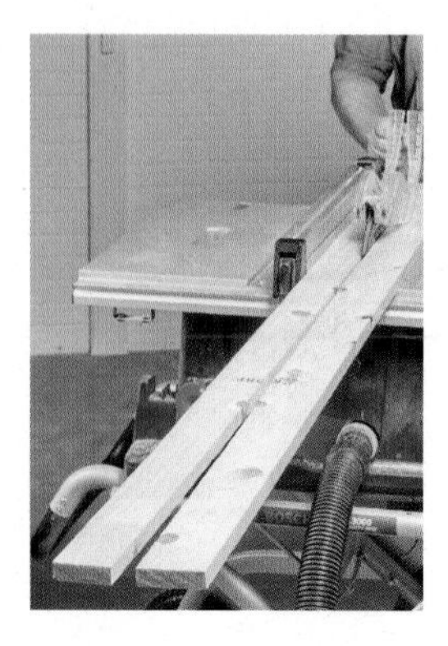

4. WOODWORKING & WORKSHOP PROJECTS & TIPS

1 Interior Projects, Repairs & Remodeling

IN THIS CHAPTER

HomeSmarts

KNOWLEDGE YOU NEED TO BE A BETTER HOMEOWNER

PEEL & STICK BACKSPLASH

Want to make a big impact on your kitchen really fast? Check out adhesive tile. To install it, pull off the backing and stick the tile into place. Misting the adhesive with soapy water gives you a little time to adjust the tile's position. Unlike with traditional tile, there's no need to glue it with mastic or thin-set and no need for grout.

These tiles are available in a wide range of designs in vinyl, ceramic, glass and metal-clad. Some of the vinyl tiles look surprisingly good; others look surprisingly bad. It's worth noting that there will be unsealed joints where the tiles meet, so the end result won't be as waterproof as a traditional tile installation.

Adhesive tile can be applied over any untextured surface. Clean all surfaces first with a degreaser such as TSP, as if you were going to paint. Allow the surface to dry completely. If you're installing the tiles on drywall, plywood, MDF or particleboard, apply primer first, allowing it to dry for 72 hours before applying the tiles. If the surface is newly painted, however, it's recommended that you allow at least 21 days for the paint to dry completely. If your wall is textured, you'll need to remove the texture.

Prices vary greatly. Vinyl is the least expensive at $8 to $10 for a pack of ten 10-in. or 12-in. square tiles. Ceramic, glass or metal clad tiles can be as much as $15 for a single 12-in. square tile. That seems expensive, but when you consider the enormous reduction in mess and labor, it might be a bargain.

CUTTING TILES IS SIMPLE

For cutting vinyl tiles, you'll only need a pair of scissors.

Cut ceramics or glass using an angle grinder with a diamond cutting wheel, or a wet saw.

Cut metal-clad tiles using an angle grinder outfitted with an abrasive wheel.

If the tile pattern allows, you'll be able to size non-vinyl tiles using only a utility knife and cutting between rows. However, you'll still need a grinder to trim the ends.

ONE-HOUR DRAWER ORGANIZER

SUPER-SIMPLE SOLUTION!

Dowels and pegboard can keep your pots and pans in order

Our kitchen drawers used to have pans crammed in however they'd fit. And it always seemed like the one we needed was at the bottom of the pile. This simple drawer organizer makes everything neat and easily accessible.

To make one, cut a piece of 1/8-in. pegboard to fit into the bottom of the drawer. Next, cut 1/2-in.-diameter dowels 6 to 8 in. long. Drill pilot holes in the dowel ends, and then attach them in rows from underneath using 1-in. screws. I used three dowels per row to accommodate any size pan.

—Sandy Hopke
Family Handyman Reader

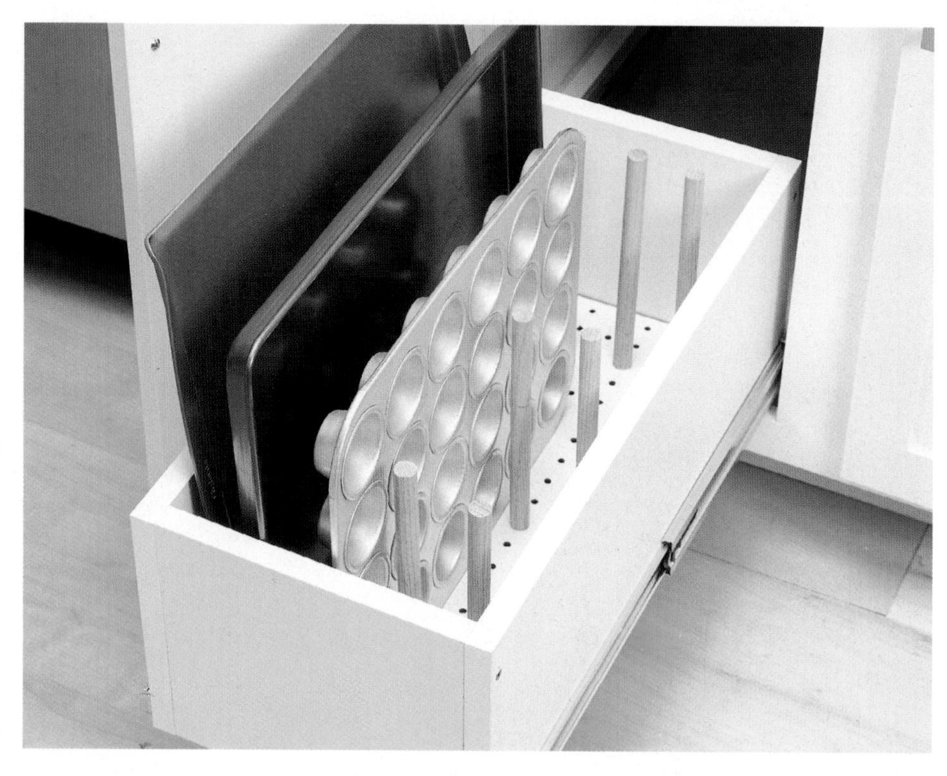

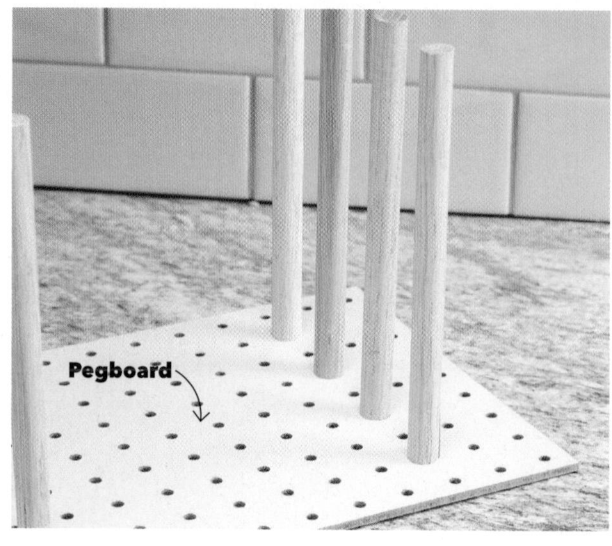

REDUCE HOME **ALLERGENS**

When pollen and mold levels are high, allergy symptoms might force you indoors. But indoor allergens are troublesome too. They can cause sneezing, a stuffy or runny nose, and itchy, watery eyes. Your best bet for beating indoor allergies is to banish the things that trigger them. For starters, vacuum regularly, preferably with a HEPA-rated vacuum cleaner so you're not blasting allergens back into the air. When you dust, use a damp cloth to help trap the allergens. Below are a few specific allergy triggers and ways to combat them.

AFRICA STUDIO/SHUTTERSTOCK

COCKROACH: PHOTOMONTAGE/SHUTTERSTOCK; POLLEN: SUE SCHWEISBERGER; DUST MITE: SEBASTIAN KAULITZKI/SHUTTERSTOCK

PET ALLERGENS

THE CAUSE: Dead skin flakes and saliva in dogs and cats, and urine in rabbits, guinea pigs, hamsters and mice. Although some animals trigger more allergic reactions than others, there is no such thing as a hypoallergenic pet.

THE FIX:

- Keep pets out of your bedroom.
- Regularly wash or replace your pet's bedding and toys.
- In extreme cases, consider replacing carpets with hard-surface floors.

MOLD & MILDEW

THE CAUSE: Dampness.

THE FIX:

- Repair roof and plumbing leaks.
- Keep damp spaces—such as kitchens, bathrooms and basements—clean and well-ventilated.
- Replace vent switches with timers to fully vent moisture during and after showers.
- Don't install carpeting on concrete or damp floors.
- Don't store items like towels, bedding or clothes in damp areas.

COCKROACHES

THE CAUSE: Saliva, feces and body parts of cockroaches, which are often found in urban areas and in the southern United States.

THE FIX:

- Block any cracks or gaps in walls and windows where cockroaches can enter.
- Repair roof and plumbing leaks to eliminate the water sources needed by cockroaches.
- Apply bug barrier products around your home's exterior perimeter.

POLLEN

THE CAUSE: Spores that make their way inside your home.

THE FIX:

- Keep doors and windows closed to prevent pollen from drifting in.
- Weatherproof around your doors and windows to seal any gaps.
- Change your air conditioner filter regularly.

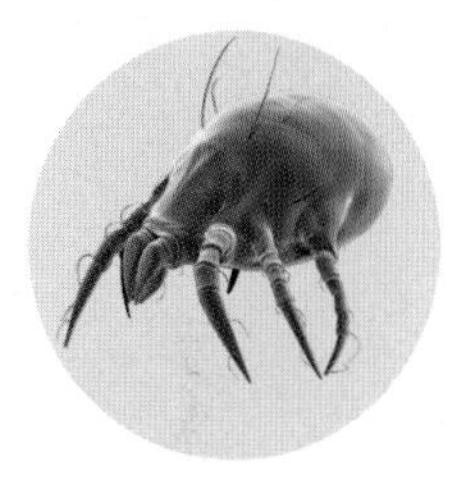

DUST MITES

THE CAUSE: Warm, humid areas such as bedding and carpeting.

THE FIX:

- Allergen-proof covers on bedding.
- Wash bedding weekly in hot water and dry with high heat.
- Consider replacing carpeting with hard-surface flooring like tile, hardwood or vinyl. If you don't want bare floors, use washable area rugs.

—Stephanie Thurrott
Contributing Editor

PERMANENT PAINT RECORD

Before you put switch or outlet covers back into place after a paint job, jot down some info. Stick on the can's color label, record the date and how much paint was needed. You may misplace your paint sample, but you'll never lose this reminder. And you won't have to wonder how much paint to buy.

MEET IN THE MIDDLE

When you have a long caulk bead to run and can't get it done in one pass, don't start again where you left off. It's hard to continue a bead without creating a glob. Instead, start at the other end and meet in the middle.

SEAL ATTIC AIR LEAKS

If you're about to add insulation to your attic and you've never heard the term "attic bypasses," you're missing the crucial part of insulating your attic. Attic bypasses are air leaks from your living space into your attic. These leaks occur where wires, air ducts or pipes go through the ceiling and into the attic. Bypasses must be sealed before adding insulation. In fact, in many states it's the law. However, in homes built before 1991, there was probably no attempt to seal bypasses. After that, there's a good chance some of the larger bypasses were sealed, but likely not all of them.

If the leaks aren't sealed, warm air is getting into your cold attic no matter how much insulation you add. But you're not just losing heat and increasing energy bills. You're also potentially causing frost and condensation in your attic, as well as ice dams, all of which lead to water/moisture damage, mold and rot. If you eliminate all attic bypasses, you'll probably eliminate most of those problems. But if you add insulation before sealing attic bypasses, you could make the frost problem worse. So, before you add insulation, seal all leaks with caulk or expanding foam. If you're hiring an insulation contractor, make sure this step is included in the work. For more information, go to familyhandyman.com and search for "how to seal attic air leaks."

CABINET DIVIDERS

Adjustable slots organize cookware for space-efficient storage

By Spike Carlsen

Cookie sheets, cutting boards, cooling racks, serving trays, pizza peels... Most of us have a disorderly pile of large, flat cookware—and the thing we need is always at the bottom of the stack. This simple system of dividers brings order to the chaos. It requires minimal skills and materials and goes together fast, which allows you to spend more time cooking and less time searching and sorting.

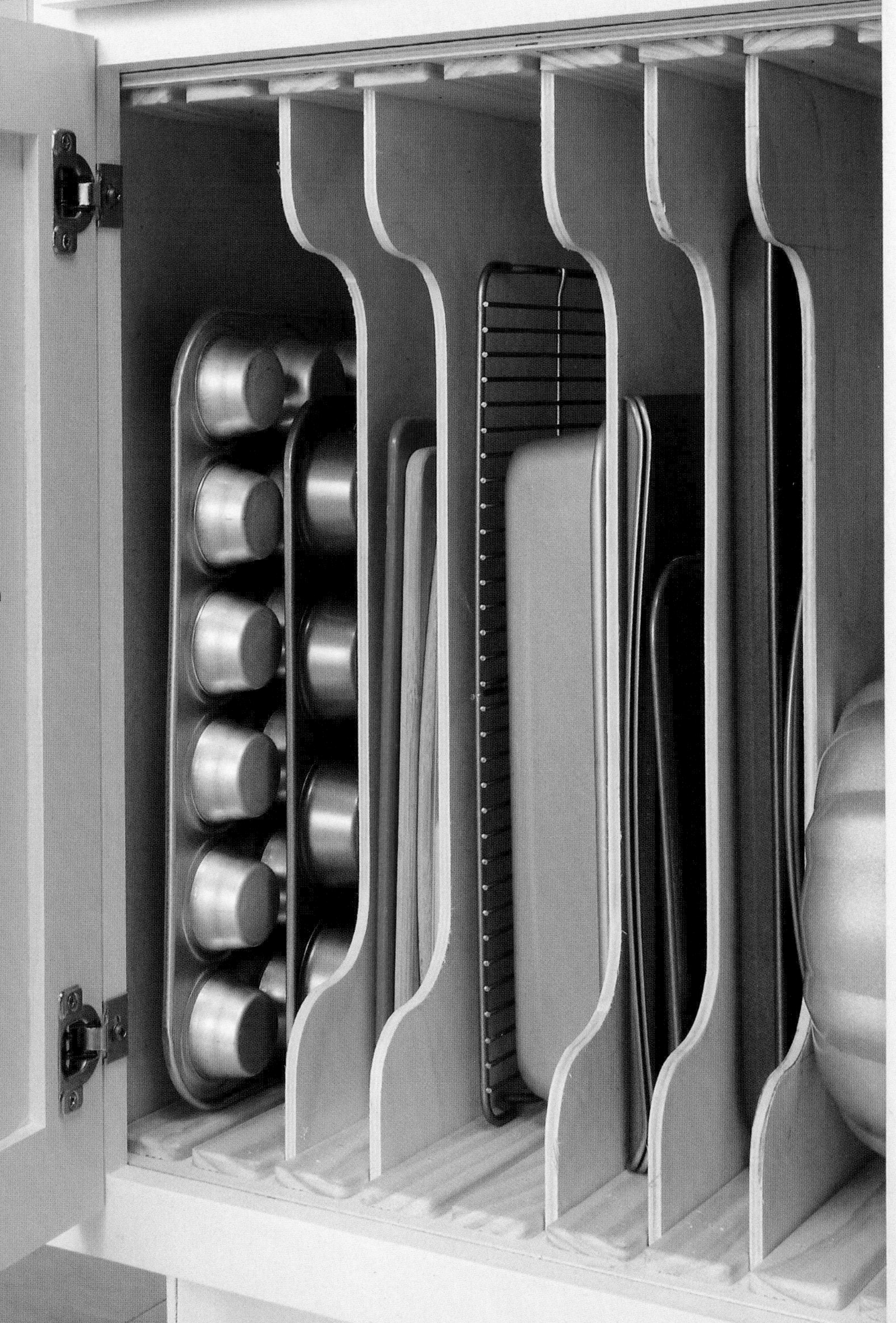

Figure A
Cabinet Dividers

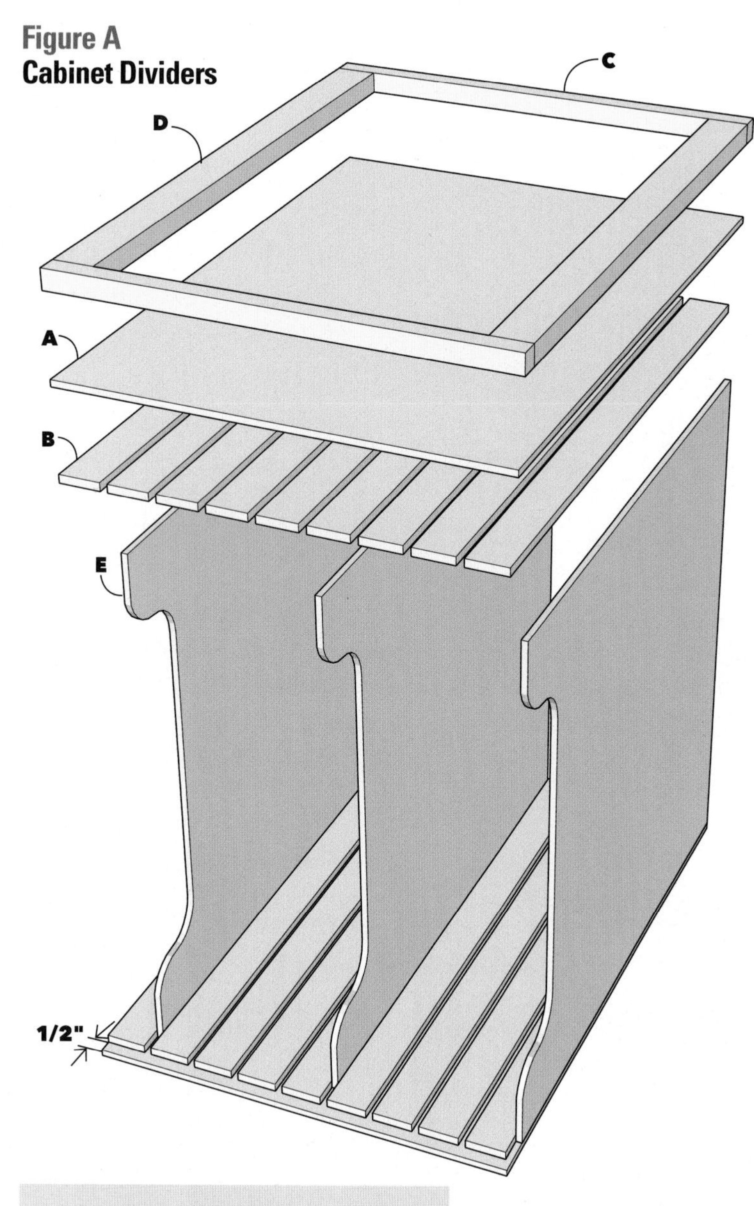

MATERIALS LIST

ITEM	QTY.
1/4" x 4' x 8' AC or better plywood	1
3/4" x 3/4" x 4' pine	1
3/4" x 1-1/2" x 4' pine	1
3/8" x 1-1/2" x 8' mull strip, available in the trim aisle at home centers	Varies

CUTTING LIST

ITEM	QTY.	MATERIAL	PART
A	2	1/4" plywood*	Top/bottom panel
B	10–20**	3/8" x 1-1/2"	Slats (mull strip)*
C	2	3/4" x 3/4" pine*	Frame front/back
D	2	3/4" x 1-1/2" pine*	Frame sides
E	4–6**	1/4" plywood*	Divider panels

Notes:

* Dimensions determined by cabinet width and length

** Quantity determined by cabinet width

WHAT IT TAKES
TIME: 2 to 4 hours
COST: $40
SKILL: Beginner
TOOLS: Circular saw or table saw, drill, brad nailer (or hammer and nails), basic hand tools

How to build it

Measure the width and depth of your cabinet (**Photo 1**), then cut two 1/4-in. plywood panels (A) to fit. If you have a double-wide cabinet (like ours), cut the plywood so it extends at least halfway beyond the vertical center stile. **Tip**: If you have a double cabinet, you can cut the plywood extra wide, install the divider strips, then cut the plywood to final width so you wind up with full-width divider strips on both ends.

Cut the slats (B) 1/2 in. shorter than the plywood and use a sander or sandpaper to lightly round the ends. Glue and nail the divider slats into place (**Photo 2**), using a scrap piece of 1/4-in. plywood and an old credit card as spacers; this extra wiggle room will allow you to slide the divider panels in and out more easily. To prevent brad nails from poking through the plywood, adjust the depth setting of your nailer and drive brads at a slight angle.

Build the top frame (C and D) the exact size of your plywood panels (**Photo 3**) and predrill the mounting holes on each end. Install this frame with the bottom edge even with the top of the cabinet opening (**Photo 4**). Screw the front in place first. Before screwing the back, make sure it's at exactly the same height as the front.

Attach the panels (A) to the bottom of the cabinet (**Photo 5**) and to the upper frame. Measure between the panels to determine the height of the dividers (E). Cut one divider panel to size (**Photo 6**) then "test slide" it through several of the openings. If all the openings are equal, use your first divider panel as a template for cutting out the remaining ones (**Photo 6**). We created a 2-in. indent on the end of the divider panels to allow easier access to the trays and other items stored between them.

1 Measure inside. Measure the width and depth inside the cabinet. Subtract 1/8 in. from those measurements and cut the top and bottom panels to that size.

2 Tack the slats to the panels. Fasten the slats with glue and 1/2-in. brads. Space the slats with a scrap of 1/4-in. plywood and a credit card.

3 Assemble the top frame. Build a frame the exact dimensions of the top/bottom panels. This frame provides a mounting surface for the top panel.

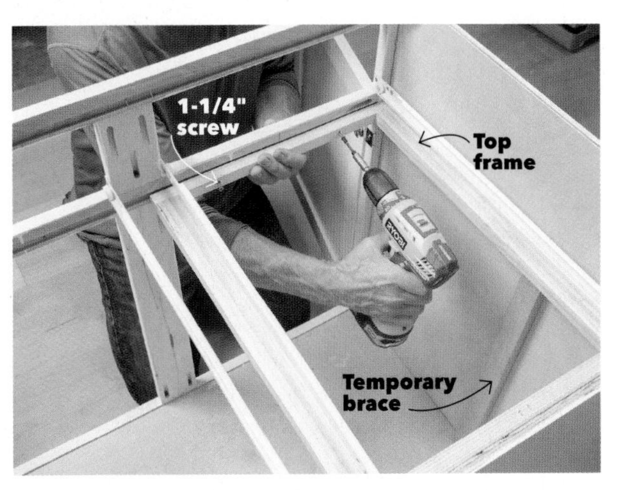

4 Install the top frame. Screw the frame to the cabinet, making the bottom edge flush with the top of the cabinet opening. Have the frame propped up with a couple braces cut from scrap wood while you work.

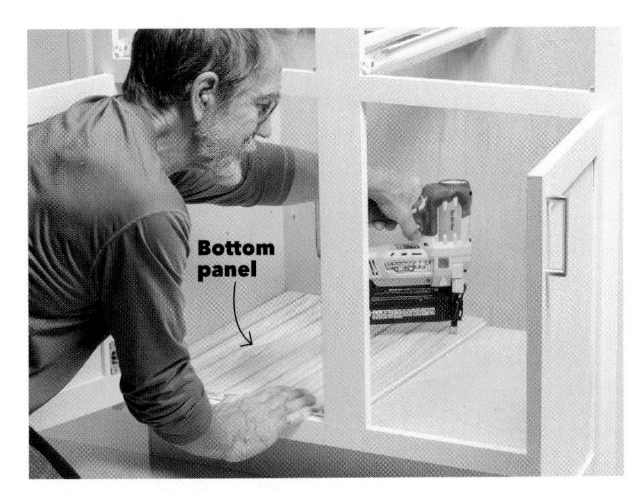

5 Install the top and bottom panels. Secure the panels to the cabinet bottom and to the upper frame using nails or screws.

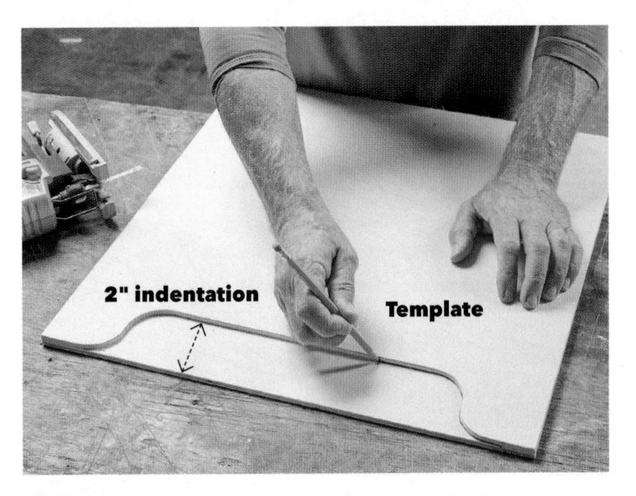

6 Measure, cut and install the divider panels. Cut one panel to size, then test-fit it in several of the openings. Use that panel as a template for making the remaining divider panels.

NEW LIFE FOR **OLD COUNTERTOPS**

The look of marble at a fraction of the cost

By Mike Berner

When I was imagining new countertops for this kitchen, it was clear to me that nothing would look as good as marble. But marble is soft and porous, making it prone to scratches, stains and chipping. It's also expensive. Then I came across this epoxy coating that you pour right over the existing countertops. I was blown away by how easy it was to mimic the look of a marble slab—at a tenth of the cost.

Everyone is amazed by the transformation. You'd have to look closely to see my mistakes that give it away: a pair of drips down one edge and a slight orange peel texture in the corner from overworking the topcoat. The countertops are tough, too; we dragged heavy pots and pans across them without damage.

If your countertops are in need of a refresh, consider covering them with epoxy for a stunning new look.

MEET THE BUILDER

Mike Berner is a carpenter and an associate editor at *Family Handyman*.

WHAT IT TAKES

TIME: 3 days

COST: $600

SKILL: Intermediate

TOOLS: Oscillating tool, 6-in. paint roller, brushes, drill, trim router, orbital sander

SUPPLIES: Four 1-qt. cups, two 2-gallon buckets, two 6-in. 3/8-in.-nap roller sleeves, wiping cloths, 80- and 220-grit sanding sponge, isopropyl alcohol, spray bottle, two paddle mixers, plastic sheet, painter's tape

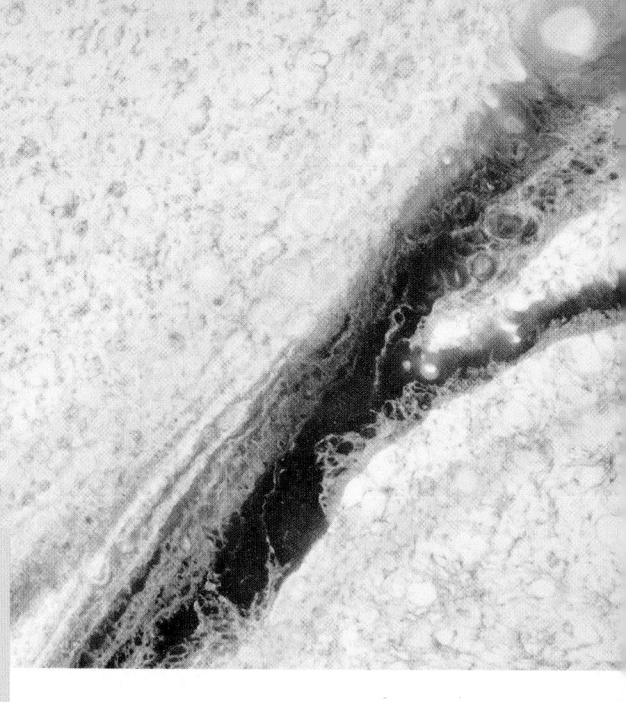

COUNTERTOP COATING KITS

If you want to coat your countertops, you have several options. Kits cost anywhere from $90 to $600 or more. We used Rust-Oleum Countertop Transformations to create the black countertop shown above. You sprinkle decorative chips in the coating to get the look of granite. To see that project, search for "renew kitchen countertops" at familyhandyman.com. Other kits, like the one we used for this marble look, require a bit more artistry to mimic the beautiful veins of natural stone. At $550, it was more expensive than others we tried, but the results were stunning. It's available from Leggari Products (leggari.com).

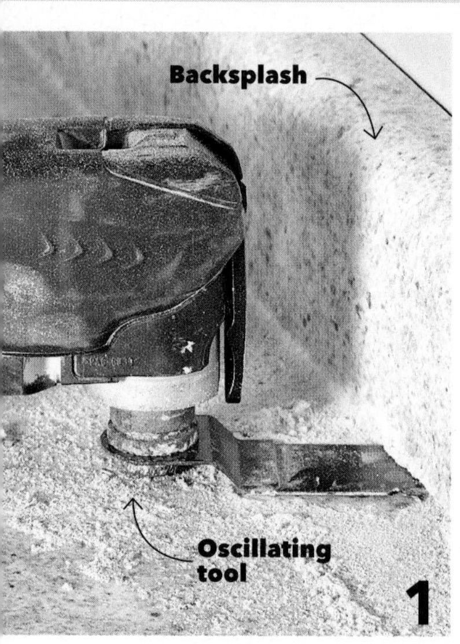

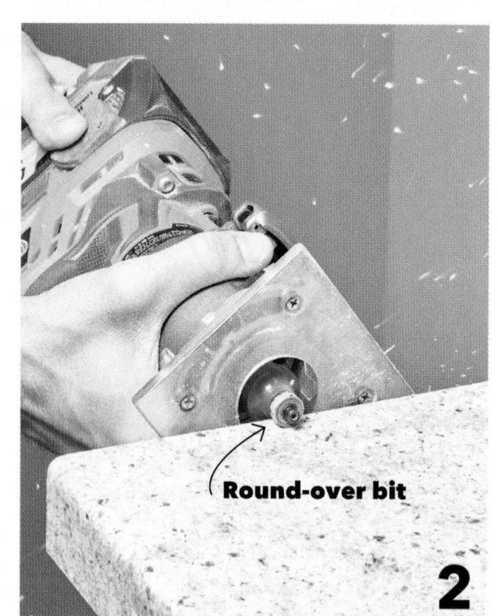

1 Cut off the backsplash. Cutting off the backsplash isn't necessary and adds extra work. But I really wanted the look of a genuine marble slab. With an oscillating tool and a carbide blade, I cut into the backsplash, flush with the rest of the counter. Once the backsplash was off, I had to glue a piece of wood between the counter and the wall to fill the gap. Then I sanded it all flat. You'll also have to remove your sink before applying the epoxy.

2 Rout the corners. An old carpenter once warned me that applying finish to sharp corners won't work; it won't work with epoxy either. Epoxy needs a rounded edge in order to bond well to the corner and to flow over it. On the ends, use a 1/8-in. round-over bit with the router positioned horizontally so the bit can follow the shape of the front edge. If the front edge isn't rounded over, use a 1/4-in. or 3/8-in. round-over bit.

3 Patch seams. Fill any gaps and seams with all-purpose body filler. This includes seams at miters, inside corners at the front edge and the gap between the counter and the backsplash. Fill and smooth out particleboard that's exposed after routing or cutting. Body filler is a two-part system that will harden in a few minutes once it's mixed together, so work in small sections and move quickly.

4 Sand it smooth. Once everything was patched, I found it easy to get rid of high spots in the body filler using a paint scraper. Then sand the top, front edge and rounded corners with 60-grit sandpaper. Scuffing up the surface helps the epoxy bond with the old top.

5 Mask everything. The epoxy is really messy. Tape plastic to the floor beneath the counters. Then drape plastic over the cabinets, tape it underneath the front edge of the counter, tuck it into the toe-kick and tape it to the plastic on the floor. For the sink opening, tape plastic to the underside of the counter to catch the epoxy. Mask off the walls, leaving about a 1/8-in. gap above the counter. Finally, I put cardboard under the counters to collect drips.

6 Prepare your materials. Once you start applying the primer coat to the counters, you're on the clock. If you have to stop to find something or run to the store, you'll be in trouble. So get organized and set everything you need from this point on within arm's reach.

7 Apply primer. The primer creates a perfect surface for the epoxy to stick to. Mix the two-part primer in a small bucket, cut into the corners with a brush and roll it on the countertops. If you notice the old counter color showing through, roll on more primer while it's still wet.

8 Premix the highlights. The primer needs about an hour to become tacky. While you wait, mix the metallic powder into part A of the highlight epoxy. Don't mix part A with part B until you're ready; it will set up in as little as 15 minutes in a bucket. You'll also want to mix metallic powder with isopropyl alcohol in a spray bottle to use later on.

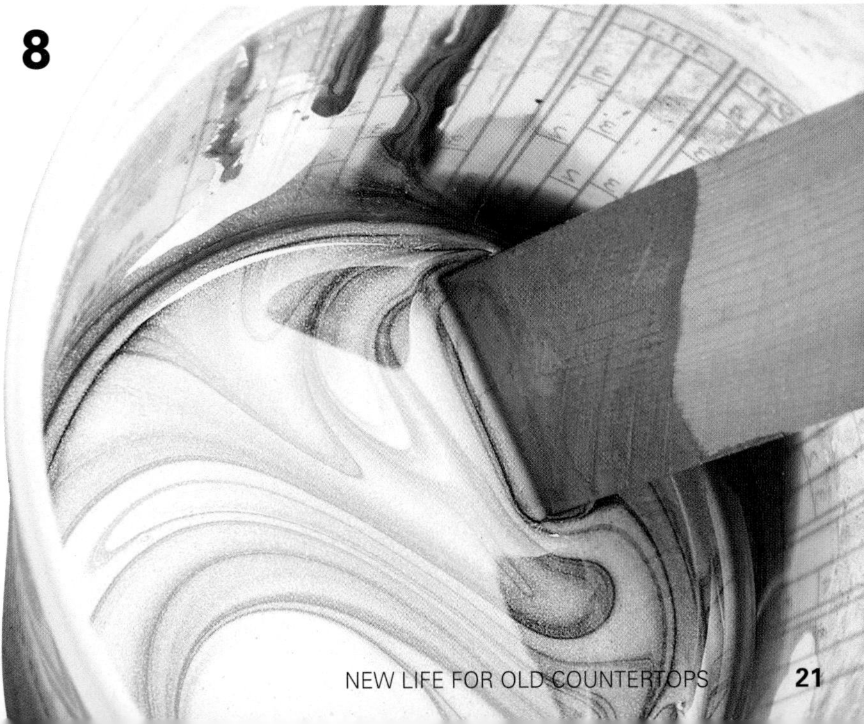

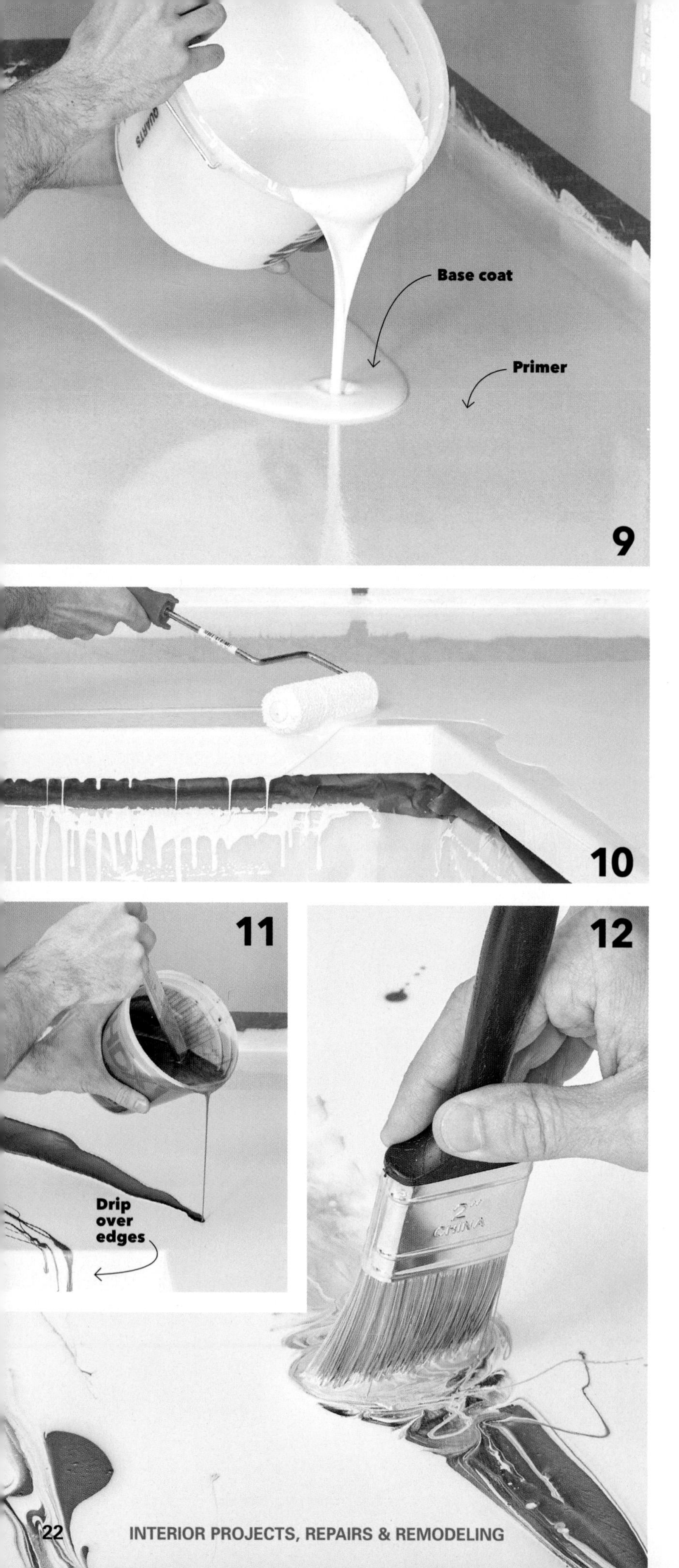

9 Pour the base coat. After about an hour, once the primer is tacky but won't leave residue when it's touched with a glove, you can mix your base coat of epoxy. The trick to getting the epoxy completely mixed and avoiding soft spots is to use two buckets. Pour the two parts into one bucket, stir with the mixing paddle for a minute or two, then pour the mixed epoxy into a new bucket and mix for another minute or two.

Pour enough down the center of the countertop to cover the entire surface, then spread it around with a roller. Keep the epoxy puddle on top of the counter at this point, but get it into the corners and near the edges. The goal is to create an even layer about 1/8 in. thick across the entire counter.

10 Roll the edges. Pour a thin line of leftover epoxy along the edges of the counter. With the roller sleeve still saturated, roll the front edge of the counter, then lightly push the thin line of epoxy over the edge. Check that the base coat is an even thickness throughout the top; if it's not, move it around or pour more epoxy. Once the base coat is on, it's time to mix the highlights, completely, just as you did with the base coat.

11 Add highlights. Drizzling the highlights is fun, but don't go overboard. You can always add more; you can't take them away. After mixing the highlights, use a combination of pouring from the mixing cup and dripping from a stir stick to create veins in the counter.

12 Drag over the highlights. Feather the highlights into the base coat by dragging a brush lightly across the top. Follow the highlights and dab the brush to give them a natural look. If you overwork the epoxy, the highlights will blend into the base coat instead of jumping out. By waiting for the epoxy to set up slightly, I found I could feather without blending. It takes about an hour for the epoxy to set up, so you can take your time on this step.

13 Spray on alcohol. Spritz the counter with the isopropyl alcohol and metallic powder solution. It works like magic: The solution disperses the epoxy

13

and gives a much more natural look. I did a few rounds of this and also made sure to spray the front edges. You can always rework the epoxy and spray again.

14 Scrape off drips. You'll need to babysit the counters for a while after you think you're done. Look for divots starting to form and fill them with a few drops of leftover epoxy. As drips form underneath the front edge, scrape them off with a stir stick. Look for dust nibs or bugs that have fallen into the coating and pick them out with a toothpick or tweezers. After about an hour of setting up, peel away the masking along the backsplash and wait a day for the epoxy to set.

15 Smooth the top. The next day you'll prepare the counter for the protective topcoat; ideally this will be about 20 hours after the pour so the topcoat will form a chemical bond with the not-yet-cured epoxy. Walk around the counters and sand out any dust nibs you find with 220-grit sandpaper. Check the bottom edge for drips and sand them out with 80-grit paper. Dust the tops and wipe them down with denatured alcohol.

16 Protect your counters. Mix the two-part topcoat in a container and apply a thick coat to the surface. Spread the topcoat on quickly and then lightly reroll the entire surface in one direction. Start along the backsplash and pull the roller to the front edge, working your way around the counter. It will take at least a week for the counters to fully cure, but once they do, they'll withstand the dents and scratches from normal kitchen use.

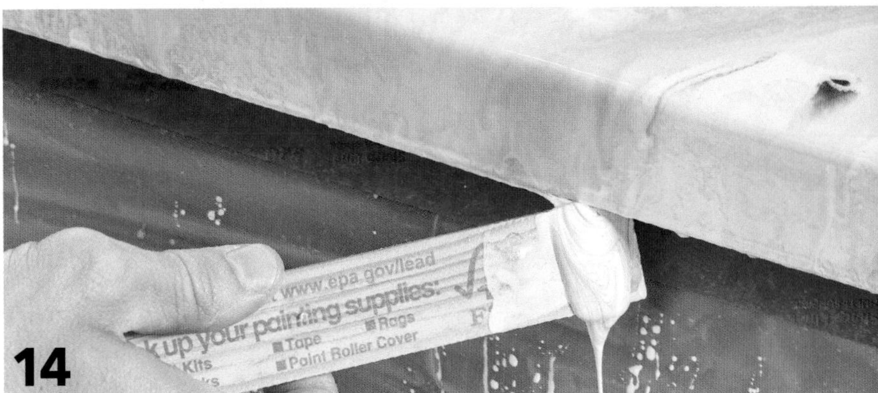

14

15

16

BUY BETTER TRIM PAINT

A quest to find the best

By Mike Berner

I installed new trim when I replaced all the doors and windows in my house a few years ago. Unfortunately, I didn't get around to painting it. I recently decided it was time to finish the job, and the first step was to determine the paint that would perform best regardless of brand, sheen or color.

To research the options—for *Family Handyman* and myself—I picked up 12 trim paints to try. After running tests and conferring with pro painters and industry experts, I singled out a few top performers.

6 FACTORS THAT MATTER

■ Cost

One thing I learned from the experts was that quality paint starts with expensive raw materials. That means cost is a pretty good predictor of the results you'll get. Using inexpensive paint could save a few bucks on the front end but cost you down the road. The paints I tested ranged in price from $35 to $90 per gallon.

■ Odor

I steered clear of any oil-based paints because of their smell, but some of the new acrylic-alkyd formulas still use solvent. These are a lot less stinky than pure oil-based paints, but some may bother sensitive noses.

■ Cleanup

With two kids under 2 running and crawling around, I don't want to mess with any solvent cleanup, and with so many great water-cleanup options, I don't think you should either.

■ Smoothness

Smoothness is king when it comes to a trim paint job. I've worked hard to make my trim look great, and I don't want to ruin it with brush marks, drips or roller ridges. A good trim paint should flatten out and become smooth as it cures. Not all the paints I tested did this well.

■ Toughness

My trim takes some abuse from my kids. It's no fun sanding and repainting when it gets dinged up. I tested the toughness of the finish by dragging a piece of 80-grit sandpaper weighted with 1-lb. boxes of screws across it. The toughest paints took the punishment with only light scuffing.

■ Workability

A good trim paint can be applied in tight areas like corners and curved profiles and smoothed out before it starts to dry. I painted an intricate profile at a mitered corner to figure out which paints were more workable.

5 THAT STOOD OUT FOR ME

Sherwin-Williams Emerald Urethane Trim Enamel ($93).
This represents a new category of paint, and it reminds me of a pigmented, water-based polyurethane—even the way it smells. This stuff produced the toughest coating of all the paints I tested. I dragged five 1-lb. boxes of screws on a piece of 80-grit sandpaper over the painted surface, and the paper just glided right along.

Emerald enamel brushes on well, has a long enough open time to work into the corners, and levels out nicely. It had less sheen than other paints; the semigloss I tested was more like a satin. If you want a super-hard finish and have $90 to spend on a gallon, this is right up your alley. It would be my choice if cost didn't matter.

PPG Break-Through! ($70).
This is one of the non-hybrid paints I tested. It's a low-VOC (volatile organic compound) formula with a strong ammonia odor, but it leveled out better than anything else on the list. According to the manufacturer, it's used to coat warehouse floors. If it can stand up to forklifts, it ought to be able to take on my son's Matchbox cars. It dries in 15 to 20 minutes, so you need to lay and smooth the paint quickly. It won't fill in dings or scratches, even small ones, so sand well before painting.

Behr Alkyd ($35).
This acrylic-alkyd hybrid may not be as tough as other hybrid trim paints, but it's still pretty tough and because it's a great value, I included it in my list of standouts. It's thicker than other hybrids and brushes on really well. It also has great leveling characteristics and could get into the tough-to-reach areas in the mitered corners of my trim-painting test.

Sherwin-Williams SnapDry ($77).
This acrylic latex ultra-fast-drying paint has great resistance to "blocking." That's the tendency of two painted surfaces to stick together, such as a door and its jamb. SnapDry's fast drying time worried me, but with some urgency, I was able to apply the paint and spread it before it became tacky. It leveled out fairly well and was one of the tougher paints I tested. It's harder to work with than others, but the super-fast drying time enables you to close your freshly painted door.

Benjamin Moore Advance ($57).
With a longer drying time, this acrylic-alkyd hybrid was the most workable of all the paints I tested, and it was also the runner-up in my toughness test. The downside is that you have to wait at least 16 hours between coats, compared with four to six hours for the other options. It also takes about 30 days to cure, so be careful reassembling parts or using the things you paint.

Tip: Always ask specialty paint stores about possible discounts. My experience tells me they're often running some sort of unadvertised sale or may have the freedom to give discounts.

The two most common options for trim paint

Acrylic Latex ($15 to $70). Most of the cans you see as you walk through the paint aisle will be labeled "acrylic." These vary drastically in both price and performance. Some gallons cost as little as $15, but I steered clear of them. Paints made of 100 percent acrylic are more expensive but will cure harder and are less porous, making them durable and easy to clean. Acrylic latex paint can be a great choice for interior trim, but it won't match the toughness of an oil-based paint.

Acrylic-Alkyd Hybrid($35 to $90). Acrylic-alkyd hybrid paints have been available to contractors for a while but are still fairly unknown to most homeowners. These paints have all the good qualities of an oil-based paint (leveling, hardness, flow and open time) while still providing easy soap-and-water cleanup and resistance to yellowing over time. Most brands have a version of these paints now, and they're definitely worth checking out.

MY CHOICE

Ultimately, I decided to go with Benjamin Moore's Advance. I've worked so hard to make my trim look nice, and I want the paint to look like it's been sprayed on. The base trim also has to stand up to vacuum cleaners, play sets and toy trucks. Advance was a good balance of price and performance, and it hung with the top performers in my tests. I am making a sacrifice in recoat and cure times—I need to figure out how to add an extra day to the weekend.

MEET THE EXPERT

Mike Berner, an associate editor at *Family Handyman*, is also a painting-expert-in-progress.

POT & PAN **PULLOUT**

A solution to stooping, searching and stacking

By Spike Carlsen

The only time our pots and pans were truly organized was when they were new in the box—since then, it's been "every pan for itself." Pots and pans are difficult to organize; if you stack them up, it's a hassle getting to the bottom ones. If you spread them out, they take up tons of valuable cabinet space.

This pot and pan pullout makes your pans easy to access and organize and—depending on your cookware—may even give you a place to stash your lids. It only takes a couple of hours, a couple of boards and a couple of drawer slides.

Note: This accessory is designed to support everyday pots and pans, not extremely heavy objects or kids doing pull-ups.

WHAT IT TAKES

TIME: 2 to 3 hours
COST: $25
SKILL: Beginner
TOOLS: Drill, jigsaw, router (optional), basic hand tools

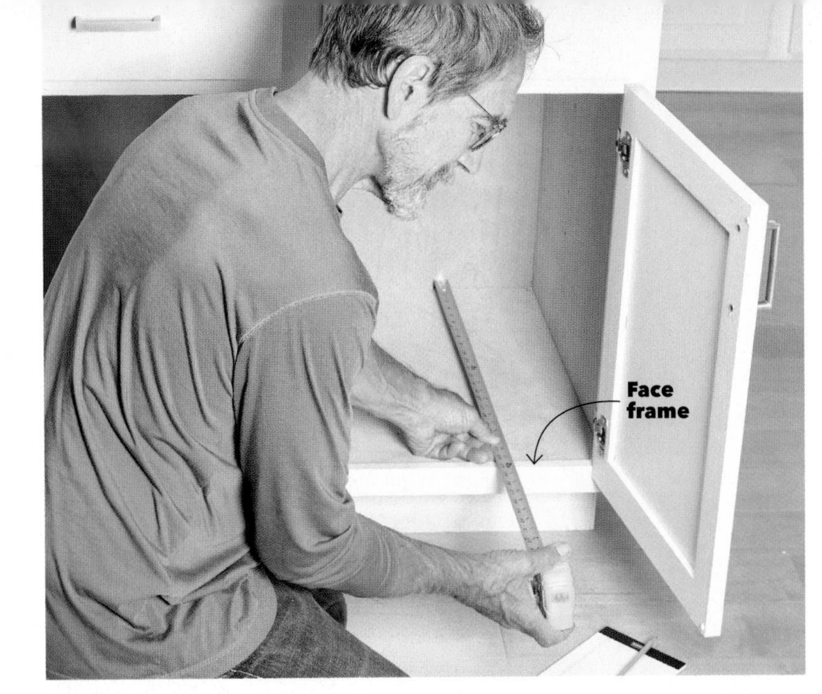

1 Measure the cabinet. Measure the depth of the cabinet from the back to the inside of the face frame. This measurement determines the overall length of the H-frame.

2 Build the H-frame. Screw the cross arms to the support slat. Predrill holes and countersink screw heads to prevent splitting.

3 Mount the drawer slides. Screw the slides into place with the back ends even with the back of the H–frame.

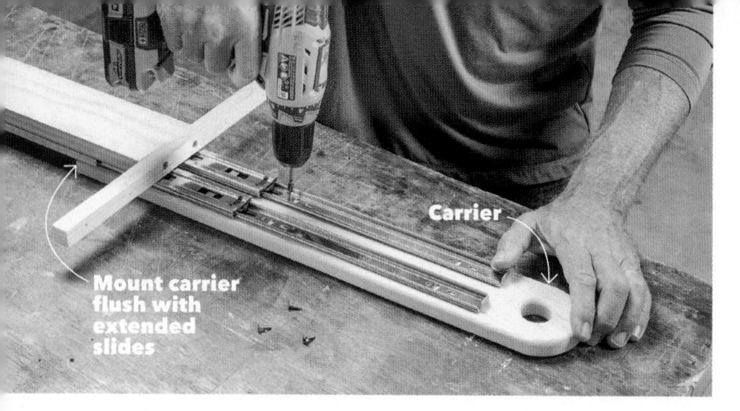

4 Screw the slides to the carrier. Cut the carrier to length, round the end and bore a finger hole, and then soften the edges with sandpaper or a router. Align the carrier with the back end of the slides.

5 Add the hooks. Secure the hooks to the carrier. Fiddle around with your pots and pans beforehand to determine the most efficient spacing.

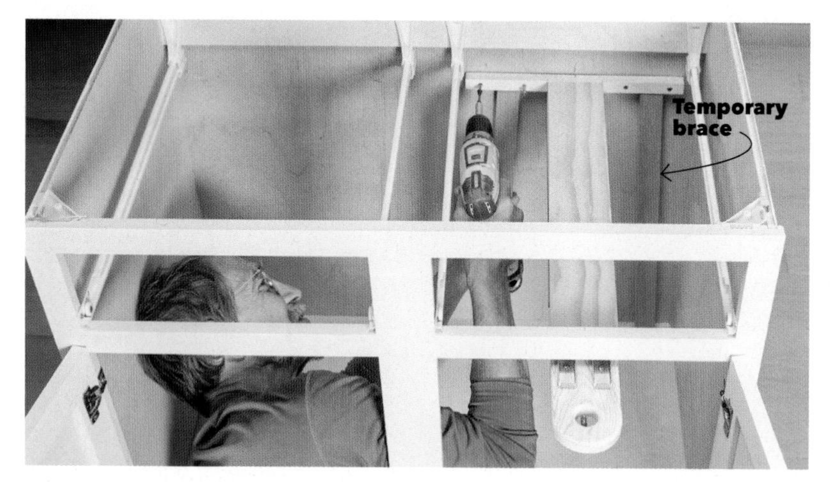

6 Install it! Position the bottom of the cross arm even with the top of the cabinet opening and attach it with screws. Then secure the back end at the same elevation, using temporary braces to prop it up.

How to build it

Empty your cabinet and measure the depth of the cabinet (**Photo 1**). Build the H-shape frame (**Photo 2**). The frame needs to be the same length as the inside depth of the cabinet, in our case 23 in. We cut our 1x4 support slat 21-1/2 in. long (two 3/4-in.-thick arms plus the 21-1/2-in. slat equals 23 in.). Predrill screw holes in the cross arms and bore countersink holes to accommodate the heads.

Screw on the two slides (**Photo 3**). Cut the carrier the same length as the depth of your cabinet. Flip the assembly over and attach the carrier as shown in **Photo 4**.

Install the hooks (**Photo 5**); we used beefy "clothesline hooks." You may want to use shorter or skinnier hooks and space them differently, depending on the sizes of your pans.

Attach the H-frame in the center of the cabinet opening (**Photo 6**). Load up your pots and pans; you may want to readjust the spacing of your hooks based on how the pans fit. Then get cooking.

Figure A
Pot and Pan Pullout

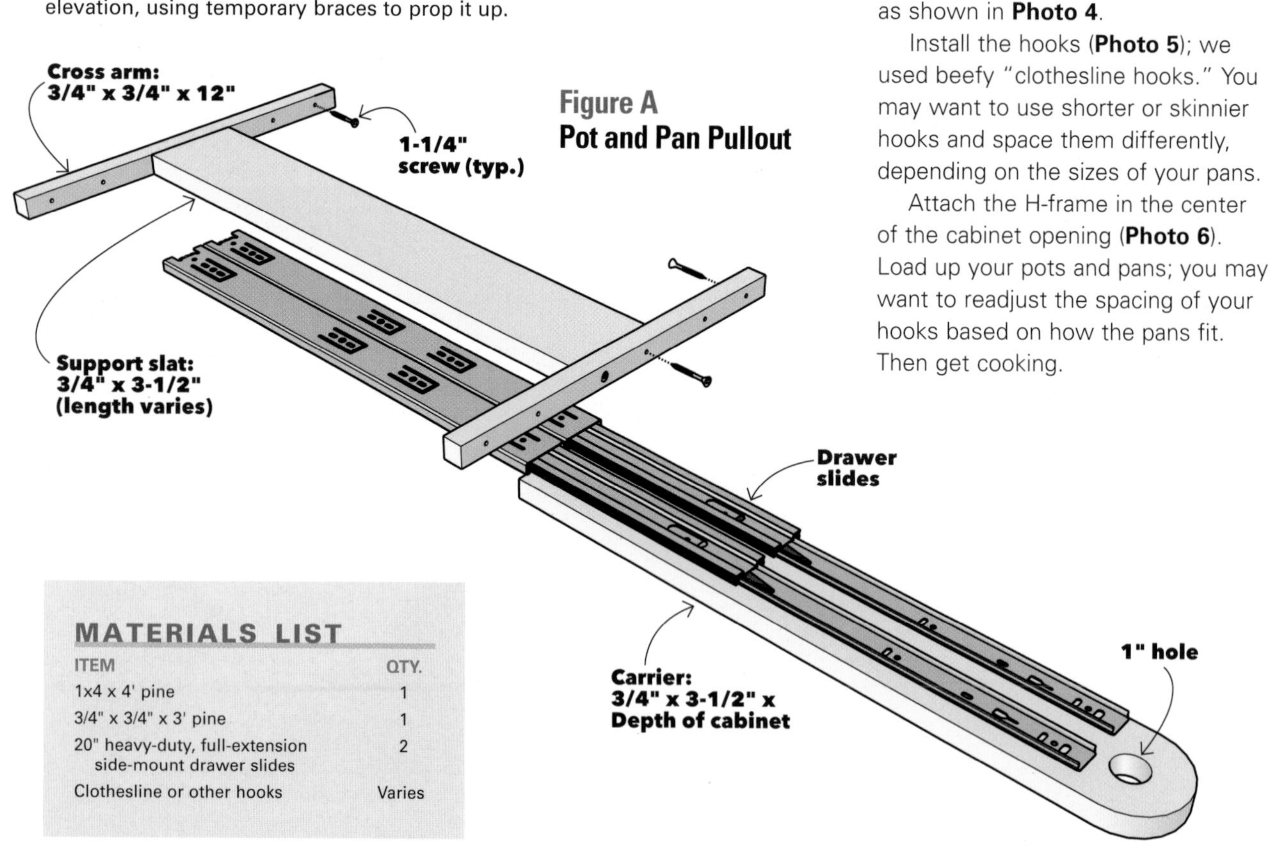

MATERIALS LIST

ITEM	QTY.
1x4 x 4' pine	1
3/4" x 3/4" x 3' pine	1
20" heavy-duty, full-extension side-mount drawer slides	2
Clothesline or other hooks	Varies

INSTANT KNIFE RACK

1-HOUR PROJECT

An easy-access organizer made from one board

By Travis Larson

This clever knife rack can be sized to suit any cabinet door and any cutlery set. And aside from waiting for glue and the finish to dry, it takes less than an hour to complete. The following pages detail the process. Here are pointers to help you along:

- Cutting the slots (**Photo 1**) requires you to remove the blade guard. Be careful!
- Our knife rack is finished with a couple of light coats of aerosol spray lacquer, but you can choose any finish you like.
- Wood shrinks and swells with changes in humidity. To allow for that movement, make sure the screw holes in the knife rack (**Photo 6**) are slightly larger than the screw diameter. When you drive the screws, make them snug but not super tight.
- If you mount this rack on a lower cabinet door and have toddlers around, you'll also need a childproof latch. There are several options costing about $3 at home centers and online.

WHAT IT TAKES
TIME: 1 hour
COST: Under $10
SKILL: Beginner
TOOLS: Table saw, two bar clamps, drill/driver
MATERIALS: A 6-ft. 1x3 board, glue, finish, 1-1/4-in. screws, finish washers

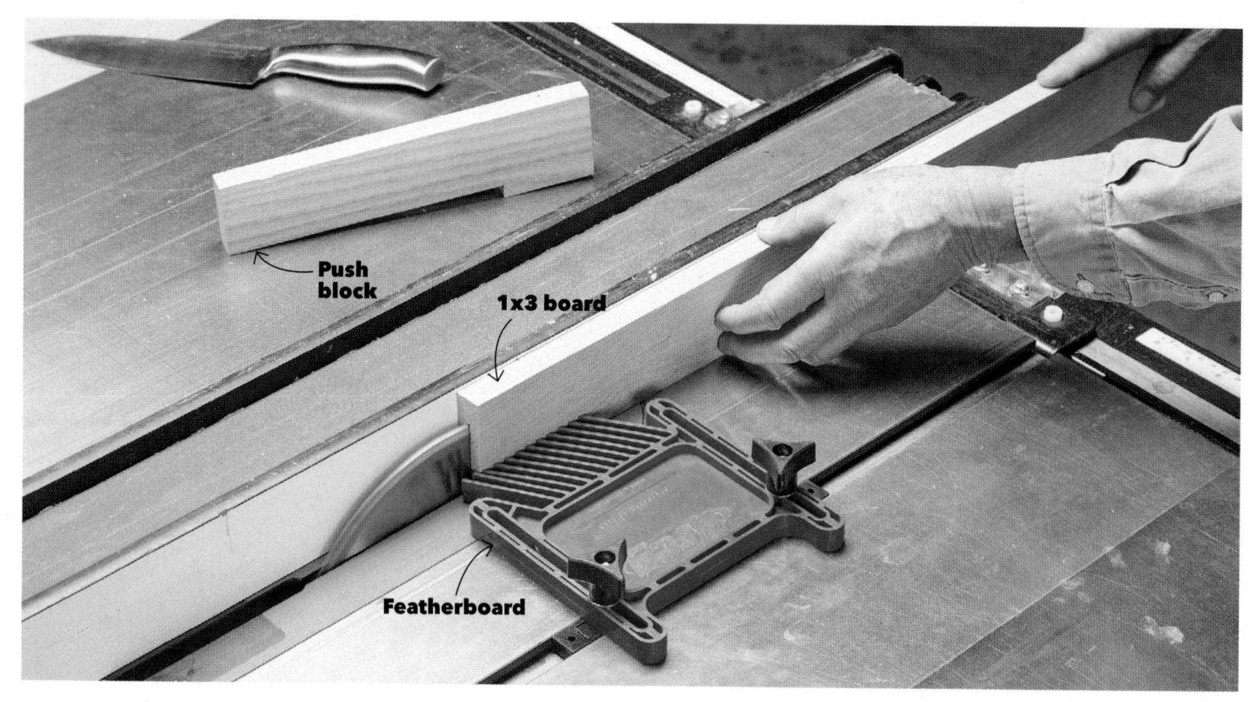

1 Cut the knife slots. Set your saw blade to cut 1 in. deep. Center the blade in the board and make a pass. Flip the board end for end and make another pass to center the slot. Raise the blade to 2 in. and repeat. Be sure to use a featherboard and push block for safety. Cut the board into six 10-in. lengths for a 16-in.-wide door.

2 Mark the end board. Remove the door from the cabinet so you can work flat. Space one edge of the assembly 3/4 in. from the door edge and mark the rip cut on the other side with another 3/4-in. block. (This allows clearance for the door to close.) Rip the end board to width.

3 Glue the slot edges. Apply a bead of glue to the edge on each side of the slots. Don't use too much or the excess will squeeze out into the slots.

Note: Start your glue-up ASAP after cutting the slots. If you wait too long, the thin sections of the wood may begin to warp.

4 Clamp it up. Flip the end board you ripped so that the last two boards are slot to slot. Clamp the boards for at least 30 minutes. Scrape away the glue squeeze-out with a chisel after it's jelled but before it's hardened.

5 Trim the edges. Attach a fence to the miter gauge and trim the edges square. Sand the surface flat and smooth. Open-grain woods like this oak only need to be sanded to 100-grit. Finish to suit your tastes.

6 Mount the knife rack. Predrill 1/8-in. holes through the rack and the door frame. (Be careful not to drill through the door front!) Add 1-1/4-in. No. 18-8 screws with finish washers and rehang the door.

ROOF VENTING BASICS

What every homeowner needs to know

By Gary Wentz

If you've never given roof ventilation a moment's thought, you're not alone. Even builders didn't think about it much until the 1950s. But eliminating warm, moist air from the attic is critical to the health of your house. A basic understanding of roof venting can help you solve big problems—or avoid them altogether.

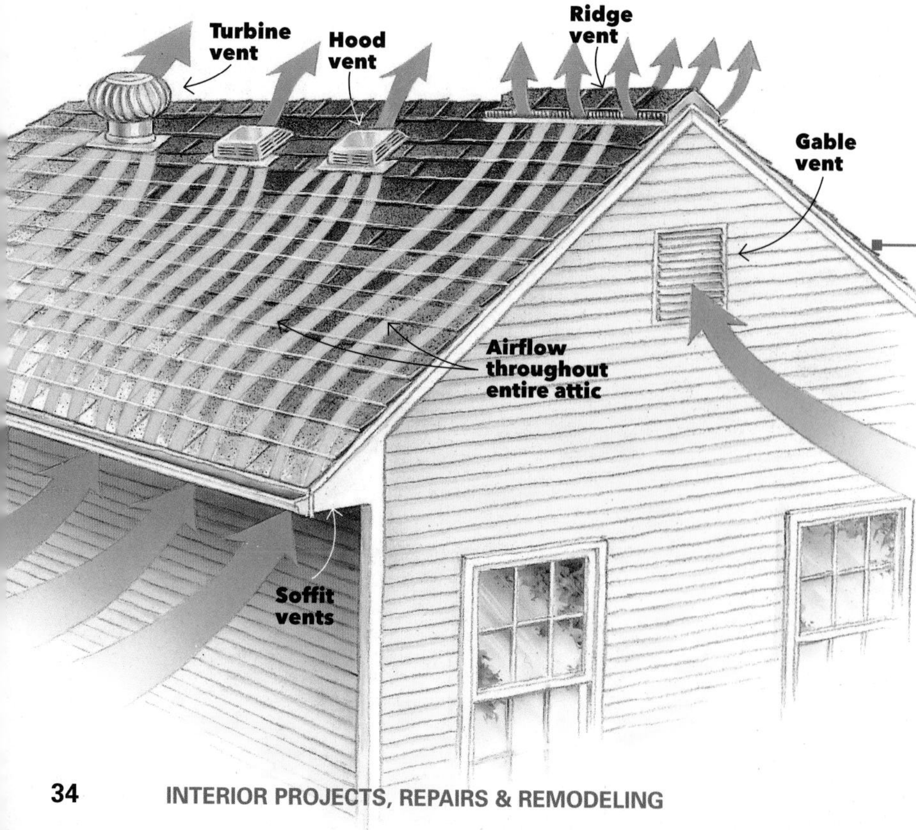

Paths to good venting

For intake air, soffit vents are best. Air can passively exit through ridge vents or hood vents. Turbine vents harness the wind to suck air out of the attic. Electric-powered vents are the ultimate air movers but aren't necessary in most situations. Gable vents can help by allowing air in or out, but they don't usually help the air flow evenly throughout the attic.

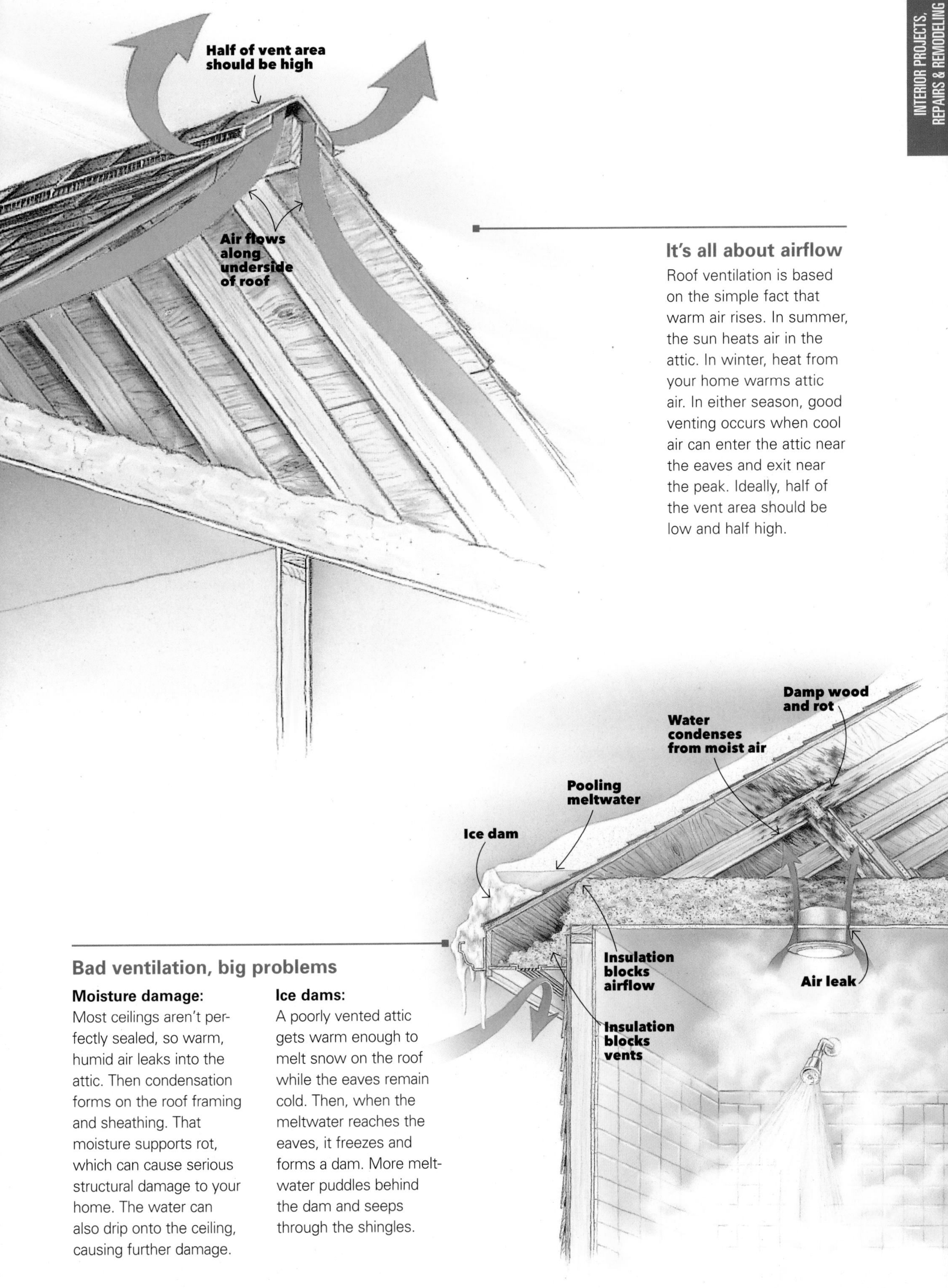

It's all about airflow

Roof ventilation is based on the simple fact that warm air rises. In summer, the sun heats air in the attic. In winter, heat from your home warms attic air. In either season, good venting occurs when cool air can enter the attic near the eaves and exit near the peak. Ideally, half of the vent area should be low and half high.

Bad ventilation, big problems

Moisture damage:
Most ceilings aren't perfectly sealed, so warm, humid air leaks into the attic. Then condensation forms on the roof framing and sheathing. That moisture supports rot, which can cause serious structural damage to your home. The water can also drip onto the ceiling, causing further damage.

Ice dams:
A poorly vented attic gets warm enough to melt snow on the roof while the eaves remain cold. Then, when the meltwater reaches the eaves, it freezes and forms a dam. More meltwater puddles behind the dam and seeps through the shingles.

■ **Spy on the neighbors**
If your roof is bare while neighboring roofs are still snow-covered, it could be a sign of trouble. While your roof may just be warmer because of its design or its more extensive southern exposure, it could also mean that you have poor ventilation or inadequate insulation.

■ **Cut cooling costs?**
Attics get super-heated by sunshine, and some of that heat is radiated to rooms below. So it's reasonable to think that better ventilation would lessen the radiated heat and reduce the load on your cooling system. But most studies find only minor savings with improved ventilation. Adding attic insulation is usually much more effective.

■ **What about 'hot roofs'?**
A "hot roof" has insulation directly under the roof sheathing and doesn't require ventilation. With careful design and installation, a hot roof can be trouble-free.

■ **Cooler shingles last longer**
Heat slowly degrades asphalt shingles. Ventilation helps to keep them cooler, extending the life of the roof. However, the effect of ventilation on shingle life depends on many factors, especially climate; venting matters most in hot, sunny regions. Most shingle manufacturers void their warranties if roof venting standards aren't met.

■ **How much is enough?**
Building codes generally require 1 sq. ft. of vent area for every 300 sq. ft. of attic floor. That assumes half of the vent area is high on the roof and half is low (in or near the eaves). Otherwise, doubling the vent area is required (1 per 150 sq. ft.) These are minimum requirements; there's no such thing as too much ventilation.

■ **Vents get plugged**
Soffit vents often get plugged by debris, cobwebs or stray insulation. You can clear them with a compressor and an air nozzle or a leaf blower. Wear eye protection!

Vocab: NFVA
"Net free vent area" is the amount of open space in a roof vent, a measurement usually given in square inches and listed on the vent. A typical hood-style vent, for example, might be labeled "NFVA: 50 sq. in."

PAINT PERFECTION

Masking tape tips for clean, straight edges

By Jeff Gorton

Masking off baseboard and other trim is a great way to get a professional-looking paint job. You'll get a crisp, clean paint line where the walls meet the trim. And the job will go quicker because you'll avoid the time-consuming "cutting in" with the paintbrush and the cleaning up of paint spatters from your woodwork. Of course, the masking process itself requires a little patience and skill. Wavy tape will result in a wavy paint line. Poor adhesion will allow "paint creep." And ragged tape in corners will leave blotches. Here are some techniques that will solve these problems and make your masking job go quickly and smoothly.

Pull from the roll to get the tape perfectly straight

One of the trickiest parts of masking is getting the tape on straight and tight against the wall. There are many techniques; here's one we know works great. Strip 8 to 10 in. of tape from the roll and use the roll itself, held tightly against the wall, to pull the tape straight (**Photos 1** and **2**). It's a little awkward at first, and it may seem slow, but the results are nearly perfect every time. Use this technique wherever you're masking at a right angle to another surface.

1 Position the end of the tape precisely and stick it down. Hold it in place while you pull about 8 to 10 in. of tape from the roll.

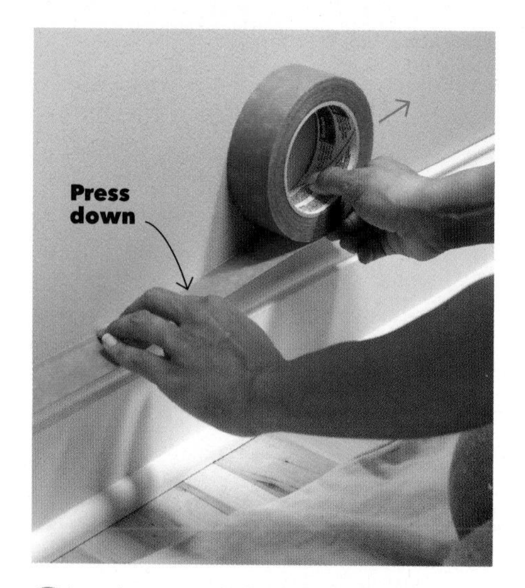

2 Lay the tape roll flat against the wall and rotate the roll to tighten and straighten it. Slide your finger across the tape to press it down.

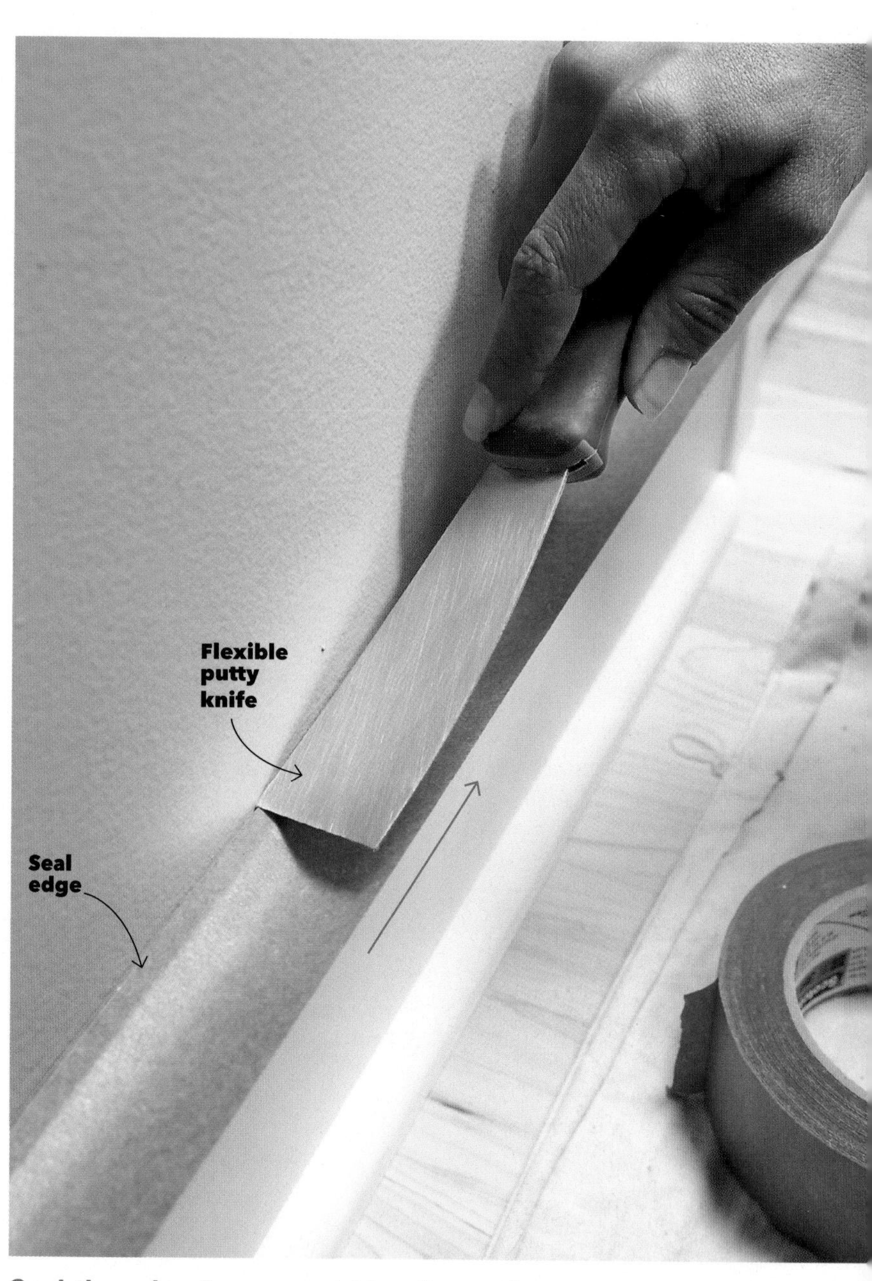

Seal the edge to prevent bleeding paint

Seal the tape to the surface by pressing it down firmly with the edge of a flexible putty knife as shown. This is the most important step in good masking, and it only takes a few moments. If you skip it, you risk a loose seal that will allow paint to seep underneath. You'll have to scrape off the seeped paint later and touch up the trim. Keep in mind that you don't have to press down the entire width of the tape. Sealing about 1/32 in. along the edge is all that's needed. Hold the putty knife at an angle as shown above. This puts pressure along the critical wall edge of the tape. Run the blade of a flexible putty knife along the edge of the tape. Apply firm pressure but avoid wrinkling or tearing the tape.

Use extra tape to make perfect inside corners

Getting two long pieces of tape to meet exactly in the corner is difficult, so don't even try. Instead, start the pieces of tape about 3/4 in. from the corner and run them using the method shown on p. 38. Then go back and finish the corner with small lengths of tape using the technique shown below.

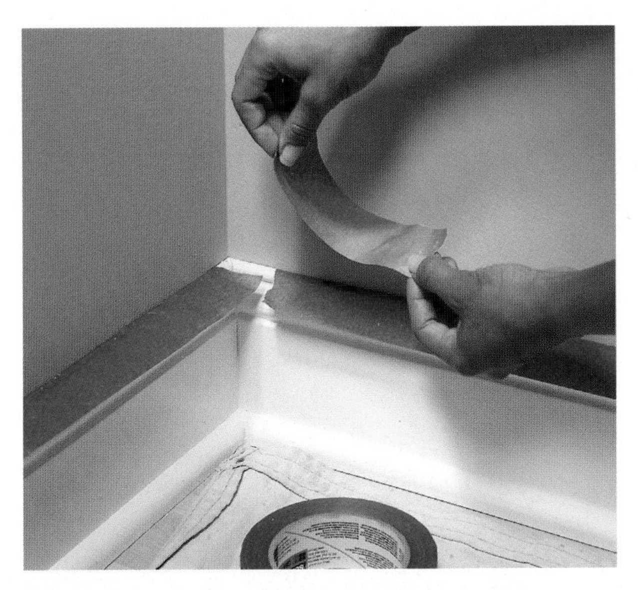

1 Press a short section of tape into the corner with the blade of a flexible 2-in. putty knife.

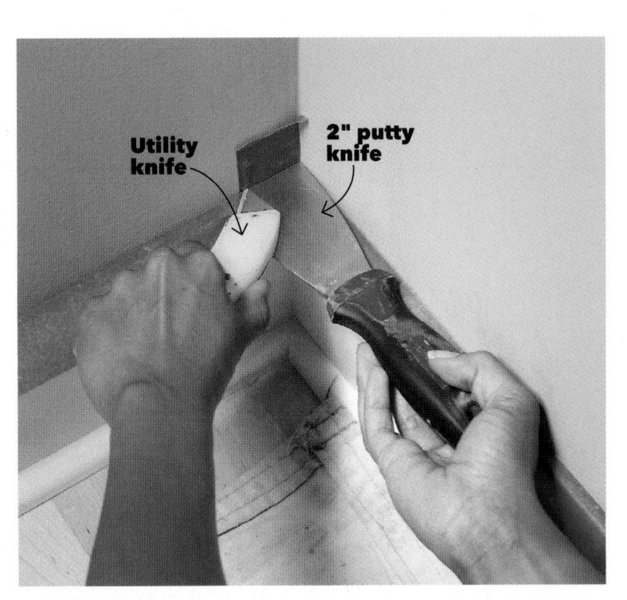

2 Cut the tape using the putty knife as a guide. Peel off the extra tape to create a perfect corner.

Tips for removing masking tape

A couple things can go wrong when you remove masking tape. If you wait too long, the adhesive will harden and remain stuck to the woodwork. Or if the paint sets but isn't completely dry, some of the wall paint may peel off along with the tape. Here are solutions to these problems.

- If you're a procrastinator, check the label and choose tape that's designed to be left on for several days.
- To avoid peeling paint, pull the tape off immediately or wait at least overnight for the paint to dry completely. Remove tape at a 45-degree angle to the painted surface. If the paint still peels with the tape, use a utility knife to cut the seal between the wall and the tape before you remove the tape.

Best Pro Tips

EXPERT ADVICE FROM THE JOB SITE

THE EASIEST FLOORING EVER

Tips to make your luxury vinyl installation fast, simple and flawless

Luxury vinyl is a beautiful, tough alternative to tile or hardwood flooring. Luxury vinyl tile (LVT) resembles stone or ceramic tile; luxury vinyl plank (LVP) mimics hardwood boards. Both can be installed over many types of flooring, so you may not have to deal with the cost and hassle of removing the old floor at all. With these tips from our expert, you can install luxury vinyl over an existing floor at a fraction of the cost in just a few hours.

MEET AN EXPERT

Brady Yeary has been tiling for 11 years. His company, Upper Crust Finishes, focuses on all things tile, from high-end Italian wall features to an expanse of commercial LVT.

CHOOSING THE RIGHT TILE

Tongue

Groove

Interlocking is easy

The tongue-and-groove design makes it easy to snap the tiles into place. Working from left to right, the short ends angle in first. Then tip the opposite end downward, lift and angle the long edge into the previous tiles and push them together.

Wear layer
The wear layer on luxury vinyl is 8 to 28 mils thick. This layer protects the decorative layer from scratches to keep it looking like new. Thicker is generally better, but your lifestyle matters more. If you wear socks around the house, 8-mil will be plenty; if you have three kids and two dogs, go for a thicker wear layer.

Decorative layer
From modern tile and stone to rustic wood designs, LVP and LVT come in many styles to fit any room.

Rigid core
Some luxury vinyl has a rigid core to provide extra durability and better sound blocking. The thicker rigid core, however, requires a flatter surface to avoid bridging low spots.

Integrated pad
Some vinyl tiles come with a built-in pad attached to the bottom of each tile to provide cushion underfoot. This eliminates the need for a separate underlayment.

Underlayment

If a tile doesn't come with a built-in pad, the manufacturer may recommend a cushion of underlayment. It acts as a pad for a softer landing, provides a vapor barrier and may reduce sound. It can also prevent some imperfections in the existing floor from telegraphing through the tile. Without underlayment, things like screw head holes, uneven seams, small high spots and even tiny grains of sand can lead to wear marks.

Install over almost anything:

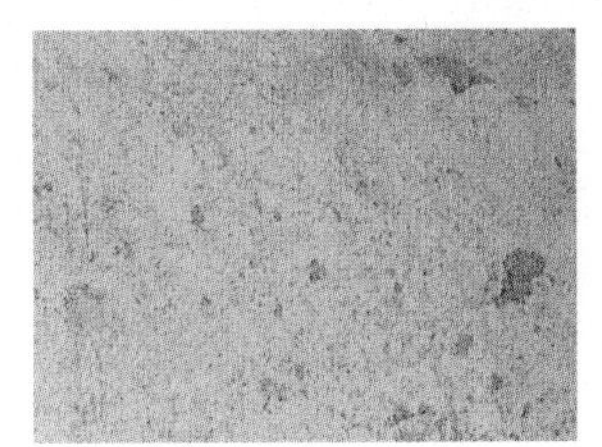

Concrete
If it's flat and smooth, you're good to go. If the surface is pitted or rough, either grind it smooth or cover it with self-leveling compound.

OSB/Plywood
Fill any gaps and screw holes with a patching compound and sand down high spots.

Sheet vinyl
Make sure seams are sound. If they're not, adhere them to the subfloor before moving on.

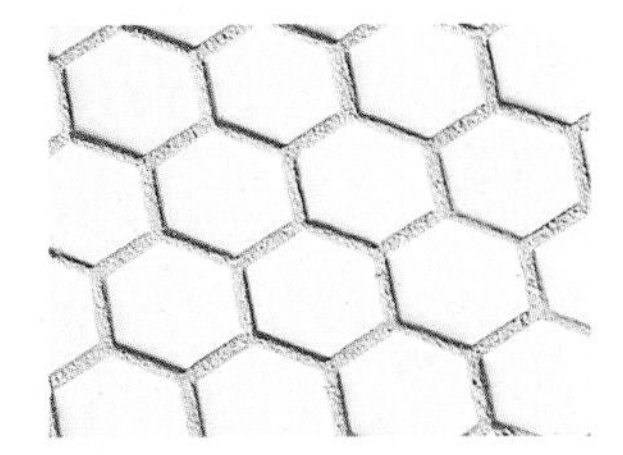

Tile
Avoid installing luxury vinyl over grouted tile. If removing the tile isn't an option, your best bet is to pour a self-leveling compound.

PLAN AND PREPARE

Spread samples all over the room

The samples will look different throughout the day. Before you buy your flooring, place samples around the room to see how they look in different light conditions.

Acclimate the tiles

Vinyl shrinks and expands slightly as the temperature changes, so let it assume room temperature before installing it. With the tiles packed together, that can take several hours. To speed up acclimation, get them out of the box.

Shuffle the tiles

Each style consists of a limited number of unique designs. To get a good random pattern, mix tiles from several different boxes. Open your boxes and pull from the top of each to make new stacks. You can cross two things off your list by doing this when you unpack the tile.

Clean the old floor

Don't leave even a tiny grain of sand on the old floor before you install the new one. It might "telegraph" through the vinyl and cause a wear mark, especially with thinner luxury vinyl.

Buy all the tile at once
Tile is produced in large batches, or "lots." Within the lots, all the tiles will be consistent, but each lot may vary slightly in size and color. Buying all the tile you need at one time will give you a better shot at getting tiles in the same lot. Double-check the batch, lot or dye number, and make sure all the boxes match.

Learn more!
For even more tips on installing this DIY-friendly tile, search for "luxury vinyl" at familyhandyman.com.

Check your substrate and level it as necessary

Use a level or straightedge to find out how flat your substrate is. Check several areas in different directions for low spots. Measure the biggest gap between the floor and the straightedge and check it against the manufacturer's specifications. For this tile, the manufacturer says the floor should be flat to within 3/16 in. over 10 ft. If the gap is bigger than what the manufacturer recommends, you'll need to address this before moving on. Use a trowel and floor patching compound to fill small low spots. For larger areas, cover the entire floor with a self-leveling compound. An added benefit of using self-leveling compound is that you can also determine exactly where the top of the flooring will finish, eliminating some bulky transitions.

Plan the layout

To avoid skinny rows along walls or cabinets, connect tiles to span the room until you can't fit a full-width tile. If the distance between the last row of tile and the wall is less than half the width of a tile, you'll want to shift the first row. You could measure the width of the space and figure out how the tiles will land along the walls, but it's best to trust your eyes and not your tape measure.

Expect out-of-square rooms

Many rooms aren't perfectly square, and it's easy to notice planks or tiles that are cut with a taper (wider at one end than the other) especially if the wall is particularly long. Crooked flooring is obvious at doorways. If you see the tiles don't line up with the door, guests will too. Shift the layout so it's crooked somewhere less visible.

BestProTips

INSTALLATION TIPS

Start rows with cutoffs

You'll end each row by cutting the last tile to fit. Instead of wasting the leftover cutoff, make it the beginning of the next row.

Change levels with transition molding

Transition molding is used to cover the cut ends of vinyl and to make up for height differences when meeting a different type of flooring. There are three common options:

Reducer strip
For transitioning vinyl floor to another floor of a different height.

T-molding
For a smooth transition between floor surfaces that are about the same height.

End cap
For transitioning from vinyl floor to carpet. Also used to terminate vinyl flooring into an exterior door.

Leave a gap under shoe molding

Pinching the flooring down with shoe mold won't allow for expansion and contraction and could cause buckling or separation at the seams. Use a 1/32-in. tile spacer or shim under the shoe to create a small gap. Be sure to nail the shoe into the baseboard, not down through the vinyl.

Stagger the seams

There's no set rule for staggering seams in vinyl planks, but if you lay your planks down and the seams end up creating a pattern, you'll notice it every time you walk on the floor. Avoid forming "H" and stair-step patterns. If you make sure seams don't line up for four or five rows, your eye will be unlikely to spot a pattern.

Leave a gap

It's surprising how much vinyl can expand or shrink with changing temperatures. A gap at the edges will ensure you won't ever come home to a buckled floor. Check with the manufacturer to see what it recommends for your tile.

Mark with a scrap

Instead of using a tape measure to transfer measurements to the tile, use some scrap. Align the tile you want to cut where it will snap in, placing it on top of the previous row. Use a full-width scrap (cut the tongue off) against the wall and scribe the tile.

Best Pro Tips

Install the planks in reverse

Being able to install vinyl tile backward is a real time-saver and makes going through doorways and installing tile under cabinets a snap. Assemble the row first, then tip the tongue underneath the groove on the previous row and pull them tight.

Heat and bend

If you run into a situation where you need to bend the tile to get it to fit under a doorjamb or toe-kick, make the tile more flexible with a heat gun. Be careful not to scorch the face of the tile.

Leave a gap at the toilet

When you're caulking around a toilet, leave a weep hole at the back. That way, water leaking past the wax ring will escape and warn you of trouble before major damage occurs.

Quick, clean cuts

Cut with a carpet knife
A carpet blade, which is much stiffer than a normal utility blade, makes it easier to score a straight line across a tile with a square as a guide. Bend the tile backward until it snaps. If the tile has built-in padding, you'll have to finish the cut with the carpet blade.

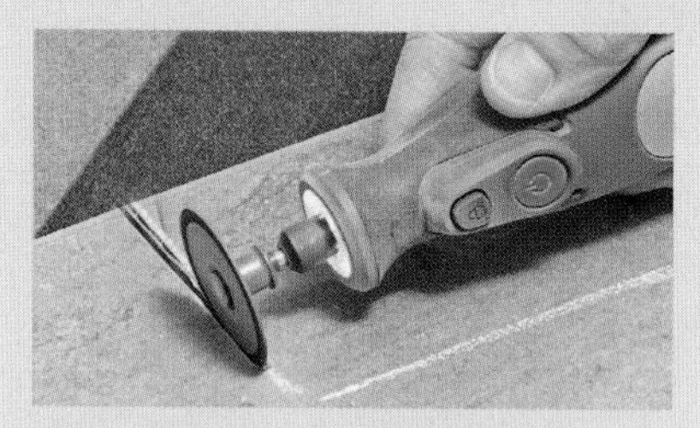

The solution for notches
With notch cuts, you can't just score and snap. Make these tricky cuts a whole lot easier by using a rotary tool equipped with an abrasive wheel for cutting plastic.

Cut faster
A slicing-style laminate cutter is great for cutting vinyl tile. Its blunt slicer punches out a 1/4-in. strip but leaves a clean-cut edge on the tile. So, if you have a lot of cutting to do, invest in this $60 tool to speed up your job. The Roberts 10-35 Laminate Cutter is available at home centers and online.

Yes, you can use a table saw!
The quickest and easiest way to cut an entire tile lengthwise is to use your table saw. Using a straightedge and a carpet blade is much slower.

HandyHints®

FROM OUR READERS

PERFECT PILOT HOLES

If you're fastening moldings by hand (without a pneumatic finish nailer), you'll need to predrill a hole the diameter of the nail so you don't split the wood. If you don't have the right size drill bit, don't worry. Predrill using one of the finish nails. Simply clip the head off the nail with lineman's pliers or wire cutters. Then chuck the headless nail into the drill. This will give you the perfect size pilot hole every time.

—Keith Clasemann

FIX FOR PAINT SPILLS ON CARPET

I used to think dropping a loaded paintbrush on the carpet meant replacing the carpet... until a carpet pro told me this little tip. Pour some denatured alcohol on a rag and scrub away the paint. Use a white rag (or one similar in color to the carpet) so the alcohol doesn't transfer unwanted dye to the carpet.

—Tom Gerdowsky

WASTE-FREE PAINTING

I have several rental properties that are always in need of repainting. Instead of throwing out leftover paint, I put it to use. I gather all my partial cans of interior latex—any color or sheen—and dump them into a 5-gallon bucket. Next, I mix the paint with a power-driven paint mixer to get a uniform color. It usually turns out off-white with an eggshell sheen. If the color is too dark, I lighten it by adding a can of white paint. Then I pour the paint into another 5-gallon bucket through a strainer bag. I lift out the strainer bag to remove any debris and pop on a lid to keep the paint fresh.

—Tom Dvorak

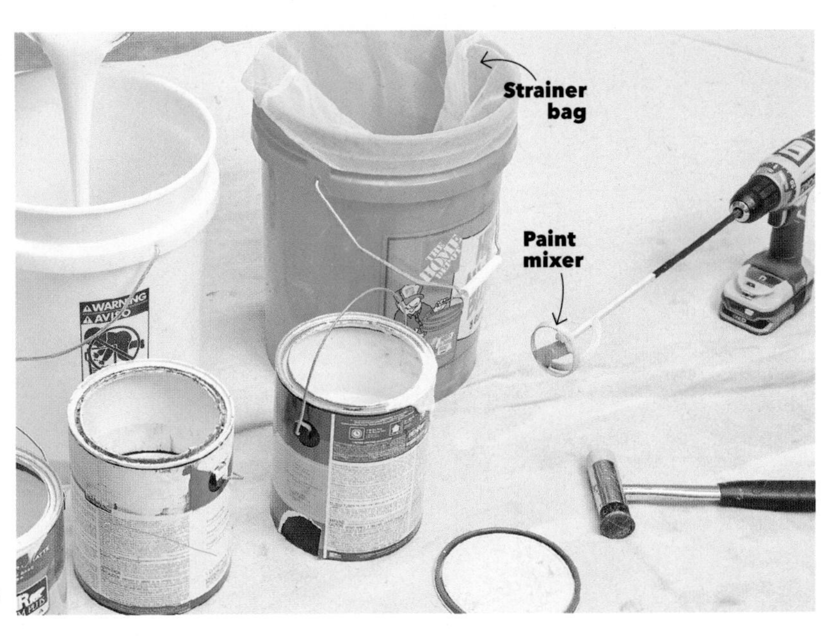

GreatGoofs®

LAUGHS & LESSONS FROM OUR READERS

10 FEET OF TRIM IN A 9-FOOT CAR

On my way to work one day, I stopped at my local home center to buy trim for my daughter's bedroom. I folded down the backseat in my car and ran the pieces of trim through the trunk, resting the front ends on the dashboard. I slammed the trunk shut, then recoiled in horror at the sound of breaking glass. The trim was too long for the car, and the slamming trunk acted like a battering ram, shoving the trim through the windshield. My little trim project suddenly got a lot more expensive—and my car was impossible to drive with the shattered windshield.

—Tom Dobbs

NAILED IT PERFECTLY!

To prepare for putting in my new wood floor, I removed all the base trim. I labeled the trim to make sure the pieces would go back in the same order. I installed the floor in a single day, and in all modesty, it looked terrific. Then I got out my compressor and trusty nail gun to reinstall the base trim. I had just nailed the last piece of base when my wife walked in and asked me why the pocket door wouldn't pull out of the pocket. I was baffled. After using every muscle in my body to try to pull the stuck door closed, I realized the problem: While reinstalling the base, I had shot nails through the trim, drywall, pocket door framing and right into the door. Oh, well. Who needs to close a bathroom door anyway?

—Will Hanson

SCREW LOOSE

To free up floor space in my kid's bedroom, I built a bed box to hold the mattress. Then I hung one side of the box from the ceiling joists with chains and screwed the other side to the wall studs.

To convince my skeptical family that the box was safely hung, I set down my tools, hopped up on it and started jumping around. As my family stood back and watched, the box pulled loose from the wall, dropping straight down and dumping me out onto the floor. The ceiling chains were secure enough, but the drywall screws in the wall pulled right out. I patched the wall and reinstalled the box with longer screws, but my family never lets me forget how I got thrown out of the bed.

—Gary Havens

THE NOSE KNEW

Recently, I bought speakers to hang from the ceiling of our family room. I tapped on the ceiling to locate the joists and then drilled small holes to make sure I'd found solid backing. Confident, I screwed the brackets to the ceiling and mounted the speakers. A few days later, we smelled something awful. We suspected our 2-year-old, who was in the midst of potty training. He denied any wrongdoing, so I followed my nose and found a stain on the speaker bracket. The "solid backing" I'd screwed the bracket into was the toilet drainpipe instead of the ceiling joist! Every time we flushed we got a small leak. I tore out the ceiling and replaced the drainpipe and offered my son a sincere apology.

—Joey Sheat

TWO INCHES OFF THE TOP

With the motto "measure twice, cut once" in mind, I borrowed my husband's tape measure and twice measured the closet floor where I was planning to install carpet. I wrote down the dimensions, grabbed my piece of carpet and headed to the garage.

I used a yardstick to measure the carpet in the garage since it held down the curling edges and provided a nice straight edge. Soon my masterpiece was ready, and I hurried to the closet to install it. When I laid it out, I was shocked to find that it was 2 in. short on two sides. I double-checked my measurements. They were right, which left me more puzzled than ever. Then my husband walked in and solved the mystery with a laugh. Weeks earlier, he'd cut 2 in. off the end of the yardstick to use as a shim. I never even noticed.

—Darlene Lockert

SPECIAL SECTION

Home Financial

TURNING YOUR **HOME INTO CASH** WITH AIRBNB

DIGITAL GENETICS/SHUTTERSTOCK

Airbnb by the Numbers

Airbnb users
151 million

Countries with Listings
191

Cities with Listings
65,000

Listings Worldwide
4 million

Stays Per Night
500,000

Joining the Airbnb revolution could help you generate revenue from a spare room, or from an apartment or house you don't use much. "It's been a great experience and very worthwhile," says Sandra Shillington, a California-based Airbnb host since 2013 and the author of the hosting guidebook, *Airbnb Toolbox*. But is hosting right for you?

Pro: The money (of course!)

While earnings vary based on size and type of space, city and neighborhood, and frequency of rentals, hosting can yield more than you might receive from even a full-time renter, Shillington says.

But keep in mind: Paying guests expect their experience "to be relatively problem-free," she says. You need to be organized, efficient and available. When the washing machine you promised breaks down, "you have to make sure someone's there to fix it." As with any business, there's also some paperwork—though that gets easier with experience, she adds.

Pro: The people

"You meet lots of interesting people from all over the world," Shillington says. "There's a sense of community that Airbnb has built its platform around." Expect fun conversations and the pleasure of introducing guests to your city or region. But keep in mind: If privacy is a priority or you don't like interacting with strangers, you may want to pass. "You're in the people business," she says. Also, while the overwhelming majority of guests are respectful of your property, "inconsiderate" guests are a possibility. Airbnb, however, does insure your rental against damage by guests, and before renting to someone, you can read reviews given by other hosts.

Tip for success

While the physical space is crucial, don't neglect your online presence. Respond quickly to queries from prospective guests and encourage reviews from those who've stayed there. Being fully engaged online may help give your property a more prominent position on the Airbnb site, Shillington says.

—Charlie Slack
Contributing Editor

WILL YOUR HOMEOWNERS INSURANCE PAY FOR BED BUG EXTERMINATION?

The cost for professional bed bug extermination typically ranges from $500 to $1,500, depending on the extent of the invasion. An infestation is a minor home disaster, so extermination must be covered, right? Not so fast. Insurance companies classify bed bugs as a home maintenance issue and thus the owner's responsibility, says Michael Barry, spokesman for the nonprofit Insurance Information Institute.

A bad risk

Although bed bug infestations occur across the United States, they are too random (and costly) to fit insurance risk models, Barry says. "No insurer wants to take this on." Nor does renters insurance cover bed bugs, although in some locales—such as New York City—landlords are required to remove them.

Bed Bugs: The (Not So) Fun Facts

500 – The number of eggs a single bed bug can lay in a lifetime

50 – U.S. states where they are found

3x – The rate of urban vs. rural infestation

7x – The amount of blood, relative to body weight, they can consume

122 degrees F – The maximum temperature at which they'll survive

Source: National Pest Management Association

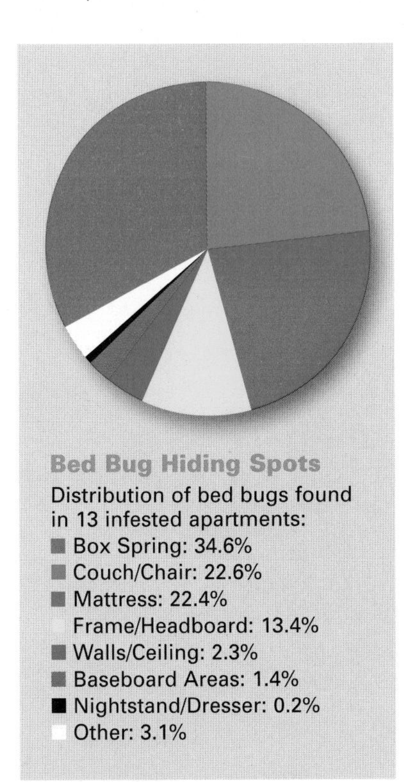

Bed Bug Hiding Spots

Distribution of bed bugs found in 13 infested apartments:

- Box Spring: 34.6%
- Couch/Chair: 22.6%
- Mattress: 22.4%
- Frame/Headboard: 13.4%
- Walls/Ceiling: 2.3%
- Baseboard Areas: 1.4%
- Nightstand/Dresser: 0.2%
- Other: 3.1%

Can you get rid of them yourself?

If you do face an invasion, it's possible to exterminate bed bugs yourself. It's a huge investment of time, but you'll save quite a bit of money. To learn how, visit familyhandyman.com and search for "how to get rid of bed bugs." For still more information, the EPA offers tips on extermination options at epa.gov/bedbugs. The National Pest Management Association offers guidance at pestworld.org. And for a detailed look at homeowners and renters insurance, visit the Insurance Information Institute at iii.org.

Focus on prevention

Without a doubt, the best way to prevent bed bugs is to not bring them home in the first place.

- Inspect used furniture before you bring it home. Live bugs are visible, as are dark spots of excrement. Crushed bed bugs leave a reddish stain.
- Vacuum frequently.
- Reduce clutter in your home, making cleaning easier.
- At a hotel, set suitcases on the luggage rack, not on the floor or bed.
- Inspect the hotel luggage rack before using it.
- Some savvy travelers even stow their suitcases in the bathtub.
- When you travel, keep dirty clothes in a trash bag and put them directly in the wash when you get home.

—Charlie Slack
Contributing Editor

Home Financial

SHOULD I CONSIDER A **REVERSE MORTGAGE?**

ITTIGALLERY

If you're retired and find yourself with unexpected medical or other expenses, or an inadequate retirement fund, the equity in your home could provide a crucial source of income, thanks to a reverse mortgage. Yet while they can be useful, reverse mortgages come with risks, so consider your situation carefully.

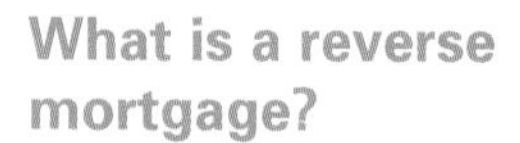

What is a reverse mortgage?

It's a type of loan offering retirees (only people 62 or older qualify) access to money without requiring regular monthly payments, and while remaining in their home. According to Peter Bell, president and CEO of the National Reverse Mortgage Lenders Association, you can draw down funds and defer any repayment until you pass away or decide to move.

What are the downsides?

"A reverse mortgage obviously helps the cash flow," Bell says, "but you still have the responsibility for maintaining the home and paying taxes, insurance and homeowner association dues. So, people need to make sure they'll have the resources to cover those expenses."

Federal Housing Administration insurance, which covers most reverse mortgages, guarantees that borrowers (or their heirs) won't owe more than what the house sells for when the loan is eventually repaid. Still, keep in mind that repaying the loan will leave you with that much less equity should you decide to sell, or that much less to leave to your heirs.

Review your overall finances

When considering a reverse mortgage, it helps to start with a detailed budget including all of your income and expenses, Bell suggests. Knowing what money you have coming in and going out each month can help you determine whether a reverse mortgage could fill the gap. This is a huge decision with huge consequences. Before you sign any papers, sit down with a financial planner who has the skills to help you decide.

—**Charlie Slack**
Contributing Editor

SHUTTERSTOCK/RAWPIXEL

HIRE CONTRACTORS **OFF-SEASON AND SAVE**

Choosing the right time to hire home contractors can save you money, get you better quality work, ensure that you'll get the job done on schedule and make the whole process a lot less frustrating. Contractors of all types have slow seasons when they're more willing to negotiate lower costs and shorten lead times and are less likely to rush through the job. If your job isn't an emergency, it's often worth waiting for a slow period.

Roofing

The busiest season for most roofers is the fall as homeowners scramble to prepare for winter. Spring is also hectic because there is a push to address problems occurring in winter and early spring. The standard rule is to schedule your roofing project between the Fourth of July and Labor Day. If your roof covering is other than asphalt shingles, such as metal, rubber or tile, then you have more flexibility and could strike a good deal for a winter job.

Exterior painting

Summer is the busiest season for house painters, in part because some homeowners prefer to have the loud, messy work done while they're away on vacation. January and February are slow months for most contractors, so if it's possible to apply paint at that time in your area, start then. Otherwise, the trade does tend to lag a bit in September and October.

Interior painting

Most people paint when they have just purchased a house (that spikes a bit in the spring) or are preparing for the holidays. Across the board, January and February are considered the slow seasons for interior painting.

Concrete work

Spring and summer are the peak seasons, so consider colder months. Concrete work is less subject to cold weather than other exterior jobs because you can pour concrete even at low temperatures. For major projects that require a concrete truck to traverse your driveway or yard, frozen ground is preferable.

Heating and air conditioning

When the weather changes—becoming hot in late spring or cold in the fall—systems break down and HVAC people get busy. Have your air conditioning system serviced or replaced in the off-peak times. Early fall and spring are good periods.

Interior remodeling

If you can work around the mess and inconvenience of a kitchen or bathroom remodeling project during November or February, the months on either side of the holiday season, there's a good chance you'll find more and better choices of contractors and be able to strike a better deal.

HOW TO FINANCE HOME IMPROVEMENT

When it's time for a major home improvement, most of us need to borrow. There are endless variations on project funding, but almost all fall into these five categories:

1. Zero percent or low-interest credit cards

If you have decent credit, you likely get offers for zero percent interest credit cards (new credit cards or checks you can use with cards you already have). Credit Karma advises that these credit card offers are best for projects under $15,000, because it's easier to pay off the loan within the low-interest-rate offer timeline (usually 12 to 18 months). Typically, these offers are easy to qualify for, and your home isn't used as collateral.

Make sure you can fully pay off the debt by the time the offer expires, or you'll end up owing a ton of interest on the full amount.

2. Personal or unsecured loans

For projects from $15,000 to $50,000, Credit Karma recommends personal or unsecured loans. These loans are easy to apply for, don't require any collateral, and tend to offer higher loan amounts than credit cards. However, interest rates are typically higher on personal and unsecured loans than they are on home equity or home equity line of credit (HELOC) loans. Compare the terms, APR (annual percentage rate), and other costs of each loan to see which one makes the most sense.

Using your home as collateral

If you have equity in your home and projects costing $50,000 or more, it's best to use loans tied to your property. To reduce risk, lenders limit the amount of loans on your home to about 85 percent of your home's value. Even so, it's easy to borrow more money than you can handle and end up owing more than your home is worth. Here are the most popular options.

1. Cash-out refinance

A cash-out makes sense in some scenarios—especially if your mortgage rate is much higher than current rates. You'll replace your current mortgage with a new one and take cash out for improvements. The long repayment period is nice, and monthly payments are lower than with a home equity loan or line of credit.

However, closing costs may be high, and your APR will be higher than if you refinanced without getting cash out. Also, you'll owe more on your mortgage. If you're 10 years into your 30-year fixed mortgage and refinance into a bigger 30-year loan, the clock restarts.

2. Home equity loans (HEL)

Home equity loans are a second mortgage on your home. They're usually a fixed interest rate, and you get the money in one lump sum. Terms vary, but many home equity loans have you pay back the principal and interest within 15 years. This is a good option if you need a set amount and have the ability to make the payments.

However, home equity loans can be pricey, with closing costs similar to those of a primary mortgage. There might also be a penalty if you pay off the loan early.

3. Home equity line of credit (HELOC)

Instead of giving you all the money you qualify for at once, a HELOC gives you a revolving open credit line. That way you can borrow money periodically. Terms vary, but many HELOCs give you 5 to 10 years to access the credit line, during which time you pay interest on what you borrow, and give you 15 or so years to pay it back in full.

HELOCs are adjustable rate mortgages, however, so rates can fluctuate and end up much higher than with a fixed home equity loan. But there are usually no closing costs on HELOCs.

—Melanie Pinola
Contributing Editor

2 Electrical & High-Tech

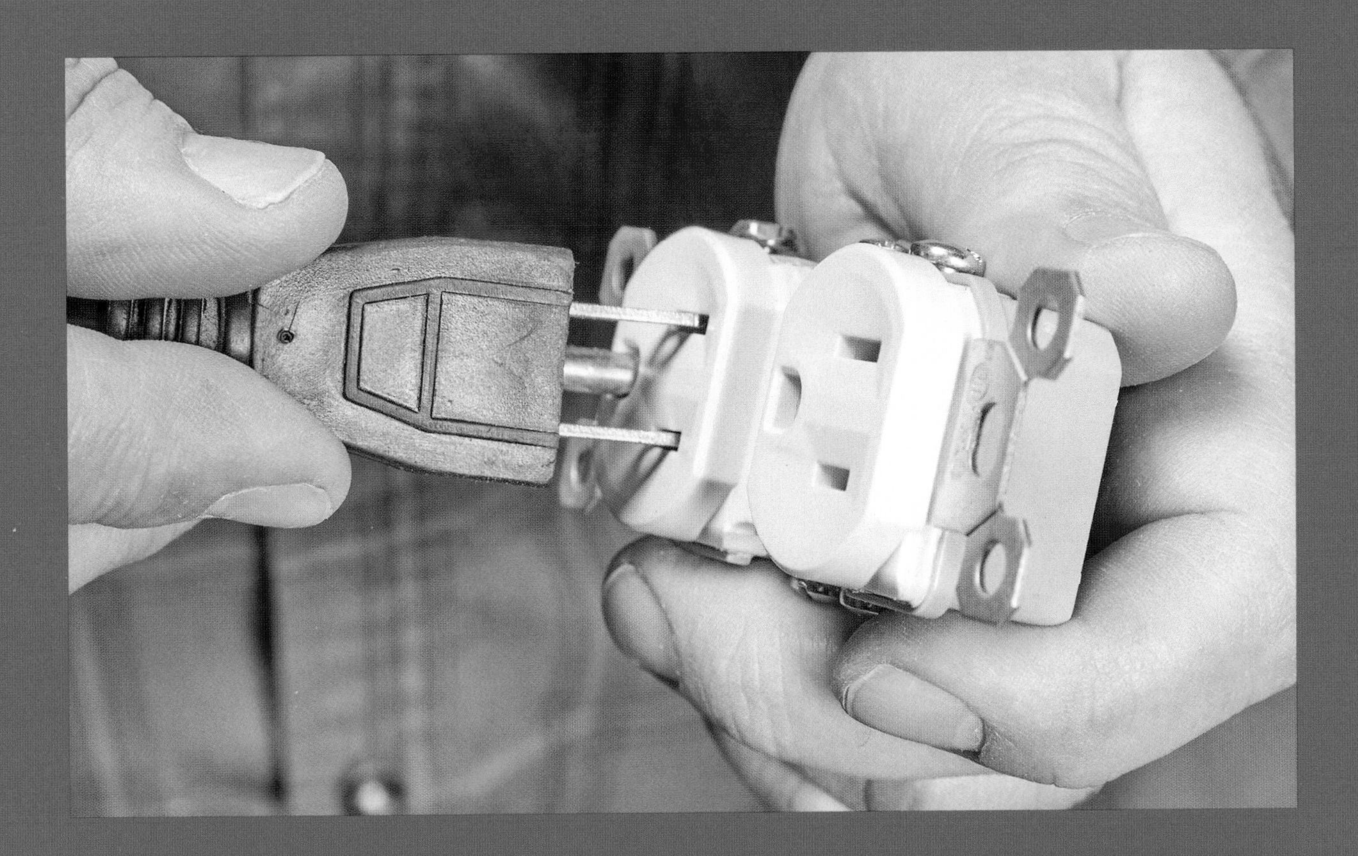

IN THIS CHAPTER

HomeSmarts

KNOWLEDGE YOU NEED TO BE A BETTER HOMEOWNER

GETTING STARTED WITH **SECURITY CAMERAS**

SHUTTERSTOCK

Just the sight of a security camera can help prevent a break-in. And if someone is snooping around outside your house, motion and sound notifications can alert you immediately. An indoor camera lets you check on your kids or pets while you're at work. You can even use a speaker on the camera to tell your kids to start their homework.

Storage and Power

There are several types of security cameras, and getting started can be overwhelming. Cameras usually include streaming on your smartphone while you're away. Some systems offer free cloud storage for a set number of days, referred to as "rolling cloud storage." For example, if you have seven days of storage, you can see only the previous seven days. But, you can download any footage you need to keep. Other systems require a subscription for storage or are equipped with a memory card. Without storage, a camera provides only a live stream. Following are several options for powering and connecting your camera.

Wired/IP

These are more traditional, heavy-duty security camera systems. Each camera connects to a recorder with an Ethernet cable. This provides you with a stable 24/7 connection, independent from the internet. The downside of wired cameras is their complicated installation.

Wi-Fi

Wi-Fi cameras connect to the internet without complex wiring. Plug your camera into a power outlet, connect it to your Wi-Fi in the app, and it's done. These are easy to set up and move, but since they depend on the internet, crashes and even hacks are concerns.

Battery Wi-Fi

Completely wire-free, battery Wi-Fi cameras work on rechargeable batteries. Install them in a tree or anywhere your internet service can reach. When it's time to recharge, the app will notify you to plug the camera in for recharging or to replace the batteries.

—Reed & Alysa Kleinman
Contributing Editors
Smarthomesolver.com

Expert Picks:

Wyze Cam V2: Super-affordable indoor camera ($26) with 14 days of free rolling cloud storage. Incredible quality for the price, and you can even record 24/7 on an SD card.

WYZE

Nest Cam: Integrates with Nest thermostats and other smart home tech. There is no free video cloud storage, but continuous video recording comes with your subscription. (Nest Cam Indoor, $200).

NEST

Arlo Pro 2: Seven days of free rolling cloud storage, works on rechargeable battery or outlet power, and is weather resistant. You cannot record 24/7 unless you have a paid subscription and plug it in. (Arlo Pro 2 VMS4230P, $450).

ARLO

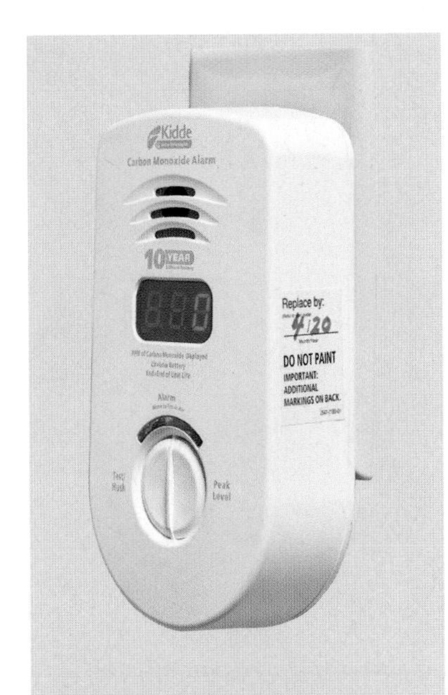

WHEN SHOULD I REPLACE MY CO DETECTOR?

Carbon monoxide detectors have a life span of five to seven years. Before you install a new one, check the manufacture date on the back, then write the replacement date in permanent ink next to it. It's a good idea to set the calendar on your smartphone or computer to send you a reminder when it's time to replace CO detectors. Make it even easier by having them all due for replacement at the same time.

Install at least one carbon monoxide detector on each level of your home, and locate them near bedrooms. For more information, search for "CO detector" at familyhandyman.com.

DO RECEPTACLES NEED REPLACING?

Over time, the internal contact springs on electrical receptacles lose their spring. If you have a receptacle that doesn't hold onto plugs (left), it's time to replace it. If you want to reuse an old receptacle from your box of electrical supplies, check its grip first by plugging in a grounded plug that's in good condition (above). If it grips well and there's no corrosion on the terminal screws, the outlet is fine to reuse. To learn how to replace a receptacle, go to familyhandyman.com and search for "replace receptacles."

—Travis Larson
Senior Editor

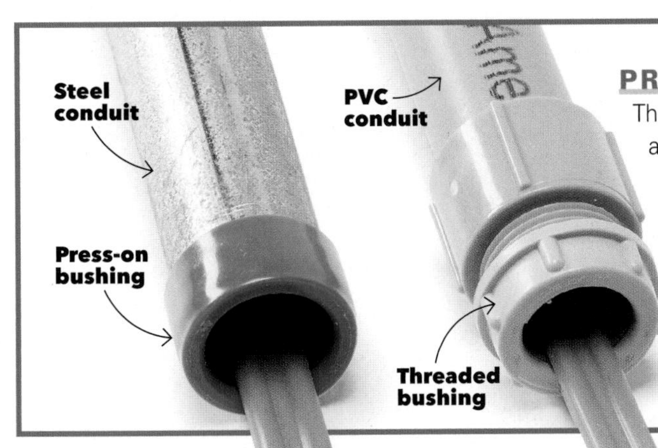

PROTECT BURIED CABLE

The end of a piece of conduit can be sharp enough to abrade electrical cable. Most installed cable doesn't move, but if it's buried, frost or settling may significantly move the cable. To protect the cable, all that's needed is a little bushing to create a smoother edge. For PVC conduit, a threaded end accepts the bushing. For steel conduit, use a press-on bushing.

—Brad Holden
Associate Editor

HomeSmarts

A VARIETY OF VOLTAGE

Terms like "110-volt circuit," "120-volt outlet," "220-volt motor" and "240-volt oven" can be confusing. That's partly because voltage standards have changed over time. In the early days of electricity, 110/220 was the standard voltage supplied to homes. In the 1930s, that changed to 115/230, and as of 1984, it is 120/240. Adding to the confusion, switches and outlets are commonly labeled "125" or "250." That's because actual voltage fluctuates by plus or minus 5 percent, so fixtures need to be able to handle slightly more than 120/240.

The bottom line: Don't worry about it—110, 115 and 120 are all the same thing. The same goes for 220, 230 and 240.

BURYING ELECTRICAL CABLE

A reader asked us to shed some light on the depth requirements for burying electrical cable. Al Hildenbrand, one of our electrical experts, explained the rules this way:

■ **Option 1:** If you don't want to dig deep trenches, you can bury individual conductors inside RMC (rigid metal conduit) at a depth of 6 in.

■ **Option 2:** You can direct-bury UF-B (underground feeder) at a depth of 12 in. In this case, PVC conduit must run to the full 12-in. depth. Also, the circuit must be limited to 15 or 20 amps and 120 volts, AND the wiring must have GFCI (ground-fault circuit interrupter) protection before the branch circuit enters the ground.

■ **Option 3:** When either the current is greater than 20 amps or the voltage is greater than 120 volts, or both, the PVC must run to a depth of 18 in. GFCI protection does not affect this rule.

■ **Option 4:** To direct-bury any circuit that isn't protected by a GFCI, the trench must be 24 in. deep. A circuit greater than 20 amps, greater than 120 volts, or both, without conduit, requires a depth of 24 in.

No. 4 No. 3 No. 2 No.1

6"

Galvanized metal conduit

12"

Underground feeder cable

18"

PVC conduit

24"

Underground feeder cable

THE SKINNY ON **SMART LIGHTS**

Smart lights let you control a bulb remotely via an app on your phone, through a smart speaker or even by talking to them. You can program when the lights go on and off, change a bulb's color as well as find your own creative uses (more on this later). Here are a few things to consider when choosing which smart lights are right for you. You can add a smart light to any light fixture or lamp. It really is as easy as changing a lightbulb: Unscrew the old one; screw in the new.

Hub vs. Hubless

Some smart lights require a hub, which is a device that plugs into your router. A hub like the one shown connects other lightbulbs, allowing you to interact with them from your mobile device and/or smart speaker.

So, how do you know which lights are compatible with hubs? When you're shopping for lights, look for the words "Zigbee" and "Z-Wave." These are names for the protocols/languages that smart devices use to communicate. Leaders in the hub market are Samsung SmartThings, Wink and Amazon Echo. Prices range from $50 to $200. Z-Wave and Zigbee protocols are both capable of creating mesh networks (which allow signals to hop from device to device, extending range) and can operate over a significantly longer range than Wi-Fi.

Hubless bulbs don't require any extra hardware or devices. They're cheaper than a bulb with a hub. These bulbs connect via your Wi-Fi or Bluetooth. Wi-Fi bulbs are more reliable and don't require a user to be within Bluetooth range (approximately 30 ft.) to control the light. Wi-Fi smart lights require no additional hardware; they use your existing router to connect to the internet. If you're interested in dipping your toe into the smart light market, a couple Wi-Fi bulbs may be the best way to go.

My Favorites:

Hubless
White
A. Kasa Smart Wi-Fi LED Lightbulb, $20

Multicolor
B. LIFX Multicolor Smart Wi-Fi LED Lightbulb, $50

Hub required
White
C. Sengled Smart LED Lightbulb, $10 (hub not included)

Multicolor
D. Philips Hue Starter Kit, $100 (includes hub and two bulbs)

AMAZON (PHILIPS HUE)

White vs. Color-Changing

Some people may be happy with just the ability to dim or turn lights on or off from their phone, while others may want more. Color-changing lights can be used like typical lightbulbs—to set the mood during a romantic dinner or even as a notification system (see below).

Make Smart Lights Smarter

- Want to know if you'll need an umbrella today? Tell the smart light located by the front door to turn blue at a certain time if rain is in the forecast.
- Do you sometimes miss important emails? Program a smart light at your desk to blink red if you get an email from your boss.
- Want your lights to turn on automatically when you arrive home? Configure them to turn on when your phone enters the range of your home Wi-Fi.
- Want to get into the team spirit with some mood lighting? Tell your lights to change to the color of your favorite sports team when a new game starts.
- Want to know when the price of one of your stocks rises? Make your lights turn green when you're making money.
- Want to be the first to know of a zombie outbreak? Set up your light to flash when the CDC sends out an alert about a deadly virus.

All these and more are possible by pairing your color-changing smart lights with a free third-party service called IFTTT (ifttt.com). The sky's the limit for what you can make your smart lights do for you; all you need is a little imagination.

—Cassidy Nelemans
Contributing Editor

ELECTRICAL BOX **BASICS**

How to pick the best junction box for any job

By Brad Holden

With the variety of different electrical boxes available at home centers, how do you know what to buy? Don't worry, it's not that complicated. We'll whittle it down to about a dozen boxes to cover almost every situation.

New work: 3 types do it all

If you have the walls opened up for remodeling or putting on an addition, these three boxes cover about 99 percent of your needs.

1. **22-cu.-in. 4-in. round box** for ceiling light fixtures, smoke alarms, carbon monoxide detectors and wall sconce light fixtures.
2. **22-cu.-in. single-gang box** for a typical outlet or switch.
3. **32-cu.-in. double-gang box** for two light switches together in the same box, or two duplex receptacle outlets.

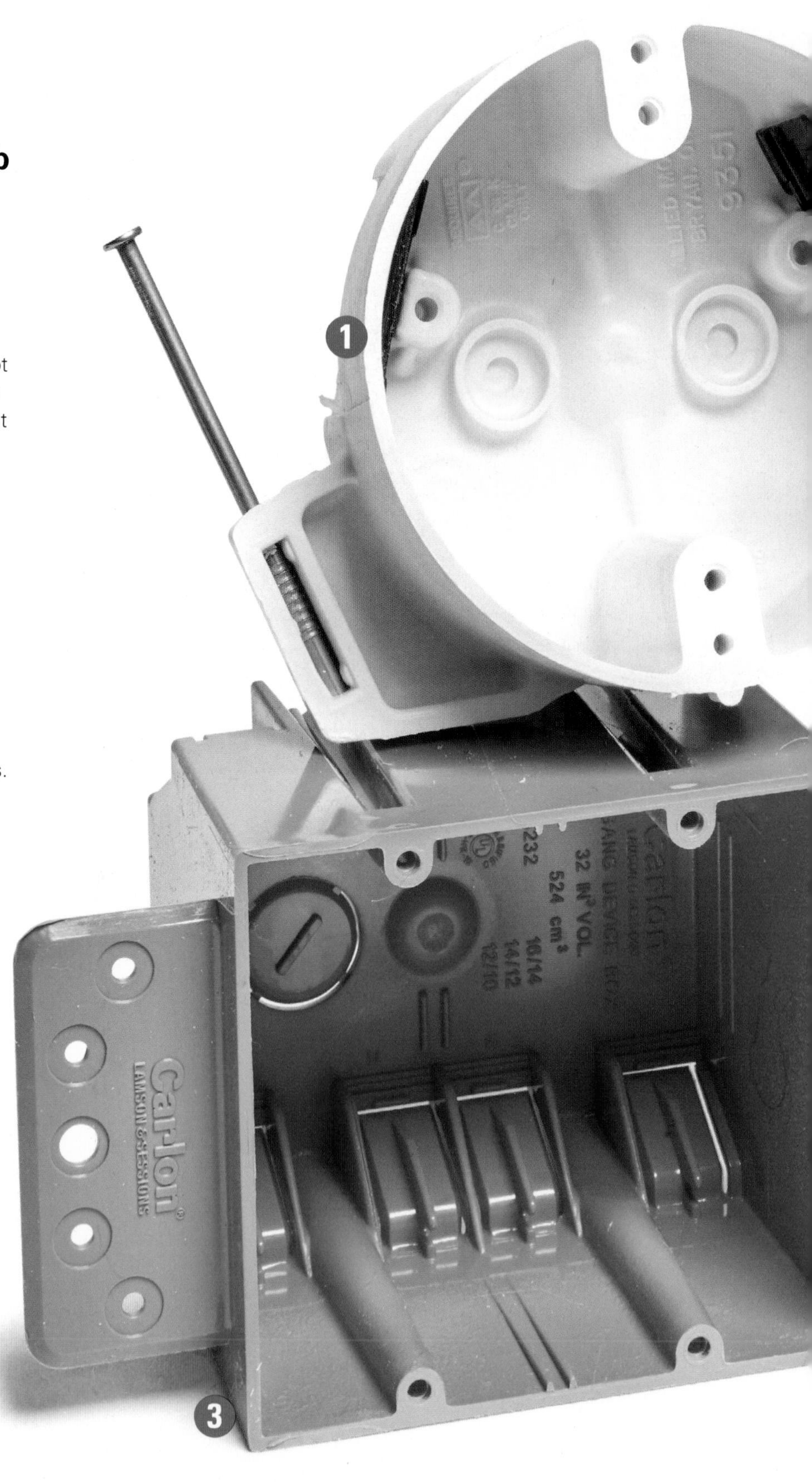

MEET AN EXPERT

John Williamson is a master electrician and electrical inspector in Minnesota.

The purpose of electrical boxes

Wiring connections—where wires join an outlet, switch or other wires—must be inside an electrical box. Here's why: Connections are the weak link in an electrical system. If they get damaged, loosened or pulled apart, you're left without power, or worse, with a fire. Electrical boxes are simply meant to protect vulnerable connections.

Box material

Indoor nonmetallic boxes are typically plastic or fiberglass. Cheap PVC boxes like the one shown at far right work fine, but they can move or distort in wood framing as the studs dry. I prefer to spend the extra 20¢ per box on heavy-duty thermoset plastic or fiberglass boxes. Unlike PVC boxes, they're super strong and maintain their shape.

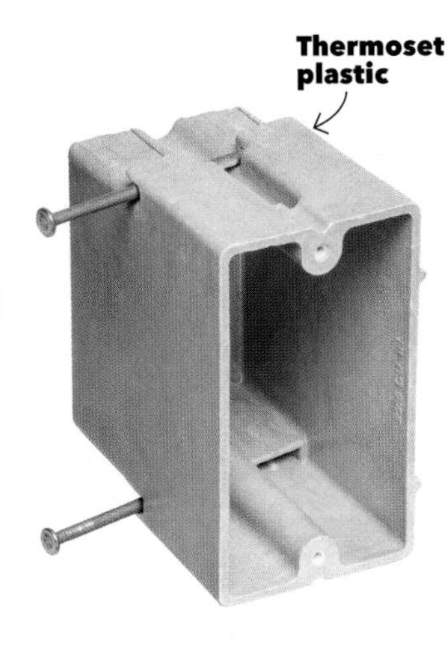

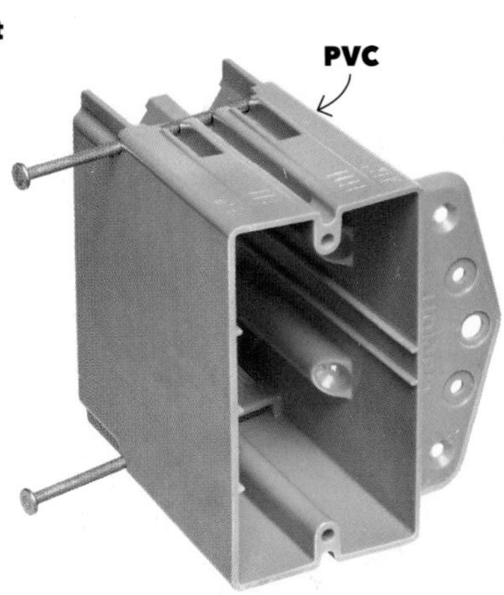

2

Box Size

Wires, receptacles and switches need adequate space. Crowded boxes can damage wires, resulting in a fire or shock hazard. You can use the chart below to calculate the required box size. Add up the numbers for the corresponding components in the box to find how many cubic inches you'll need. In most cases, I skip the math and just buy the largest volume box available in the style I need. I've never been frustrated by having a box that was too large!

BOX VOLUME CALCULATOR

CONDUCTOR SIZE	14 AWG*	12 AWG	10 AWG
Each insulated wire	2	2.25	2.5
All grounding wires combined	2	2.25	2.5
Each switch or receptacle	4	4.5	5
All internal cable clamps	2	2.25	2.5

*American wire gauge

EXAMPLE:

A BOX WITH FOUR 14-2 TYPE-NM CABLES WITH GROUND

8 insulated wires	= 16 cubic in.
All 4 grounding wires	= 2 cubic in.
1 switch	= 4 cubic in.
1 receptacle	= 4 cubic in.
All cable clamps	= 2 cubic in.
Minimum box volume	**= 28 cubic in.**

SPECIALTY BOXES

Ceiling fan boxes

If you're hanging a ceiling fan, you'll need a box designed to support the extra weight. These boxes for ceiling paddle fans are sold as kits, with a wide variety of mounting options for new work and old work (defined below). Boxes that are the sole support of the fan have to be rated for up to 70 lbs. If the fan is supported independently of the box, you can use a general-purpose box.

Adjustable boxes

If you know you'll be installing ceramic tile or wood paneling or wainscoting, buy adjustable boxes. They're mounted to the framing members like any other box; you just turn a screw to adjust the depth flush with the wall treatment. The adjustment screw is accessible even after the wall treatment is applied.

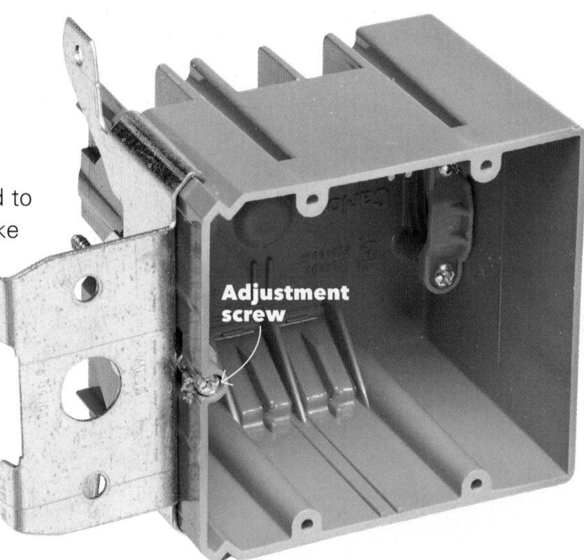

Exterior surface-mount boxes

Exterior surface-mount boxes—often molded PVC—have either threaded or glued hubs and are used with PVC electrical conduit. I like cast-aluminum boxes for outdoor projects. They're extra durable and weatherproof. They often come as a kit, including a ground-fault circuit interrupter (GFCI) receptacle and a weatherproof cover, or as a lighting kit with gaskets and lamp holders for floodlights.

Surface-mount boxes

On concrete or block walls, surface-mount boxes and conduit are the way to go. These boxes can be plastic or metal. Because they're exposed, they need to be mounted perfectly plumb and level. They also require conduit to protect the wires.

Pan boxes

Four-inch round pan boxes (short for "pancake") come in handy if a ceiling joist is right where you need to install your dining room light fixture. Cutting a notch in the ceiling joist would weaken it. Pan boxes are only 1/2 in. deep and only have a volume of 6 cu. in., but they will safely accommodate the three wires you need for your light fixture.

Gasket boxes

Energy code boxes are for insulated walls and ceilings. They typically have a molded flange with a foam gasket as well as foam-lined cable entries. This helps form an airtight seal to keep out drafts. I like to caulk the box flange right to the vapor barrier.

Metal boxes

You can wire a whole home using only nonmetallic boxes, but metal boxes still come in handy for certain situations. They're extremely sturdy and work well where you need lots of volume in the box—for example, for a welder receptacle in your workshop or for a hub where multiple cables meet. As with nonmetallic boxes, get the large ones, which are 4 in. square by 2-1/8 in. deep. You'll find cover options for most configurations of switches and receptacles, as well as mud rings.

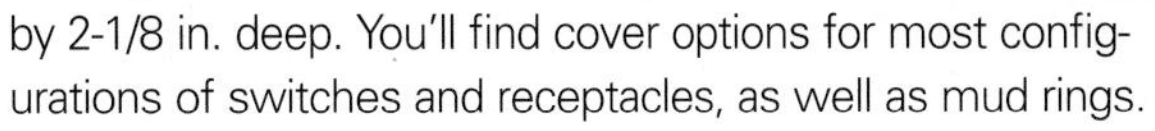

"Old work" boxes

Old work (or "remodeling") boxes are for walls that are covered with drywall or other material. They don't need to be fastened to a stud, so you can install them anywhere. There are several types. The one shown has flip-out tabs that squeeze the box flanges against the drywall. Using the box face as a marking template, you'll get a nice, close fit.

Low-voltage brackets

Unlike in the old days when homes had one or two phone jacks, today we have much more low-voltage wiring for computers, cable TV, home entertainment systems, and whole-house audio, security and temperature control systems. Save time and money by installing low-voltage brackets instead of electrical boxes. Low-voltage wiring doesn't necessarily need an enclosed box. In fact, you often don't want an enclosed box because it may require the wires to make a sharp bend, which impedes the performance of some cables.

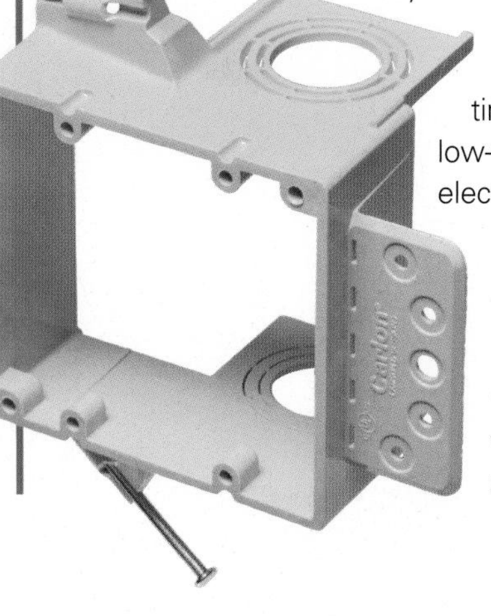

FLOOD YOUR KITCHEN WITH LIGHT

And transform it into a place you'll love to be

By Brad Holden

I've tackled several kitchen projects over the years, but I've never made such a major improvement with so little time and money. I spent less than $350 and just four hours brightening our kitchen. My original intent was strictly practical: I just wanted better light to make food prep and cleanup easier. But replacing the single fixture with bright LEDs transformed the room, surprising me and amazing our guests.

Planning the job

If you have an attic above, you can access the joists from there instead of working from below as I did. That simplifies fishing wires, but you'll still have to dig through insulation.Before starting the job, remove the ceiling fixture and look inside the junction box. My box had just one incoming cable. If your box contains more cables, wiring will be a bit more complicated. You may need to install a second junction box because the box for these LED fixtures can house only two 14-2 cables. I replaced the existing fixture with an LED like all the others.

If you want a standard fixture in the center of your ceiling, you'll still have to remove the existing junction box (**Photo 2**) to access the joists. Then, after installing the new lights, install a remodeling box in the same hole. I found everything I needed at a home center. Two special tools made the project much easier: an adjustable drywall circle cutter ($30) and a 54-in. flexible drill bit ($50).

WHAT IT TAKES
TIME: 1 days to $500
SKILL: Beginner
COST: $30 per light
TOOLS: Drywall circle cutter or manual drywall saw, wire cutter, wire stripper, drill, flexible drill bit

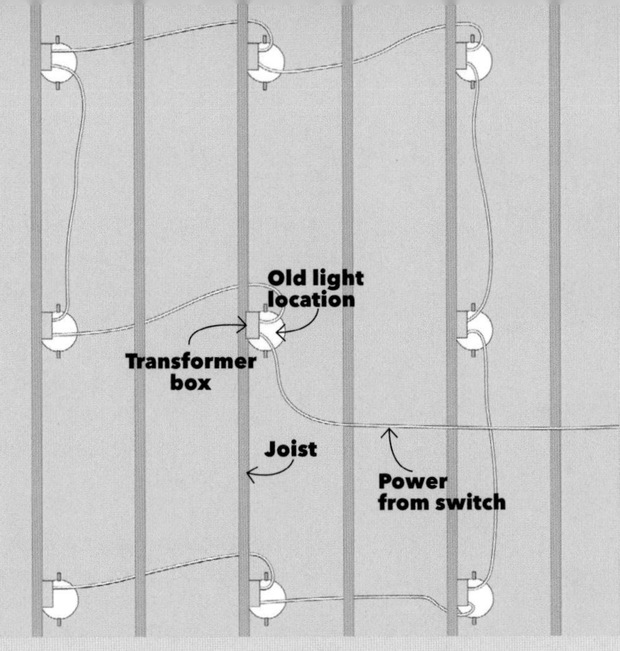

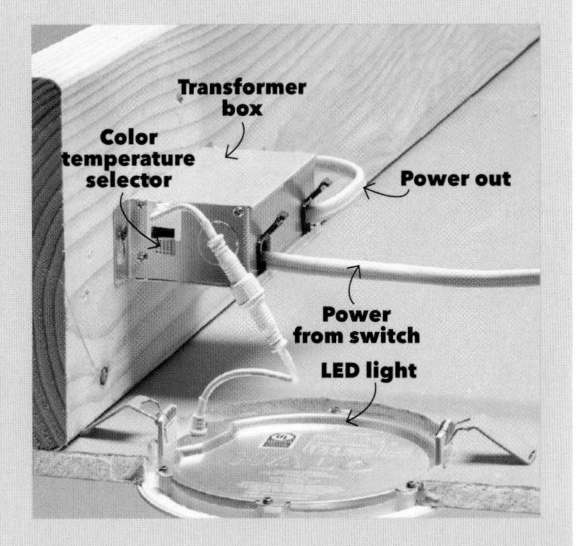

Low-profile LEDs made it easy

Initially, I thought I'd install recessed can lights for a sleek look and lots of light. Then, I ran across these ultra-slim Halo LEDs by Eaton ($30 each). These LED lights are super bright (900 lumens) and have such a low profile (less than 1/2 in.) that you can even locate them directly under a joist if needed. They're rated for insulation contact and wet locations, so you can use them in a shower or even outdoors. A switch on the side of the box lets you adjust the color temperature. They're also dimmable. All you need is a power supply, a means to cut round holes, 14-2 NM-B cable, basic electrical tools and a drill. The transformer box converts 120V to low voltage, and it's UL-listed as a junction box with room for power in and power out. That lets you take power from the first box and string together as many lights as you want. You might need to fish wire, but aside from that, installation is easy. Several companies make a similar product, but this was in stock at the local home center.

1 Lay out the new light locations. Mark all the joists involved in the installation using strips of tape. Then mark the location for each new light with tape. The lights can go anywhere, but I kept them close to the joists to get better access for attaching the transformer boxes to the joists.

2 Remove the old ceiling box. Shut off power to the fixture at the breaker panel. Use a noncontact voltage detector to verify that there's no current, and then pull out the old ceiling box. Depending on how the box is attached and what it's made of, this may entail different methods. For instance, you could break a fiberglass box to remove it. Ours was a plastic box, nailed to the joists, so I was able to pry it out.

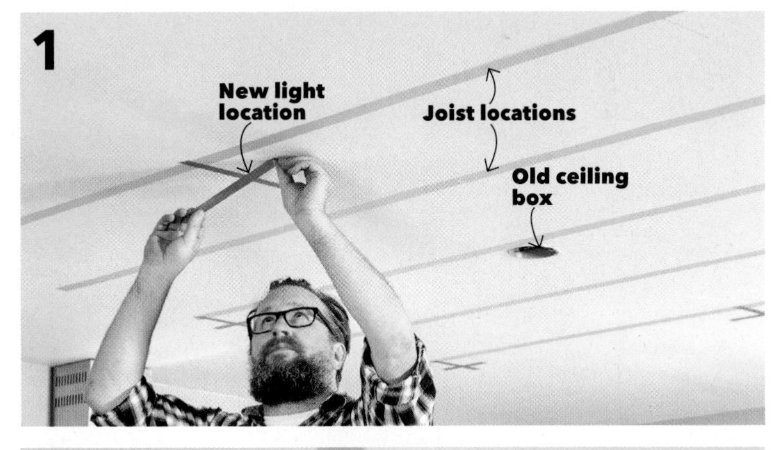

MEET AN EXPERT

Brad Holden, an associate editor at *Family Handyman*, has been a furniture maker and remodeler for 30 years.

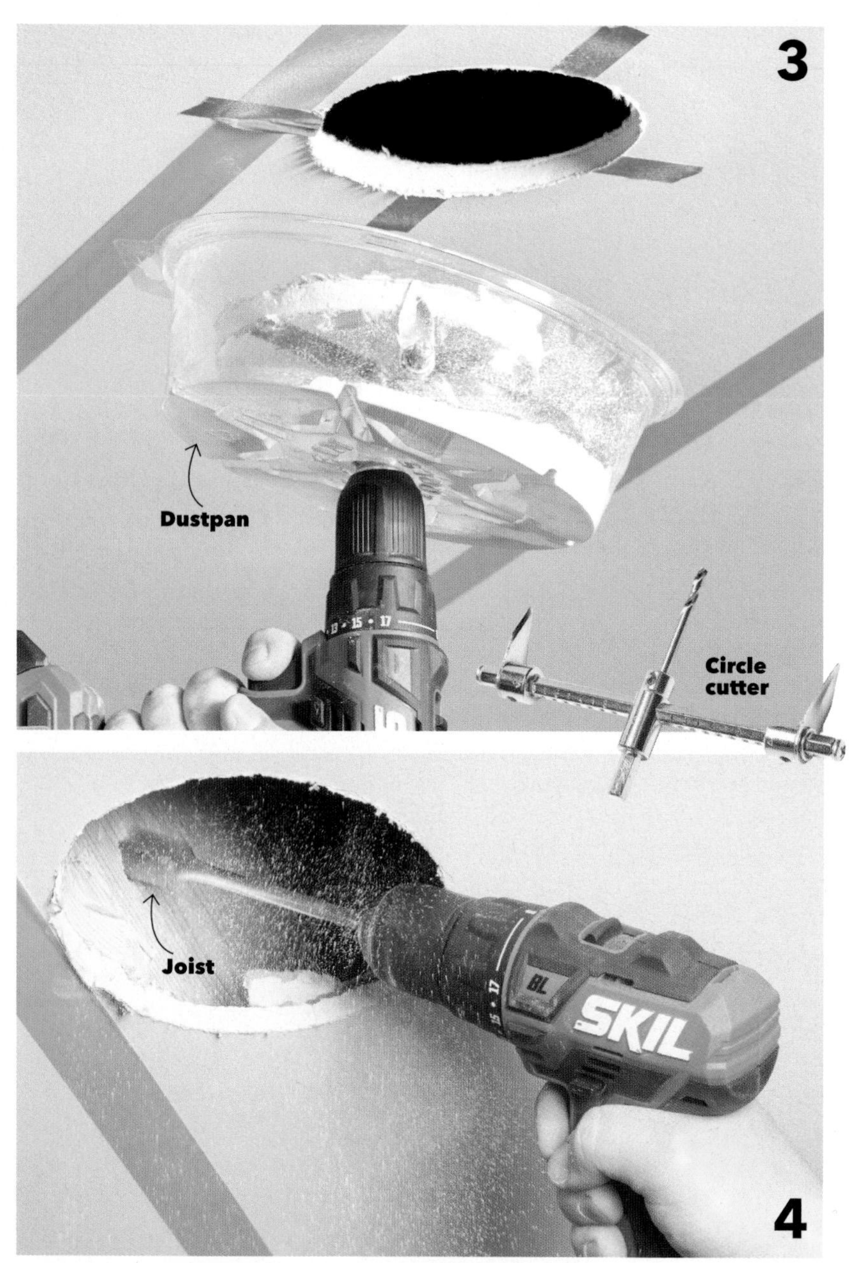

3 Cut new holes. Cut all the holes for the new lights. This adjustable drywall circle cutter (left) slices out perfect holes, saving lots of time. It includes a pan to catch the dust. But it can't be used to enlarge the existing hole that held the old box. For that, trace the provided template and cut it out using a manual drywall saw. Now it's time to fish wires.

4 Drill through the first joist. Drill through the joist at least 2 in. from its bottom edge. I drilled a 1-in.-diameter hole here to make it easier to maneuver the long, flexible bit in the next step. If you're just going through one joist, you won't need the flexible bit.

5 Drill through the next joist. Pass a flexible bit through the hole you just drilled until it hits the next joist. Flex the bit downward to get close to the center of the joist. Unless you have access from above, this is guesswork. Drill through the joist, and then loosen the drill's chuck and set the drill aside, leaving the bit in the hole.

6 Fasten cable to the drill bit. Run one of the wires from a new cable through the hole in the bit's tip and bend it over. Twist the other wires together and wrap everything with electrical tape.

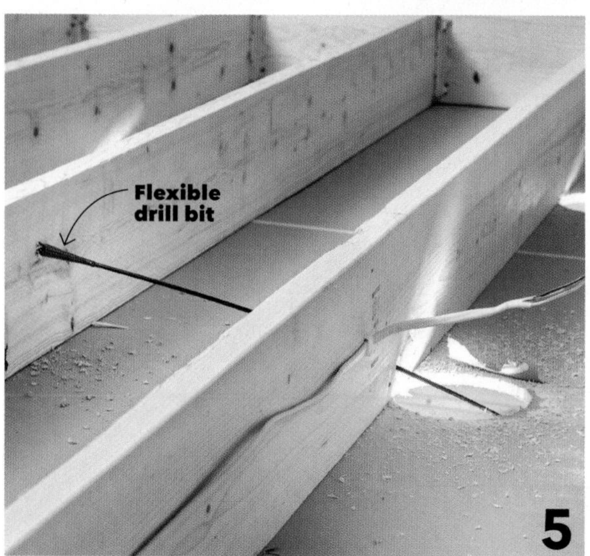

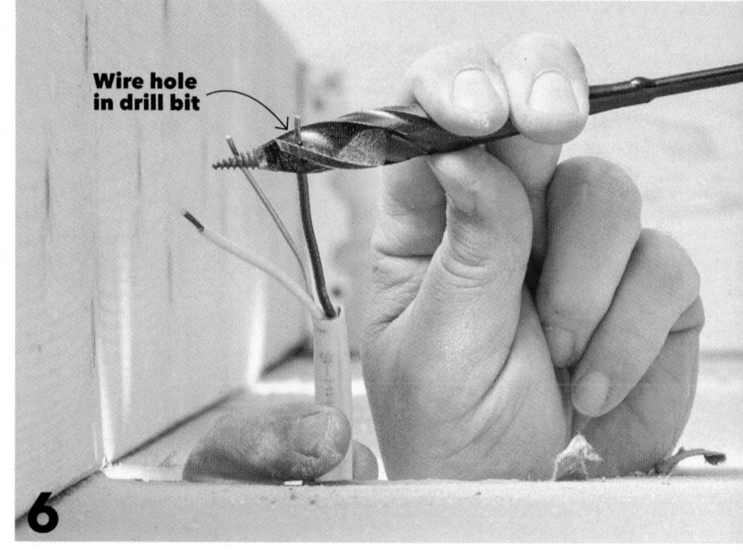

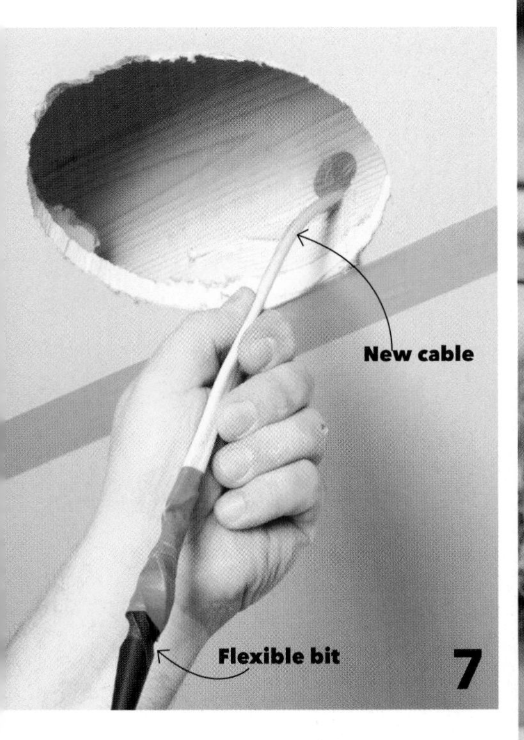

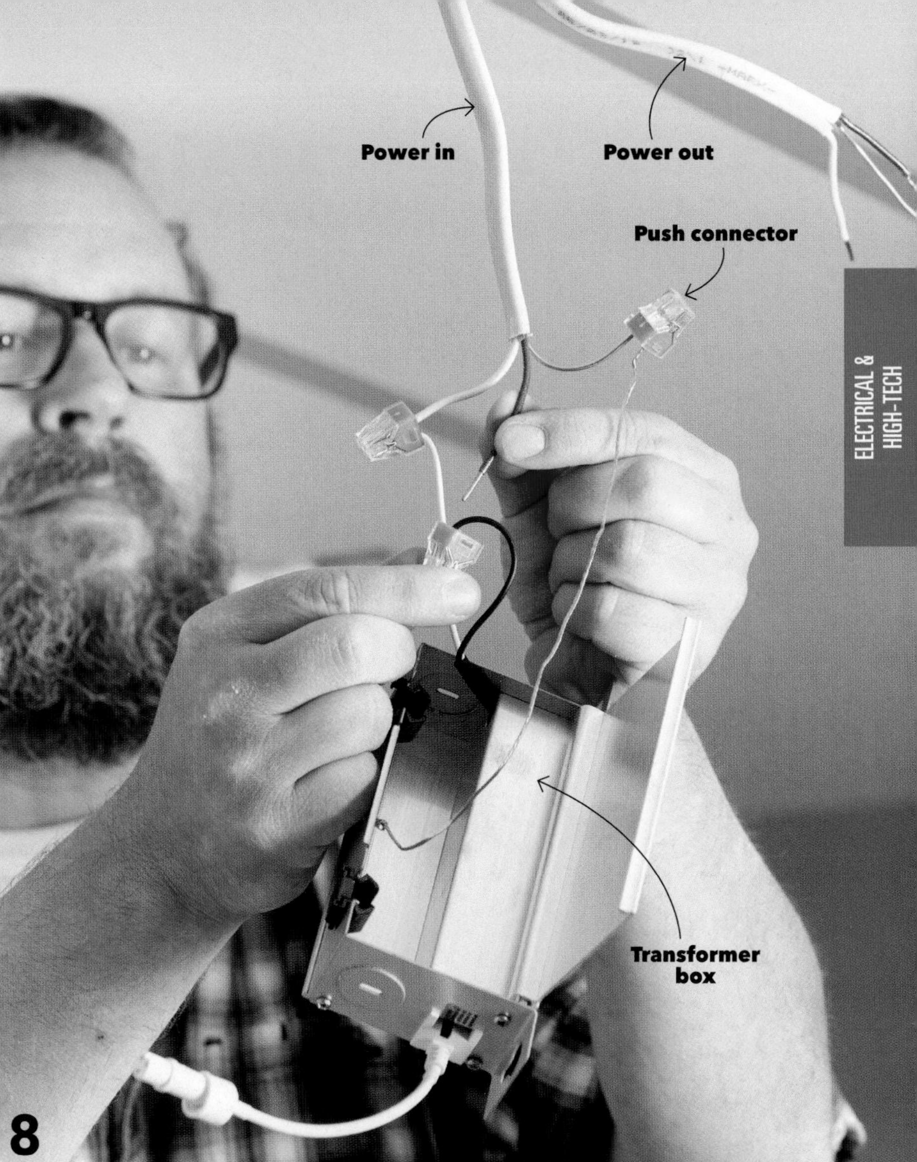

7 Pull in the new cable. Pull the bit back through the hole along with your new cable, and then unwrap the tape. Each light cutout (except the last one in the chain) requires two cables: power in and power out. As you're running wire from hole to hole, leave plenty of extra length. It'll be much easier to make the connections.

8 Connect power to the transformer. Connect the power source to the first transformer box. Connect your "downstream" cable to power the next box in line. These lights are outfitted with push connectors, which are far simpler to use than wire nuts and take up less space. Secure the cables using cable clamps in the knockouts or the built-in cable traps. In this situation, code doesn't require the cable to be secured to the joists.

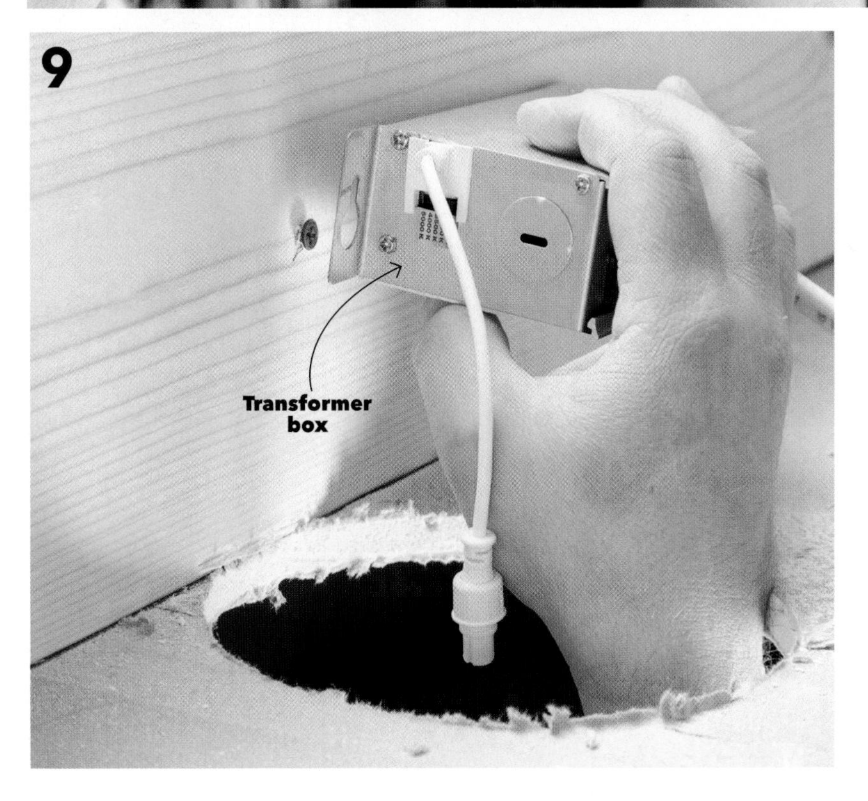

9 Hang the transformer. Hold the transformer box against the joist and mark the keyholes. Set the box aside and install the two screws. Hang the box, and then tighten the screws with a screwdriver. Working space is limited, so hang the box directly above the hole.

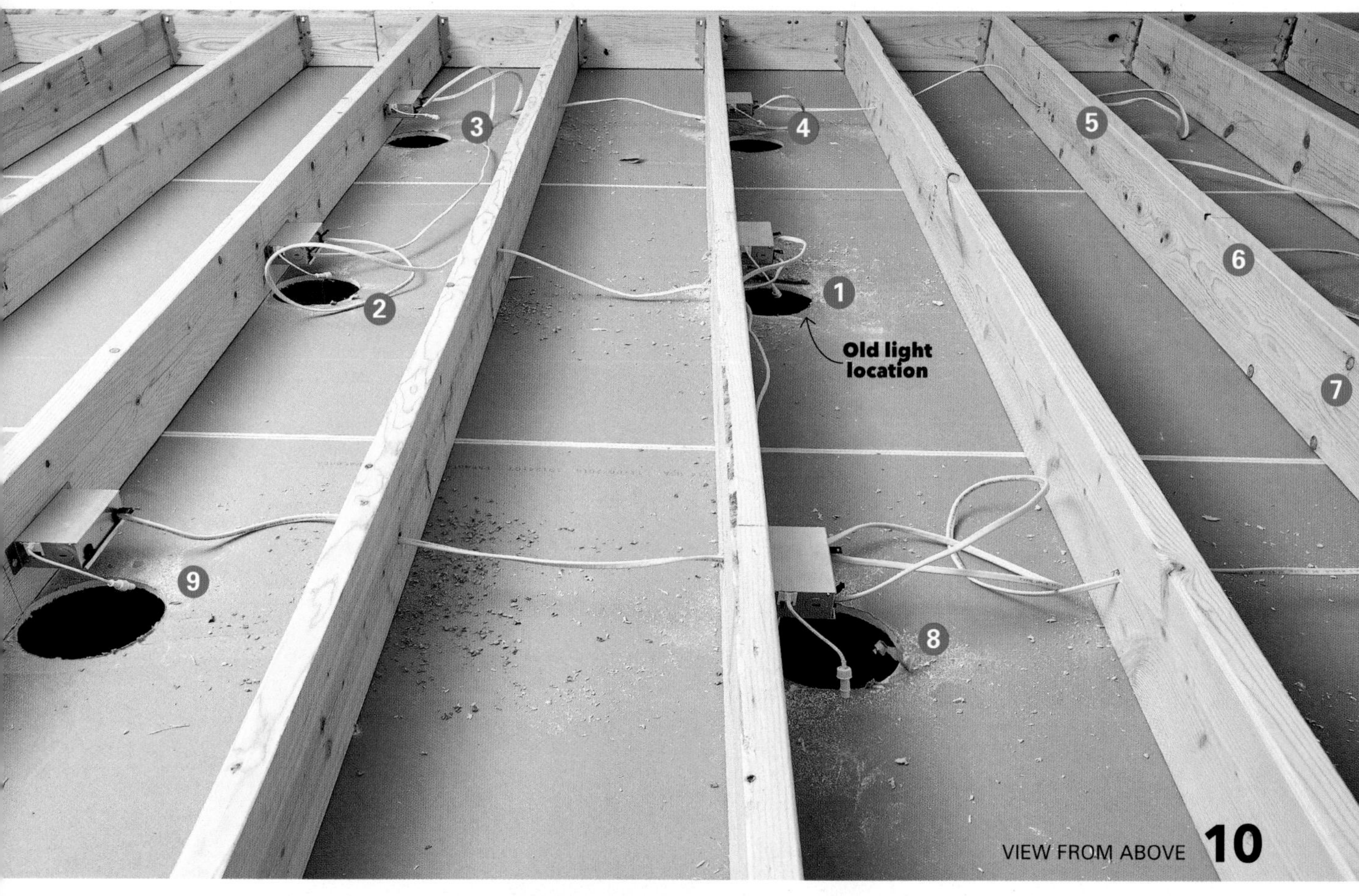

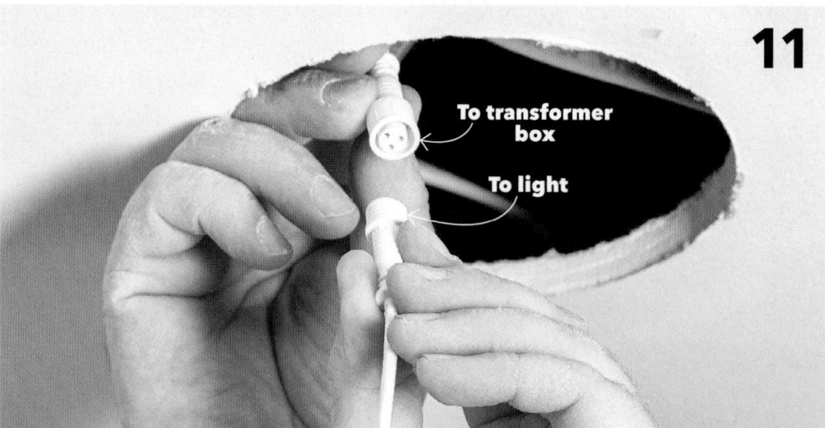

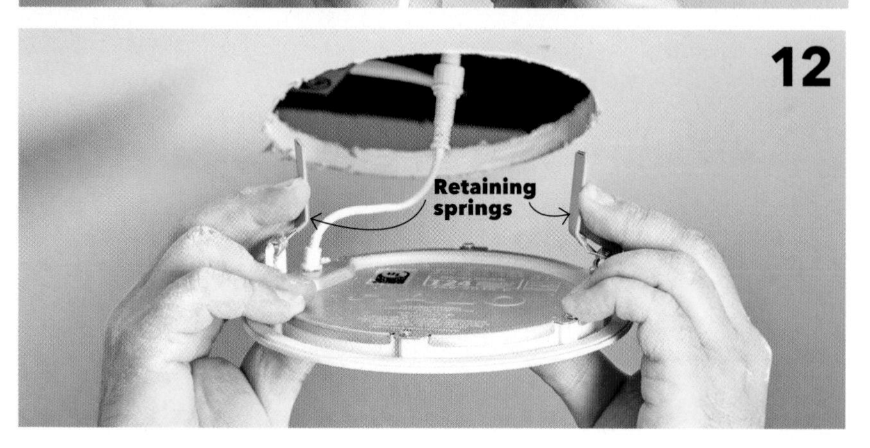

10 Connect all the transformers. Connect power to each box and hang all the transformers. Each box has power in and power out except for the last one.

11 Connect the lights. Plug the low-voltage cables from the lights into the cables from each transformer box. Set the desired color temperature using the switch on the side of each transformer box.

12 Snap in the lights. Press the retaining springs upward and pop each light into place, and then switch the power back on at the breaker panel. If you want to change the color temperature after the lights are installed, carefully pull down on the light's flange to remove it, keeping your fingers clear of the mousetrap-like retaining springs!

Best Pro Tips

EXPERT ADVICE FROM THE JOB SITE

ELECTRICAL & HIGH-TECH

AVOID **ELECTRICAL MISTAKES**

How to recognize and correct wiring blunders that can endanger your home

CAUTION: Turn off the power at the main panel when you're doing electrical work.

MISTAKE:

Overfilling electrical boxes

Too many wires stuffed into a box can cause dangerous overheating, short-circuiting and fire. The National Electrical Code (NEC) specifies minimum box sizes to reduce this risk.

THE RIGHT WAY:

Install a larger box

To figure the minimum box size required, assign numerical values to the items in the box:

1 - for each hot wire and neutral wire entering the box
1 - for all the ground wires combined
1 - for all the cable clamps combined
2 - for each device (switch or outlet—but not light fixtures)

Multiply the total by **2** for 14-gauge wire and by **2.25** for 12-gauge wire to get the minimum box size required in cubic inches. Then choose a box with at least this much volume. Plastic boxes have the volume stamped inside, usually on the back. Steel box capacities are listed in the electrical code. Steel boxes won't be labeled, so you'll have to measure the height, width and depth of the interior. Then multiply to find the volume.

MEET AN EXPERT

John Williamson is a master electrician and an electrical inspector in Minnesota.

BestProTips

MISTAKE:

Poor support for outlets and switches

Loose switches or outlets look bad (**photo right**); worse, they're dangerous. Loosely connected outlets move around, causing the wires to loosen from the terminals. Loose wires can arc and overheat, creating a potential fire hazard.

THE RIGHT WAY:

Add plastic spacers

Fix loose outlets by shimming under the screws to create a tight connection to the box. You can buy spacers like the ones shown below at home centers and hardware stores. Small washers or a coil of wire wrapped around the screw work as well.

Plastic spacer

Plastic spacers

MISTAKE:

Reversing hot and neutral wires

Connecting the black (hot) wire to the neutral terminal of an outlet creates the potential for a lethal shock. Unfortunately, you may not realize the mistake until someone gets shocked, because lights and most other plug-in devices will still work; they just won't work safely.

THE RIGHT WAY:

Identify the neutral terminal

Connect the white wire to the neutral terminal of outlets and light fixtures. The neutral terminal is always marked, and usually has silver- or light-colored screws. Connect the hot wire to the other terminal. If there's a green or bare copper wire, that's the ground. Connect the ground to the green grounding screw or to a ground wire or grounded box.

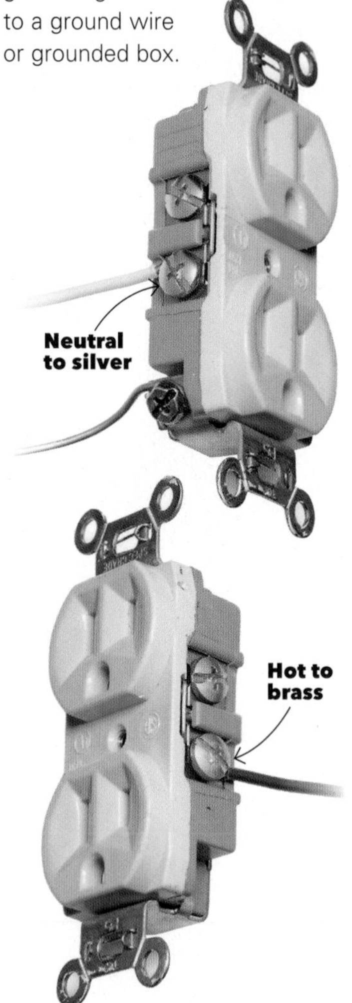

MISTAKE:
Wiring a GFCI backward

GFCI (ground-fault circuit interrupter) outlets protect you from a lethal shock by shutting off the power when they sense slight differences in current. They have two pairs of terminals. You'll lose the shock protection if you mix up the line and load connections.

THE RIGHT WAY:
Connect power to the "line" terminals

One pair of terminals is labeled "line," for incoming power for the GFCI outlet itself. The other set is labeled "load" and provides protection for downstream outlets. Each pair of terminals receives a hot and a neutral wire.

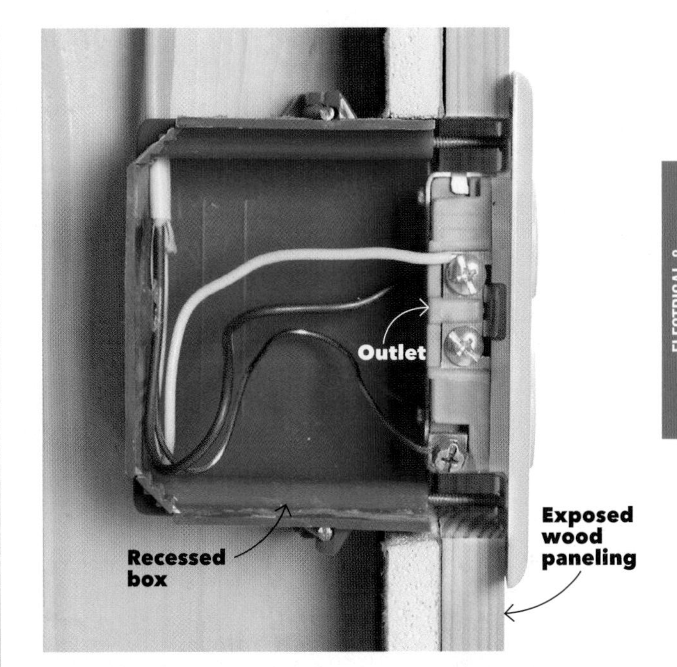

MISTAKE:
Recessing boxes behind the wall surface

Electrical boxes must be flush to the wall surface if the wall surface is a combustible material. Boxes recessed behind combustible materials like wood present a fire hazard because the wood is left exposed to potential heat and sparks.

THE RIGHT WAY:
Add a box extension

The fix is simply to install a metal or plastic box extension. If you use a metal box extension on a plastic box, connect the metal extension to the ground wire in the box using a grounding clip and a short piece of wire.

ELECTRICAL & HIGH-TECH

BestProTips

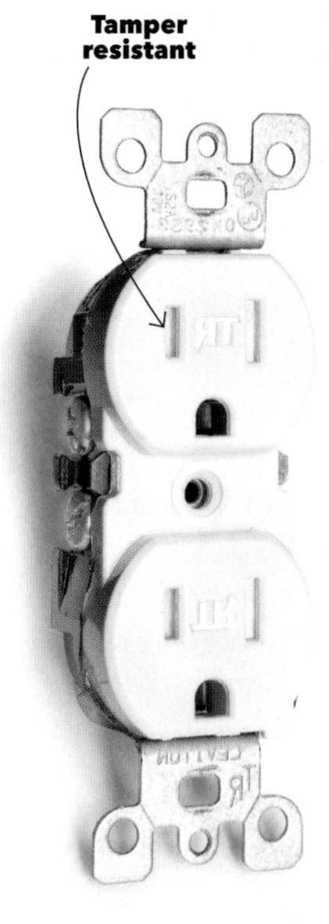

MISTAKE:
Not using tamper-resistant receptacles

Conventional receptacles are available at home centers, so many people use them when replacing an outlet.

THE RIGHT WAY:
According to the NEC, when you replace an outlet, the new one must be a tamper-resistant receptacle.

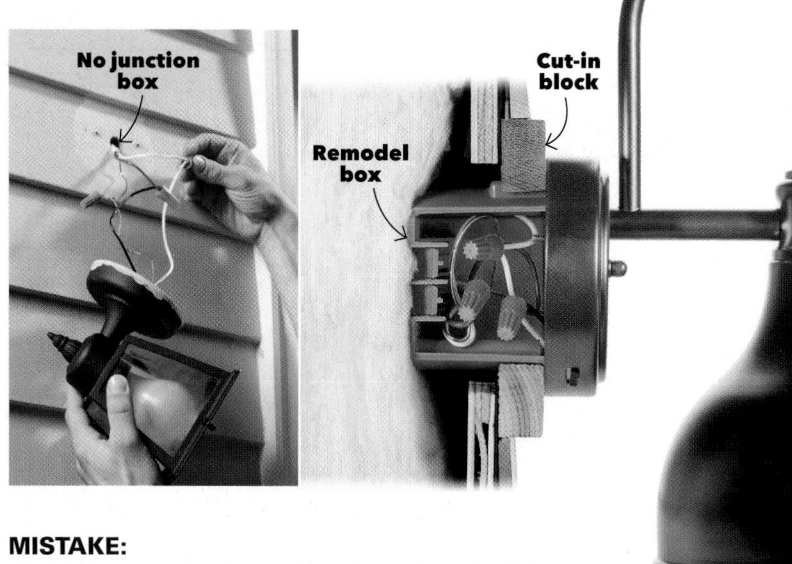

MISTAKE:
Making connections outside electrical boxes

Never connect wires outside electrical boxes. Junction boxes protect the connections from accidental damage and contain sparks and heat from a loose connection or short circuit.

THE RIGHT WAY:
Add a box

Where connections aren't contained in an electrical box, install a box and reconnect the wires inside it. The photo above shows one way to do this for an exterior light mounted on wood siding.

MISTAKE:
Installing a flat, weather-resistant cover on an outdoor receptacle

Flat covers provide protection only when a receptacle isn't in use, but it's not uncommon for extension cords to be plugged in for extended periods of time—for example, for holiday lights.

This product may still be available at home centers, but it no longer meets code.

THE RIGHT WAY:
Install a bubble cover

All new exterior outlets must have a "bubble" or "in-use" cover identified as "extra-duty." And don't forget the weather-resistant receptacle. The NEC requires that all 15- and 20-amp receptacles be rated as weather-resistant and tamper-resistant when installed in both wet and damp locations.

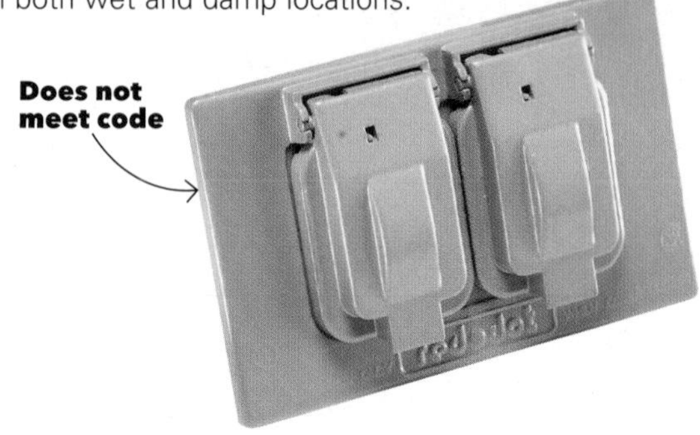

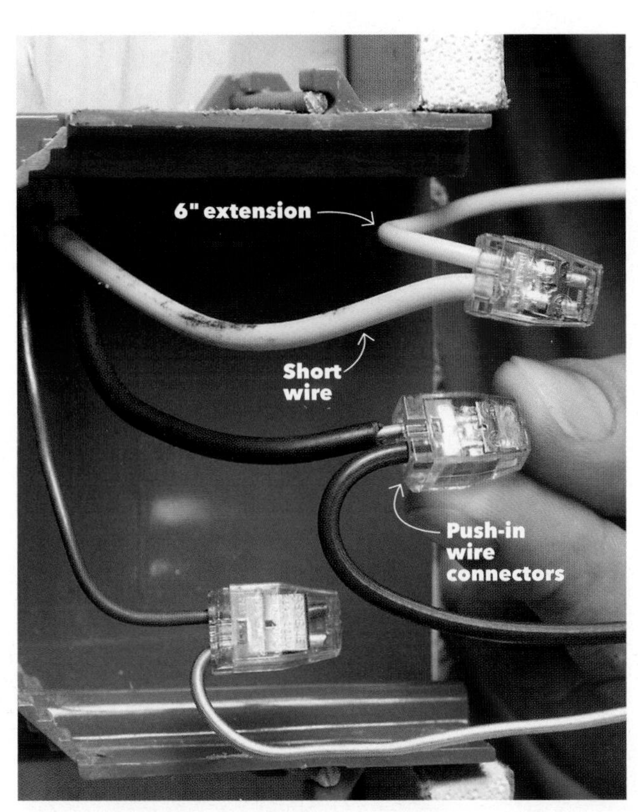

MISTAKE:
Cutting wires too short

Wires that are cut too short make wire connections difficult and—since you're more likely to make poor connections—dangerous.

THE RIGHT WAY:
Extend wires

Leave the wires long enough to protrude at least 3 in. from the box. If you run into short wires, there's an easy fix. Simply add 6-in. extensions to the existing wires. The push-in wire connectors shown below are easier to install in tight spots. You'll find them at hardware stores and home centers.

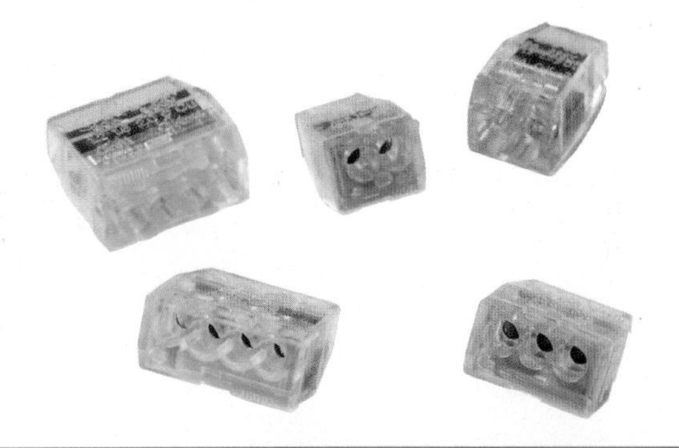

MISTAKE:
Installing cable without a clamp

Cable that's not secured can strain the connections. In metal boxes, the sharp edges can cut the insulation on the wires.

THE RIGHT WAY:
Install a clamp

Single-gang plastic boxes do not require internal cable clamps, but the cable must be stapled within 8 in. of the box. Larger plastic boxes are required to have built-in cable clamps, and the cable must be stapled within 12 in. of the box. Cables must be connected to metal boxes with an approved cable clamp. Make sure the sheathing on the cable is trapped under the clamp, and that about 1/4 in. of sheathing is visible inside the box. Some metal boxes have built-in cable clamps. If the box you're using doesn't include clamps, buy clamps separately and install them when you add the cable to the box (**photo right**).

BestProTips

MISTAKE:
Installing a three-slot receptacle with no ground wire

If you have two-slot outlets, it's tempting to replace them with three-slot outlets so you can plug in three-prong plugs. Don't do this unless there's a ground available. Use a tester ($7 to $10 at home centers) to see if your outlet is grounded. A tester indicates whether the outlet is wired correctly or what fault exists.

THE RIGHT WAY:
Install a two-slot outlet

If you discover a three-slot outlet in an ungrounded box, either replace it with a two-slot outlet, or tamper-resistant GFCI outlet. Tamper-resistant, two-slot outlets don't exist, so the new GFCI must be labeled "No equipment ground."

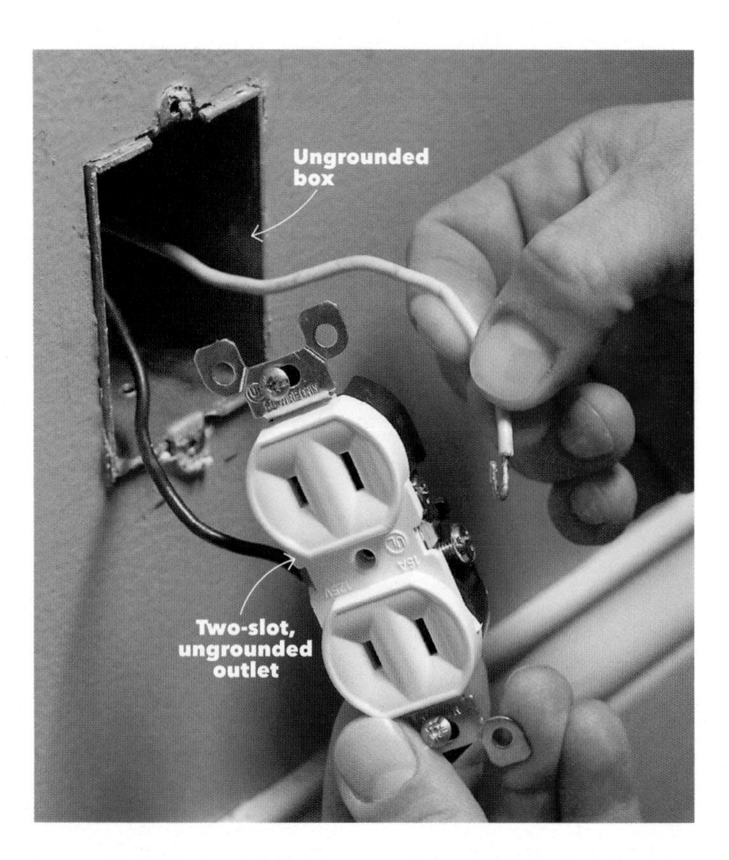

MISTAKE:
Leaving plastic-sheathed cable unprotected

It's easy to damage plastic-sheathed cable that's left exposed between framing members. That's why the electrical code requires cable to be protected in these areas. Cable is especially vulnerable when it's run over or under wall or ceiling framing, as shown here.

THE RIGHT WAY:
Install a 2x2

Protect exposed cable by nailing or screwing a 2x2 board alongside the cable as shown above. Staple the cable to the board every 4-1/2 ft. or less, as needed.

3 Plumbing, HVAC & Appliances

IN THIS CHAPTER

HomeSmarts

KNOWLEDGE YOU NEED TO BE A BETTER HOMEOWNER

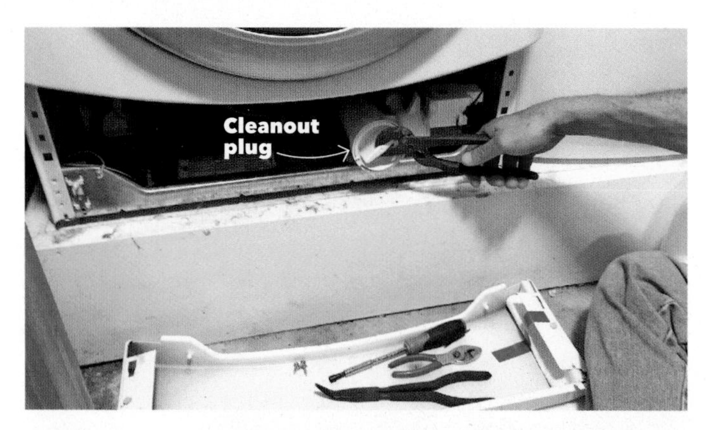

EASY FRONT-LOAD WASHER FIX

Our washing machine stopped pumping out water during the discharge cycle and shut itself down. Instead of calling an appliance repair service, I took off the front access panel to poke around a bit. Seeing the big, obvious PVC cleanout plug, I unscrewed it to see what it was all about. Holy smokes! About a gallon of water poured out before I pulled out what appeared to be a filter drawer. Inside were $2.52 in change, a clothing tag, a house key, three bobby pins, a golf tee, wadded pieces of paper, a jean rivet, a couple of nuts and a washer, plus some unidentifiable debris. I cleaned the drawer and put everything back, and the washer now works perfectly. If your washer stops working, give this a try. If this solves the problem, you've probably saved about $100 for a service call, not to mention the embarrassment of watching the repair technician pull off the same easy operation.

—Travis Larson
Senior Editor

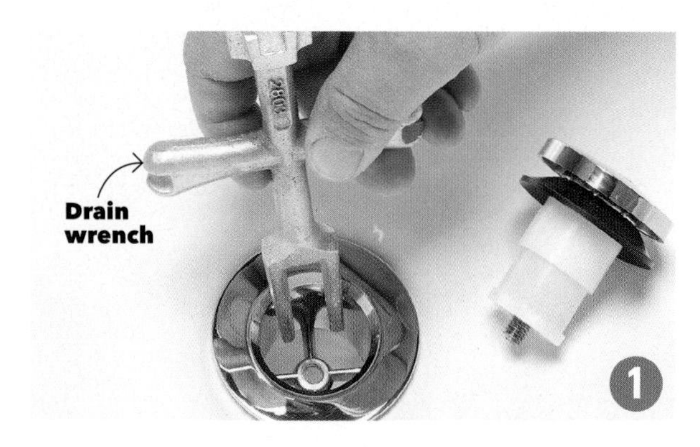

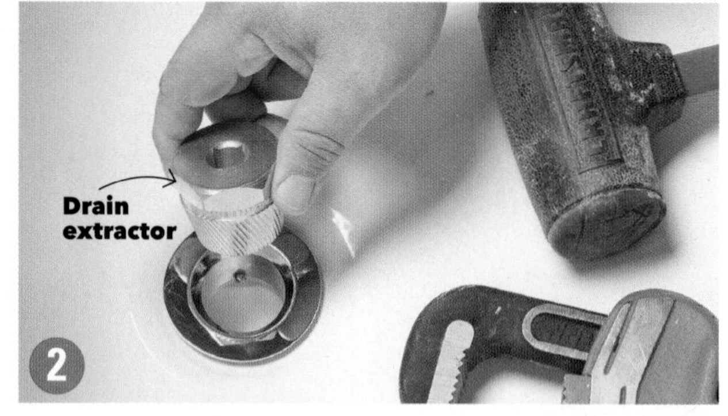

REMOVE A BATHTUB DRAIN

Need to replace your tub drain? Removing the old one can be a real chore. Typically, you'd remove the drain with a drain wrench ($10 online; **Photo 1**), but if the drain's crossbars are gone, you'll have to use a drain extractor ($20 online; **Photo 2**). If the drain is really old, sometimes even a drain extractor isn't enough; you'll first have to knock it loose using an old chisel to bite into the metal (**Photo 3**). Once the drain is loosened a bit, turn it the rest of the way with the drain extractor.

—Brad Holden
Associate Editor

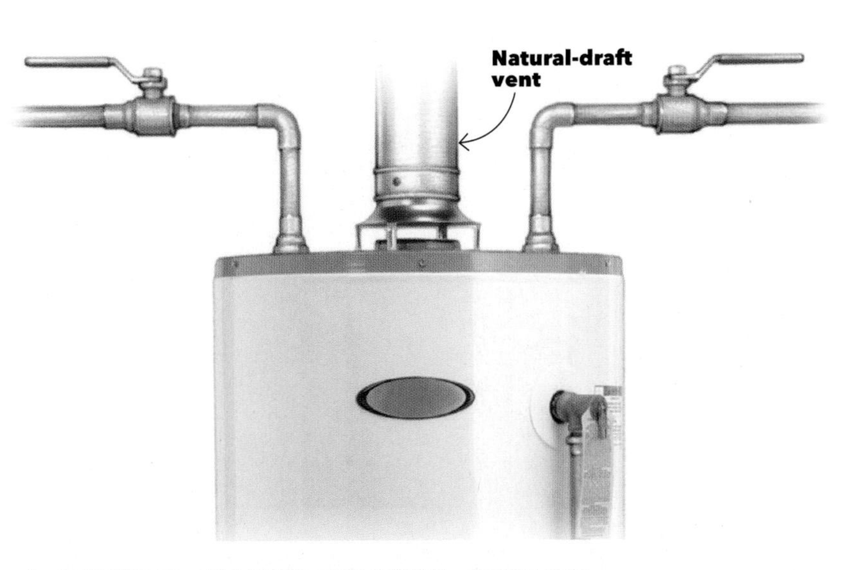

A BETTER WATER HEATER OPTION

Q We've been getting high electric bills and want to replace our old electric water heater with a natural gas model. But I'm afraid that running the exhaust vent will be a hassle. Is there an easy way to do it?

—Michael Banks,
Portland, OR

A It's much easier to run the vent if you install a "power-vented" type of natural gas (or propane) water heater. This type of venting system is different from what you see on most gas water heaters. Most have a "natural-draft" type of vent (**photo above**), where the hot waste gases rise through an open draft diverter and into metal pipes, which eventually lead to the outdoors. Running one of these vents is complicated and may be expensive.

In contrast, a power-vented type (**right**) uses a fan to blow the exhaust gases out. Since this method doesn't rely on the natural buoyancy of hot air, the vent pipes don't have to go upward. They can run horizontally, which usually makes them much easier to install. Further, the fan dilutes the exhaust with cooler air so you can run the vents with easy-to-assemble PVC pipe. Power venting is an especially good solution for more energy efficient, tightly built homes, where a good natural draft is difficult to establish.

However, you should be aware of several drawbacks:

- You may notice the sound of the fan. Ideally the water heater will be in a room away from the main living area so it doesn't become bothersome.
- You have to provide a standard electrical receptacle near the unit to supply power for the fan.
- You have to be sure you have adequate "makeup" air to replace the air being blown out.
- And finally, power-vented water heaters cost at least 50 percent more than natural-draft water heaters. Figure somewhere in the $450 to $650 range, plus installation. You can find power-vented water heaters wherever water heaters are sold; almost every major water heater manufacturer makes them.

If you decide to install one yourself, read the instructions carefully and make sure to follow all venting procedures. Also, call your local building department to ask if you need a plumbing permit to do the work.

—Gary Wentz
Editor-in-Chief

SECURE TOILET BOLTS TO THE FLANGE

When I install a toilet, I always fasten the flange bolts to the floor flange with a second set of nuts. Better flange bolt kits come with an extra set of nuts just for this purpose. The extra nuts anchor the bolts as you set the toilet in place. Use only corrosion-resistant brass or stainless-steel bolt kits.

—Les Zell
Master Plumber

TROUBLESHOOT YOUR TOILET: DO THE BUCKET TEST

If your toilet's flush is weak, the first thing you need to determine is whether the problem is in the drain or the toilet. Before you snake out the drain or replace your fill valve, try this. Dump a bucket of water into the bowl. If it flushes slowly, the problem is in the drain. If it flushes quickly, the problem is in the toilet. This doesn't fix the problem, but at least it tells you where to start looking. For solutions to all kinds of toilet trouble, search for "toilet" at familyhandyman.com.

—Malcolm McAdam

RUBBER COUPLERS—YES OR NO?

I've installed at least a hundred rubber couplers on ABS, PVC and metal pipes, in my own houses and others. Never had a problem. Not once. But recently I heard a couple experts call them "unreliable." So I'm hoping that pro plumbers can help settle the issue. Do you use rubber couplers? Have you seen them leak, tear or crack? In the areas I've worked, inspectors allow the types with full metal sleeves (shown at right), but not the kind with just two band clamps (left). Which kind do you use? Thanks for sharing your expertise!

Metal sleeve

—Gary Wentz
Editor-in-Chief

PEX VS. PE-RT

You'll find both PEX and PE-RT in the plumbing department at home centers along with the fittings and tools needed for installation. They look similar, so what's the difference? PEX is certified safe for use in residential plumbing for potable water. PE-RT, on the other hand, is certified for use in radiant floor heating applications only, not for drinking water.

3 REASONS TO FILTER YOUR **WATER**

SHUTTERSTOCK/ALEXXNDR

While the lead crisis in Flint, Michigan, raised serious questions about the risks in public water supplies, most supplies in the United States are very safe. Still, there are good reasons you might want to filter your home's water:

Hard water

The dissolved minerals in hard water can make your laundry feel scratchy, decrease the efficacy of shampoo and soap, and affect your water's taste. Iron can stain your clothes and dishes, even at levels allowed by the EPA.

The solution: Install a whole-house system, which will filter every drop of city or private well water that comes into your home.

Safety

While the water leaving your provider should be clean, the quality could decline before the water reaches your taps. Even the pipes inside your home could be to blame.

The solution: First, have your home's water tested to identify lead, pesticides, minerals, bacteria and other substances. The Environmental Protection Agency offers a list of certified water testing labs on its website, epa.gov.

In most cases, you'll only be concerned about your drinking water. That means a system connected to your kitchen faucet may be all you need and will save you lots of money compared with a whole-house system.

Bad taste

It's the disinfectants added at the water treatment plant—often chlorine—that people generally find distasteful. "The chemicals are there for a good reason, but many people do prefer to have them removed," says Tom Bruursema, associate executive director of the Water Quality Association. Once the water has reached your house, the chemicals have done their job and can safely be filtered out.

The solution: A simple under-sink filtration system removes chlorine taste and odor. But you might not need to install a filtration system. A simple NSF-certified pour-through pitcher filters out chlorine taste and odor, and costs $30 or less. Some of these pitchers also filter out contaminants such as copper, cadmium and mercury. There are pitchers for about $40 that remove lead.

—Stephanie Thurrott
Contributing Editor

Whole-house filtration system

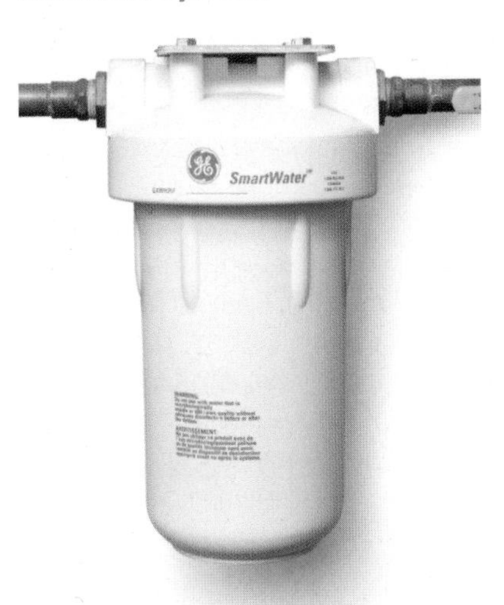

Under-sink filtration system

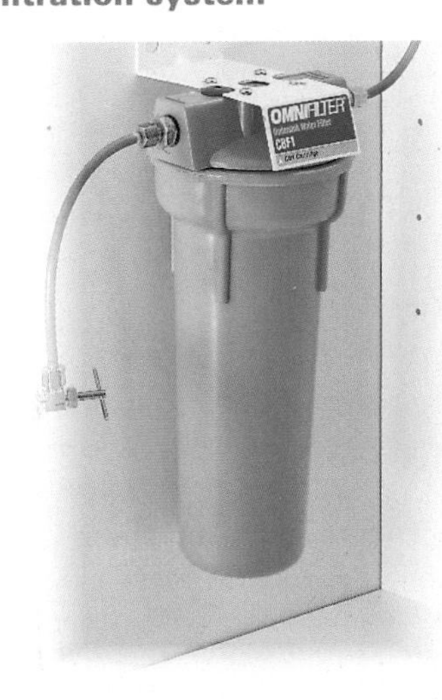

Pour-through pitcher

For more information on choosing and installing water filters, search for "water filters" at familyhandyman.com.

PLUMBING, HVAC & APPLIANCES

SMART FAUCET: AN EXTRA HAND IN THE KITCHEN

By Jason Ingolfsland

By tapping into a virtual assistant such as Google Home, a smart faucet turns on and off, fills containers by exact measurement, programs "experiences" and changes water temperature, all by voice command. Smart faucets aren't cheap, ranging from $500 to $800. At first glance, it seemed like a novelty, but I was intrigued. So I picked up a Kohler Konnect Sensate ($518 on Amazon), a smart faucet that connects to my Google Home, to test it out in my own kitchen.

Same install—but with wires

Smart faucets install like standard faucets; you connect supply lines to the faucet. After that, as you might expect, there are multiple wires to connect a solenoid valve and other sensors. It looked daunting, but all was easy and intuitive, and installation was done in about an hour. Some smart faucets require an electrical outlet underneath the sink. If you don't have an outlet under your sink, search "outlet" at familyhandyman.com to learn how to install one. Other faucets are battery-powered; with them, you'll have the nuisance of periodic battery changes.

Control with voice commands

Voice commands are easy but not always intuitive. For the model I installed, rather than saying "Hey Google, turn on the faucet," I had to say "Hey Google, ask Kohler to turn on the faucet." Not a big deal, but kind of a mouthful. This model doesn't offer voice temperature control, but some smart faucets do. Smart faucets also have a manual override, so they can also be operated the old-fashioned way.

Program different containers

You can program "experiences" for specific containers, such as coffee pots, dog bowls or watering cans. This way, you don't need to remember exact amounts for each container. I programmed an experience called "spaghetti." After telling my virtual assistant to "start spaghetti," the pot filled to 4 quarts while I prepared other things.

Keep your faucet germ-free

After handling raw meat, I'd rather not smear it on the faucet handle. So I asked the smart faucet to turn on, washed my hands and turned it off with the motion sensor, never touching it.

Measure water with precision

While making pancakes, I put a container under the faucet and asked for two cups of water. In the meantime, I got a skillet from the cupboard and turned on the range. When I returned to the sink, two cups of water was waiting. It was magic.

The bottom line

I tested this faucet for a week. After I replaced it with our "analog" faucet, my wife and I were surprised to find we missed the convenience. Smart faucets are still very new and will undoubtedly improve, but even this early model made me think about installing one permanently in the near future.

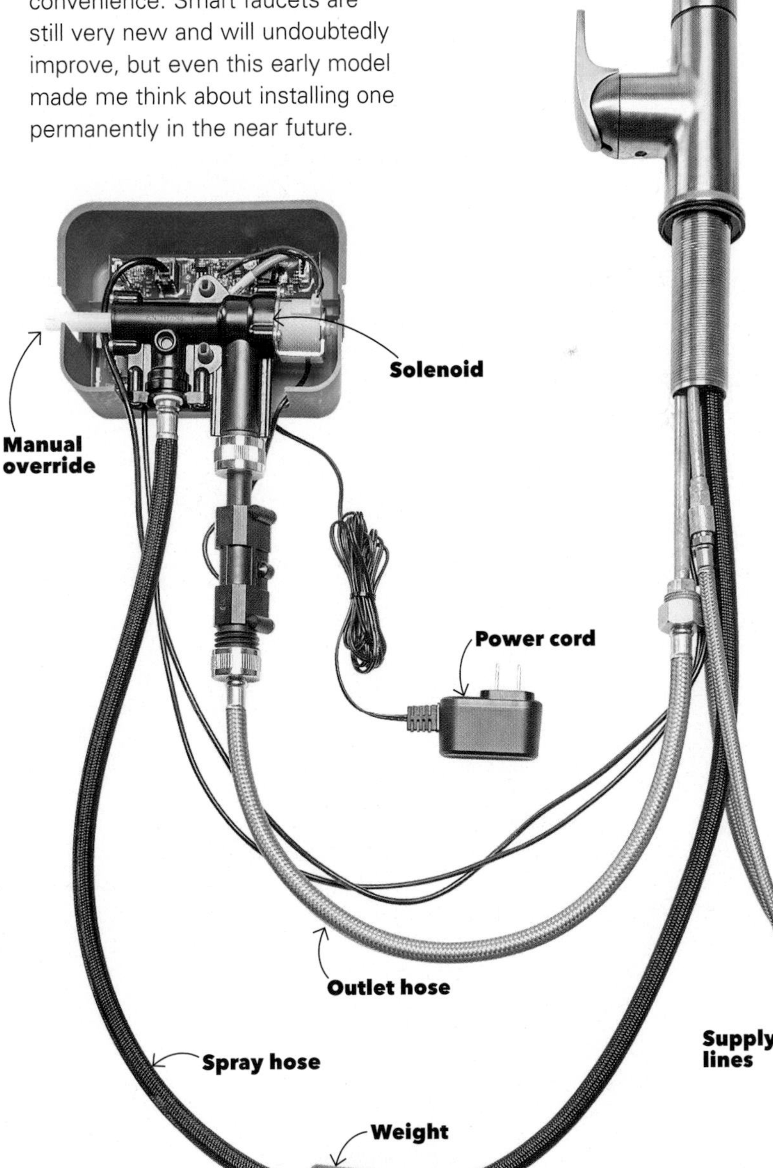

HOW A TOILET WORKS

Learn the basics so you can fix it yourself—and save!

By Brad Holden

Possibly the most used yet most taken for granted household fixture, the toilet is a marvel of engineering simplicity. Even typical modern toilets still employ just a couple basic mechanical components. The rest of the flush relies on the natural forces of gravity and siphoning action.

But sooner or later, every toilet develops problems like weak flushing, clogs or constant running. When that happens, most homeowners just live with the problem or pay a plumber a lot for a simple fix. You don't have to. If you know how a toilet works, you can diagnose and solve problems yourself, often in just a few minutes. So let's lift the lid to see the magic that happens in the bowels of this underappreciated fixture.

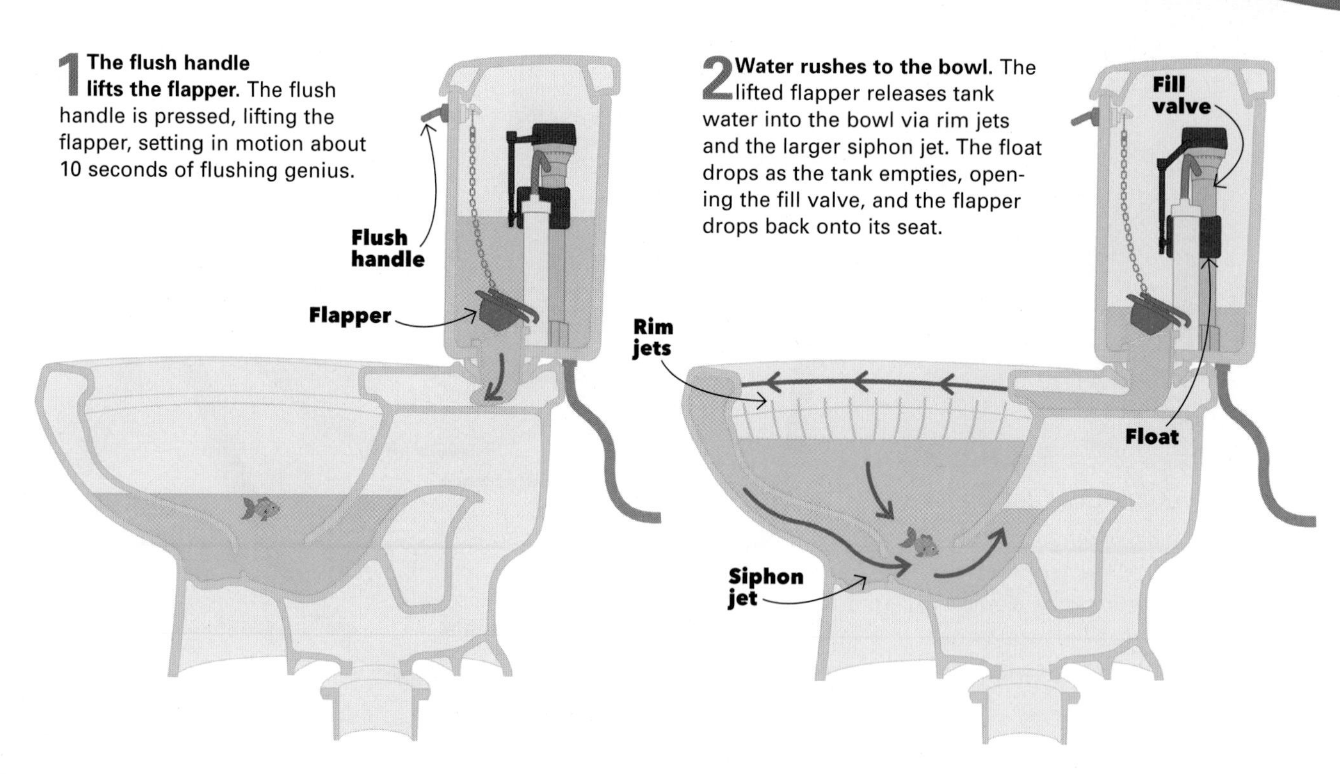

1 The flush handle lifts the flapper. The flush handle is pressed, lifting the flapper, setting in motion about 10 seconds of flushing genius.

2 Water rushes to the bowl. The lifted flapper releases tank water into the bowl via rim jets and the larger siphon jet. The float drops as the tank empties, opening the fill valve, and the flapper drops back onto its seat.

Toilet History

The oldest known "flushing" toilet, located in a small castle on the island of Crete, is about 4,000 years old.

Watch the Video!

To see an animation of the flush and fill process, search for "how a toilet works" at familyhandyman.com. You'll also find easy fixes for all kinds of toilet trouble.

3 Gravity happens. The bowl fills, and gravity forces water into the trapway, causing it to overflow the top of the trapway.

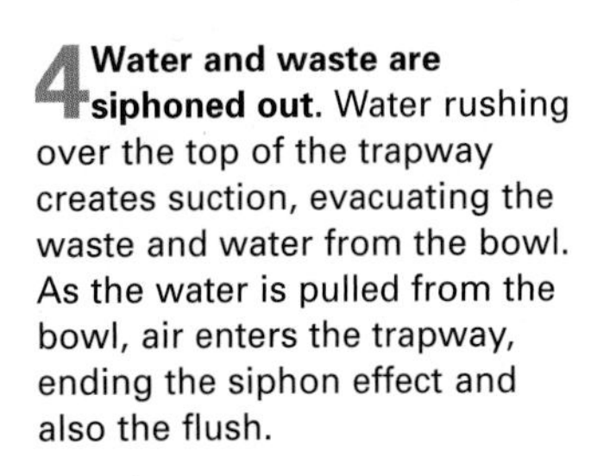

4 Water and waste are siphoned out. Water rushing over the top of the trapway creates suction, evacuating the waste and water from the bowl. As the water is pulled from the bowl, air enters the trapway, ending the siphon effect and also the flush.

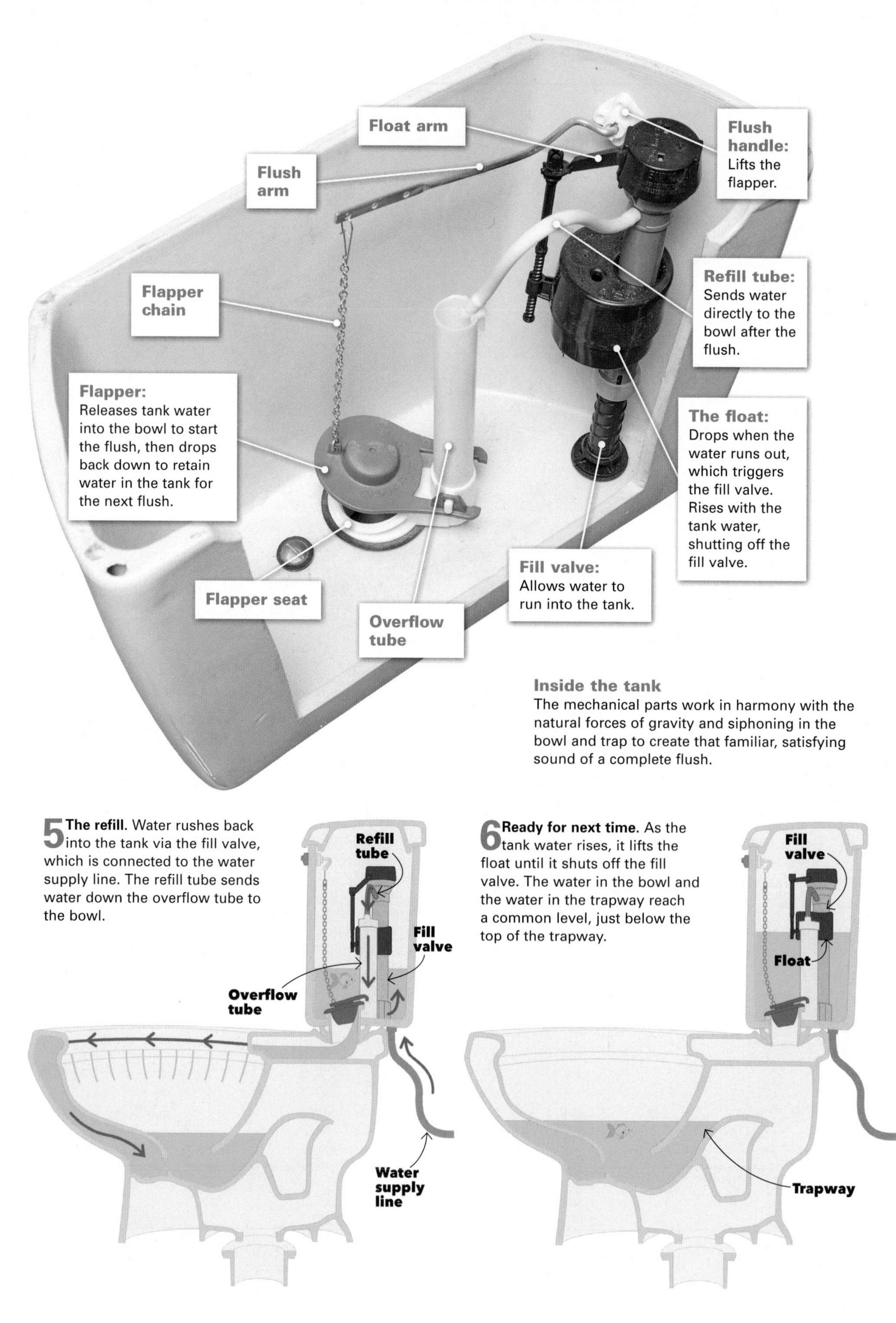

Inside the tank
The mechanical parts work in harmony with the natural forces of gravity and siphoning in the bowl and trap to create that familiar, satisfying sound of a complete flush.

5 The refill. Water rushes back into the tank via the fill valve, which is connected to the water supply line. The refill tube sends water down the overflow tube to the bowl.

6 Ready for next time. As the tank water rises, it lifts the float until it shuts off the fill valve. The water in the bowl and the water in the trapway reach a common level, just below the top of the trapway.

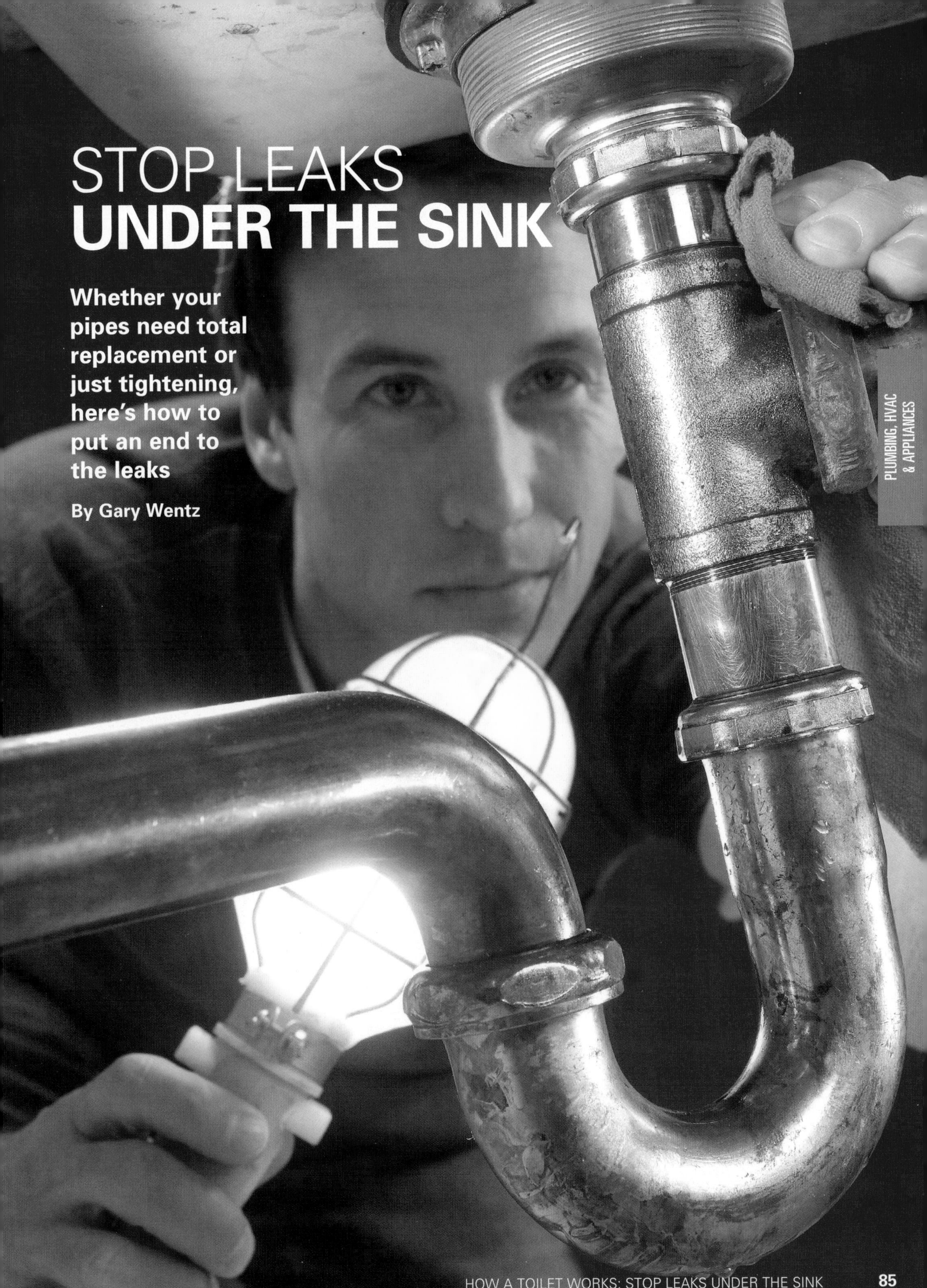

STOP LEAKS
UNDER THE SINK

Whether your pipes need total replacement or just tightening, here's how to put an end to the leaks

By Gary Wentz

Before you can stop a leak, you have to find its source. That can be tricky. Water that escapes your pipes can travel a long way before it drops onto your cabinet's floor.

Here's how a drip detective tracks the source of a leak: Fill both bowls of the sink with lukewarm water, not cold. (Cold water can cause beads of condensation to form on the pipes, making it impossible to find the leak.) Then get under the sink with a trouble light. Dry off all the pipes and examine the seals around the basket strainers. If you don't see any droplets forming, remove both sink stoppers and watch for telltale dribbles. Joints are the most likely source of leaks, but old metal pipes can develop pinhole leaks anywhere, especially in the trap.

If you can't find any leaks in the drain system, check the water supply lines that serve the faucet. Finally, check for "splash leaks," spots where water seeps under the sink rim or faucet base. To find these leaks, use a rag to dribble water around the faucet and sink rim, then get underneath and look for drips.

1. Straighten pipes and tighten nuts

The washers that seal pipe joints won't hold water unless one section runs straight into the other. The "ground" joint on the trap has no washer, but it too will leak if it's misaligned (see p. 89). Eyeball the leaking joint to check its alignment. If it's crooked, simply loosen the nut, straighten the pipe and retighten. Since the whole assembly is interconnected, you might misalign one joint while straightening another. Don't be surprised if you end up loosening and tightening several joints to straighten just one.

If a joint is aligned but leaks anyway, tighten the slip nut. Use two slip-joint pliers on metal pipes: one to hold the pipe, the other to tighten the nut. If you have old metal pipe, you might find that it has worn thin and collapses when you put a pair of pliers on it. With plastic pipe, hand-tighten first. If that doesn't stop the leak, use pliers. But be gentle; plastic threads are easy to strip.

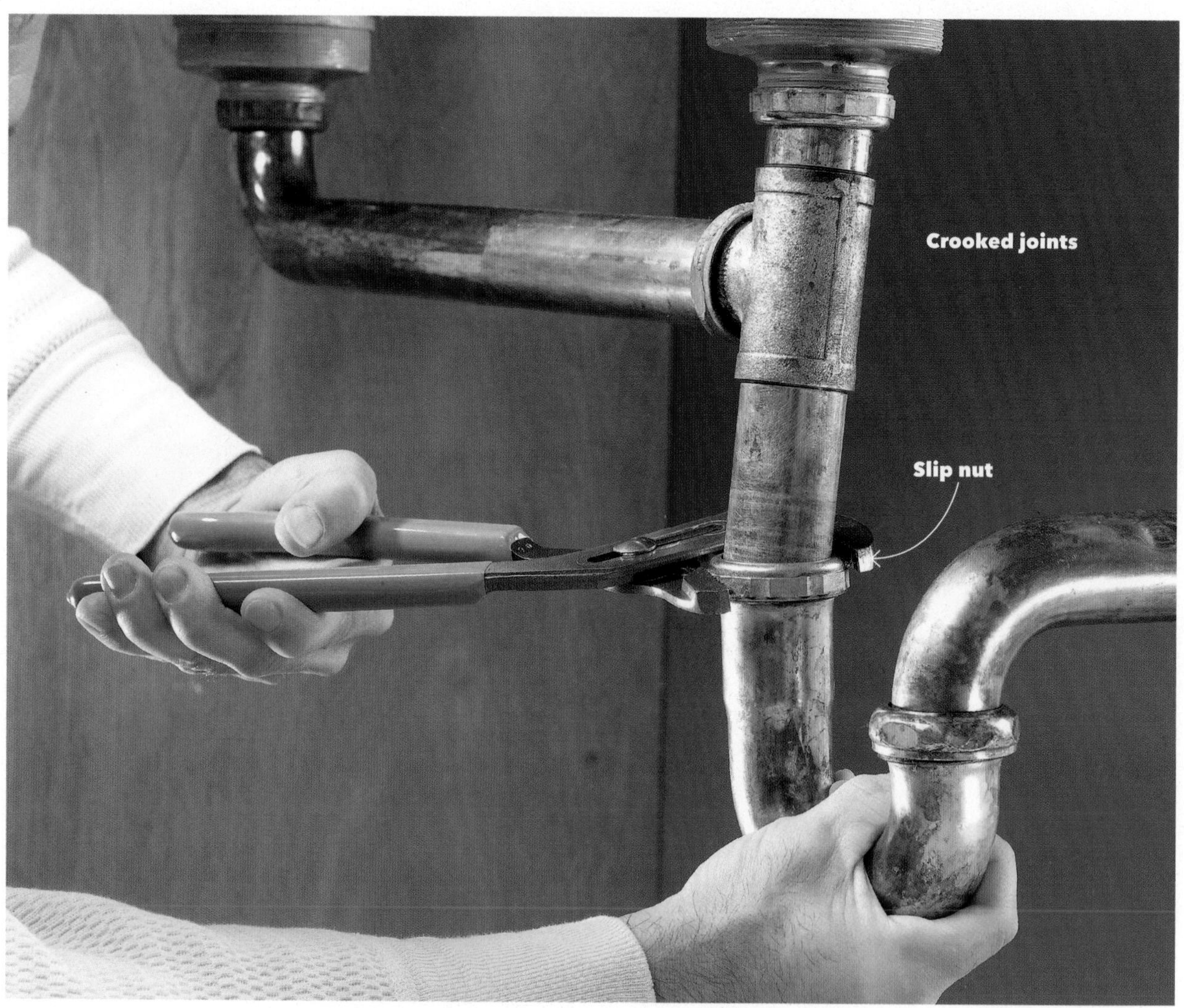

Loosen slip nuts, then straighten crooked pipes. Retighten metal nuts with slip-joint pliers. With plastic nuts, hand-tighten first. If that doesn't stop the leak, gently snug up the nuts with pliers.

Basket Strainer Assembly

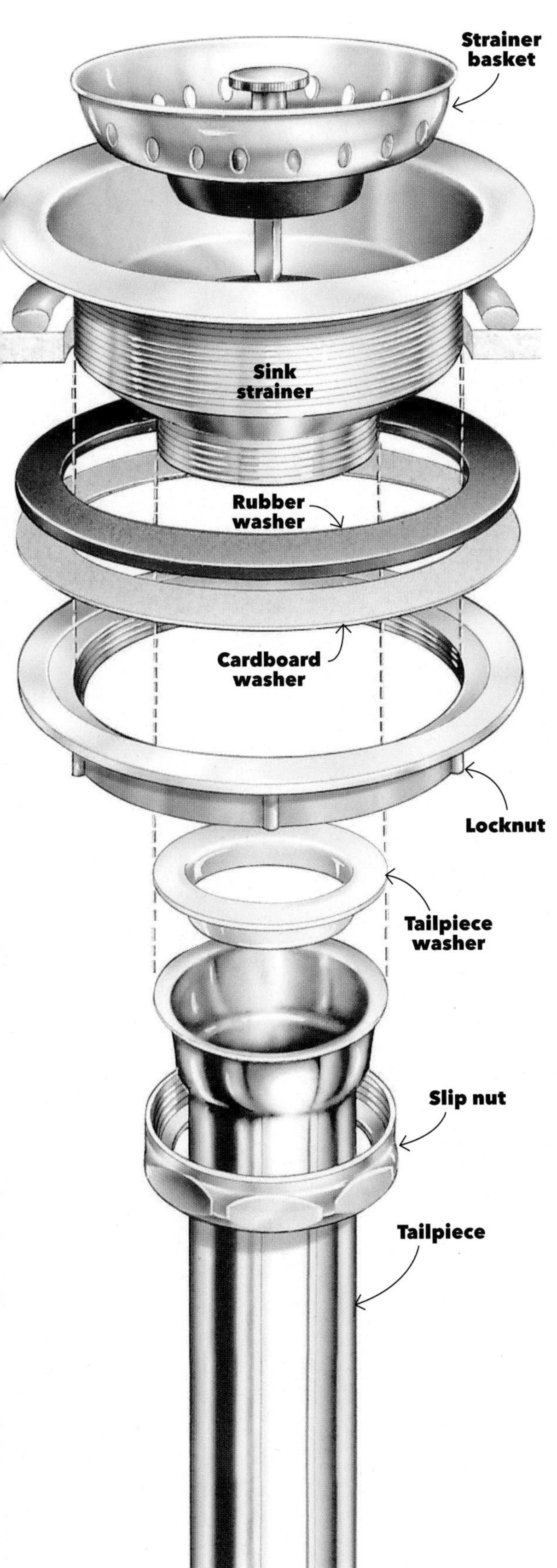

2. Reseal a leaky strainer

The primary seal around a basket strainer is plumber's putty, which doesn't last forever. Over the years it can harden, shrink or crack. Sometimes you can stop a leak by tightening the locknut. But in many cases, the only cure is a new dose of putty. **Photos 1 – 4** below show you how. You can reuse the old strainer if all the parts are in good shape, but it usually makes sense to replace it. Expect to spend at least $15—cheaper strainers are less reliable. Since you have to take apart most of the drain assembly to get at a leaking strainer (**Photo 1**), consider replacing the drain lines if they're old (see p. 88).

The hardest part of this job is unscrewing the old locknut, which is often welded in place by mineral deposits or corrosion. A special wrench designed just for locknuts, called a "spud wrench" or "locknut wrench" (**Photo 2**), costs about $15. Big slip-joint pliers ($25) with a 3-1/2-in. jaw opening will work too, plus you can use them for other jobs. Whatever tool you use, you might find that the locknut won't budge. In that case, a single cut with a hacksaw blade is the only solution (**Photo 3**). It's almost impossible to do this without cutting into the strainer threads, so plan on buying a new strainer.

With the locknut removed, pull out the strainer and scrape old putty off the sink with a plastic putty knife. Installing a new strainer is simple (**Photo 4**). Just remember that the rubber washer goes on before the cardboard washer. Tighten the strainer using the same method you used to remove it.

1 Disassemble the drain assembly so you can remove the leaky strainer. Turn slip nuts counterclockwise, using a second set of pliers if necessary to keep the pipes from turning.

2 Turn the locknut counterclockwise to remove the strainer. Have a helper stick the handles of the pliers into the strainer holes and keep the strainer from turning using a screwdriver.

3 Cut the locknut with a hacksaw if you can't unscrew it. Cut at a sharp diagonal angle and be careful not to cut into the sink.

4 Encircle the drain opening with plumber's putty or waterproof caulk. Install the rubber washer and the cardboard washer and tighten the locknut using the same method you used to remove the old one.

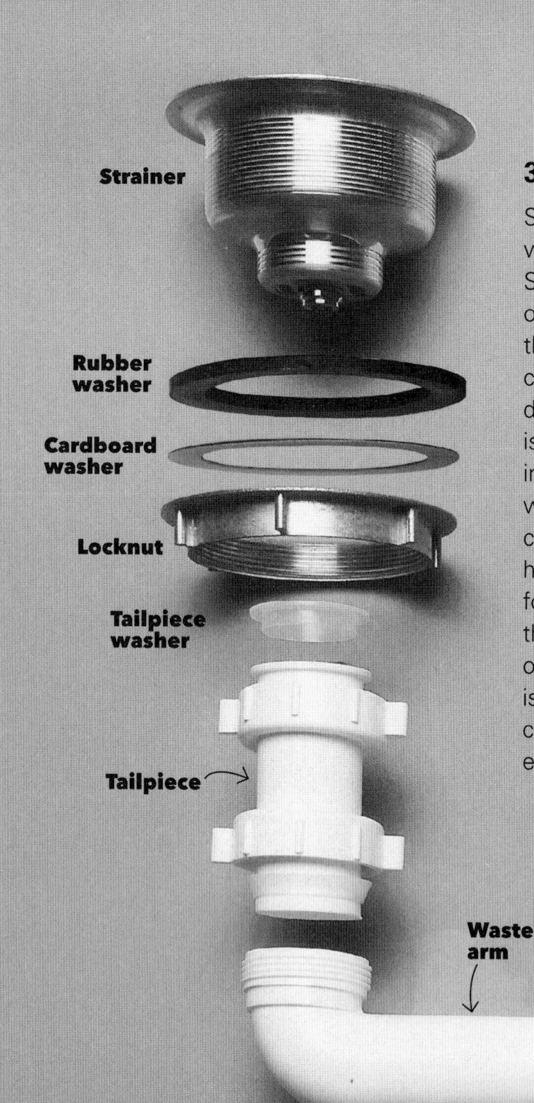

3. If the pipes are old, replace the whole works

Some leaks can't be stopped with straightening or tightening. Stripped nuts won't tighten and old washers won't seal because they're stiff and distorted. You could get new nuts, washers or drain parts. Since plastic pipe is so inexpensive and easy to install, the smart, reliable fix is a whole new drain assembly. You can buy everything you need at home centers for about $20. Kits for side outlet assemblies (like the one shown here) or center outlet assemblies (where the trap is beneath the center of the sink) contain most of the essential parts.

But you might also need:

- **Long tailpieces (Photo 1)**. The tailpieces that come with kits are often only a couple of inches long.
- **A trap arm extender (Photo 2)**. The arm that comes with the kit may not reach the drainpipe that protrudes from the wall.
- **A dishwasher wye** that has a connection for your dishwasher hose.
- **A disposer kit** that allows the waste arm to connect to a garbage disposer.

1 Attach the tailpiece to the basket strainer, but don't fully tighten it yet; you'll have to remove and cut it later.

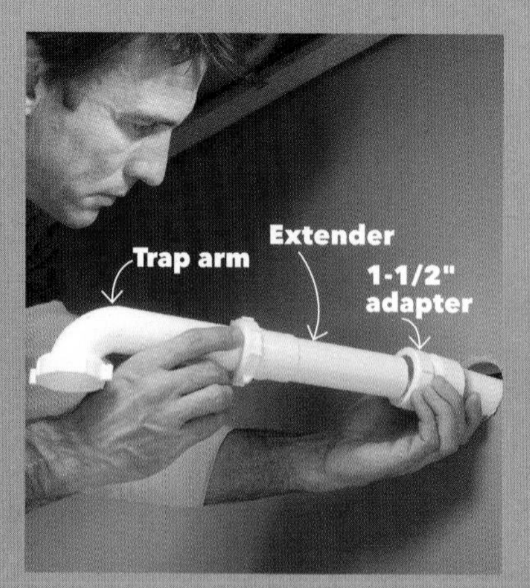

2 Slide the trap arm into the adapter. Then attach the trap and slide the arm in or out to position the trap directly under the tailpiece. You may need to cut the arm or add an extender.

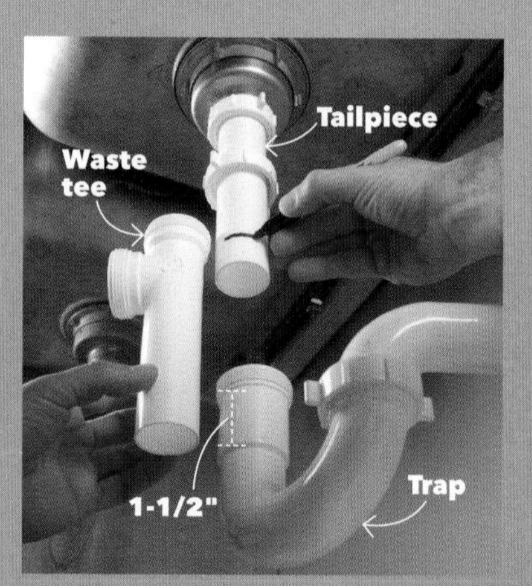

3 Hold the waste tee alongside the tailpiece about 1-1/2 in. below the top of the trap. Mark the tailpiece 1/2 in. below the top of the tee. Cut both tailpieces to the same length and install them.

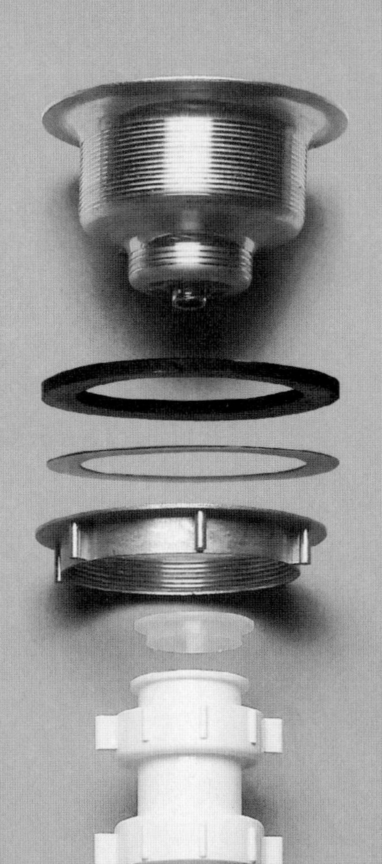

Tips for success:

- You'll have to cut a few pipes: both tailpieces, the waste arm and maybe the trap arm. A fine-tooth hacksaw works best.
- When in doubt, mark and cut pipes a bit long. Better to cut twice than cut too short and make an extra trip to the hardware store.
- Don't forget to insert tailpiece washers (**Photo 1**). Other joints require cone washers. The only joint without a washer is the ground joint at the trap.
- Connect everything loosely until the whole assembly is complete. Then tighten all the slip nuts.
- Hand-tighten the slip nuts. If any joints leak when you test the new assembly, tighten them slightly with slip-joint pliers.
- Lastly, check for leaks. To see how, search for "finish a plumbing job" at familyhandyman.com.

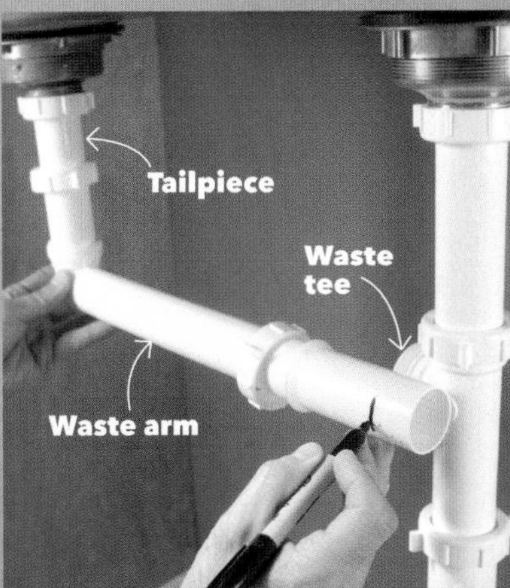

4 Slip the waste arm onto the second tailpiece, make it extend about 3/4 in. into the tee and mark it. Cut and install it.

5 Loosen the slip nuts and slide the tee up or down so the waste arm slopes slightly down toward the tee. Tighten all the nuts.

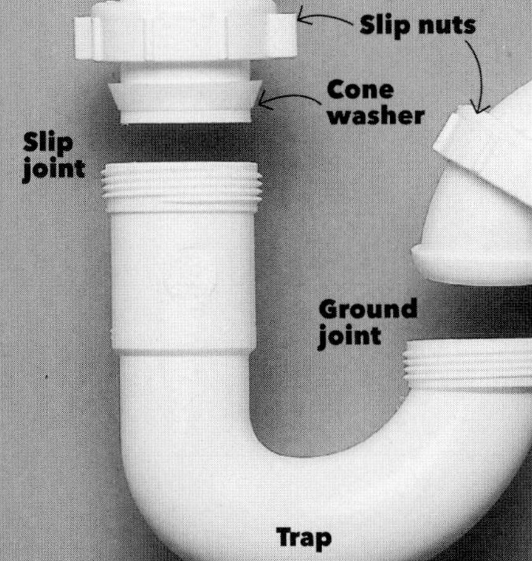

Slick Tip:

Brush a little Teflon pipe thread sealant on male threads. It lubricates the threads and makes slip nuts much easier to tighten. Check the label to make sure the sealant is safe for plastic.

DIY DUCTLESS AIR CONDITIONING

Installing cooling is surprisingly easy with a mini-split system

By Matthew Knopp

Adding an A/C system sounds like a job for pros only. And usually it is. But two non-pros installed this ductless "mini-split" system in a garage in one day.

The installation was fast and easy because of the special line set (top right). It comes prefilled, or "precharged," with refrigerant and includes connectors that don't require special skills or tools. Just mount the two main units and connect the line set to the condenser. Some mini-splits include an easy-install line set, but most don't.

A mini-split system can be installed in a home, a garage, a cabin or a shed. Some offer heating as well as cooling, and some include multiple evaporators to serve multiple rooms. Depending on features and size, most DIY mini-splits cost from $700 to $2,000.

Choosing the system

Very few brick-and-mortar stores carry DIY systems, so online shopping may be your only option. Luckily there are many online suppliers. The size of the system is listed in BTUs (British thermal units). The higher the number, the greater the cooling capacity. To select the right size mini-split, calculate the heat loss of the room. Several websites simplify these calculations. Don't just guess; an undersized system won't keep up, and an oversized system will cycle on and off too frequently, shortening the condenser's service life. We installed a 12,000-BTU heating and cooling system that costs about $1,100 at climateright.com. The other necessary materials totaled about $275.

Providing power

Scan the photos on the following pages and you'll see that installation is mostly basic DIY stuff: measuring, drilling holes, driving screws… Usually the biggest challenge is running power to the system. With a small system, you may be able to draw power from a nearby underloaded 20-amp circuit. More likely, you'll want to install a new circuit dedicated to the mini-split. That can be a small job or a major project depending on how easy it is to run cable from the main panel to the unit.

By cutting—and later patching—three small holes in drywall, we were able to run cable from the basement up through the garage wall, through the attic, then down and out the exterior wall and into a disconnect box. (The disconnect provides an easy, certain way to turn off power when servicing the unit.) Power then runs from the disconnect to the condenser. Cable running alongside the line set powers the evaporator. Our bill for electrical supplies was about $160. A local electrician estimated that work at about $500.

If you have some electrical know-how but need extra guidance, don't forget your local electrical inspector. It's not an inspector's job to act as a consultant, but most will give you some advice and outline code requirements. Expert help and certainty that the job is done right—not bad for the cost of an electrical permit.

Other materials

The condenser needs a level surface to rest on. You could pour a concrete pad, but a plastic condenser pad ($50 and up online) is instant and easy. We mounted ours on condenser wall brackets ($60 online).

The fabric sleeve covering the line set isn't attractive or easy to keep clean. The solution is a plastic line set cover kit, which costs about $50 online.

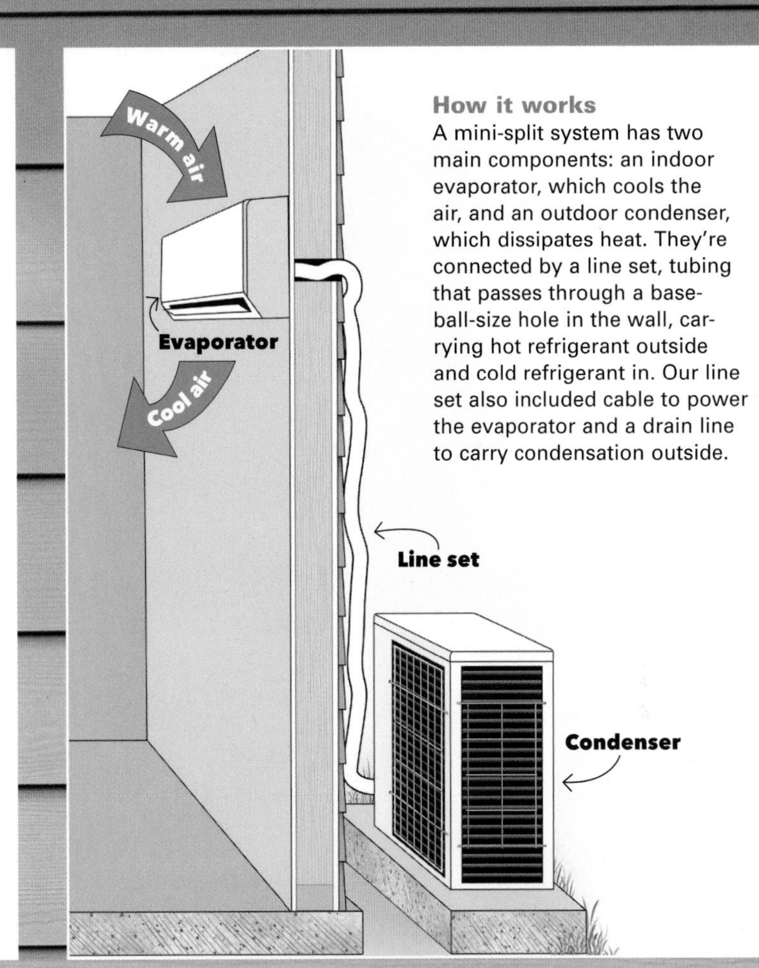

How it works

A mini-split system has two main components: an indoor evaporator, which cools the air, and an outdoor condenser, which dissipates heat. They're connected by a line set, tubing that passes through a baseball-size hole in the wall, carrying hot refrigerant outside and cold refrigerant in. Our line set also included cable to power the evaporator and a drain line to carry condensation outside.

PLUMBING, HVAC & APPLIANCES

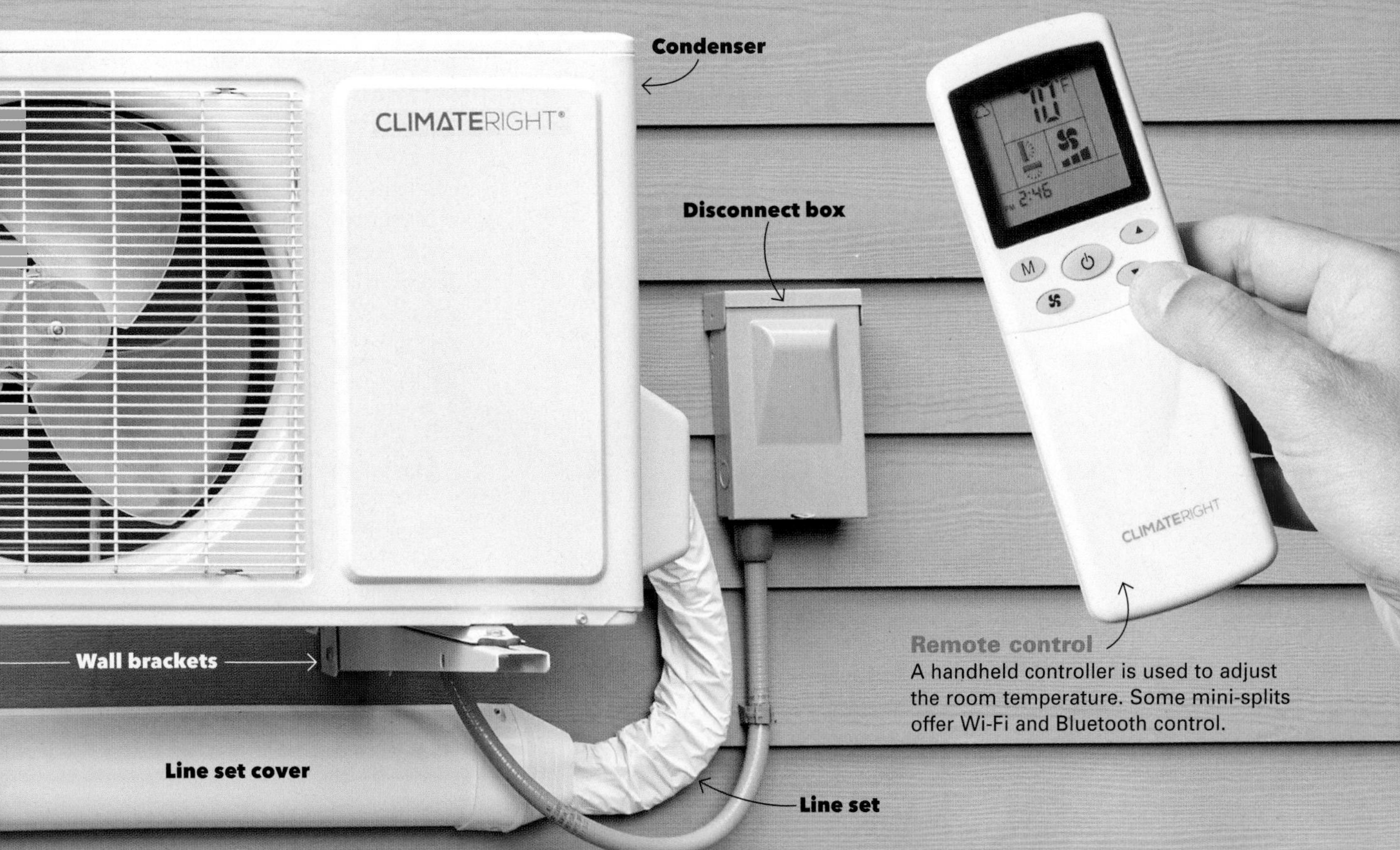

Remote control

A handheld controller is used to adjust the room temperature. Some mini-splits offer Wi-Fi and Bluetooth control.

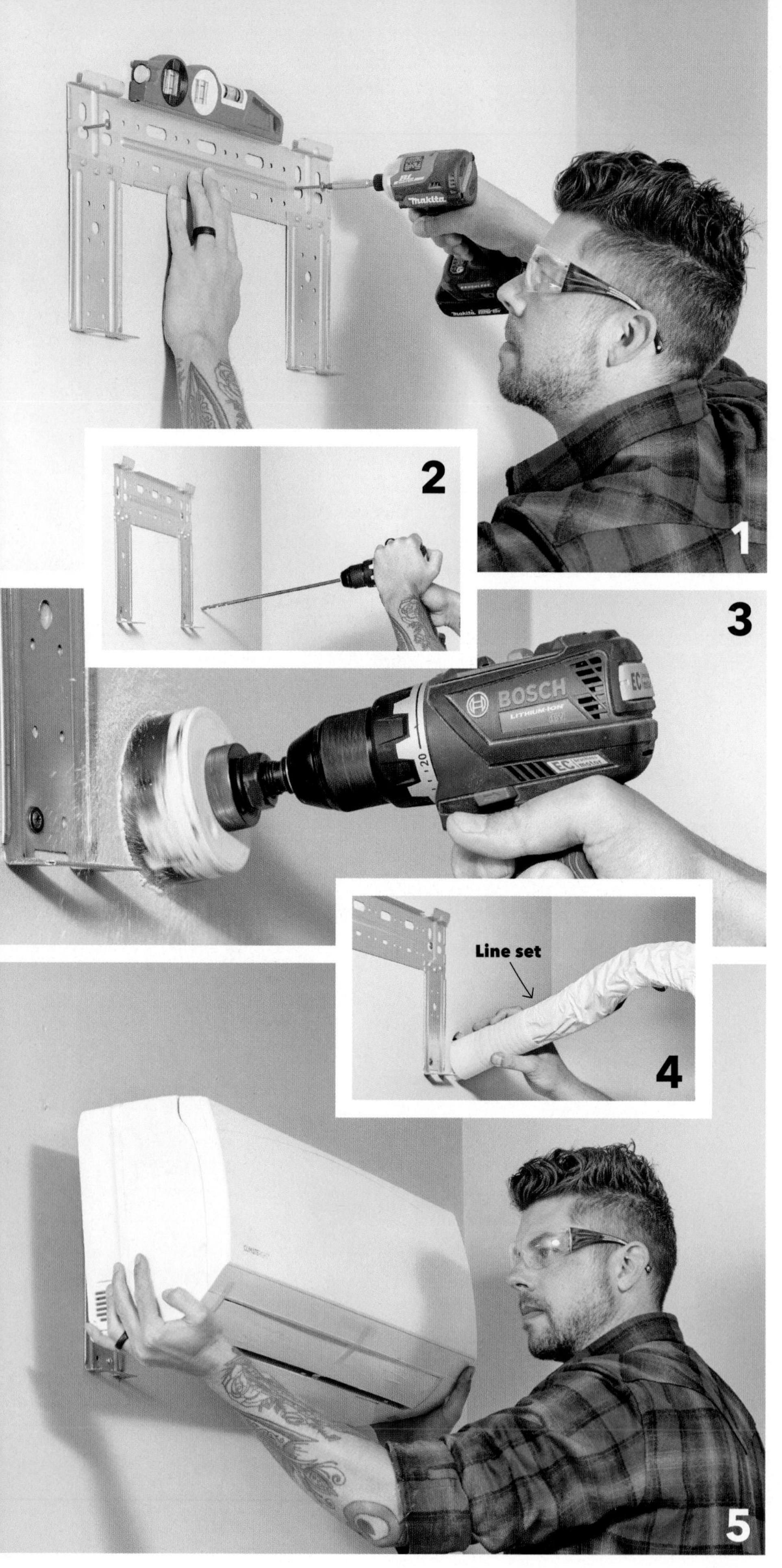

1 Install the mounting bracket. Mount the evaporator inside the room on an exterior wall away from direct sunlight, doorways and sources of dust. Make sure this area of the wall is free of wires, pipes and ducts that would interfere with making a hole for the line set. Mark the stud locations and fasten the bracket to them with screws.

2 Drill a pilot hole. The line set hole must slope slightly downward to the outside so condensate from the evaporator can drain outside. Begin by drilling a pilot hole from inside to outside. Then go outside and make sure no trim or other obstructions will complicate drilling the full-size hole.

3 Bore the full-size hole. Cut with a hole saw from inside, move aside any insulation and inspect the wall cavity for obstructions. Finish the hole by drilling from the outside.

4 Run the line set. Carefully uncoil the line set from the back of the evaporator. With an assistant outside, feed the line set through the hole. As it emerges, the assistant should gently bend the line set downward and to the side as needed to reach the condenser. Keep the rigid plastic collar surrounding the line set at the end that connects to the condenser. The drain line is shorter and goes through last, below the other lines. Add the drain extension and wrap the joint with electrical tape to keep it secure.

5 Install the evaporator. Wrap the foam sleeve around the section of line set within the hole and replace any insulation in the wall cavity that was disturbed. Then hang the evaporator on the mounting bracket. Your helper may need to feed a few more inches of the line set outside as you do this. On the outside, insert the two-piece plastic trim into the hole to prevent any rough edges from damaging the line set.

6 Install the condenser. Set the condenser on a pad on the ground or mount it on a wall bracket so that the refrigerant lines can reach it easily. Route the line set so it stays tight to the building exterior and doesn't leapfrog any obstructions. This makes it easier to install a cover. Ensure the condenser has the recommended clearance from walls and bushes. Avoid placement where ice or packed snow could fall on it or where other appliances vent. A location on the east or north side of the structure maximizes cooling efficiency.

7 Connect the refrigerant lines. This step varies by manufacturer. With this system, a locking lever presses the line connections together. Before powering up, inspect the refrigerant lines for kinks and verify the electrical connections. Then go inside and set the temperature using the handheld controller.

8 Cover the line set. Insulate and seal the hole in the outside wall, then cover the line set using sections of plastic or metal channel cut to length. Place the back half of the channel behind the line set, plumb it and anchor it to the wall with self-tapping screws. Our line set travels horizontally to the compresser, so when we added the channel corner (see p. 90), we drilled a hole in it to allow the drain line to exit straight down.

PROTECT YOUR **FURNACE**

Filter failure can cost you thousands

By Travis Larson

If you're negligent about replacing your furnace filter regularly or you're not using the correct one, listen up. You're not just compromising your indoor air quality. You're also spending more money than necessary on utility bills and repairs, and you may even have to replace your furnace.

MEET AN EXPERT

Seth Roe holds an HVAC journeyman card, is NATE certified and has been with Standard Heating & Air Conditioning for 15 years. He is one of the lead trainers for incoming techs.

You should still get your furnace serviced

You might think frequent filter switch-outs would keep your furnace in tiptop condition, but you'd be wrong. It's still a good idea to have your furnace professionally serviced. The technician will clean internal components and the condensate line, as well as perform a combustion analysis for O_2, CO and CO_2 to make sure your furnace is performing safely and up to par. Most important, the technician will ensure your heat exchanger is intact, and that's a big safety issue. If you live in an exceptionally clean house, you may be able to go two or more years between services. Ask the technician for advice.

Fiberglass is a poor filter

There's a reason that light passes through fiberglass filters so well—they're very porous. That's why they last so much longer than pleated filters. Because they don't capture the finer debris, they don't clog as fast as higher-quality filters. That fine dust stays in your indoor air and also circulates within the furnace, where it will damage mechanical and electronic parts. Use pleated paper filters instead.

A higher "MERV" rating isn't always better

Furnace filters are "MERV" rated according to the size and quantity of particles they filter. MERV stands for "minimum efficiency reporting value," and the range is from 1 to 16, with 1 being the most porous and 16 the finest. One might think that the higher the MERV rating, the better. But for most homes, a filter in the 8 to 12 range is plenty good. It will filter the vast majority of airborne particles and protect your furnace components.

MERV filters rated higher than 12 plug up much faster and need more frequent replacement. Only households with respiratory issues, serious allergies or low-immunity issues should bother with them, and you really have to stay on top of filter changes.

MERV RATINGS

FILTER QUALITY	POLLEN	DUST & LINT	SMOKE	PET DANDER	BACTERIA	VIRUS CARRIERS	MOLD	MICROSCOPIC ALLERGNES	ODOR	DUST MITES
MERV 13	✔	✔	✔	✔	✔	✔	✔	✔	✔	✔
MERV 11	✔	✔	✔	✔	✔	✔	✔	✔		✔
MERV 8	✔	✔		✔	✔		✔			✔
MERV 6	✔	✔		✔						✔

The Home Depot rates filters differently

If you shop at The Home Depot, you'll find the filter aisle dominated by filters made by 3M and Honeywell. And you'll be confused because the MERV ratings are replaced by an "FPR" (filter performance rating). That is The Home Depot's own rating system—you won't find it at other stores. FPRs are not equivalent to MERV ratings. Roughly, a MERV rating of 8 matches an FPR of 5, and a MERV 11 is close to an FPR of 7. Our advice? Next time you have your furnace serviced, ask the technician to recommend a filter to suit your home air-quality needs and protect your furnace.

MERV	FPR
13	10
11	7
8	5
6	N/A

Replacement frequency varies

You should change your filters when you need to—not on some arbitrary schedule. Depending on your filter and home environment, filters may need replacing anywhere from 20 days to a full year.

How do you tell? First of all, always have at least one new replacement filter on hand. Every 20 to 30 days, take a few seconds to pull the filter from your furnace and compare it with the new one. You'll be able to tell whether the filter is covered with dust and needs to be replaced. Never go more than 60 days between changes for any 1-in. filter.

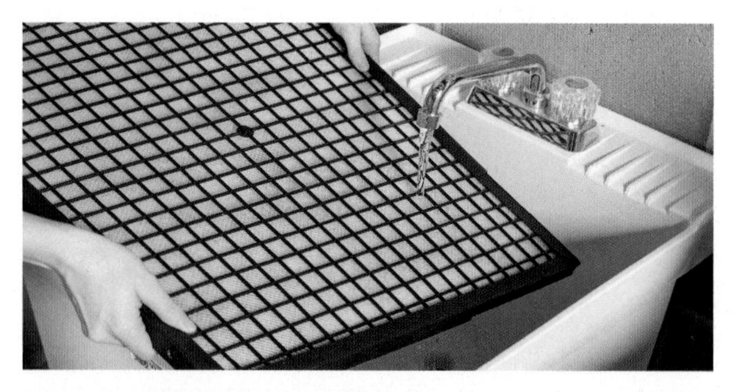

Be wary of washable filters

Washable, reusable filters require far more effort than simply swapping a dirty disposable filter for a new one. Plus, it's difficult to get washable filters completely clean. Most washable filters offer MERV ratings only in the 1 to 4 range, so they don't provide good filtration either. Since they cost $80 to $100, you'll have to decide if the benefit is worth the price, trouble and substandard filtration. If you choose this route, shop around to find washable filters with MERV ratings of about 9.

Clogged filters wreck furnaces

A clogged furnace filter is more serious than it sounds. When a filter clogs, the air simply bypasses the filter and introduces debris into all the important furnace components and the air you breathe. And because the airflow is slower, the furnace electronics can overheat. To prevent damage, the furnace is designed to shut off when that happens. And if it happens often enough, over long periods, the furnace is likely to fail completely.

Buy in bulk

Here's why it pays to have extra filters on hand: When you buy in bulk, you'll save money. When you're checking a filter to see if it needs replacement, you'll have a new one for comparison. And finally, you'll be able to install a new filter right away.

Replace filters in summer, too

Whenever your HVAC system is running, the filter is getting dirty. That's not only during the heating season but also through the warmer months. During the cooling season, the air flows through the furnace exactly the same way it does when you're heating the house. So it's important to check your filter all year long. However, if you live in a mild climate where the furnace is off for long stretches, you can skip the regular filter checks during those periods.

BestProTips

EXPERT ADVICE FROM THE JOB SITE

FIX A **LEAKY TOILET**

If your toilet is leaking around the base, there's a problem with the toilet-to-flange connection. It may be as simple as a wax ring that needs replacement. It's important to stop leaks as soon as possible; even minor ones can cause substantial damage over time. Here are the most common problems you'll find under the toilet and how to address them.

MEET AN EXPERT

Les Zell has been a plumber for almost 30 years and an invaluable resource to *Family Handyman* for the past decade. He's the owner/operator of Zell Plumbing & Heating.

BestProTips

FLANGE FIX-IT OPTIONS

■ Two-part repair ring

Steel flanges that surround plastic flanges can rust away. The easiest solution is to install a two-part (or hinged) ring ($15) that locks under the plastic rim. Badly corroded steel rings can be pried and peeled away. If you have to get aggressive, cut it away with an angle grinder or oscillating tool fitted with a metal-cutting blade.

■ Eared reinforcement ring

If you have just a small amount of rot surrounding the flange, or screws won't be able to grip the wood under a repair flange, you might get away with an eared reinforcement ring. The ears may extend beyond the rot enough to get a good grip in the subfloor for the screws. Use six 1-1/2-in. No. 8 oval-head stainless steel screws to anchor it in wood. If you have concrete, use 1-1/4-in. flat-head concrete screws.

■ Repair ring

Plastic flanges often bend or break, but there's an easy fix. Just screw a stainless steel repair ring ($6) over the plastic flange with at least four 1-1/2-in. stainless steel screws. Consider doing this even if you find that the flange is in good shape and you only need to replace the wax ring. It's cheap insurance against trouble. The repair ring raises the flange about 1/4 in., so before you install the ring, rest it over the flange and then see if the toilet rocks when you set it on top. If it does, you'll need to shim under the toilet to allow for the extra height.

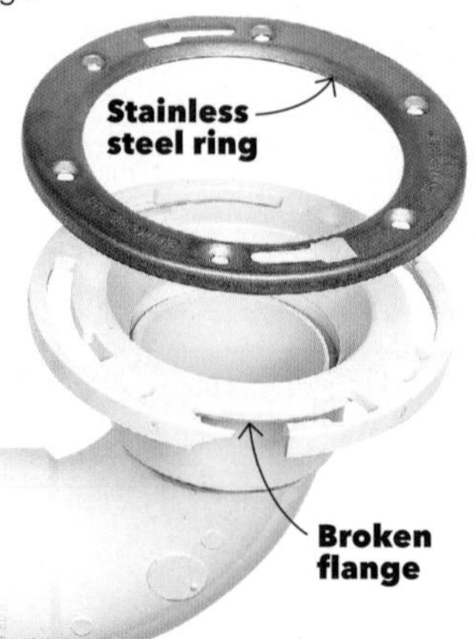

■ Repair brackets

Cast iron flanges often break on one or both sides. If only the bolt slot is damaged, slip a repair bracket ($5) under the cast iron lip. It will be held in place by the unbroken cast iron lip and provide a new slot for the flange bolt.

■ Repair flange

If the flange is in bad shape, you can install a plastic flange ($25) that slips inside (shown above). Home centers carry one or two versions of these. Or you can add a brass ring ($7) similar to the stainless steel ring shown at left. If necessary, break away the cast iron flange with a cold chisel.

Buy every flange fix sold!

You never know what you're going to find when you pull the toilet, so you have to be prepared so you can get your toilet working again fast. You can always return the items you don't use. (Don't buy the cast iron repair parts unless you have cast iron drain lines.) In addition to the flange fixes, get two wax rings, a new set of brass toilet flange bolts, plastic toilet shims and a tube of tub/tile caulk.

Don't ignore a rocking toilet!

If your toilet is rocking or wobbling, don't ignore it, even if it's not leaking. Eventually the wax ring/toilet base seal will fail and you'll have a leak. Shim under the toilet with plastic toilet shims until it's steady. Trim the shims and snug up the flange nuts. Then caulk around the base of the toilet with tub/tile caulk.

Choose flanges with stainless steel rims

If you have access under the toilet, replacing a bad or corroded flange is sometimes the best and easiest solution. Because all plastic flanges are prone to breakage, and plastic flanges with ordinary steel rims are prone to rotting away, the best choice is a plastic flange surrounded with stainless steel. Go downstairs and investigate. Depending on access, you may need elbows, more pipe and a coupling to tie in the new one.

Best Pro Tips

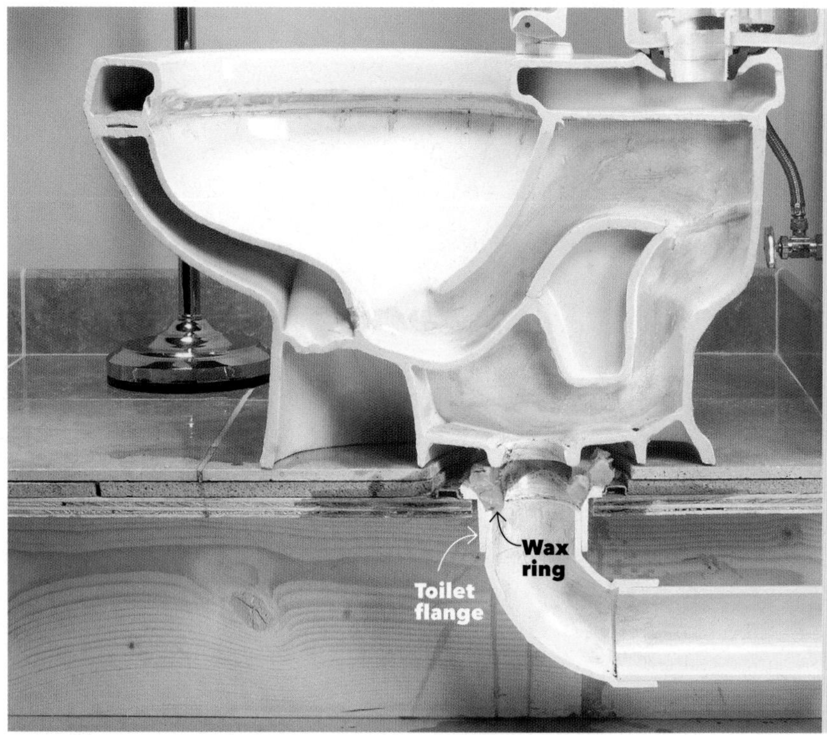

How a wax ring works

A wax ring is the most commonly used seal between the toilet and the toilet flange. There are synthetic versions, but traditional wax rings (made from real beeswax) are the go-to choice for most plumbers—pros and amateurs alike.

When the toilet is set, the wax is compressed and reshaped to form a watertight seal. Because the wax doesn't harden or degrade, the seal will last for a very long time if the toilet is set properly and firmly bolted down.

DEALING WITH FLOOR ROT

If your toilet has been leaking for some time, you're likely to have rot. Finished flooring traps water, which accelerates and spreads the problem. The rot can range from a little bit around the flange to a full-blown case that requires tearing up the flooring and replacing subflooring and possibly framing.

■ Moderate rot

If the rot extends beyond the range of an eared flange but is still contained within the footprint of the toilet, step up to a flange support bracket ($20). These transfer the load past the rotted areas of the subfloor.

■ Extensive rot

Don't freak out if you have bad floor rot. It's easier than you think to cut out the bad flooring and replace it with new wood and additional framing if needed. Just make sure you go far enough to cover the entire area of rotted wood. Bad framing can usually be left in place and reinforced with new 2-by material, if you can screw it into solid wood. Don't worry about removing the rotted framing. With the leak fixed, the rot won't continue. The worst part is that you'll also need to replace the finished floor.

Great Goofs®

LAUGHS & LESSONS FROM OUR READERS

SEWER WITH A SECRET

We bought our home six years ago and have had problems with the sewer backing up. After having the sewer line snaked, jetted and scoped, we learned that the backflow valve cap had broken off and likely become lodged in the line. We hired someone with a backhoe to dig up the line, but we couldn't find the broken cap. Puzzled, we again called the company that scoped it to locate the lodged cap.

Meanwhile, the backhoe operator asked my husband if he'd checked the cleanout drain. "Cleanout drain?" my husband repeated, turning pale. Sure enough, under a piece of carpet in the basement was the drain, and inside it was the broken cap. Then we went upstairs to take a good, long look at our dug-up backyard. It was like buying a price tag with no clothing attached.

—Katie Hein

THAT QUIET LITTLE DRIP!

The water dispenser in my refrigerator door wasn't working, so I figured the solenoid valve was shot. After a one-hour trip to the parts store for a new $60 valve, I installed it. Guess what? Still no water! After 30 minutes of troubleshooting and checking the electrical connections and the water hookup, I was as perplexed as ever. That's when my 7-year-old daughter waltzed in and asked me what I was doing. Then she told me that she'd pressed the water lock button on the fridge door after learning about water conservation in school. I felt like a big drip!

—Tony Jackson

A NEW TOILET TO GO WITH THAT SEAT

My dad waited until I came home from college to ask me to install the soft-cushion toilet seat he'd just bought. I sprayed the old, rusty toilet seat bolts with a heavy dose of lubricant and then got out the wrench and went to work on them. Unfortunately, the wrench slipped off the lubricated bolt and the handle busted a nice hole in the toilet, sending water all over the floor. With my tail between my legs, I had to tell my dad that he needed a new toilet to go with his new seat.

I replaced the toilet, but haven't had my dad ask me to do anything around the house since. (I guess that means it worked out for the best after all!)

—Martin Todd Dorris

SPECIAL SECTION

Buy, Sell or Stay!

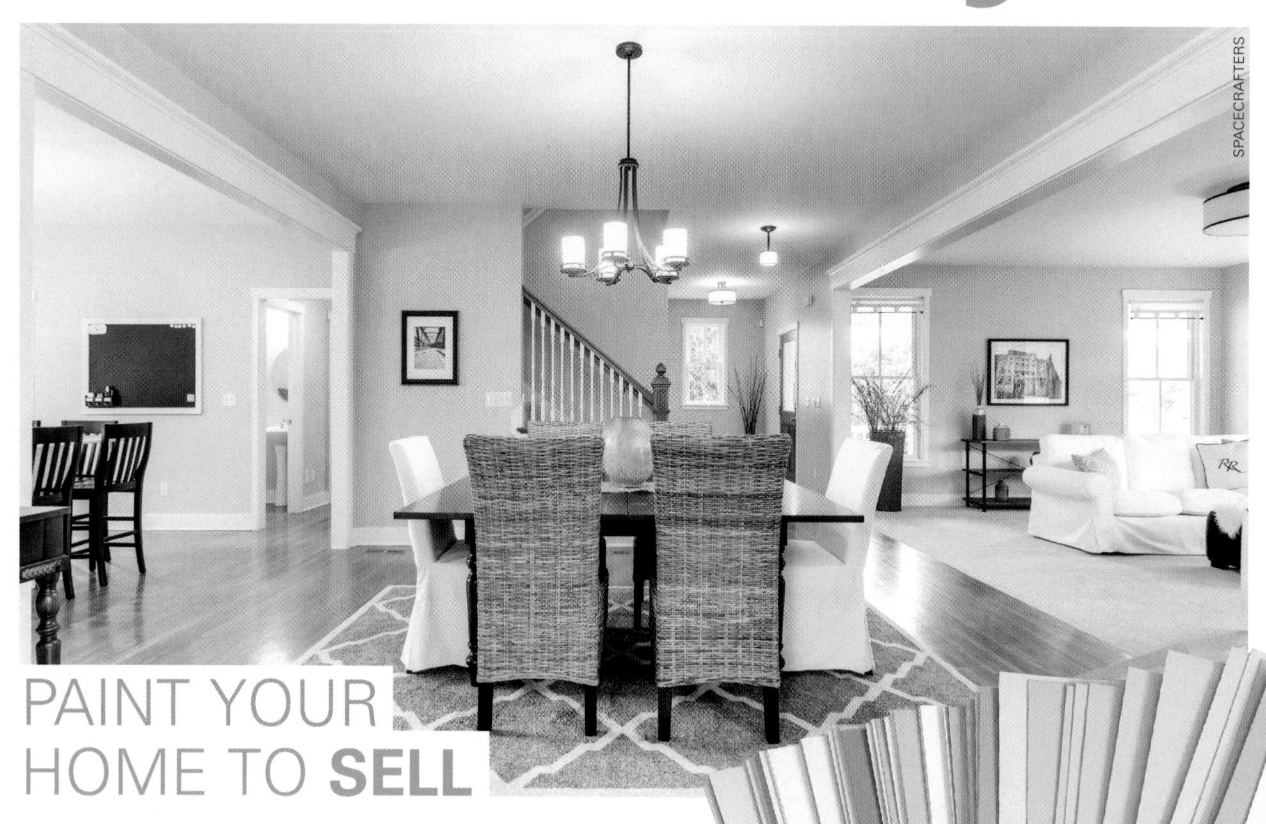
SPACECRAFTERS

PAINT YOUR HOME TO SELL

A fresh coat of paint is hands down the best way to spend your time and money to get the biggest payback when you sell your home. It's far less expensive than remodeling, and it's something you can do yourself. But choosing the right colors is the key.

Experts say you should paint all the rooms a neutral color. But what exactly does that mean? "Neutral" depends on what other colors are present in the room. All paint colors have undertones that may not really come out until they are in a room where other elements such as woodwork and furniture bring them out.

In my home staging kit, I carry 75 samples of "neutral" colors to see which one appears truly neutral in any given room. There are three that I come back to most often: For a room with white trim, I use Sherwin-Williams "Agreeable Gray," shown at right. For a room with dark woodwork or dark wood elements, I use Sherwin-Williams "Accessible Beige," shown above. In a room with honey oak, I use Benjamin Moore "Manchester Tan." Any paint store can match these colors using other paint brands.

—Melanie Zaelich
Stager & Stylist

MEET AN EXPERT

Melanie Zaelich is a certified home stager and stylist, and the owner of Happy Place Interiors (happyplaceinteriors.com).

BEFORE: Dark walls

TIP: Give your front door some color. Brick red is the most common, followed by navy blue.

SHUTTERSTOCK/DAVID PAPAZIAN

"In the U.S., trends start on the coasts and work their way to the middle. Right now, in coastal cities, I'm seeing a trend moving away from gray and beige in favor of creams and whites."

AFTER: "Agreeable Gray" wall color

SIMPLE SIGHT STUDIOS

Buy, Sell or Stay!

SEAL AN ASPHALT DRIVEWAY

The driveway is often where you take your first step when checking out a property. This project is a bigger investment in time and money, but a weekend of work and $200 to $400 worth of material could land you an offer. Even if you're not selling, a coat of sealer will extend the life of your driveway. For detailed instructions, go to familyhandyman.com and search for "asphalt driveway."

TUNE UP OR REPLACE YOUR STORM DOOR

Before replacing a storm door that's not working quite right, see if either of these fixes helps.

- **The damper.** Don't let the storm door slam shut and catch your heel or force you back to pull the door closed. Adjusting the pressure of the pneumatic closer is a simple turn of a screw at the end of the closer. It might take a few tries to get the door to ease into the latch just right.
- **The handle.** If the handle isn't working properly or is an eyesore, buy a replacement and install it yourself. There are several handle configurations, so be sure to get one that's compatible with your door. You may have to drill new holes in the door; just follow the instructions included in the package.
- **Replace.** If the door is beyond repair, you'll be glad to know that replacing it isn't difficult. For an easy-to-install door, you may spend $200 to $300, but you can go from your old door to the new door in an hour with minimal tools. For detailed instructions, search for "storm door" at familyhandyman.com.

WHAT SHOULD MY REAL ESTATE AGENT DO **FOR ME?**

SHUTTERSTOCK/GPOINTSTUDIO

Whether you're buying or selling a house, remember that the real estate agent you hire is there to negotiate for you, says Antoine Thompson, national executive director of the National Association of Real Estate Brokers. When challenges arise, "you want to have a good advocate working on your behalf."

Here are some services you should expect:

When you sell

- **Setting a fair price, and boosting value.** Your agent should bring a deep understanding of the local market, including current economic conditions and new developments that could affect values, to help you set a reasonable price, Thompson says. The agent should also have a keen eye for modest improvements (say, a new coat of paint in a popular color) that could significantly improve your home's appeal to buyers, he adds.
- **A marketing strategy.** There should be a clear plan in place for publicizing your home, from professional photography and staging (setting up your house for showing) to getting the word out via social media and multiple websites, says Vicky Scarnuley, a licensed real estate agent in Trumbull, Connecticut. "They should help you evaluate offers and negotiate the best price," and help arrange ancillary services such as attorneys, title services and even moving companies.
- **An open house.** Open houses take time and money to arrange, and not all agents offer them. Even so, "I encourage sellers to ask their agents to do open houses," Thompson says. "That gets traffic into the property, which reduces the amount of time it might be on the market."

When you buy

- **A price advocate.** Your real estate agent should help you understand current market conditions for your area and the type of home you're interested in, and whether specific properties that catch your eye are priced fairly, Scarnuley says.
- **Help with inspections.** Your agent should recommend qualified inspectors to thoroughly examine any home you're thinking of buying. "They should attend every inspection and be with the buyer every step of the way," Scarnuley says.
- **Negotiating fixes.** If the inspection reveals flaws, particularly safety or health risks such as structural problems, mold, septic, or asbestos issues, or water damage, a buyer's agent "should have the client's best interest in mind," Scarnuley notes. That should include negotiating with the seller to ensure problems are fixed before you move in.

Shop around

Real estate is a relationship business, so interview potential agents. In addition to their experience and knowledge, consider whether you enjoy spending time with them. "You'll be working together through what can be a lengthy and stressful process," Scarnuley says. "If the personalities aren't a good match, you should be able to find a better fit with someone else."

—Charlie Slack

Buy, Sell or Stay!

DIY RADON TESTING & REMEDIATION

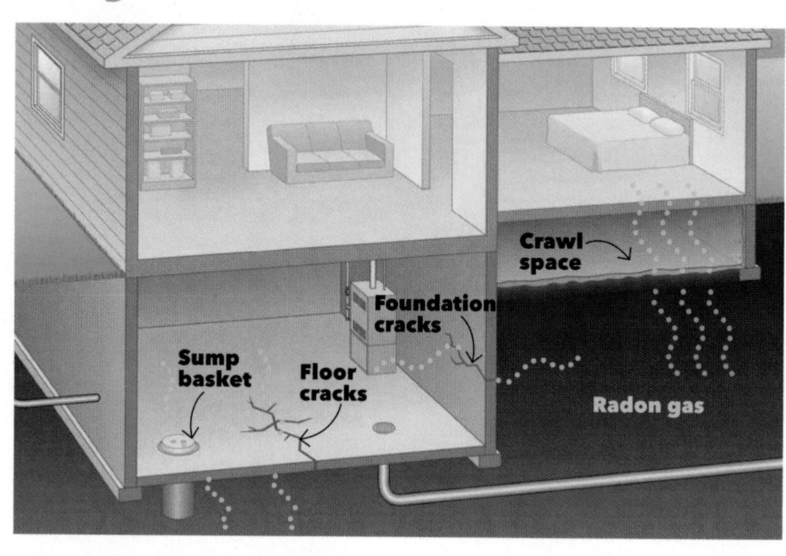

Radon is a colorless, odorless radioactive gas that's produced by decaying uranium. Radon is present in nearly all soils, and very low levels of radon gas are found in the air we breathe every day. Long-term exposure to high levels of radon trapped in your home can cause lung cancer.

How does radon gas enter a home?

Radon gas moves from the soil into a home. Although small amounts of radon can seep directly through pores in concrete, the major entry points are cracks in basement floors, sump baskets and the perimeter of slabs. Any house, of any age, can have elevated radon levels. It really depends on the way your specific house interacts with the surrounding soil. Your neighbor's radon level may differ significantly from yours.

How do I test for radon?

- Start with a short-term test for a quick assessment to see if further testing is warranted. Most are activated charcoal–based and measure radon levels for two to seven days. Mail the tests to a lab for the results. Short-term tests are available at home centers, hardware stores and online retailers for $10 to $40. If your reading is above 4 picocuries per liter (pCi/L), do a second test.
- If your short-term tests are high or borderline, try a long-term test kit. Long-term tests measure levels for 90 days to one year. Most are based on alpha particle tracking. This is a more accurate indicator of average annual levels, which can vary significantly from day to day and month to month based on factors such as a drop in air pressure, gusty winds, soil moisture and snow cover, which traps radon gases. Long-term radon tests are available through state radon agencies and online retailers.
- If you live in an area with high radon levels, or just because of the fluctuating nature of radon levels, consider a continuous electric monitor, such as the Safety Siren Pro Series digital meter. These monitors plug into a standard outlet and can be used for both short- and long-term testing to give you a running average. They use an ionization chamber and sample the air continuously. Continuous monitors are available at home centers and online, and typically cost $150 to $200.

When to take action

The EPA (Environmental Protection Agency) recommends doing a second test if an initial short-term test registers 4 (pCi/L) or higher. A long-term test gives the most accurate information, but a short-term test is acceptable if you need the results quickly, such as for a real estate transaction, or if your first levels registered 8 pCi/L or higher. If a second test registers above 4 pCi/L, consider taking steps to reduce radon levels in your home.

How to reduce radon levels

Here are a few easy steps you can take that may reduce radon levels:

- Caulk foundation cracks, construction joints and other openings with polyurethane caulk.
- Install an airtight cover on your sump pump (choose a cover that allows access to your sump).
- Cover soil in crawl spaces with polyethylene plastic sheeting tightly attached to the walls. Use sheeting with a minimum thickness of 6 mil (available at home centers).
- Seal concrete. Note that the EPA has found concrete sealers to be a temporary solution at best.

These solutions are DIY friendly, and if your level is only slightly high, they might solve the problem. If not, they'll make further steps more cost effective and efficient. Once you've tackled these, retest. If levels are still high, consider installing a radon mitigation system. You can install one yourself or hire a pro.

—Val Riedman

For more information, go to familyhandyman.com and search for "radon."

SMART LOCKS

Have you ever had the uneasy feeling you didn't lock the door when you left for work? Adding a smart lock gives a sense of security and enables other automations.

As with all smart devices, smart locks speak a variety of protocols (Wi-Fi, Bluetooth, Z-Wave and Zigbee). Knowing how you intend to interact with the smart lock—close range or remotely—will help you choose the right one. Z-Wave, Zigbee and Bluetooth are all close-range protocols, and Wi-Fi is for remote accessibility.

ALEXANDER KIRCH/SHUTTERSTOCK

Close-range use

For close range, Bluetooth is the way to go. It works when your phone is within range of your lock, usually about 30 ft. Don't want to fumble with your groceries and keys in the rain? You can unlock the door before you get out of the car.

A number pad is an inexpensive close-range option. You can operate your lock with your smartphone or the number pad, and set temporary key codes for guests or a dog walker when you're away.

Remote accessibility

Most smart locks—even those with number pads and Bluetooth capability—have remote access capability. But you'll need a Wi-Fi signal, your smartphone, an app and possibly a gateway/bridge, which is a device on your home network that allows communication with a smart device that's not on the home network. You can lock the door, get notified when family get home, or even unlock the door for a package delivery—from anywhere.

Zigbee- and Z-Wave–compatible locks require a smart hub because smartphones don't speak these protocols natively. Samsung SmartThings and Wink are the front-runners in the smart home space and are compatible with many smart locks. Zigbee and Z-Wave allow easy communication between multiple devices by creating a mesh network. With Zigbee, all the devices need to be within 60 ft. of each other. With Z-Wave, the range increases to about 300 ft.

Lock types

Locks come in two main configurations: dead bolt replacements and dead bolt retrofits. Dead bolt retrofits attach to your existing dead bolt and automate its movement.

Automation possibilities

Adding a smart lock to your setup not only provides added security but also unlocks some cool options if you integrate it with other smart devices. You can:

- Automatically have your lights turn on when the door is unlocked.
- Automatically lock your door when you leave or unlock as you approach.
- Trigger a certain playlist to play on your smart speaker whenever you arrive home.
- Turn on your A/C when you arrive home for the day.
- Log every lock/unlock action to a Google spreadsheet.
- Activate a security camera when you leave for the day.
- Lock your door using Alexa or Google Home.

—Cassidy Nelemans

Some lock options

August Smart Lock Pro: Works with August Connect Wi-Fi Bridge

Nest x Yale Lock: Works with Nest Connect

Schlage Sense Smart Lock: Works with Schlage Sense Wi-Fi adapter

Buy, Sell or Stay!

MOBILE STORAGE CONTAINERS

SHUTTERSTOCK/ROB CRANDALL

Ever wonder about those containers you see outside people's homes? If you need a place to put stuff temporarily, these storage containers are the perfect solution. Whether you're moving, decluttering or preparing to renovate, mobile storage containers offer the ultimate in convenience and flexibility. PODS, Pack Rat, Smartbox, U-Pack and U-Haul are a few companies that provide them. All you need is a level, paved surface for the container and maybe some professional or volunteer help to fill it.

Get the best deal

With so many storage options to choose from, pricing is competitive. To compare bids, complete the form at each company's website. You'll need the zip codes where the container will be going (both empty and full), your anticipated dates of delivery, and the size and number of containers you want. Promo codes may be provided. If not, ask your real estate agent or contractor. You'll save money by using your own packing supplies, including blankets, boxes and bubble wrap, and by packing efficiently. All the companies offer videos on how to pack their containers. Booking a container in the winter for a project you're doing in the summer can save you as much as 30 percent.

Reserve containers early

Most storage companies allow you to book containers without any down payment or deposit, so shop for a container as soon as you know you'll need one. "It doesn't matter how many containers you order," a salesman at PODS told me. "It's how many containers you receive." Plus, you can change the delivery dates without an additional charge.

How it works

Before taking delivery, make sure you have all the permits required by your city, apartment complex or homeowner's association. After the container is delivered, you'll typically have three to 30 days to fill it before the company comes for it. Or you can leave it on-site if that's what your project calls for. If you opt for off-site storage of your container, most companies will allow you to access your container with 24 hours' notice. You can store your containers as long as needed or, if you're moving, have them delivered to your new home. If you store more than one container, keep a list of the container numbers and what each one holds.

Is my stuff safe?

In most cases, the container's contents are covered by your renter's or homeowner's insurance. Once the container leaves your property, however, the coverage drops, typically to 10 percent of the policy's full value. You can also buy coverage from the storage companies.

—Matthew Knopp

Reasons to use mobile storage containers

- Preparing your house for sale or rent
- Decluttering your house or garage
- Renovations
- Sorting out an estate
- Storage of home office materials or equipment
- Emergency repairs

Other options

If you're moving the contents of a small apartment, it might be cheaper to use FedEx, UPS or Amtrak instead of a temporary storage container. While you'll sacrifice some convenience, you could save hundreds of dollars. It depends on the weight of the shipment and the distance it will travel.

Major suppliers

1-800-Pack-Rat: 1800packrat.com
PODS: pods.com
Smartbox: smartboxmovingandstorage.com
U-Pack Moving: upack.com
U-Haul (U-Box): uhaul.com

INSTANT **IMPACT**

Easy upgrades—whether you're buying, selling or staying put

By Mike Berner

We recently sat down with home-staging expert Melanie Zaelich of Happy Place Interiors. She flooded us with great tips for home sellers—we could hardly write them down fast enough. Then it struck us: This would be great advice for everyone. We all want our homes to "show" better, whether we're selling a house, moving into a new home or apartment, or staying in place for years.

Get rid of rugs—maybe

If you're staying in your home, you probably want the softness and silencing effect of area rugs. But if you're selling, remove them. They chop up the room in photographs and hide your nice flooring. Melanie tells her clients, "You're selling the floor, not the rug." There is an exception to this rule: In a large, open layout, rugs help to define the space. For example, a rug can make a seating area distinct from an adjoining dining area.

BELINDA FONTES/OFFSET.COM

Buy, Sell or Stay!

INSTANT IMPACT continued

TRIM TREES THAT BLOCK VIEWS OR LIGHT

Natural light is something everyone craves, especially during the shorter days of the year. To let in as much light as possible, trim trees or shrubs that are creating shade. If the branches are within arm's reach, use a lopper or reciprocating saw with a pruning blade. Use a pole saw if the sun-blocking limb is higher than that.

UPGRADE LIGHT FIXTURES

In many homes, it's the most powerful, effective thing you can do: Replace dated lights with more stylish fixtures, especially in "public" rooms like the living room and kitchen. It doesn't have to be expensive, since home centers carry up-to-date fixtures starting at about $50. (The fixture above is $89 at judylighting.com.) Nor is it difficult, even if you have no experience with electrical work. To see how, search for "light fixture" at familyhandyman.com.

Make sure lights match in color and brightness from room to room. The bulbs in recessed lights should be the same, and the bulbs in fixtures should all match as well. Melanie suggests using GE Crystal Clear incandescent bulbs. She thinks they show off the interior best.

INSTANT BACKSPLASH

An attractive kitchen backsplash can transform a kitchen. Melanie recommends a peel-and-stick backsplash as an easy DIY solution. You just peel off the backing from the sheet of tile and stick it to the wall. The tiles are available in all types of materials from natural stone to gel tile and cost $3 a sheet and up.

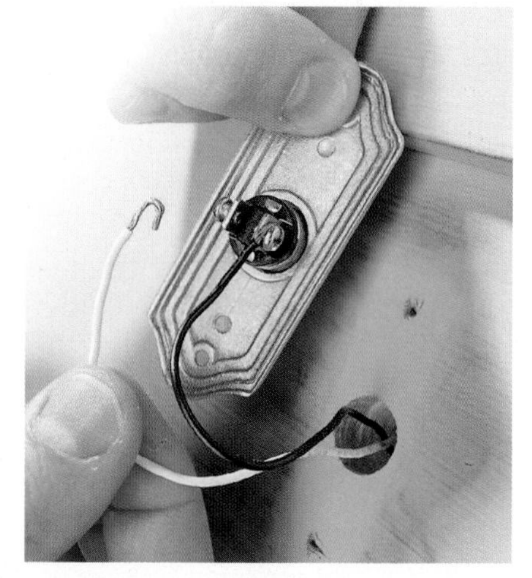

REPLACE A DOORBELL BUTTON

If the first thing buyers notice as they approach a house is a stuck, broken or ugly doorbell button, it will affect their impression as they check out the rest of the house. Replacement is easy; there are just two low-voltage wires to connect. To solve other doorbell problems, go to familyhandyman.com and search for "doorbell."

BLOCK THE VIEW, NOT THE LIGHT

People like bright, sunlit spaces. So if you want to block the view of your neighbor's backyard junk collection, go with translucent window film rather than opaque window coverings. Window film is also ideal for bathroom privacy.

During showings, potential home buyers first notice things at eye level, then they look up, and lastly, they check near the floor. Keep that in mind when choosing the projects you want to prioritize.

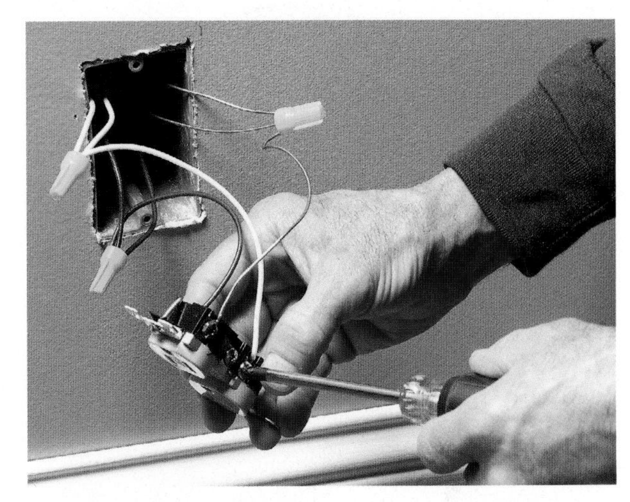

REPLACE OUTLETS AND SWITCHES

Switches, outlets and cover plates get dirty, damaged and discolored, giving your home a worn look. New ones give your home a remodeled feel. Replacing them is usually easy and inexpensive ($2 to $3 each).

RESTORE GROUT

If the grout lines in your tile are dingy and dark from grime, you can easily get the grout to look like new again with a grout restorer. Some are kits that come with two solutions—a tile-and-grout cleaner and a color sealer. Other products consist of just a colorant. Either way, clean the grout and wipe it dry, apply the colorant according to the manufacturer, then wipe off the excess. Products range from less than $15 to $30 and can be found at home centers.

REPLACE CABINET HARDWARE

Changing out old cabinet hardware for an updated style can drastically change the way the entire room looks. Updating the cabinet knobs and pulls will cost as little as $2 to $5 apiece, and each can be done in a matter of minutes. If the shape of the knob is up to date, but the color or shade isn't, give it a few coats of spray paint.

Buy, Sell or Stay!

INSTANT IMPACT continued

MAKE SPRAY PAINT YOUR FRIEND

All homeowners should get familiar with laying a nice coat of spray paint over all kinds of faded, rusty or outdated things around your home. The key to a good spray-paint job is a good cleaning with a degreaser followed by several very light coats of paint, starting with a primer. Spray-paint appliance handles, HVAC registers, bath fan covers and light fixtures to give them new life. If the material you're painting is plastic, use a paint formulated for plastic.

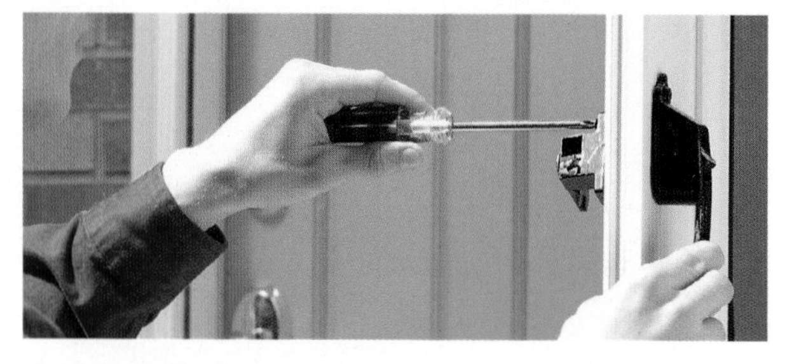

FIX DOORS

If you've lived in your home for a while, you've learned to tolerate your sticking, stubborn doors. But to other people, they're a frustration and a turnoff. The good news: You can solve most problems in less than an hour. Familyhandyman.com has how-to help for any type of door trouble. Search for "door repair."

The front entry is first priority. buyers typically know within 10 seconds whether or not they're interested.

ADJUST CABINET DOORS

Make sure those cabinet doors are aligned properly. It will make a huge difference and it's really easy. On euro hinges, there are two screws you can tighten and loosen to align the doors and make sure gaps between them are consistent.

COVER UP CLAW MARKS

Claw marks from pets need to be fixed. If the door is painted, it's easy to fill the gouges with wood filler or patching compound and repaint. On a stained door, try gel stain. Lightly sand the area and then, using a dry brush, start with a light stain and darken it to match the old finish. Keep the brush on the drier side by wiping excess stain off on a clean rag. When you're done, feather from the newly stained area with a clear spray finish into the surrounding area.

FIX IT BEFORE YOU LIST IT!
This includes torn window and storm door screens, doorbells and bifold and sliding doors inside the house.

REPLACE TORN SCREENS

This is an easy DIY project that involves a special screen roller and just a few basic tools. You start by removing the old spline, the stringy rubber piece that holds the screen in the groove, then you'll be able to take off the old screen. Place the new screen over the frame and use the screen roller to press in a new spline. After cutting away the excess screen, you'll have it back in the opening in half an hour.

MASK CEILING STAINS

If you have a water-stained ceiling, a stain-blocking primer is mandatory to prevent the stain from bleeding through a fresh coat of paint. KILZ Upshot and Zinsser Covers Up are both stain-blocking primers, and both have nozzles that shoot upward. These primers attempt to match aged ceilings, so you may be able to get away without repainting the ceiling. You can pick up a can at any home center for about $7.

Hide wall damage

If you've got dings or dents around your outlet, or made a mistake cutting tile or drywall around an outlet or switch, install a jumbo cover plate to hide those gaps or dents. In fact, consider replacing all your old, yellowed or dirty cover plates: they cost less than $1 apiece.

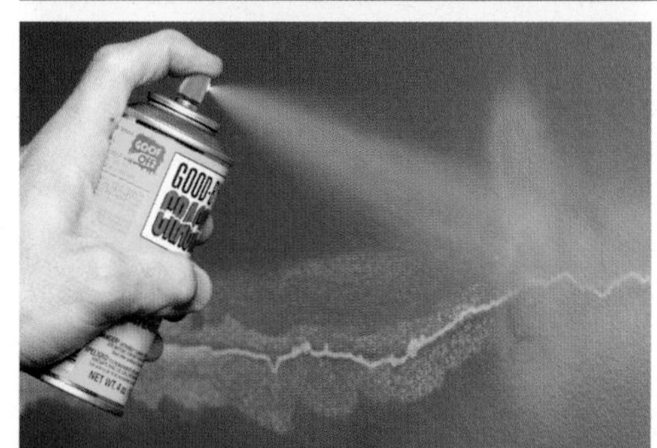

Adiós, Good-Bye Cracks

Our favorite solution to cracks in plaster and drywall was Good-Bye Cracks, an elastic spray-on coating that flexes along with wall movement. After filling the gaps with patching compound, you spray on two coats, then repaint. However, it has been discontinued and will soon be gone for good. A 4-oz. can is $4. Stock up while you can!

Cover doorknob dings

Doorknobs are some of the main culprits when it comes to doing damage to your walls. If the accident has already happened, you can prevent further damage and cover up the dent with a bumper. And if your wall is still in good condition, you can keep it that way. You can find door bumpers online or at home centers for about $5.

Buy, Sell or Stay!

EXTREME CLEANING

A home improvement with a huge payoff

By Brad Holden

You probably don't think of cleaning as home improvement, but a thorough cleaning really is a powerful way to improve your home. Things that look old, worn and in need of replacement sometimes just need a good scrubbing! Some of us at *Family Handyman* have learned that lesson recently.

NATALI_ MIS/SHUTTERSTOCK

If you're buying

The house my wife and I bought was pretty dirty, which triggered some buyer's remorse. So we spent a long, hard day cleaning. It was worth it. The grime left by the previous owners is gone, and the place feels like ours.

—Mike Berner

If you're selling

To show our house in the best light possible, we cleaned everything and every corner. Dirt is unattractive, and somebody else's dirt is especially so. You'll get more and better offers if potential buyers see your house as "move-in ready."

—Marcia Roepke

If you're staying

A long weekend of cleaning cut my list of remodeling chores in half. The grout, the kitchen sink and fixtures, the entryway walls—they didn't need a redo. A deep cleaning made them look like new. Well, almost.

—Gary Wentz

Declutter first

Cleaning your house is far easier once you remove clutter, and that's something most of us need to do anyway. If you're selling, don't just put everything in the garage. That's a turnoff for potential buyers. Move your stuff off site.

Donate it. Donating your goods is a nice way to get rid of usable items without the hassles of selling them. Perfect if you have a lot of stuff and limited time.

Sell it. If you have time and you'd like to make a little extra cash, sell unwanted things online. Keep in mind that you'll have to check messages and be available for people coming over to buy your stuff. It can be a big hassle.

Put it on the curb. Setting free stuff on the curb is probably the quickest and easiest way to get rid of it. People will take anything that's free! The drawback is that if you itemize deductions on your tax returns, you won't get a receipt to count it as a charitable donation. You can also list free items on Craigslist.com.

Trash it. If you have a lot of junk, throwing it all in a dumpster or Bagster bag is an easy and gratifying experience. A small dumpster (about 10 cu. yds.) typically costs about $300.

Store it. For the items you're keeping but not using for staging, mobile storage containers are the way to go. Have one dropped at your house, fill it up, and then the company will haul it off to a temporary storage facility or your new home. The cost varies depending on the container size and the distance of the move. A long-distance move is about $800.

Buy, Sell or Stay!

EXTREME CLEANING continued

Focus on the bathroom

Cleaning the bathroom might take you more time than the rest of the house combined. But it's essential, especially if you're selling. If there's one room potential buyers are extra picky about, it's the bathroom. It should be spotless.

Glass shower doors: Built-up soap scum seems impossible to remove. Pick up polishing compound at a home center or an auto parts store and use it with an auto buffer to polish off the offending scum. If you don't own a buffer, you can buy one for as little as $20 or borrow one from a gearhead friend. If possible, take the doors out to the garage to avoid messing up the bathroom.

Exhaust fan: Turn on the fan and blast out the dust with "canned air." The fan will blow the dust outside. This works on the return air grilles of your central heating/cooling system too. Run the system so the return airflow will carry the dust to the filter. You'll find canned air at home centers, usually in the electrical supplies aisle.

Rust stains: To clean rust from toilets and other porcelain surfaces, add three parts water to one part rust remover (Acid Magic is one brand we like). Use a sprayer, brush or foam pad to apply the mixture to the rust stains, then watch them dissolve. Rinse with clear water. You can also use it full strength for stubborn stains. Avoid getting the acid on metal parts because they can discolor. Acid Magic is available online and at hardware stores.

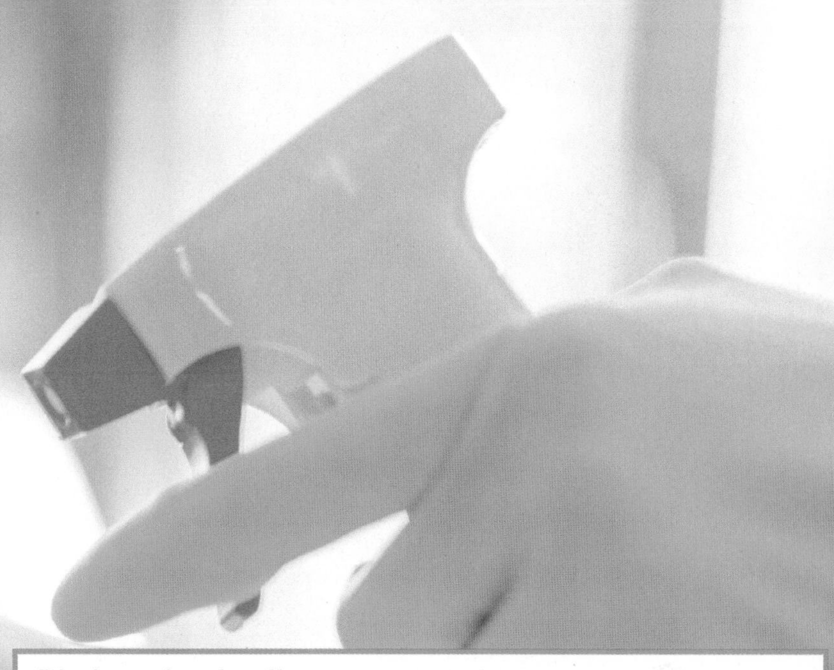

Faucets and fixtures: Scrub faucets and fixtures with a calcium, lime and rust remover, such as CLR, and an old toothbrush.

Tile grout: Try a bleach pen to transform your grout from grungy to great. This method is tedious, but the payoff is crisp, clean grout lines. Use the pen to "draw" bleach across the grout lines. The pen allows you to target the grout without getting bleach all over the tile. Wait 10 minutes, then rinse.

Tile: Magic Eraser sponges (or other brands) make short work of cleaning tile. Just dampen the sponge and rub it on the offending mess. In most cases, the mess will come right off. These sponges are especially useful for removing ground-in dirt from porous floor tile and cleaning those pesky nonslip strips in the bottom of your tub.

SHUTTERSTOCK/DANIEL JEDZURA (BACKGROUND PHOTO)

Dig into the details

Some cleaning jobs get overlooked, either because we're so used to these areas not being clean, or because we just don't like doing them. Pay attention to the following:

- Ceiling fan blades
- Light fixtures
- Baseboards/trim/door frames
- Handrails
- Furniture feet
- Fingerprints
- Furnace exterior
- Water heater exterior
- Exposed pipes and ductwork
- Washer and dryer
- Inside cabinets and drawers
- Walls and ceilings
- Curtains
- Under appliances
- Trash cans
- Doorknobs
- Dishwasher
- Throw pillows

Windows

Your windows present the view as well as let in natural light. You can hire a window cleaning service, but if you'd like to do it yourself, go to familyhandyman.com and search for "how to clean windows."

Carpet

If the carpet is reasonably clean, don't go beyond vacuuming it. Carpet is the last thing buyers look at and doesn't give a big return on investment. If there's hardwood underneath, consider removing the carpet.

Get a cleaning service

You can hire a pro to do a deep cleaning. At about $500 for a 1,400-sq.-ft. home, it's definitely worth considering. Check off a solid weekend's worth of drudgery by writing a check!

Don't clean; replace

Some things just aren't worth the effort to clean. You'll save time and money and get better results by simply replacing the following items with new:

- Shower curtains
- Switch plates
- Mini blinds
- Showerheads

Buy, Sell or Stay!

GET THE MOST FROM YOUR HOME INSPECTION

Expert advice for home buyers

You've chosen a home, made an offer and had it accepted. You're ready to charge ahead and tempted to hire the first (or cheapest) home inspector you find so you can check that item off your list. But slow down. With a little extra time and knowledge, your home inspection can be much more than just a standard requirement in the buying process.

SEEKING AN INSPECTOR? READ A SAMPLE REPORT

When hiring an inspector, ask for recommendations from people you trust and read online reviews. But also go to the inspector's website and read a sample report. If there isn't one, I'd look further. A good report contains these elements:

- Photos should accompany the items discussed in the report.
- The report should be written in plain English, understandable to anyone. You shouldn't need a degree in building science to understand it.
- The report should cover three aspects of each potential problem: what the issue is, why it's an issue and what should be done.
- Every report includes disclaimers. Like everyone else, inspectors don't want to be sued. But a good report keeps them to a minimum.
- Many reports are filled with recommendations for further testing or inspections. When I see that, I get the feeling the inspector aims to avoid lawsuits more than to provide great service.
- Look for statements that mention an issue but also say it isn't a significant problem. Anyone can identify an issue and recommend further action. But it takes deep experience and knowledge to say an issue isn't worth worrying about. That's often the sign of a great inspector.

SELLING? DON'T RISK AN INCOMPLETE INSPECTION

If you're selling, you'll want me to complete my job. If I label it an "incomplete inspection," that may delay or even sink the sale. Good preparation is mostly about providing easy access. Keep in mind that it isn't the inspector's job to move barricades of boxes or stacks of paint cans.

- Make sure I can get to and open the main electrical panel and any subpanels.
- Clear a path around the furnace and water heater.
- If you have a detached garage, leave keys or an opener so I can get in. I don't know how to pick locks.
- If you have crawl spaces, make sure the doors to them are accessible.
- Secure any pets that might escape through open doors—or worse, attack me. I'm not a burglar!
- If the house has been unoccupied, make sure the water, gas and electricity are turned on.

MEET AN EXPERT

Reuben Saltzman is the owner of Structure Tech Home Inspections. His blog is a gold mine of information, stories and opinions. Check it out at StructureTech1.com.

THE REPORT IS NOT A NEGOTIATING WEAPON

Buyers sometimes use the inspection report as an excuse to renegotiate the price of the house. Unless the problems are dangerous or major, this is a bad idea. Defects like peeling paint, sidewalk cracks or wall damage are considered "known conditions." In other words, they were already obvious when you first toured the house. Asking for compensation after the agreement will poison your relationship with the seller and real estate agents.

The same goes for old construction that doesn't meet newer building codes. If old stair balusters, for example, are spaced farther apart than current code allows, the report will note it. But that doesn't mean the seller should pay for correction.

A "known condition"
This railing is unsafe and doesn't meet building codes. But since it's an obvious problem and one that you saw before the inspection, it's not a good reason to renegotiate the sale of the house.

A camera on a cable
A sewer inspection camera and a trained eye can spot cracks before they cost you big bucks.

GET A SEWER INSPECTION

For about $200, I can hire my sewer guru to run a camera through the waste pipe that runs from the house to the city sewer system. I used to recommend this for old homes only. But after seeing dozens of fractures in newer lines—and repairs that cost thousands—I know better.

BIG PROBLEMS MIGHT MEAN RENEGOTIATION

If the inspection uncovers dangerous or expensive problems—like aluminum wiring, a cracked heat exchanger or structural flaws—it's reasonable to rethink the agreement. There are four options:

- **Lower the price:** This is often a fair way to compensate the buyer. But even though the home loan will decrease along with the sale price, the buyer will have to pay for those repairs. And that's often burdensome on top of the ordinary costs of buying a home.
- **Ask the seller to make the repairs:** This also can be fair—if the seller can afford to pay. But the buyer should keep this in mind: The seller will want the work done quickly and cheaply and may not be too concerned about the quality of the job.
- **Cancel the sale:** This is usually the worst option. Both parties have invested time and money to reach an agreement. Killing that agreement is a huge step backward for everyone.
- **Do nothing:** Since all the other options raise new complications, this is often the best response to problems—as long as those problems don't pose an immediate health threat.

A serious, expensive issue
Aluminum wiring can be a fire hazard, and making it safe can cost thousands. If your inspector finds it, renegotiation is justified.

Buy, Sell or Stay!

GET THE MOST FROM YOUR HOME INSPECTION continued

High-tech help
A moisture meter is one of the tools that inspectors use to track down the water problems that feed mold.

Plugged plumbing vent
Plumbers sometimes forget to remove the plug in rooftop vents. Some owners of new homes live with the results for years—slow, gurgling, stinky drains.

NEW HOMES NEED INSPECTIONS TOO

During construction, a house gets several inspections by city building inspectors. So it's reasonable to assume that a new house won't have problems. But you shouldn't assume that. I've seen hundreds of serious problems in new homes over the past few years—homes built by big, reputable builders.

FOUNDATION CRACKS? DON'T FREAK OUT

When the walls that support an entire building are cracked, it seems pretty scary. But here's the deal: All foundations have some cracks, and most will never become a problem, even in a hundred years. A good inspector will make note of cracks but will rarely recommend further inspection by an engineer.

Cracks are normal
Keep in mind that the majority of foundation cracks will never become a structural problem. They might let in some groundwater, but that's usually an easy fix.

SKIP THE MOLD TEST

I can provide mold testing, but I usually talk my clients out of it. Testing costs hundreds of dollars and rarely provides practical information. And since mold issues are caused by moisture problems, moisture testing is a better path to the root of any problems.

4 Woodworking & Workshop Projects & Tips

IN THIS CHAPTER

HomeSmarts

KNOWLEDGE YOU NEED TO BE A BETTER HOMEOWNER

THE CASE FOR THE **COMPACT ROUTER**

My full-size routers have been gathering a lot of dust since I purchased a compact router for trimming plastic laminate. Compact routers only accept 1/4-in.-shank bits, which limits the size bits you can use. But my compact router can handle about 75 percent of my routing tasks: light edge profiles, shallow dadoes and rabbets, round-overs and chamfers. One-handed operation is a nice bonus.

If you're new to routers, a compact router is a good introduction. They're less intimidating than their full-size siblings. You can grab a basic compact router for as little as $30. Or, you can spend about $200 for an entire kit that includes various bases and attachments.

—Gary Wentz
Editor-in-Chief

Basic kit: $30

Complete kit: $200

CAN WOOD MAKE **YOU SICK?**

We all know that sawdust and fine dust particles floating in the air don't just make your shop a mess; they're also health hazards. Typically, we think of distant consequences like breathing problems in old age. But often there are immediate effects.

It's not just about dust. Oils and compounds in wood cause adverse reactions, and people can become sensitized to a particular species. It's impossible to predict who will be susceptible to which woods. Reactions range from mild to severe, and they can be immediate or build up over time. Many wood species are known sensitizers, but some are worse than others. The yew tree, for example, is flat-out toxic. Other known sensitizers include common species such as oak, cedar, birch, walnut, and spruce, which is mixed in with most bins of construction lumber. Several websites, such as wood-database.com, list woods with a reputation for being sensitizers.

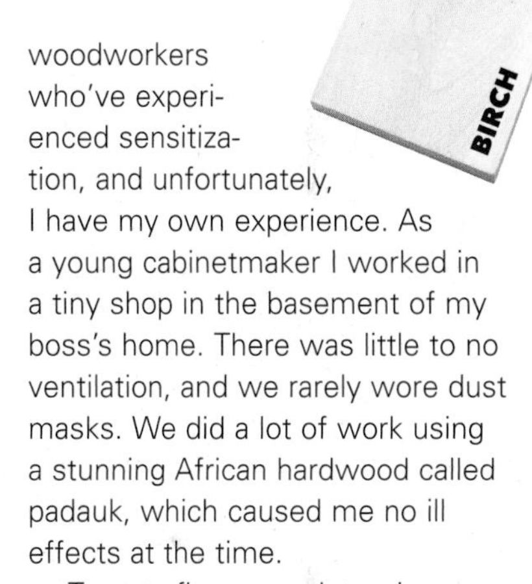

I know several professional woodworkers who've experienced sensitization, and unfortunately, I have my own experience. As a young cabinetmaker I worked in a tiny shop in the basement of my boss's home. There was little to no ventilation, and we rarely wore dust masks. We did a lot of work using a stunning African hardwood called padauk, which caused me no ill effects at the time.

Twenty-five years later, I was commissioned to build a project using padauk. After making one rip on the table saw, I started to feel it: runny nose, watering eyes. Within the next five minutes, I experienced shortness of breath and general malaise. I quickly locked up the shop and went home for the day. My clothes and I both required a good laundering before I felt better. Working with padauk is no longer fun!

I still had to finish the project, which meant I needed long sleeves, nitrile gloves, a canister filter mask and goggles. So, if you want to continue your favorite hobby, take precautions now: Wear a dust mask, use dust collection and install an air cleaner. Had I taken these precautions in those early years, I likely wouldn't have developed this sensitivity.

—Brad Holden
Associate Editor

HomeSmarts

ADJUSTABLE
HARDWARE BINS

Build these bin racks with removable partitions to suit the size of the hardware you're storing

On a table saw, cut 3/16-in.-deep slots every 4 in. across the 24-in. x 7-1/8-in. piece of plywood. Make the slots just wide enough for the 1/8-in.-thick partition to slide in smoothly. Now saw the slotted piece into strips 4-1/2 in. and 2-1/2 in. wide. Use 1-in. brads and glue to assemble the sides and angled ends, then nail and glue the floor on. Drop the angled partitions into the slots, mount the rack to a wall, and go nuts sorting and organizing your scattered hardware.

—Bruce Wiebe
Contributing Editor

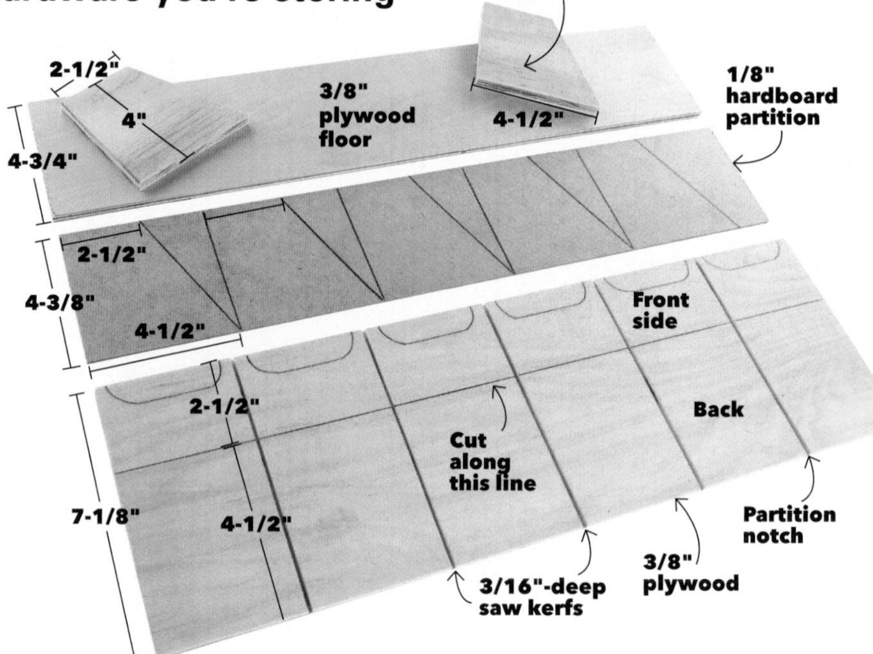

WHICH FINISHES ARE FOOD-SAFE?

The short answer is, all of them. Some finishes used to contain lead as a drier, but that was banned years ago. The key is to allow finishes to fully cure, which takes up to 30 days. There are essentially two types of finish: oil, which penetrates the wood, and film forming, which lies on top of the wood.

If your wooden bowl or cutting board gets rough treatment with knives and utensils, use an oil finish like tung, mineral, linseed, or even an edible oil, such as olive or walnut oil. Just refresh the finish as needed with another coat of oil. Film finishes develop cracks with heavy use. These cracks allow water to get into the wood but don't allow easy escape, and refinishing involves sanding the whole piece back to bare wood. If your item isn't used for cutting, a film finish is fine.

—Brad Holden
Associate Editor

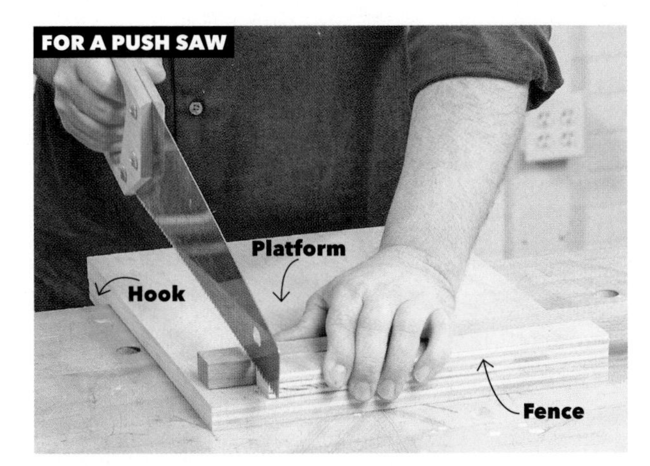

UNIVERSAL BENCH HOOK

A bench hook is an indispensable tool for hand-sawing at the workbench. Cut the hook to the width of the platform and cut the fence slightly shorter than the platform. Next, glue the fence and hook to opposite ends and sides of the platform as shown. This allows the bench hook to grab the front edge of your workbench. Hook it on the front edge of your bench for use with a saw that cuts on the push stroke, or on the back of the bench for a saw that cuts on the pull stroke.

HOME CENTER **LUMBER**

Home centers carry more lumber species (both hardwood and softwood) than they used to, but the selection is still hit-or-miss. Stores even within the same company might stock more species than another, so you'll need to check around. Traditional lumberyards or specialty hardwood stores carry the best lumber and far more options for thicknesses and species. But with these tips, you may find everything you need at a home center.

Hardwood vs. softwood

These are confusing terms, as they really don't refer to the actual hardness of the wood. Balsa, for example, is a hardwood, but you could practically cut it with your fingernail. The term "hardwood" simply indicates that the wood comes from a deciduous tree, the type that loses its leaves in the fall. "Softwood" refers to conifers, which are generally trees with needles, like pine, spruce, fir and cedar. The vast majority of home construction is done with fast-growing softwoods.

What you'll find at home centers

(The prices listed are for an 8-ft. 1x6.)

Standard Pine ($4)
Eastern white pine is the most widely used wood for home construction. Knots and resin are common. Doesn't take stain evenly.

Select Pine ($10)
Same as standard pine but completely knot free. Nice for paint or natural finish.

Cedar ($12)
Western red cedar is lightweight and rot resistant, making it popular for outdoor furniture. Knots and splits are common.

Poplar ($13)
Yellow poplar is generally light-colored, with hues ranging from yellow to green to purple. Excellent for painted woodwork because grain doesn't show through.

Red oak ($17)
Red oak is the most ubiquitous cabinet wood of the last 75 years. It's strong, durable and takes finish well.

Less common

Cherry ($40, not shown)
Black cherry is a "medium hard" hardwood. It's easy to work with hand or power tools and takes a finish well, turning darker as it ages. Used for high-end cabinetry and furniture.

Aspen ($12)
Aspen is a soft, lightweight hardwood with subtle grain. It's excellent as a base for paint or as a secondary wood (see p. 128).

Red Alder ($21)
Red alder is a soft, lightweight hardwood. Its reddish brown color and grain texture make it resemble cherry. Stable and easy to work, it's a good choice as either a primary or secondary wood (see p. 128).

Mahogany ($24)
Philippine mahogany is a soft hardwood. Typically has uniform grain and texture. The home center variety is less showy than African mahogany, but it's a stable, easily worked primary or secondary wood.

Hickory ($25)
Hickory, a tough hardwood, is well suited for tool handles and baseball bats. It's hard to work with hand tools but finishes beautifully.

Maple ($26)
Hard maple is durable and fine textured. It's a popular choice for cabinetry. Doesn't take stain evenly.

Special order
Some home centers will special-order a wide variety of species for you. We don't recommend this unless it's your only option. You won't see the exact boards you're getting until they arrive, and unless they're somehow unusable, you won't be able to reject them.

Nonstandard boards

If you're serious about woodworking, you'll want a jointer and planer in your shop eventually. But if you don't have these tools yet, know that many home centers carry hardwood thicknesses other than nominal 1-by (3/4 in. actual). You can regularly find thicknesses ranging from 1/4 in. to 1-1/2 in.

If you need wide stock, you'll also find large 1-in. or 1-1/4-in. edge-glued panels in one or two species. This is a better option than buying really wide boards, which are prone to cupping. Solid wood stair treads are another handy option.

Buy extra

After you've figured out how much lumber you need for a project, add 10 to 20 percent. This allows for the inevitable mistakes, as well as trimming off split ends of boards and cutting around defects.

Cut out defects

Construction lumber tends to have a lot of knots. When you're shopping, be aware of your project's part sizes. Often, you can buy an inexpensive board and cut around the defects.

Primary and secondary boards

If you look at antique furniture, you'll notice that a beautiful quarter-sawn oak dresser, for example, uses expensive wood for parts that show and cheaper woods for parts that don't. So take a page from the old masters and use the showy stuff only where it counts.

Working with rough-sawn boards
Serious woodworkers prefer to buy rough-sawn wood and then flatten and machine those boards down to their desired thicknesses and widths. The advantage is that the boards have warped to their final shape, so when they're flattened, they stay perfectly flat, straight and stable. However, that calls for two specialty tools, a jointer and a planer. To learn about this process, go to familyhandyman.com and search for "how to plane rough lumber."

Use the outer edges

The way a board is cut from a log affects its stability. Quarter-sawn boards are the most stable; they don't "move" as much with changes in humidity. Home centers don't carry quarter-sawn lumber; it's too expensive. But when you're sorting through the piles, look at the end grain. Sometimes you'll find growth rings running perpendicular to the board's face on the outer edges. This is essentially quarter-sawn lumber. You can rip these edges free of the less stable center.

Inspect boards

Sight down the edge of a board to see how flat and straight a board is. Chances are you won't find perfect boards, only better and worse. Use the best boards for larger/longer project parts. Cut smaller parts from less perfect boards. As you cut these boards into shorter lengths, their imperfections will be less pronounced. Reject boards that twist along their length.

Match grain

Even though you may be buying only one species, look closely and choose matching grains and colors, especially for glue-ups. These boards are all red oak, but one of them is very different and would look hideous glued up in this panel. Even stained, their colors would be different.

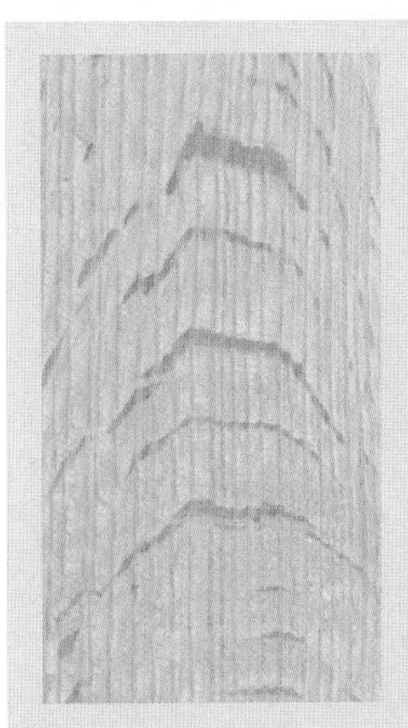

Look for gems

Home centers don't stock premium lumber like quarter-sawn oak and curly maple. But sometimes they have it by accident, and the people who are looking for precious lumber aren't shopping at the home center; they go to a lumberyard. So keep your eyes open. This lovely piece of quarter-sawn oak was mixed right in with the common stuff!

Buy the width you need

Hoping to save some money by ripping wide boards into narrower pieces? When you rip wide boards, internal stresses change, and they'll likely warp a bit. This means restraightening an edge between rips. You'll need a jointer or other straightening method for this. Instead, find the straightest boards you can that are closest to the width you need. Ripping off 1/4 in. is far less likely to cause a board to warp.

Lumberyards & online ordering

If you're looking for a larger selection of hardwoods—and typically nicer lumber—go to a local lumberyard. You can find one by searching for "hardwood lumber" online. Buying lumber online is another good option. Reputable online lumber sellers provide photos, dimensions and descriptions of the actual boards you're buying.

TINA SARGEANT

ONE-DAY **STORAGE BENCH**

Elegant outside, enormous space inside!

By Brad Holden

While looking for patio bench ideas, I came across a sleek modern design with tons of storage inside. Perfect. The price tag—over $1,000—wasn't a problem because I knew I could build my own version, and in just a day. And so can you. It's really just a plywood box dressed up with solid wood slats.

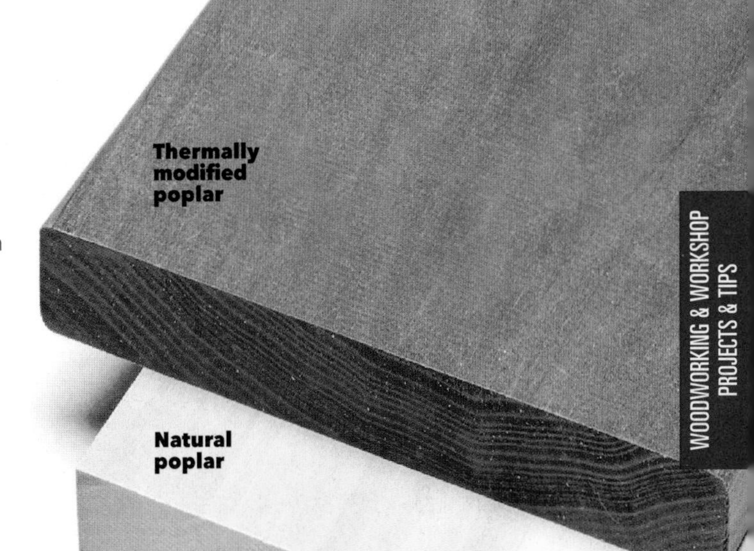

Thermally Modified Wood

I chose thermally modified poplar for this bench. Normally, poplar would be a poor choice for an outdoor project, but thermal modification changes the rules. Thermally modified wood (TMW) has essentially been cooked, removing the organic compounds. The chemical-free process makes wood more stable and resistant to decay and insects.

This process naturally darkens the wood. Left unfinished, it will weather gray like any other wood. The price of TMW varies. My supplier had pine for $1.25 per linear ft., poplar for $3.80 and ash for $4.20. To find TMW, ask your local hardwood lumberyard or search online.

WHAT IT TAKES

TIME: 1 day
COST: $100 to $600*
SKILL: Beginner
TOOLS: Circular saw or table saw, drill/driver, clamps

*About $300 if you use cedar and less expensive lid supports

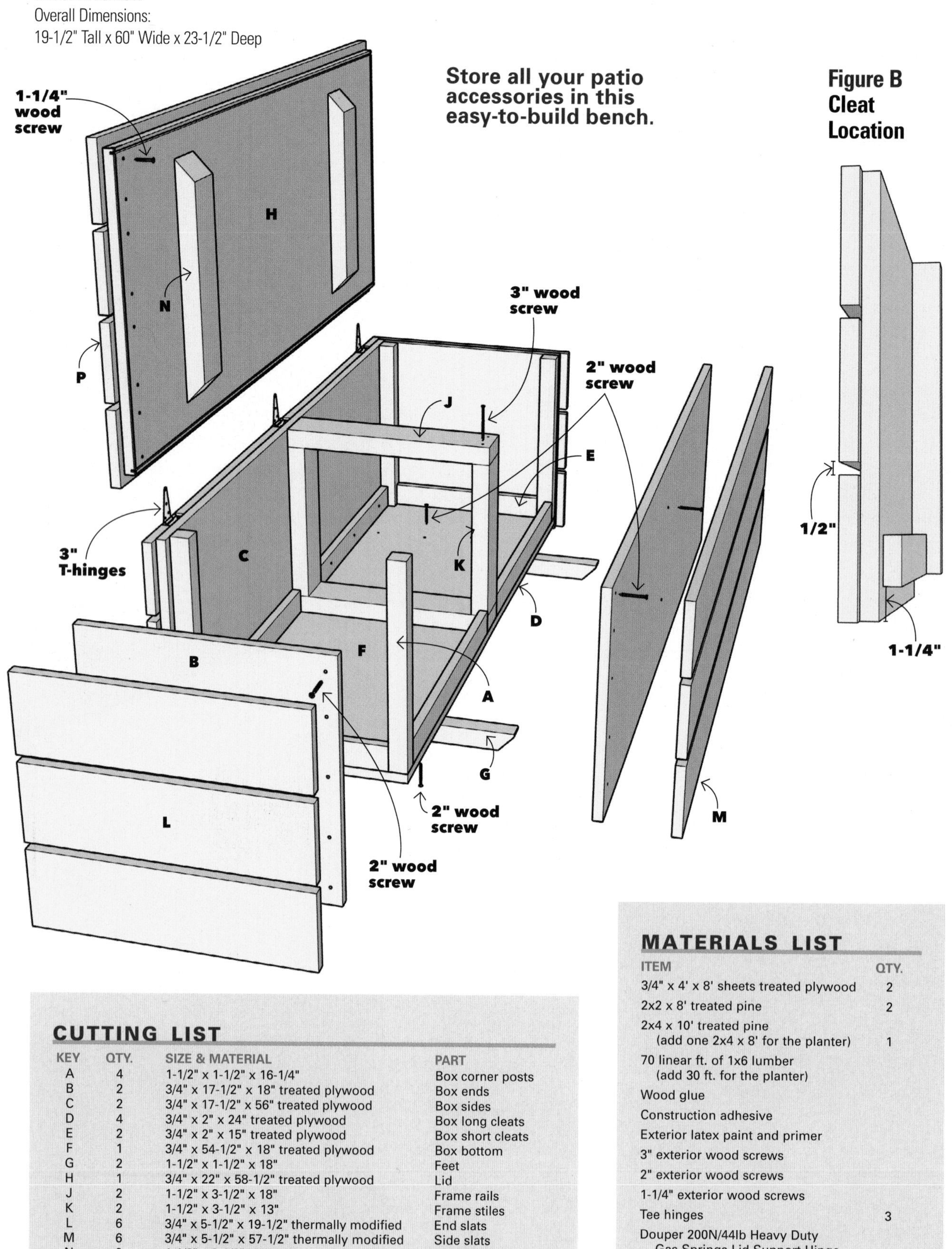

CUTTING LIST

KEY	QTY.	SIZE & MATERIAL	PART
A	4	1-1/2" x 1-1/2" x 16-1/4"	Box corner posts
B	2	3/4" x 17-1/2" x 18" treated plywood	Box ends
C	2	3/4" x 17-1/2" x 56" treated plywood	Box sides
D	4	3/4" x 2" x 24" treated plywood	Box long cleats
E	2	3/4" x 2" x 15" treated plywood	Box short cleats
F	1	3/4" x 54-1/2" x 18" treated plywood	Box bottom
G	2	1-1/2" x 1-1/2" x 18"	Feet
H	1	3/4" x 22" x 58-1/2" treated plywood	Lid
J	2	1-1/2" x 3-1/2" x 18"	Frame rails
K	2	1-1/2" x 3-1/2" x 13"	Frame stiles
L	6	3/4" x 5-1/2" x 19-1/2" thermally modified	End slats
M	6	3/4" x 5-1/2" x 57-1/2" thermally modified	Side slats
N	2	1-1/2" x 3-1/2" x 17-1/2"	Lid battens
P	4	3/4" x 5-1/2" x 60" thermally modified	Lid slats

MATERIALS LIST

ITEM	QTY.
3/4" x 4' x 8' sheets treated plywood	2
2x2 x 8' treated pine	2
2x4 x 10' treated pine (add one 2x4 x 8' for the planter)	1
70 linear ft. of 1x6 lumber (add 30 ft. for the planter)	
Wood glue	
Construction adhesive	
Exterior latex paint and primer	
3" exterior wood screws	
2" exterior wood screws	
1-1/4" exterior wood screws	
Tee hinges	3
Douper 200N/44lb Heavy Duty Gas Springs Lid Support Hinge, $36/pair	1 pr.

Money and materials

This bench is mostly treated plywood, which stands up to the elements but can be unfriendly to work with. It's often slightly damp, if not soaking wet, so let it dry in your shop for a week or two before cutting. Store it flat to minimize warping as it dries. Caution: Warped boards are dangerous to cut on a table saw. A circular saw with a cutting guide is a safer option.

I used TMW for the bench's exterior (see "Thermally Modified Wood," p. 131), which drove up the cost to $600. Building the bench with cedar decking, which is rot-resistant, would cost $300. The least expensive choice is construction-grade pine ($100), which would give the bench a more rustic look.

1 Assemble the box sides. Attach the corner posts (A) flush with the long edges and tops of the box ends (B). Glue and screw the sides (C) and ends together. Be sure to use a waterproof glue.

2 Install the bottom. Glue and screw the bottom cleats (D and E) around the inside of the box (see **Figures A** and **B**). Apply glue to the underside of the cleats, drop the bottom (F) into place and fasten it with screws. Glue and screw the feet (G) to the bottom.

3 Cut a drip groove. Cut a kerf all the way around the lid's (H) underside so that rainwater will drip off the lid instead of clinging to the lid and running into the box. Apply exterior latex to the outer faces and visible edges of the lid and box.

4 Install the frame. Fasten the center frame (J and K) inside the box using glue and screws. The frame gives the box rigidity and helps flatten out any warping in the plywood.

WOODWORKING & WORKSHOP PROJECTS & TIPS

5 Attach the first slat. Attach the bottom end slat (L) flush with the box's bottom edge using exterior construction adhesive and driving screws from inside the box. Apply a bead of exterior caulk along the top edge of the slat so water can't seep behind the slat.

6 Attach remaining slats. Fasten the remaining end slats, using spacers and caulking the top edges as you go. Attach the side slats (M) using the same method. These short (1-1/4-in.) screws don't have a lot of pulling power, so maximize it by predrilling and countersinking clearance holes through the plywood before driving the screws.

7 Fasten the lid battens. Tack the lid battens (N) to the underside of the lid using glue and screws. Flip the lid right side up and secure the battens with longer screws. The battens help keep the lid flat.

8 Assemble the lid. Clamp the lid slats (P) together, placing 1/2-in. spacers between each pair of slats. Apply construction adhesive to the slats, and then center the lid on the slats. Drive screws through the lid into the slats. Again, predrill the screw holes for maximum pulling power.

9 Install the hinges. Attach the hinges to the lid, centering the hinge barrels 1/2 in. from the lid's edge. Then prop the lid in position near the box edge. Mark the hinge mortise locations on the top slat. The mortise depths are equal to the hinge barrel's diameter.

10 Cut hinge mortises. There are many ways to cut hinge mortises. I used an oscillating multi-tool with a square, flush-cutting blade. It's well suited to the task, acting as both chisel and saw. Once all the mortises are cut, attach the lid.

11 Install lid stays. I chose these pneumatic props to hold the lid open and add a little assistance in lifting the heavy lid. Substitute less expensive lid supports if you like. Apply the exterior finish of your choice. We used an exterior penetrating oil stain.

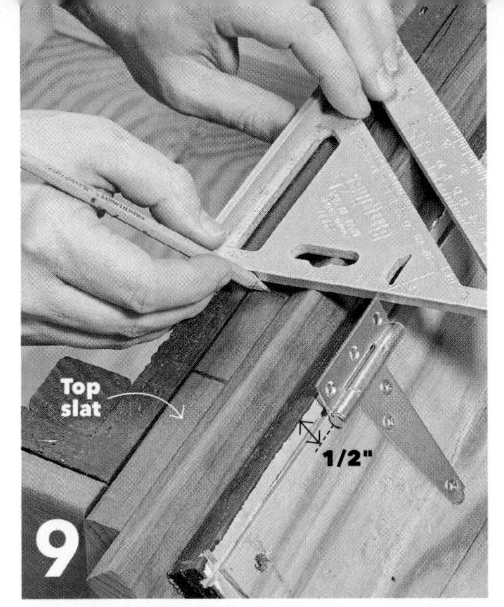

Matching Planter
The planter is even simpler to build than the bench because the inner box has no top or bottom. Glue and screw the sides together, screw in the diagonal braces and then paint any visible surfaces. Add the slats using the same method as for the bench. Position the side cleats at a height suitable to the pot you're setting in the planter. Don't attach the platform slats. If they rot, they'll be easier to replace.

Figure C Planter

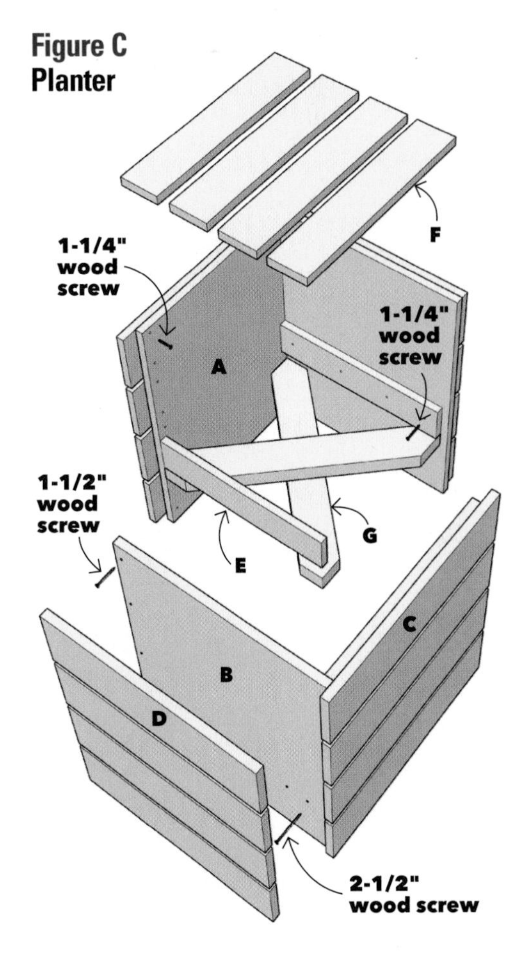

CUTTING LIST

KEY	QTY.	SIZE & MATERIAL	PART
A	2	3/4" x 24-1/2" x 18" treated plywood	Box short sides
B	2	3/4" x 24-1/2" x 19-1/2" treated plywood	Box long sides
C	8	3/4" x 5-1/2" x 21" thermally modified	Long slats
D	8	3/4" x 5-1/2" x 19-1/2" thermally modified	Short slats
E	2	3/4" x 2" x 18" treated plywood	Platform cleats
F	4	3/4" x 3-1/2" x 18" treated plywood	Platform slats
G	2	1-1/2" x 3-1/2" x 25-1/2" (2x4 cut to fit)	Diagonal braces

MASTERPIECE CUTTING BOARD

An eye-catching project—made from scraps!

By Gary Wentz

This cutting board dazzles the eye, but making it is easy: Just cut strips of wood and glue them together. I used walnut and maple scraps cut at increments of 1/8 in., but the variations are endless. I made four versions of this design and got smarter with each—and I've shared my lessons on the following pages.

Watch the process
April Wilkerson's cutting board is the inspiration for this project. To see how April made hers, watch the video at wilkerdos.com.

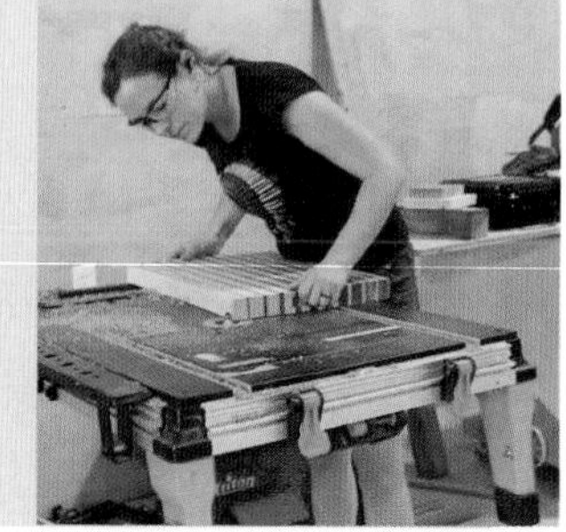

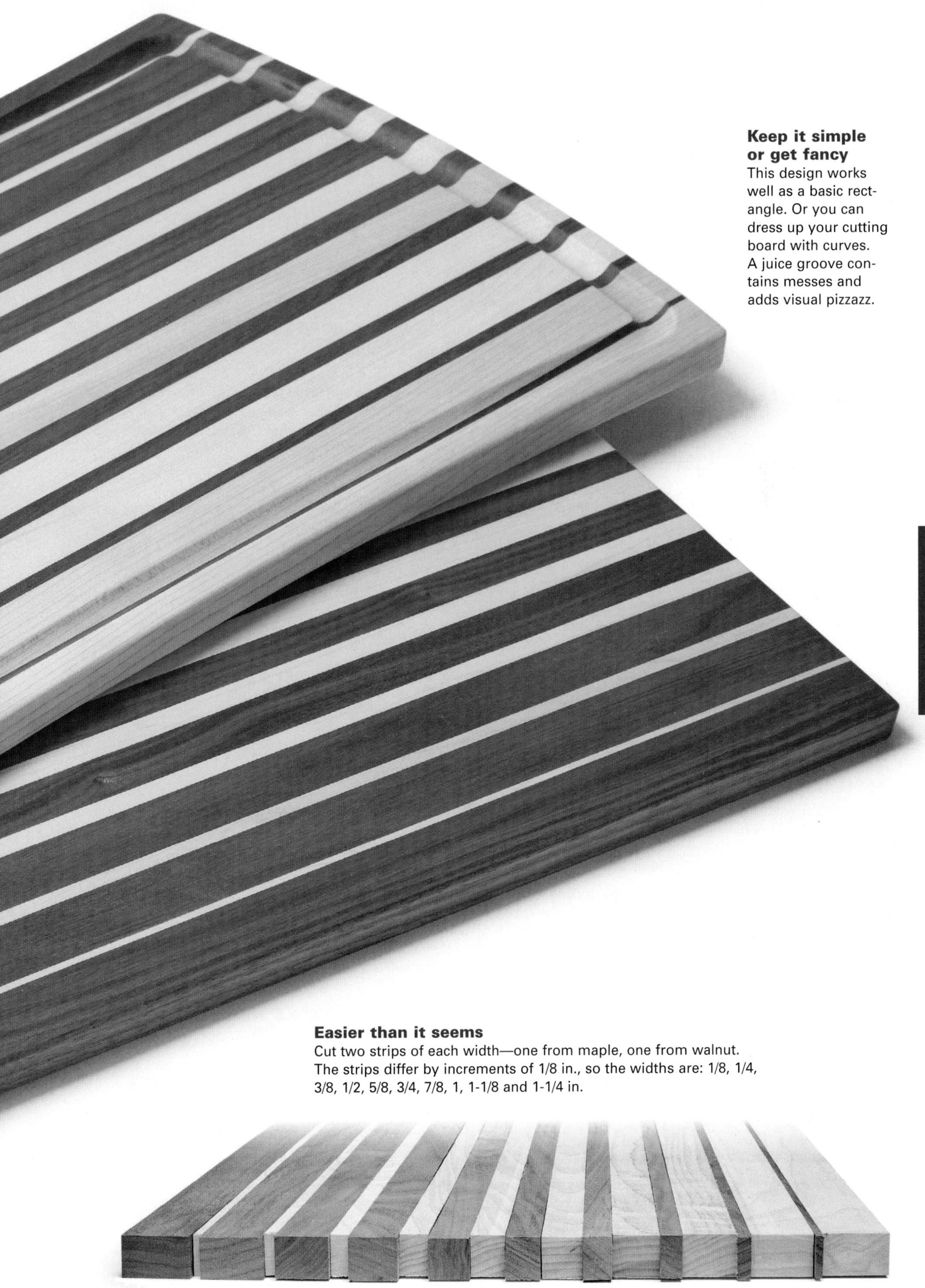

Keep it simple or get fancy
This design works well as a basic rectangle. Or you can dress up your cutting board with curves. A juice groove contains messes and adds visual pizzazz.

Easier than it seems
Cut two strips of each width—one from maple, one from walnut. The strips differ by increments of 1/8 in., so the widths are: 1/8, 1/4, 3/8, 1/2, 5/8, 3/4, 7/8, 1, 1-1/8 and 1-1/4 in.

Tips for flat, tight results

■ **Start with long strips:** Before cutting strips, cut your boards at least 1 in. longer than the final length of the cutting board. That way, you won't have to align the ends perfectly during glue-up. Trim off the imperfect ends after glue-up.

■ **Tune up your table saw:** Clean, precise cuts are critical. Grab a square and make sure the blade is square to the tabletop. Also check that the fence is perfectly parallel to the blade. Your owner's manual will show you how. This is a good time to install a fresh, sharp ripping blade too.

■ **Lay out the strips:** Arrange the strips with their best faces up. Then mark a guideline across them. During glue-up, that line will help you keep them arranged correctly (see photo, right). Also check the overall width of the combined strips.

■ **Do a dry run:** Once you start to spread glue, you have to work fast. So first clamp and caul the cutting board without glue. This dress rehearsal will reveal problems like a misfit joint or alert you to the need for another clamp.

Rip thin strips safely
Cutting thin strips with just the fence is dangerous and leads to bad cuts. This simple jig will keep your fingers far from the blade and will prevent strips from getting trapped along the fence. It's exactly 5 in. wide, so you get 1/4-in. strips, for example, by setting the fence at 5-1/4 in. I used it to cut all the strips that were thinner than 1 in. and then cut wider strips against the fence using a push stick.

Cauls keep it flat
To guarantee a flat glue-up, I cut three pairs of cauls from a 2x6 and taped the edges to keep glue from sticking. I set the strips on the lower cauls, applied a generous bead of glue to both sides of every other strip and lightly tightened the upper cauls. I added clamps, applying only light pressure at first. Then I gradually tightened down both the cauls and clamps, alternating between them.

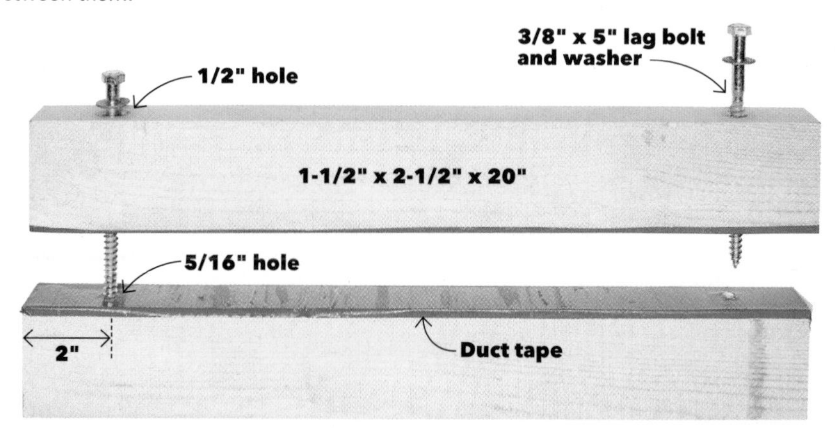

Dress it up

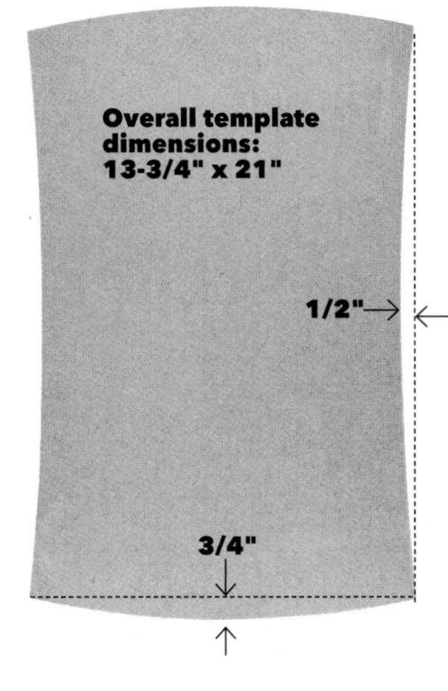

■ **Ease the edges:** Dull the sharp edges with sandpaper or a router. I used a 1/8-in. round-over bit.

■ **Finish it with oil:** Oil finishes are best for this project because they're easy to renew. When the finish wears, just wipe on a fresh coat of oil. There are oils intended for cutting boards, but I used mineral oil from the drugstore (after sanding the entire cutting board with 80- and 120-grit).

Materials

■ 3/4-in.-thick boards at least 22 in. long and a total width of at least 8-1/4 in. for each species. The cost for walnut and maple is about $20 per cutting board.

■ 2x6 x 6 ft. of pine (for cauls)

■ Six 3/8-in. x 5-in. lag screws and washers

■ 1/8-in. MDF (for templates)

■ Waterproof wood glue such as Elmer's Wood Glue Max or Titebond III

■ Sanding supplies

■ Mineral oil, duct tape, double-sided tape.

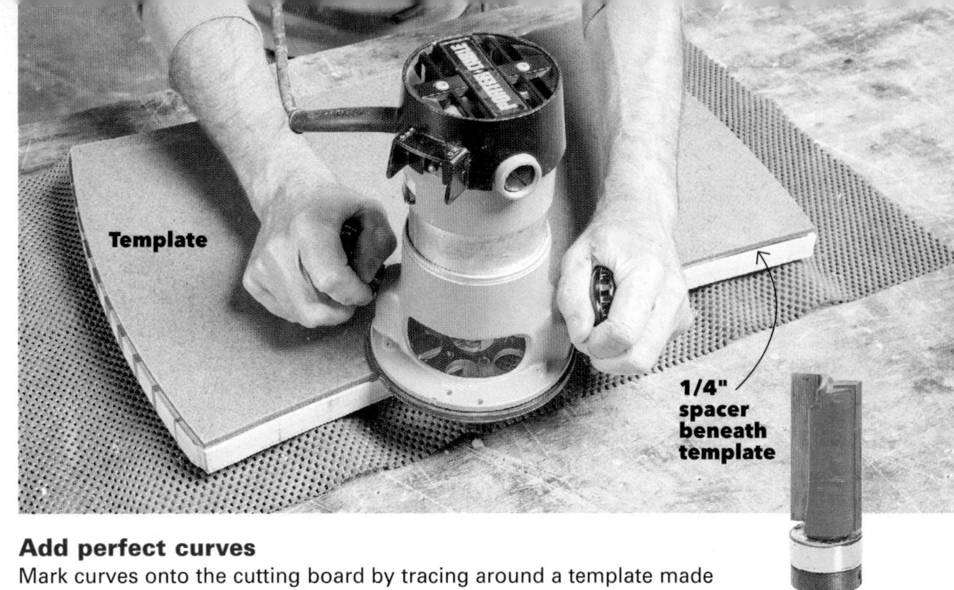

Add perfect curves

Mark curves onto the cutting board by tracing around a template made from 1/8-in MDF. Rough-cut the shape with a band saw or jigsaw, keeping the blade about 1/8 in. from the line. Then fasten the template to the cutting board with double-sided tape. A pattern bit guided by the template produces perfect curves. I glued a scrap of 1/4-in. plywood to the underside of this template and to the juice groove template. That elevates the template and allows the bearing to make full contact with it.

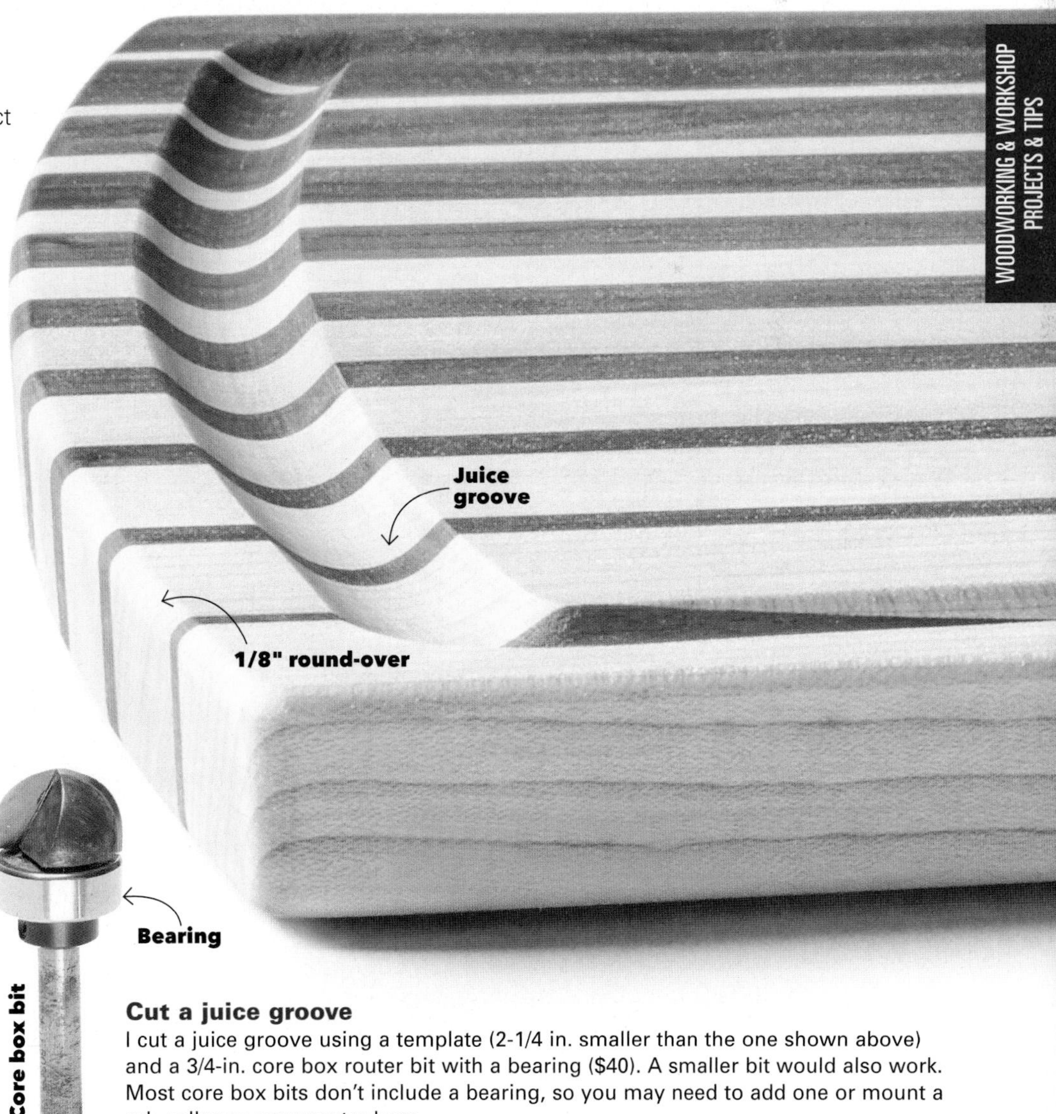

Cut a juice groove

I cut a juice groove using a template (2-1/4 in. smaller than the one shown above) and a 3/4-in. core box router bit with a bearing ($40). A smaller bit would also work. Most core box bits don't include a bearing, so you may need to add one or mount a rub collar on your router base.

ULTIMATE FOLDING WORKBENCH

By Brad Holden

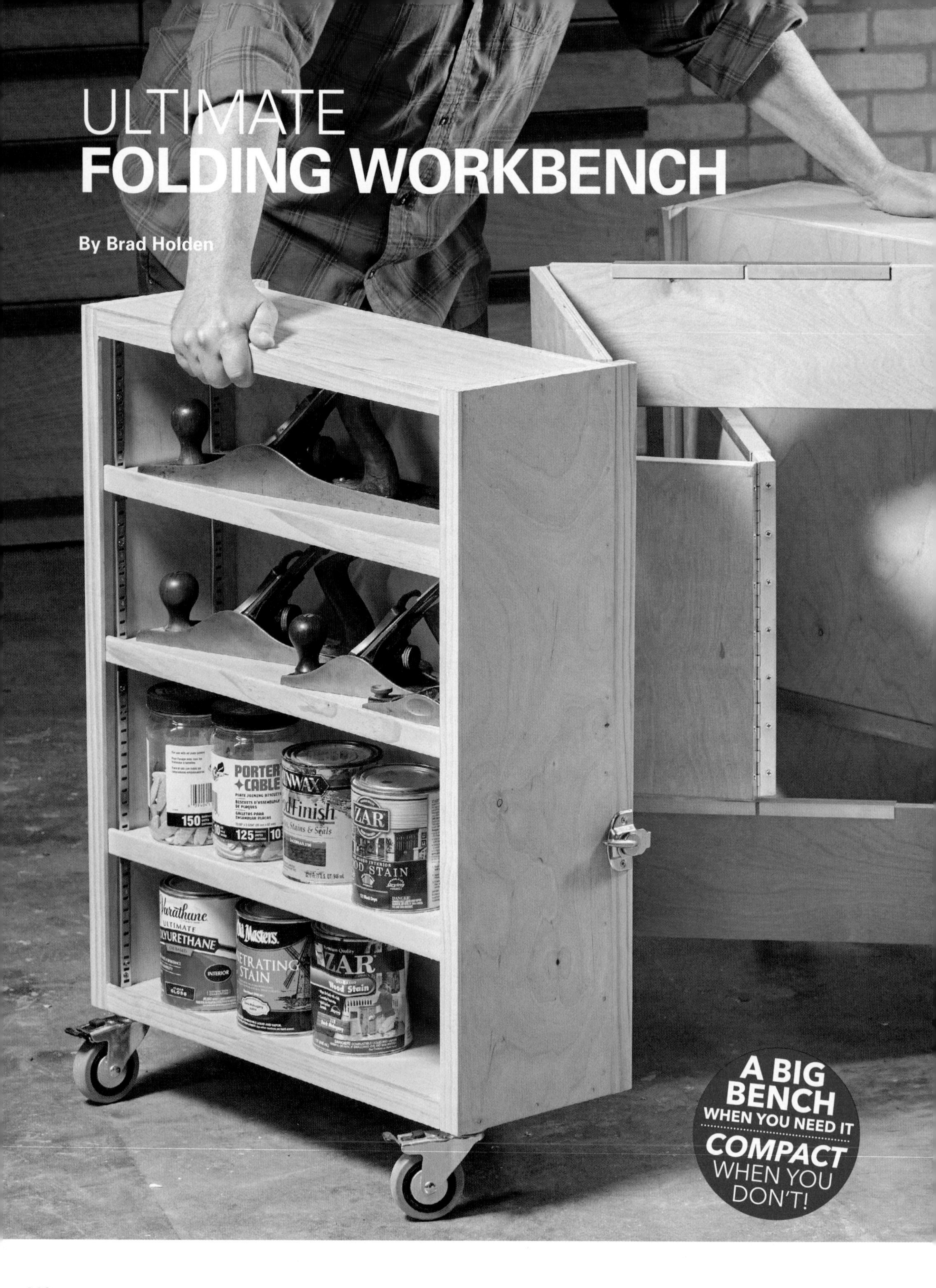

I built a folding workbench for *American Woodworker* magazine about 20 years ago—I think it was one of the first ever built. It has served as a lumber cart, finishing stand, cutting station, job-site workbench and as an assembly table. Because it's been so useful, I designed a deluxe anniversary model with extra features. If you want to build the original, simpler version instead, search for "folding workbench" at familyhandyman.com.

5 Fresh Features:

1 A tough work surface
For a durable, smooth work surface, I glued a layer of tempered hardboard over plywood.

2 Two tops
The large top allows ample room for work and tools. When the bench is folded up, the small top is just right for a benchtop tool like a drill press or miter saw.

3 A large lower shelf
This big space is the perfect spot to park tools during projects. The shelf's ends clip into the cabinets, making the bench extremely rigid.

4 Adjustable shelves
I replaced the end frames on the original with cabinets. This one holds adjustable shelves.

5 Deep drawers
The drawer cabinet is the same size as the shelf cabinet, so you could opt for two shelf cabinets or two drawer cabinets.

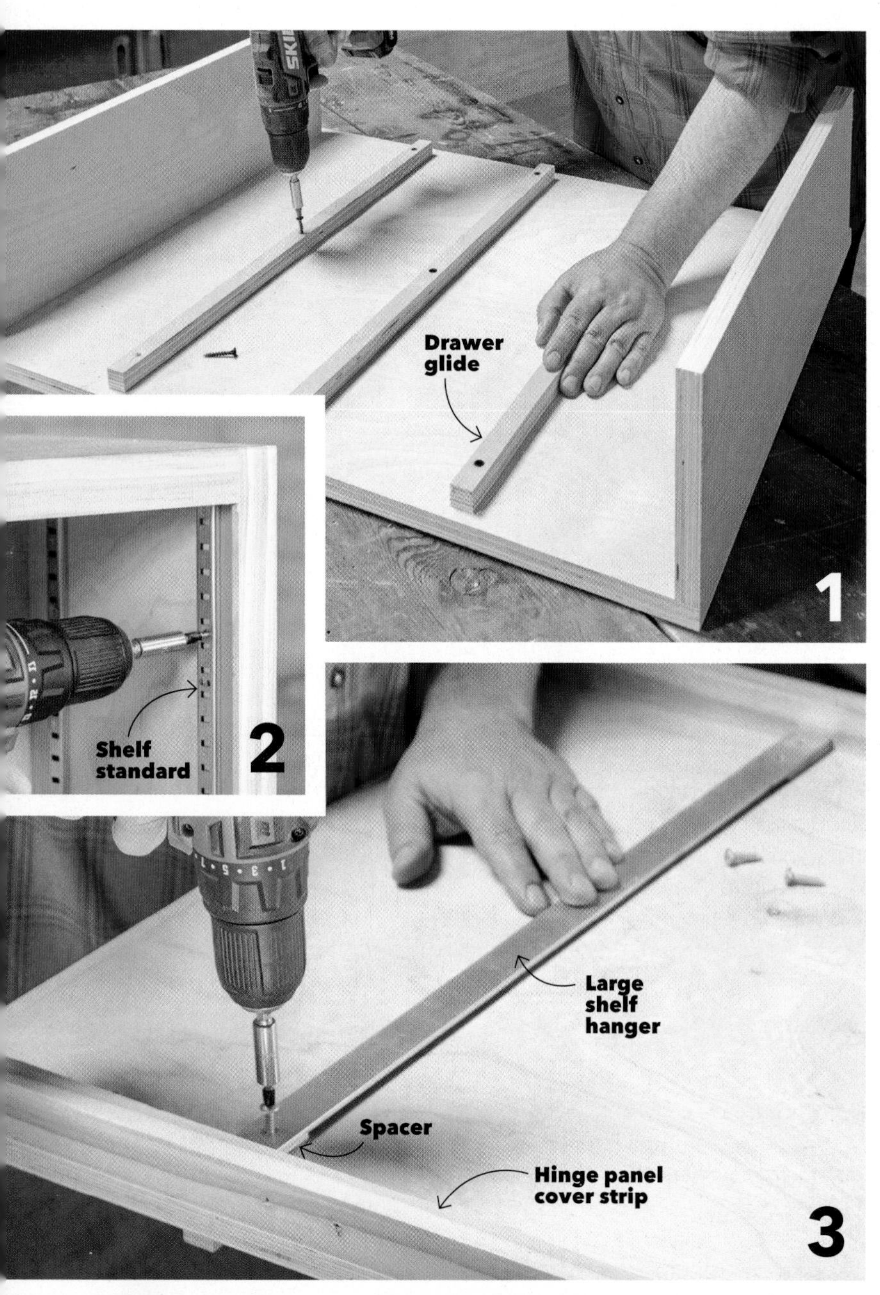

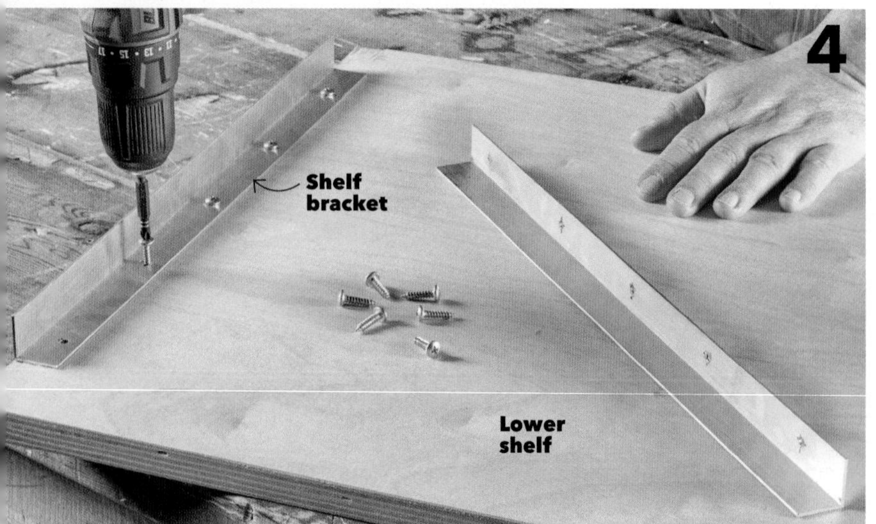

1 Build the cabinets. Cut all the cabinet parts to size. Plywood thicknesses vary slightly, so double-check dimensions as you build. Sand all the parts, and then screw the drawer glides to the drawer cabinet sides (don't use glue, in case you need to make adjustments). Assemble both cabinets.

2 Install shelf standards. Cut the shelf standards to length. Install the standards using No. 6 x 3/4-in. screws, with the factory ends of the standards set on the cabinet's bottom. Attach the hinge panel cover strips to both cabinets. Apply finish.

3 Attach shelf hangers. Cut to length the hangers and spacers that support the lower shelf. Attach the hangers to the cabinets using pan-head screws.

4 Attach shelf brackets. Cut the large shelf and shelf brackets to size. Attach brackets flush with the ends of the shelf using pan-head screws.

5 Attach casters. Fasten the casters near the outer ends of the cabinet bottoms using washer-head screws. I used swiveling casters that lock to prevent rolling as well as pivoting, so the bench stays put while in use.

Figure A
Folding Workbench

Overall Dimensions:
34" High x 27-1/2" Deep x
73-1/2" Wide

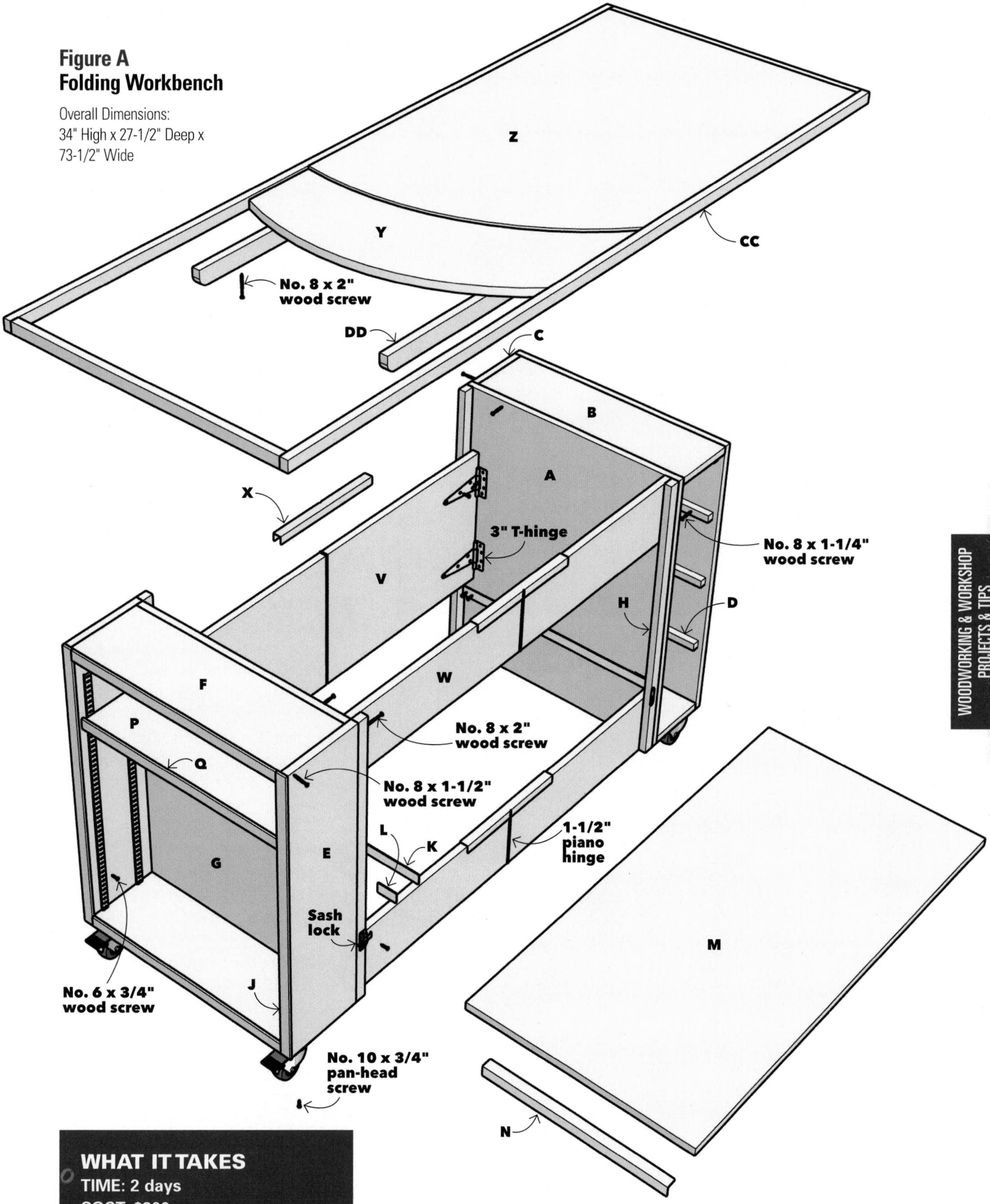

WHAT IT TAKES

TIME: 2 days
COST: $300
SKILL: Intermediate
TOOLS: Circular saw, table saw, clamps, drill, jigsaw, hacksaw

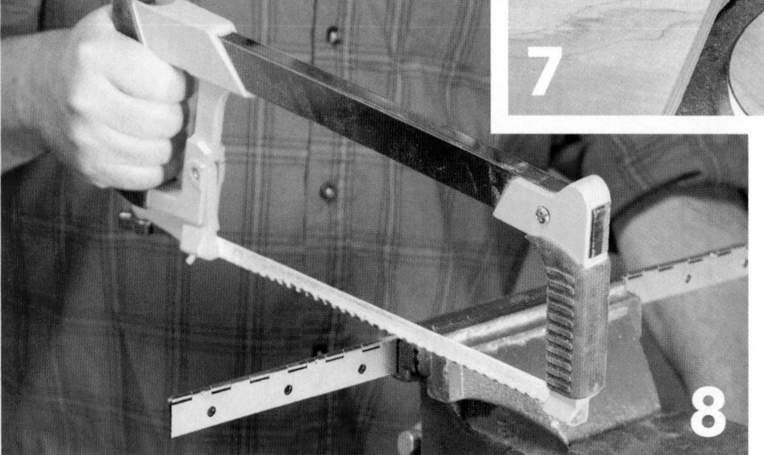

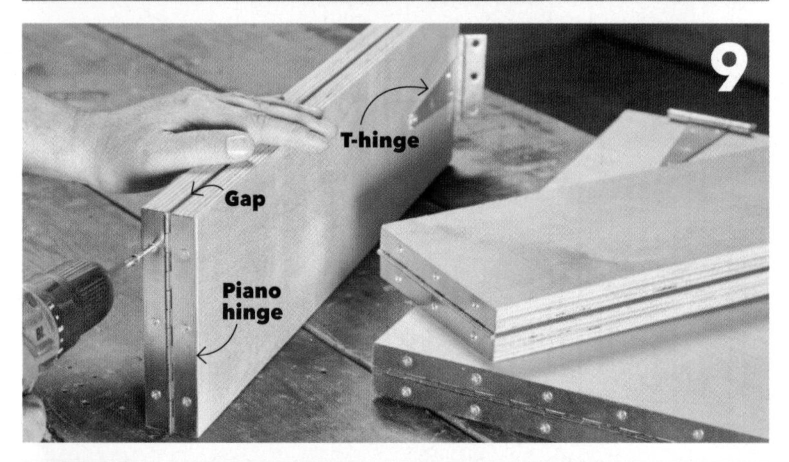

6 Build the shelves. Cut the small shelves to size, allowing about 1/8 in. of play between the shelf standards. Sand the shelves and then attach the shelf lip. The lip overhangs the tops of the shelves to keep contents from sliding out. Sand the shelves and apply finish.

7 Build the drawers. After cutting the drawer parts, draw an arc on one of the drawer fronts using a roll of tape or a paint can as a guide. Cut out the arc and sand it smooth (sandpaper stapled to the cutout works well for this). Repeat for the other drawer fronts. Dado the fronts and sides to accept the bottoms. Assemble the drawers using glue and brad nails, and then apply finish.

8 Cut the hinges. Secure the piano hinge in a vise and cut the lengths needed for the hinge panels using a hacksaw. File the cut edges smooth.

9 Assemble the hinge panels. Join each pair of hinge panels using a section of piano hinge and No. 8 x 1-1/4-in. wood screws, predrilling for the screws. Leave a gap equal to the hinge barrel's diameter. Install the T-hinges on the free ends of each panel.

10 Position and attach hinge panels. Attach the top and bottom hinge panels flush with the top and bottom of the cabinets, directly behind the hinge panel cover strips. Mount the center hinge panel on the opposite side of the cabinets, on a line 1/2 in. below the top hinge panel.

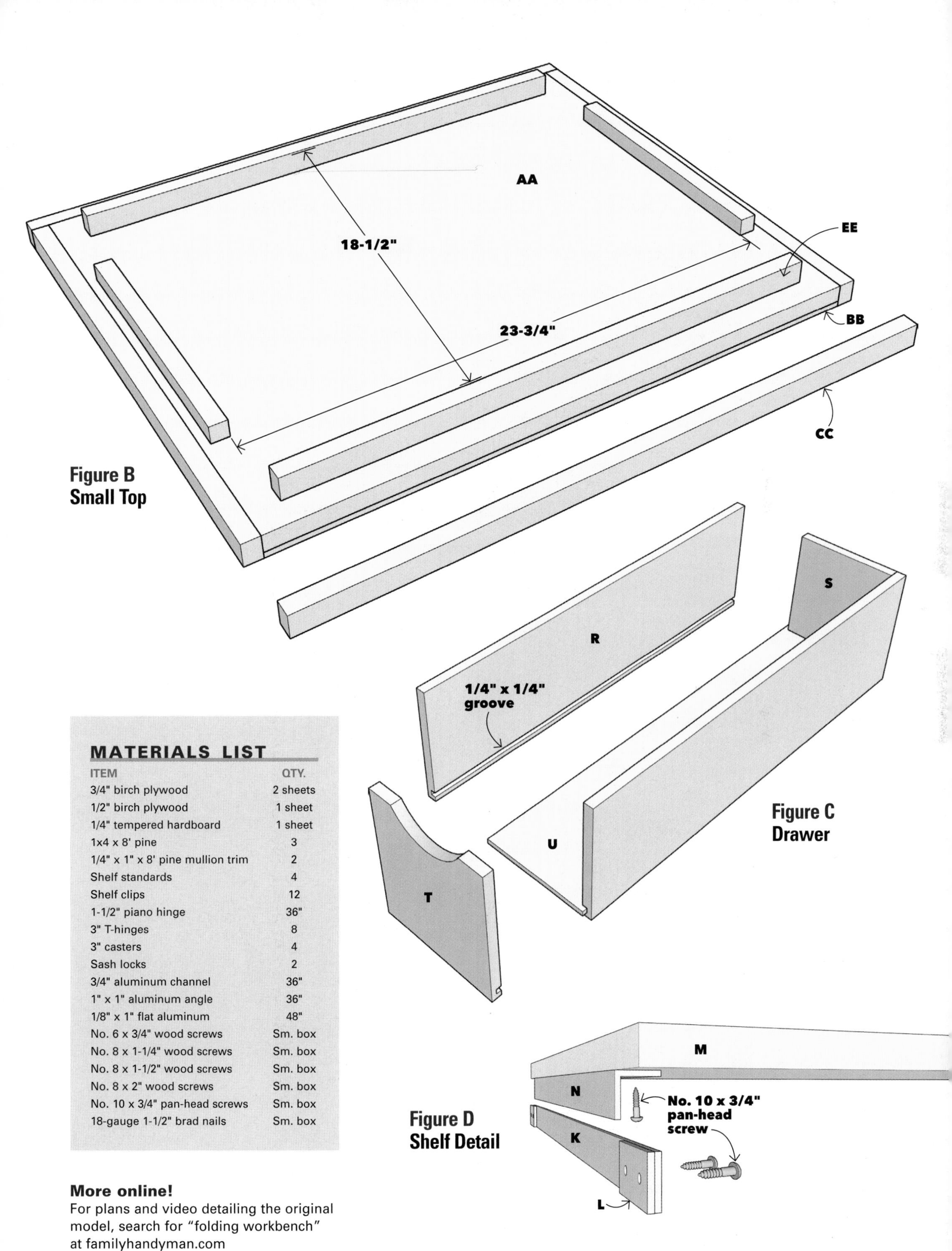

MATERIALS LIST

ITEM	QTY.
3/4" birch plywood	2 sheets
1/2" birch plywood	1 sheet
1/4" tempered hardboard	1 sheet
1x4 x 8' pine	3
1/4" x 1" x 8' pine mullion trim	2
Shelf standards	4
Shelf clips	12
1-1/2" piano hinge	36"
3" T-hinges	8
3" casters	4
Sash locks	2
3/4" aluminum channel	36"
1" x 1" aluminum angle	36"
1/8" x 1" flat aluminum	48"
No. 6 x 3/4" wood screws	Sm. box
No. 8 x 1-1/4" wood screws	Sm. box
No. 8 x 1-1/2" wood screws	Sm. box
No. 8 x 2" wood screws	Sm. box
No. 10 x 3/4" pan-head screws	Sm. box
18-gauge 1-1/2" brad nails	Sm. box

More online!
For plans and video detailing the original model, search for "folding workbench" at familyhandyman.com

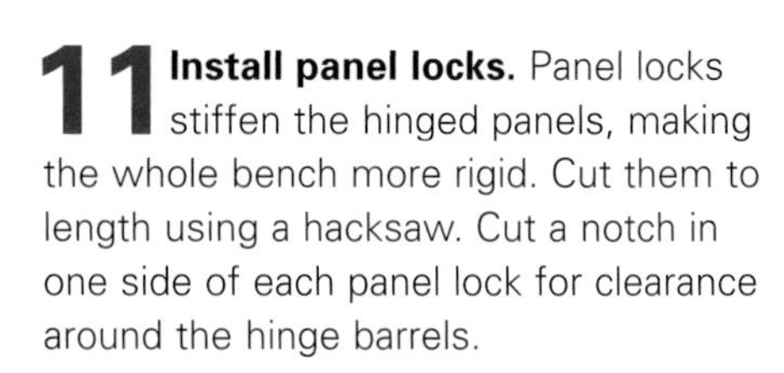

11 Install panel locks. Panel locks stiffen the hinged panels, making the whole bench more rigid. Cut them to length using a hacksaw. Cut a notch in one side of each panel lock for clearance around the hinge barrels.

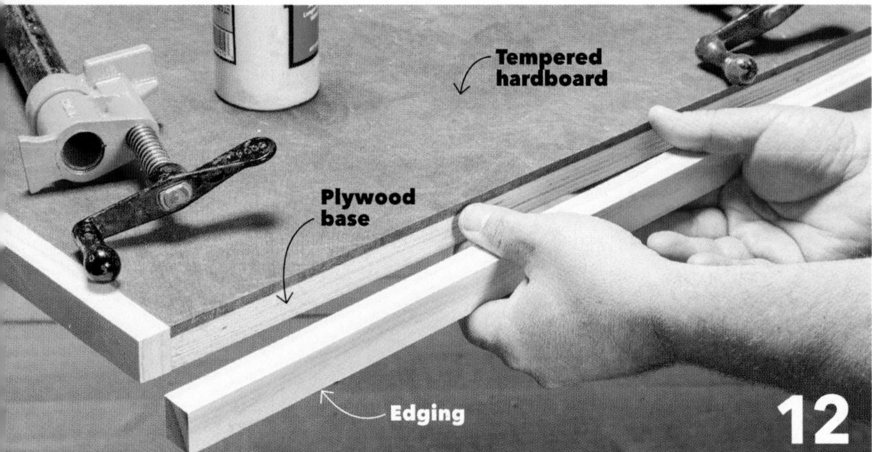

12 Build the tops. Hardboard "skins" provide a smooth, tough surface for the large and small tops. Cut the top bases and skins slightly oversize, and then glue the skins to the bases. When the glue is dry, cut the tops to finished size. Attach the edging using glue and clamps.

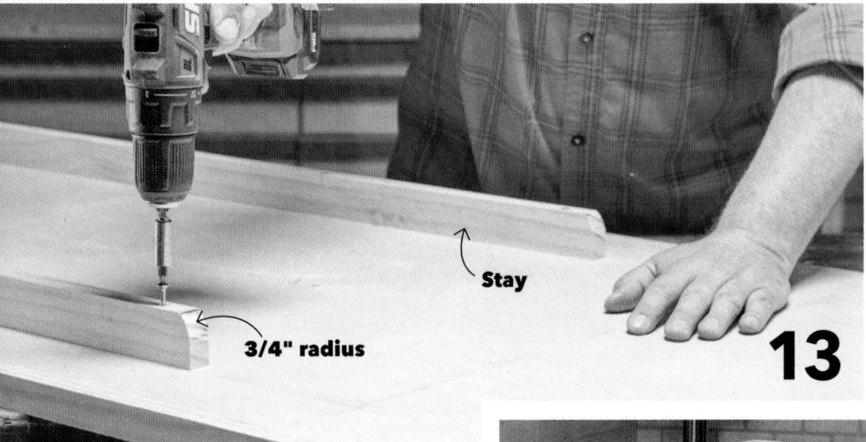

13 Attach stays to tops. Glue and screw the top stays to the underside of both tops. The stays on the large top lock the two cabinets in their open position. The small top stays lock the cabinets in their closed position and prevent the top from sliding.

14 Install sash locks. To hold the cabinets together, install sash locks on the hinge panel cover strips 6 in. from the bottom of both sides of the cabinets.

15 Add the shelf. Drop the shelf into place, slipping the shelf brackets behind the shelf hangers. This addition makes the bench very rigid.

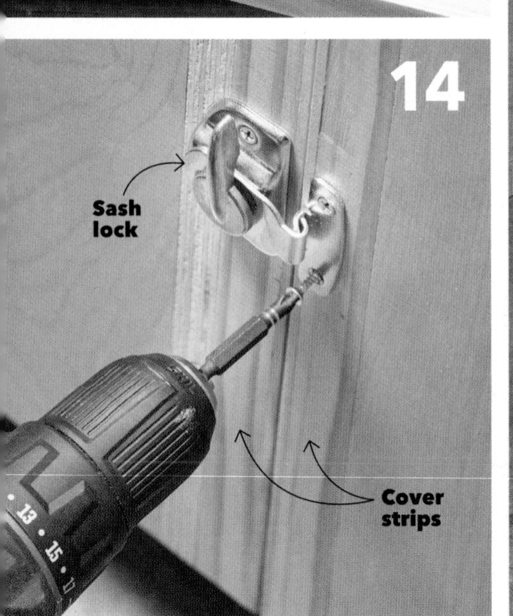

Figure E
3/4-in. Plywood

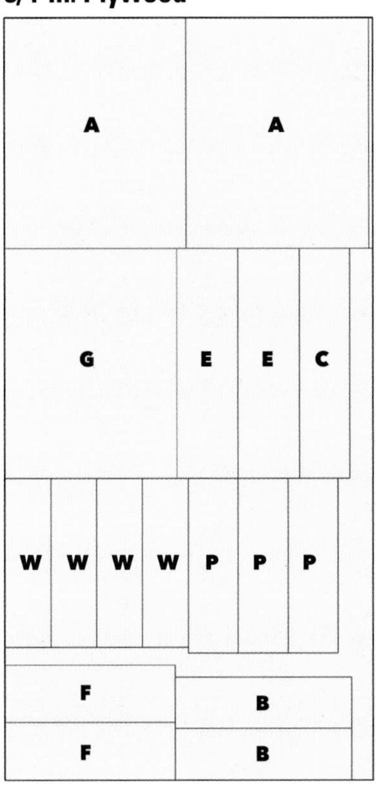

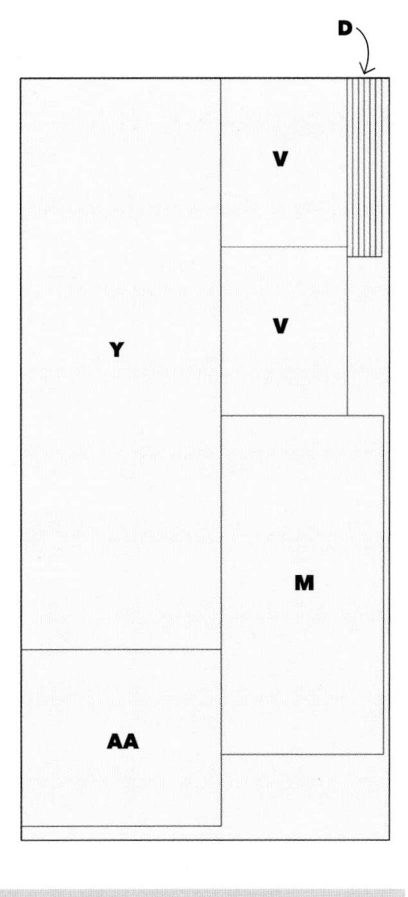

With a few basic tools, you can build this versatile workbench in a weekend. Even if you build just the original design, you won't regret it. Mine has been in constant use for 20 years!

Figure F
1/2-in. Plywood

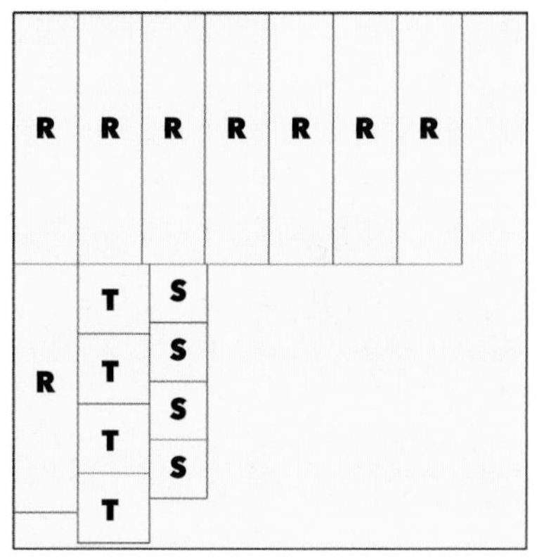

Figure G
Tempered Hardboard

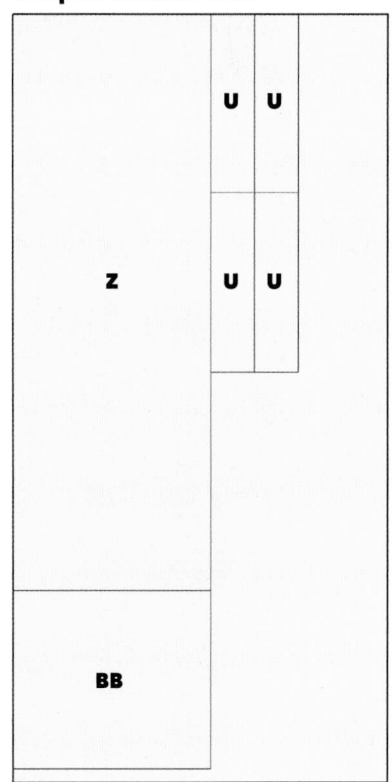

CUTTING LIST

KEY	QTY.	DIMENSIONS	MATERIAL	PART
A	2	3/4" x 23-3/4" x 29"	3/4" birch plywood	Drawer cabinet sides
B	2	3/4" x 6-1/2" x 23"	3/4" birch plywood	Drawer cabinet top & bottom
C	1	3/4" x 6-1/2" x 29"	3/4" birch plywood	Drawer cabinet back
D	6	3/4" x 3/4" x 22-1/2"	3/4" birch plywood	Drawer glides
E	2	3/4" x 8" x 29"	3/4" birch plywood	Shelf cabinet ends
F	2	3/4" x 7-1/4" x 22-1/4"	3/4" birch plywood	Shelf cabinet top & bottom
G	1	3/4" x 22-1/4" x 29"	3/4" birch plywood	Shelf cabinet back
H	4	3/4" x 1-1/8" x 29"	1x4 pine	Hinge panel cover strips
J	1	1/4" x 1" (cut to fit)	Pine mullion	Shelf cabinet trim
K	2	1/8" x 1" x 22-1/4"	Flat aluminum	Shelf hangers
L	2	1/8" x 1" x 2"	Flat aluminum	Shelf hanger spacers
M	1	3/4" x 21-1/4" x 42-11/16"	3/4" birch plywood	Large shelf
N	2	1" x 1" x 17-1/2"	Aluminum angle	Shelf brackets
P	3	3/4" x 6-1/2" x 21-7/8"	3/4" birch plywood	Small shelves
Q	3	1/4" x 1-1/2" x 21-7/8"	Pine mullion	Shelf lips
R	8	1/2" x 6" x 22-1/4"	1/2" birch plywood	Drawer sides
S	4	1/2" x 5-1/2" x 5-1/4"	1/2" birch plywood	Drawer backs
T	4	1/2" x 6-3/4" x 6-1/4"	1/2" birch plywood	Drawer fronts
U	4	1/4" x 5-3/4" x 22-1/2"	Tempered hardboard	Drawer bottoms
V	2	3/4" x 14" x 21-1/4"	3/4" birch plywood	Wide hinge panels
W	4	3/4" x 6" x 21-1/4"	3/4" birch plywood	Narrow hinge panels
X	3	3/4" x 3/4" x 12"	Aluminum channel	Panel locks
Y	1	3/4" x 26" x 72"	3/4" birch plywood	Large top base
Z	1	1/4" x 26" x 72"	Tempered hardboard	Large top skin
AA	1	3/4" x 22-1/4" x 26"	3/4" birch plywood	Small top base
BB	1	1/4" x 22-1/4" x 26"	Tempered hardboard	Small top skin
CC	8	3/4" x 1" (cut to fit)	1x4 pine	Top edging
DD	2	3/4" x 1-1/2" x 42-11/16"	1x4 pine	Large top stays
EE	4	3/4" x 3/4" x 6' (cut to fit)	1x4 pine	Small top stays

ELEGANT **KEEPSAKE BOX**

Show off treasured wood—and lock other treasures inside

By Brad Holden

TO SEE HOW THE **INGENIOUS SECRET LOCK** WORKS, FLIP TO P. 154!

Small boxes like these allow you to showcase the beautiful details of a piece of wood. It could be an unusual color, a highly figured pattern or just an eye-pleasing wave of grain. You could splurge on an exotic species or simply use choice leftovers from another project. I made the box in this article from mahogany scraps that were too small for most projects but way too nice for the fireplace.

Showcase the wood

Splurge! Consider bird's-eye maple, burled walnut or some exotic
species you've never even heard of before. Wood-database.com is a great source for images and working properties of various wood species.

Cut parts consecutively.
Try to cut all your parts in order from a single board. When you assemble your box—particularly one with mitered corners—the grain will look seamless as it wraps around the corners.

Select the best.
Cut out cardboard windows, sized to each of your box parts. Position the windows on your boards to find the most attractive section of grain for each piece.

1 Prep the sides and ends. Cut each side as a single piece, including one end each, to finished width and rough length. The end pieces will be cut off later.

2 Groove the sides and ends. Mill the grooves for the top and bottom. Both grooves are the same distance from their respective edges. Plane the bottom to fit the groove.

3 Miter the corners. Cut the miters on the ends and sides, trimming each piece to final length. Then rip the short end to finished height.

4 Assemble the box. Lay out the box parts in a line, with tape at the corners. Glue the miters, slip in the bottom, and then fold the box together. Reset each piece of tape, stretching them to pull the corners tight.

Make the parts

This box is made from 1/2-in.-thick material. Most home centers carry 1/2-in. boards in a few common species like oak and poplar. If you want more choices and don't own a planer, shop online (rockler.com is one good source).

Since the ends (B and C) are so short, leave each end and side (A) as a single board for now (**Photo 1**). Then cut them free after milling the grooves, leaving extra length.

Mark the outside face of the side/end boards. Keep that side facing up as you cut the grooves. The easiest way to cut these grooves is with a dado set. Make one pass for the bottom groove, spin the board and make one pass for the top groove (**Photo 2**). To cut these grooves with a regular blade, you'll just need to make several passes to get the right dimension.

Cut the bottom (D) oversize for now, and then plane it to proper thickness. It should be just thin enough to fit in the groove easily without being loose.

Attach a long, straight fence to your miter gauge. If you have two miter gauges, attach the fence to both of them so they work like a sled. Tilt the blade to 45 degrees, cut a miter on a piece of scrap, then verify that the angle is accurate and the cut is straight. Make any necessary adjustments, then cut the miters on the sides and ends (**Photo 3**). Rip the short end to final height.

Cut the lid (E) and bottom to final dimensions. To get exact dimensions, dry-assemble the box using tape to hold the corners together. Measure the interior width and add 7/16 in. to get the width for the lid and bottom.

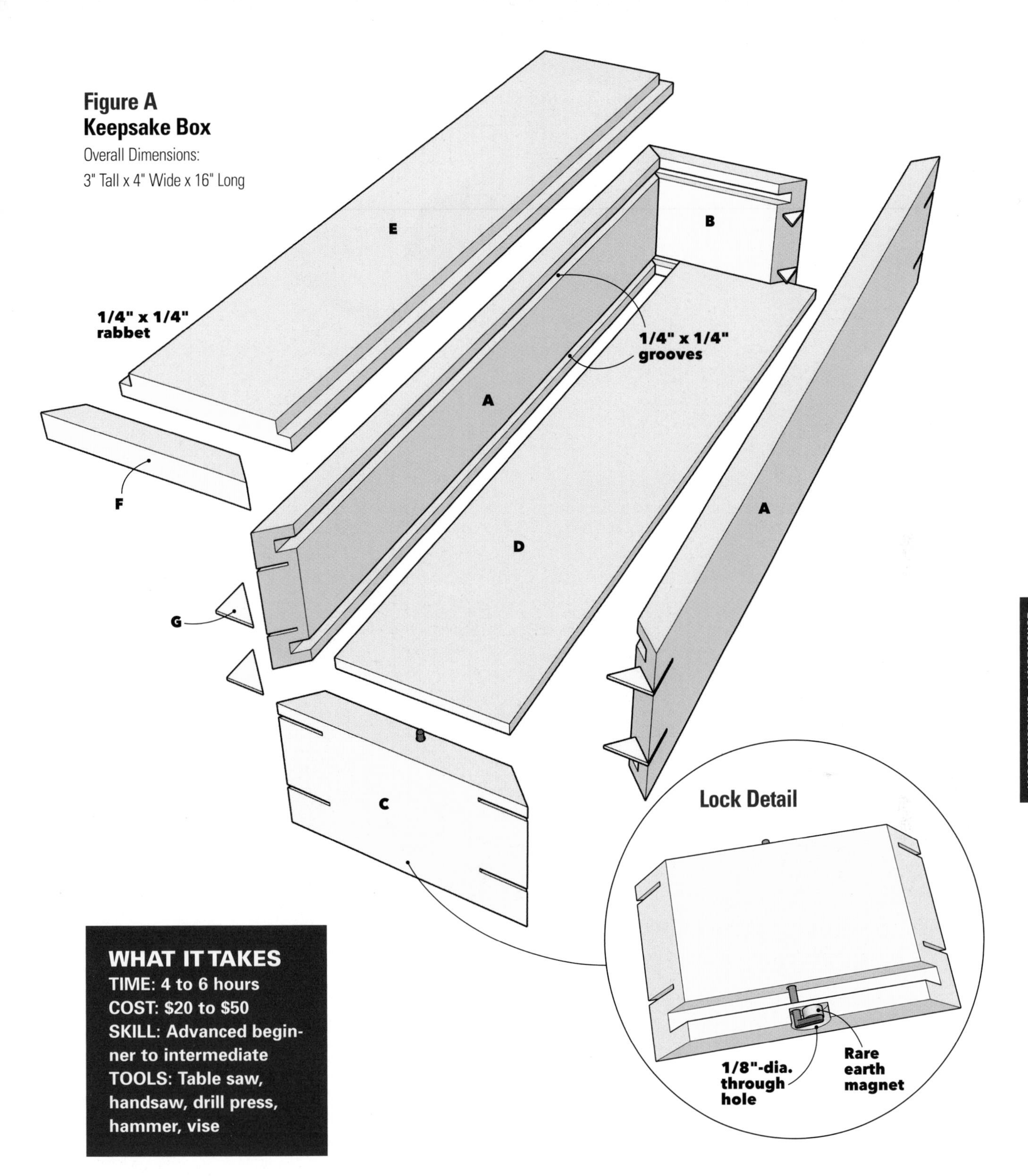

WHAT IT TAKES
TIME: 4 to 6 hours
COST: $20 to $50
SKILL: Advanced beginner to intermediate
TOOLS: Table saw, handsaw, drill press, hammer, vise

CUTTING LIST

KEY	QTY.	SIZE & DESCRIPTION
A	2	1/2" x 3" x 16" (sides)
B	1	1/2" x 3" x 4" (tall end)
C	1	1/2" x 2-15/32" x 4" (short end)
D	1	1/4" x 3-7/16" x 15-1/2" (bottom)
E	1	1/2" x 3-7/16" x 15-1/4" (lid)
F	1	1/2" x 1/2" x 4" (lid end)
G	1	1/16" x 3/4" x 24" (corner keys)

MATERIALS LIST

ITEM	QTY.
1/2" x 4" lumber	6'
1/4" x 4" lumber	16"
1/16" x 1" key stock	12"
16d nail	1
1/4" x 1/8" rare earth magnet	1

All grooves and rabbets are 1/4" x 1/4"

5 Rabbet the lid. Rabbet both sides and one end of the lid, using a dado set with a sacrificial board to protect the fence.

6 Fit the lid. Adjust the lid as needed so that it slides smoothly in the grooves, and then attach the mitered lid end using glue and tape.

7 Kerf the corners. Lay out and cut the kerfs for the corner keys. Painter's tape marks a clear stopping point for the kerf ends.

8 Widen the kerfs. Widen the kerfs with a thicker blade, such as a fine-tooth reciprocating saw blade.

Measure the interior length of the box and add 7/16 in. for the length of the bottom. The lid length is the interior dimension plus 3/16 in.

Assemble the box

It's difficult to sand inside the box after assembly, so sand all the interior surfaces up to 180-grit before assembly. Lay out the box parts in a line and glue the miters. Slide the bottom into its groove and fold the box together, stretching the tape across the corners (**Photo 4**). Wipe off any excess glue inside the box with a slightly damp rag. This will raise the grain a bit, but you can lightly sand those spots after the glue dries. Let the glue dry for at least an hour.

Rabbet the lid

While the box is drying, pop in your dado set again. Clamp a sacrificial board to your saw's fence so you can slide the fence right up against the blade. Rabbet both edges and one end of the lid (**Photo 5**), testing the fit in a grooved offcut. The finished, visible surface of the lid should be equal to the inside width of the box minus about 1/16 in.

Slide the lid into its grooves. If it's too tight, thin the rabbeted edges using a sanding block until the lid slides home smoothly. Once you're satisfied with the fit, cut the lid end (F) and glue it on (**Photo 6**).

Key the corners

The corner keys (G) are optional. They're mainly decorative, but

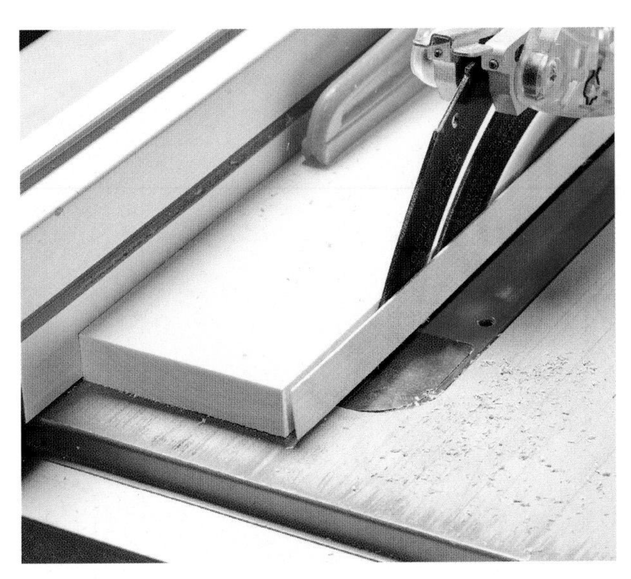

9 Cut key stock. Rip key stock from the outer edge of a wide board. It might take a few attempts to get the thickness just right.

10 Install the keys. Cut the keys with a fine-tooth handsaw or utility knife. Glue the keys and slip one key into each kerf.

11 Finish up. Trim the keys flush, and then sand and finish the box.

they do add some strength. If you choose to use them, lay them out on the box corners however you like. Clamp the box in a vise and make a single cut on each line with a handsaw (**Photo 7**). I wanted my keys to be a little bit thicker than my handsaw's kerf, so I widened the kerfs using a fine-tooth reciprocating saw blade (**Photo 8**).

Rip the key stock from the outer edge of a wide board (**Photo 9**). You might have to try a few times to get the thickness just right. The key stock should be just thick enough to slide in easily without wiggling in the kerf; if you have to force it, it's too thick. Cut the key stock into short sections just long enough to fill the saw kerfs, using a fine-tooth handsaw or utility knife. Apply glue to each key and then slip them into the kerfs (**Photo 10**). Let them dry for at least an hour, then trim and sand them flush (**Photo 11**). Finish-sand the whole box to 180-grit.

Apply finish

To get a rich, satin sheen on my box, I applied three coats of tung oil, allowing each coat to dry overnight and doing a light 400-grit sanding between coats. Finally, I applied paste wax with "0000" steel wool. Wipe the wax off immediately for a satin finish, or let it dry first for a glossier finish. If the lid doesn't slide as freely after finishing, lightly sand the underside of the edges. Rubbing the edges with a candle also helps.

ADD A HIDDEN LOCK

Everyone loves a secret. To add this hidden lock, you'll need a 16d nail and a 1/4-in. rare earth magnet (available at home centers). A drill press is highly recommended.

1 Make a recess. Drill a recess in the bottom edge of the box's short end using a Forstner or brad point bit, so the bottom of the recess is flat.

2 Drill the nail passage. Drill the hole for the 16d nail all the way through the short end, offset to one side of the recess.

3 Install the magnet. Glue the magnet in the recess, opposite the nail hole.

4 Bend the nail. Cut off the nail's head and grip it in a vise with about 3/8 in. protruding. Hammer the nail over, creating a "foot." Hammer the foot until it's flat.

5 Drill into the lid. Slide the lid into place and drill into it through the nail hole to mark the spot. Remove the lid and drill halfway through, using a tape flag as a stop. Cut the nail to length. It should contact the magnet and engage the hole in the lid. File any sharp edges.

6 Lock the box. To engage the lock, slide the nail through the hole and pivot the foot onto the magnet. To disengage it, pivot the foot off the magnet and slide the nail out.

UNDER-BED **DRAWER**

Easy to build—even easier to fill!

By Matt Boley

WHAT IT TAKES
TIME: 1 hour
COST: $50
SKILL: Beginner
TOOLS: Miter saw, drill, clamps, brad nail gun

This project is really just a box on rollers. What makes it unique is that it glides on appliance rollers instead of casters. They're low profile and super strong, and they roll smoothly over carpet and hard flooring. Appliance rollers cost about $20 per pair at home centers and online. The project cost depends on the wood you choose. Before building, measure the height beneath your bed frame and alter our dimensions to suit.

1 Build the box. Drill countersink holes and fasten the sides (B) to the ends (C) with wood glue and 2-in. screws. Attach the base (A) using the same method.

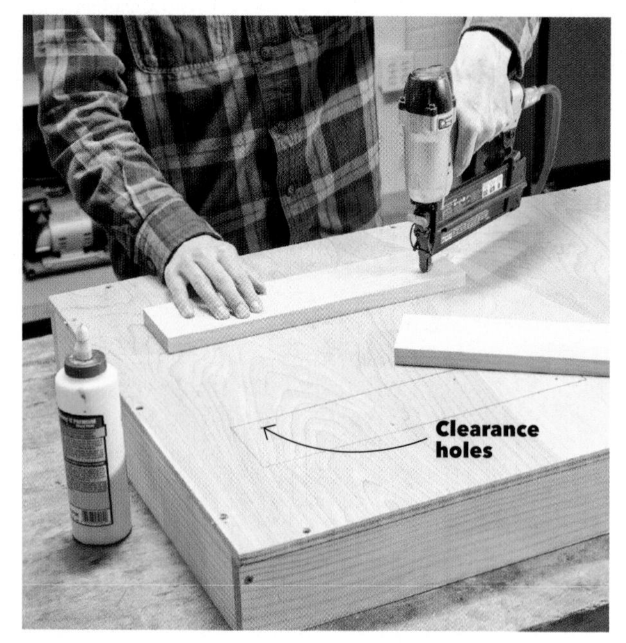

2 Locate and fasten the cleats. Mark the cleat (D) locations, 2 in. in from the front/back and 5 in. from each side. Set the cleats in position and trace them. Drill four clearance holes in each cleat outline. Glue the cleats and tack them in position with 1-in. nails. Flip the box over, countersink the clearance holes and then drill pilot holes in the cleats (D). Fasten the cleats with 1-in. screws.

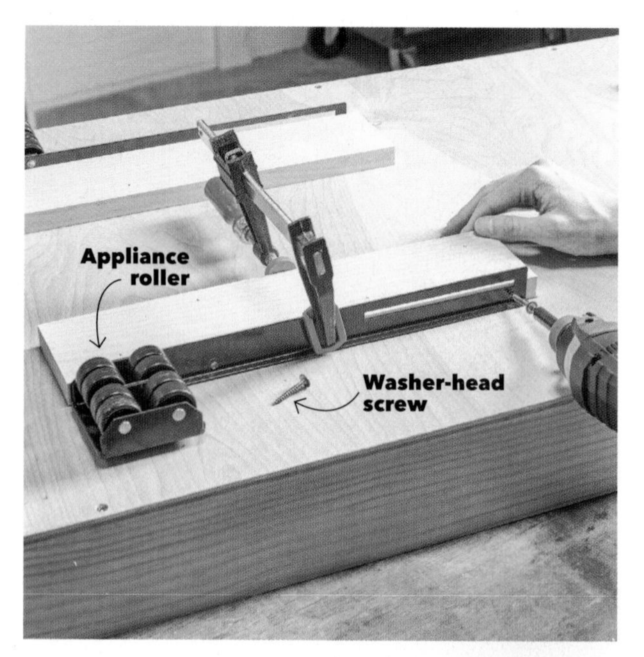

3 Attach the rollers. Separate the halves of the appliance rollers. Drill two clearance holes in each half of the rollers with a sacrificial board underneath. Clamp the rollers to the cleats (D) and fasten with 1-1/4-in. washer-head screws.

4 Attach the drawer front. Drill six screw clearance holes through one box end. Clamp the drawer front (E) to the box end with a 1/2-in. spacer underneath. Drill pilot holes in the drawer front, and then attach it with 1-1/4-in. washer-head screws.

5 Install the handle. Drill three evenly spaced clearance holes in the handle (F), and then clamp it to the top edge of the drawer front. Drill pilot holes in the drawer front and fasten with 1-1/4-in. washer-head screws.

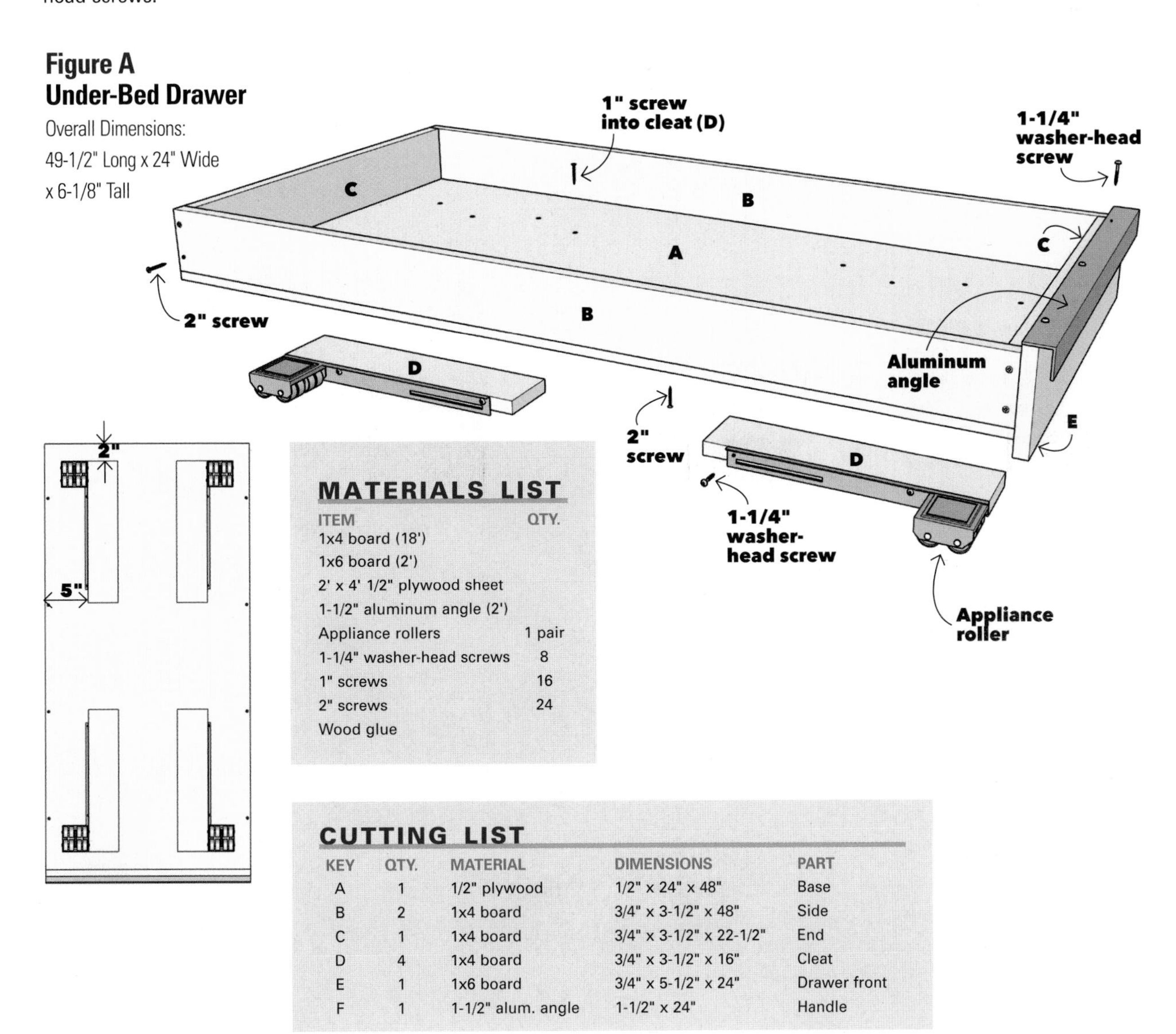

Figure A
Under-Bed Drawer

Overall Dimensions:
49-1/2" Long x 24" Wide
x 6-1/8" Tall

MATERIALS LIST

ITEM	QTY.
1x4 board (18')	
1x6 board (2')	
2' x 4' 1/2" plywood sheet	
1-1/2" aluminum angle (2')	
Appliance rollers	1 pair
1-1/4" washer-head screws	8
1" screws	16
2" screws	24
Wood glue	

CUTTING LIST

KEY	QTY.	MATERIAL	DIMENSIONS	PART
A	1	1/2" plywood	1/2" x 24" x 48"	Base
B	2	1x4 board	3/4" x 3-1/2" x 48"	Side
C	1	1x4 board	3/4" x 3-1/2" x 22-1/2"	End
D	4	1x4 board	3/4" x 3-1/2" x 16"	Cleat
E	1	1x6 board	3/4" x 5-1/2" x 24"	Drawer front
F	1	1-1/2" alum. angle	1-1/2" x 24"	Handle

4 SIMPLE JOINERY **OPTIONS**

Make strong, long-lasting joints without years of practice or a big budget

Traditional hand-cut joinery requires skill and a great deal of practice to master. But are those fancy joints necessary? Nah. I still use mortise-and-tenons or dovetails when a project calls for it. But for most projects, I just need joinery that's strong and simple.

My go-to methods include pocket screws, dowels, biscuits and the Beadlock system. There's no reason to have all of them in your arsenal. Most serious woodworkers choose one or two, become proficient and use them for virtually all joinery. These four methods are strong enough for typical joinery, and they're all affordable.

Pressure's on! We put these joints to the test! See p. 163 to find out how they held up.

POCKET SCREWS

You can get a basic pocket hole kit for about $30. You'll need a supply of different lengths of special self-drilling washer-head screws (coarse threads for softwoods, fine threads for hardwoods).

You likely already have a drill/driver, which is the only necessary tool. That's a big plus—it saves you money as well as space in your shop. Once you've become a convert, you can pick up more clamps, accessories and jigs to really step up your production. The only downside to pocket screws is that without special clamps, they don't automatically align parts during assembly.

Pros

- Fast
- No large clamps required
- Benchtop or portable

Cons

- Visible holes
- Parts alignment not automatic

1 Drill the holes. Clamp your workpiece in the jig and drill the steeply angled holes. This unusual jig has two pairs of holes: one pair for thinner stock and one pair for thicker. It costs about $65 at harborfreight.com. The included drill bit bores a flat-bottom hole with a short pilot hole at the center to guide the screw into the adjoining part. A stop collar regulates the hole depth.

Pocket screw tips
Search for "pocket screws" at familyhandyman.com

2 Drive the screws. Apply glue, clamp the parts into alignment and drive the screws. Some pocket hole jigs are portable; you can clamp them onto a workpiece that's too large to put on your workbench.

DOWELS

A solid, easy-to-use doweling jig will set you back about $70. As with the pocket hole method, the only tool you'll need is a drill. Then you'll also need a supply of dowels. The dowels for joinery are different from the standard dowel rods found at hardware stores. Joinery dowels are grooved to keep glue from getting trapped in the bottom of the hole and preventing the parts from pulling together. Unlike pocket screws, dowels align the parts and make both sides of the joint look the same (that is, no exposed screws). That's good when both sides will be visible.

Dowels

Pros

- Automatic alignment in both directions
- Mating dowel holes can be positioned anywhere using dowel centers (below)

Cons

- Clamping required
- Slow

1 Drill the holes. The Dowl-It jig I use is self-centering, with an integrated clamping mechanism. You can buy the latest version for about $70 online. Mark the hole locations on both parts, clamp the jig into place and drill the hole.

Dowel centers

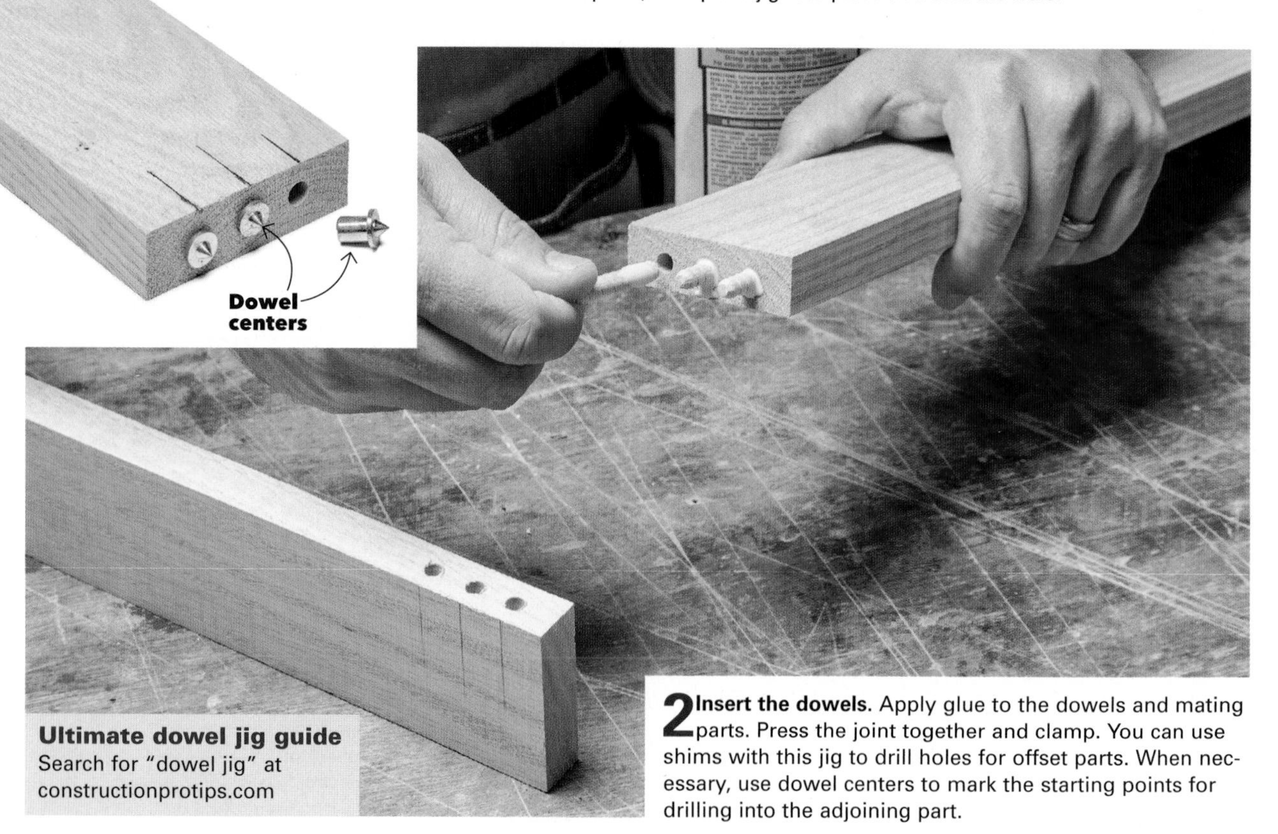

2 Insert the dowels. Apply glue to the dowels and mating parts. Press the joint together and clamp. You can use shims with this jig to drill holes for offset parts. When necessary, use dowel centers to mark the starting points for drilling into the adjoining part.

Ultimate dowel jig guide
Search for "dowel jig" at constructionprotips.com

Slot

Biscuit

BISCUITS

A plate (aka biscuit) joiner runs anywhere from $70 to $700. The $700 variety is really nice, but it's not necessary for an amateur woodworker. A modestly priced model works just fine. A plate joiner cuts a semicircular slot in adjoining parts to accept a plate/biscuit, which is then glued into place. Biscuits come in different sizes to accommodate various part dimensions.

Pros

- Fast
- Easy to use
- Easy to offset parts
- Effective dust collection
- Automatic alignment in one direction

Cons

- Clamping required
- Parts can slide during clamping

1 Cut the slots. Mark joint centerlines on adjoining parts. Set the plate joiner to the desired cutting height, and set the cutting depth to match the biscuit size you're using. Line up the guide mark on the joiner's fence with your mark and plunge the cut. The latest version of this Ryobi plate joiner costs about $100 at homedepot.com.

Biscuit tips galore
Search for "biscuit" at familyhandyman.com

2 Insert the biscuits. Apply glue to the mating surfaces and in the slots. Insert the biscuit, press the joint together and clamp.

BEADLOCK

A Beadlock jig facilitates drilling mortises in adjoining parts, again using only a drill. A basic Beadlock kit like the one shown is $30 at rockler.com. This is one of many "loose tenon" systems. Instead of the tenon's being cut from one of the adjoining parts, precut tenon stock is glued into a mortise in both parts.

Beadlock mortises are just a series of overlapping holes, and the tenon stock looks like a stack of dowels. You can buy tenon stock, or you can buy router bits to make your own tenon stock. But you'll need a router table for that, and it's a bit fussy.

Pros

- Easy to use
- Automatic alignment in both directions
- Extremely strong

Cons

- Slow
- Clamping required

1 Drill the mortises. Mark the joint centerline on both parts, position the jig using its alignment guide and then clamp the jig into place. Drill the first set of holes, slide the drilling block to its second position and drill the second set of holes. Repeat the process on the mating part.

2 Insert the tenons. Apply glue to the mating parts and the Beadlock tenon. Press the joint together and clamp.

JOINT STRENGTH TEST

We made 24-in. x 24-in. L-joints from red oak for all four of these joinery methods. Then we applied increasing tension with a turnbuckle and measured the failure point with a scale.

While admittedly not very scientific, the results were surprising. And it's always fun to break things!

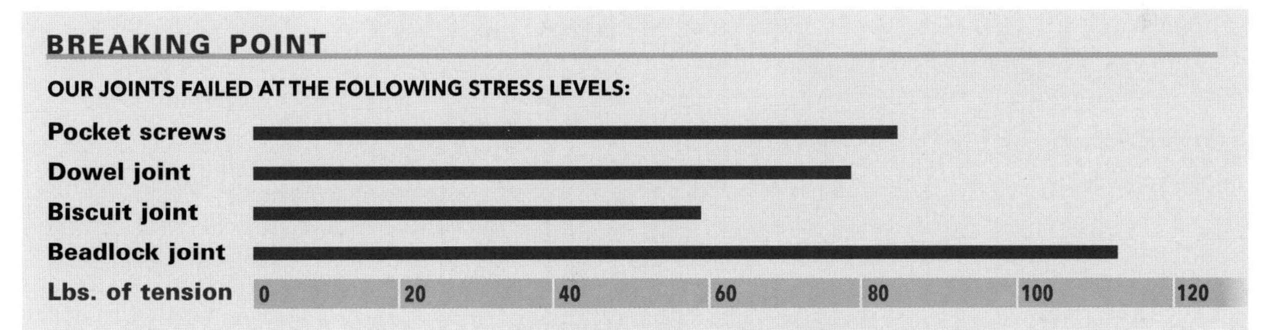

Pocket screws
The pocket screw joint is the only one that didn't break at the glue joint. The wood broke instead!

Dowels, biscuits and Beadlock
While the Beadlock joint was the strongest, these three joints eventually failed the same way: The glue joint broke and the wood pulled free of its reinforcement.

BOTTOM LINE

Strength is not the main consideration
All of these methods are plenty strong for typical woodworking uses. Unless the joint has to be especially strong, choose your method on the basis of speed or convenience rather than on strength.

MEET AN EXPERT

Brad Holden, an associate editor at *Family Handyman*, has been building cabinets and furniture for 30 years.

HandyHints®

FROM OUR READERS

SANDPAPER TEARING BLADE

Cutting sandpaper will dull scissors and utility knife blades in no time. Here's a better technique: Fasten a hacksaw blade to the edge of your workbench. Slip a washer behind the blade at each of the mounting holes so a sheet of sandpaper can easily slide in behind the blade. I fold the paper to the finished size I want, then cut along the fold.

—Darrell Novacek

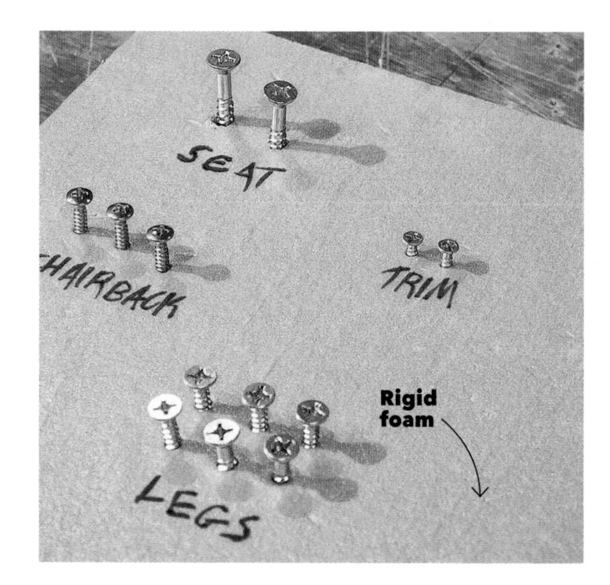

SCREW ORGANIZER

When you disassemble a piece of furniture that needs to be repaired or moved to a new home, poke the screws and nails into a piece of rigid foam. Group similar fasteners together or arrange them in the order they were removed. Use a pen or marker to label the groups or make notes that will be helpful for reassembly.

—J. Krech

NO-FUSS VENEER TRIMMING

You don't need a special veneer trimmer or even a router to trim wood veneer. But don't try to trim the veneer from the finished side. Flip the workpiece over on a flat work surface instead. Then slice the veneer with a sharp utility knife from the back side. If the project is too big to set on a workbench, hold a backer block against the veneer face as a cutting surface.

—Matt Boley

RUST PREVENTION POUCH

It's difficult to keep your tools free of rust if your toolbox is in an unconditioned garage or in the bed of your truck. Moisture in the air invades those spaces in a hurry, causing tools to rust. To absorb the moisture and prevent rust, I put a scoop of silica crystal cat litter in a rag and then tie it shut. I drop a pouch in every toolbox and replace them once a year.

—Rick Ambrasas

HandyHints®

BUILT-IN BLADE HEIGHT GAUGE

Here's a quick way to set your blade or dado height for non-through cuts on the table saw. Make a scale directly on your table saw's fence using a fine-point permanent marker. You'll have to refresh the marks once in a while; they'll get rubbed off by stock sliding against the fence.

—Norm Matuska

NO-ROLL PENCILS

Carpenter's pencils are handy because they don't roll off your workbench or countertop. But I prefer regular pencils for precise marking. To keep them from rolling off the workbench, I put a tape "flag" around the end.

—David Schmidt

SOFT-TOP SAWHORSES

Most of my sawhorses see rough use. If they get beat up, it doesn't matter. But I have a few that I use for assembling projects, so I stapled carpet scraps to them to provide a non-marring surface.

—Dan Brown

PENCIL TRICK FOR SANDING

When you're sanding an edge flush to the adjacent surface, first draw a squiggly pencil line across the joint. Use the marks as a guide to help you sand flat and avoid sanding through the plywood's veneer.

—Timothy Manka

PLASTIC BAG STORAGE

In a workshop, it's easy to find plenty of uses for plastic grocery bags. To store lots of bags in a small space, I stuff as many as possible into empty paper towel tubes. I can fit more bags in the drawer when they're contained this way, and it's easy to pull out just one bag at a time when I need it.

—Chris Annoni

FIDDLE STICKS

When you're using a belt sander, you need to make sure the piece you're sanding stays put. You can't just clamp down the board—the clamps will block the belt sander from reaching the edges. The trick is to screw boards, sometimes called "fiddles," to a corner of your workbench. As you sand, the spinning motion will push the workpiece against the fiddles, holding it in place.

—Travis Larson

DIVIDING ODD WIDTHS

Say you have a board that's 11-3/8 in. wide and you need to divide it into four equal parts. No problem. Angle your tape across the board until it reads a number easily divisible by four, such as 16. Then, with the tape angled, make marks at 4, 8 and 12 in.

—Bryan Malm

HandyHints®

PLYWOOD HANDLE

Carrying a sheet of plywood by yourself is awkward and hard on your back. The best method I've found involves making a loop from an 18-ft. rope. Wrap it around the bottom two corners of the plywood sheet. The rope makes a perfect handle.

—Ken Porter

SAFETY SUPPORT

A miter saw makes quick work of accurately cutting aluminum angle. But given the often wide gaps between the fences and in the throat plate, using the saw this way is also dangerous. If the blade grabs, it can pull the aluminum angle into those gaps, destroying the piece and possibly causing injury. To make the cut safely, glue up two boards as shown. This way, the aluminum angle is fully supported, greatly reducing any chance of a mishap.

—Josh Risberg

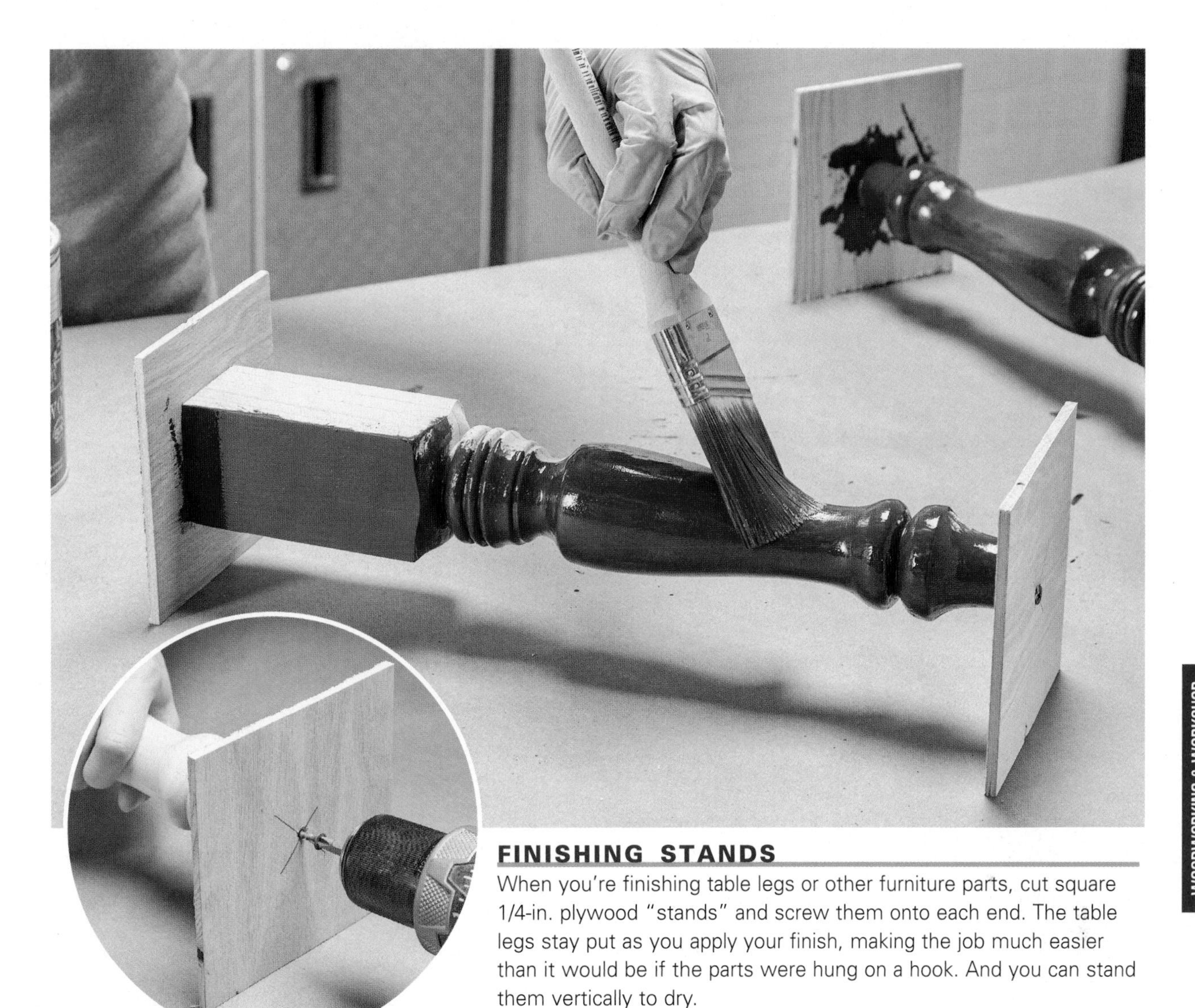

FINISHING STANDS

When you're finishing table legs or other furniture parts, cut square 1/4-in. plywood "stands" and screw them onto each end. The table legs stay put as you apply your finish, making the job much easier than it would be if the parts were hung on a hook. And you can stand them vertically to dry.

—Doug Macqueen

MITER SLOT STOP

When you trim parts with a hand plane, a board in the miter slot makes a perfect stop.

—Mike Berner

3/4" scrap in miter slot

HandyHints®

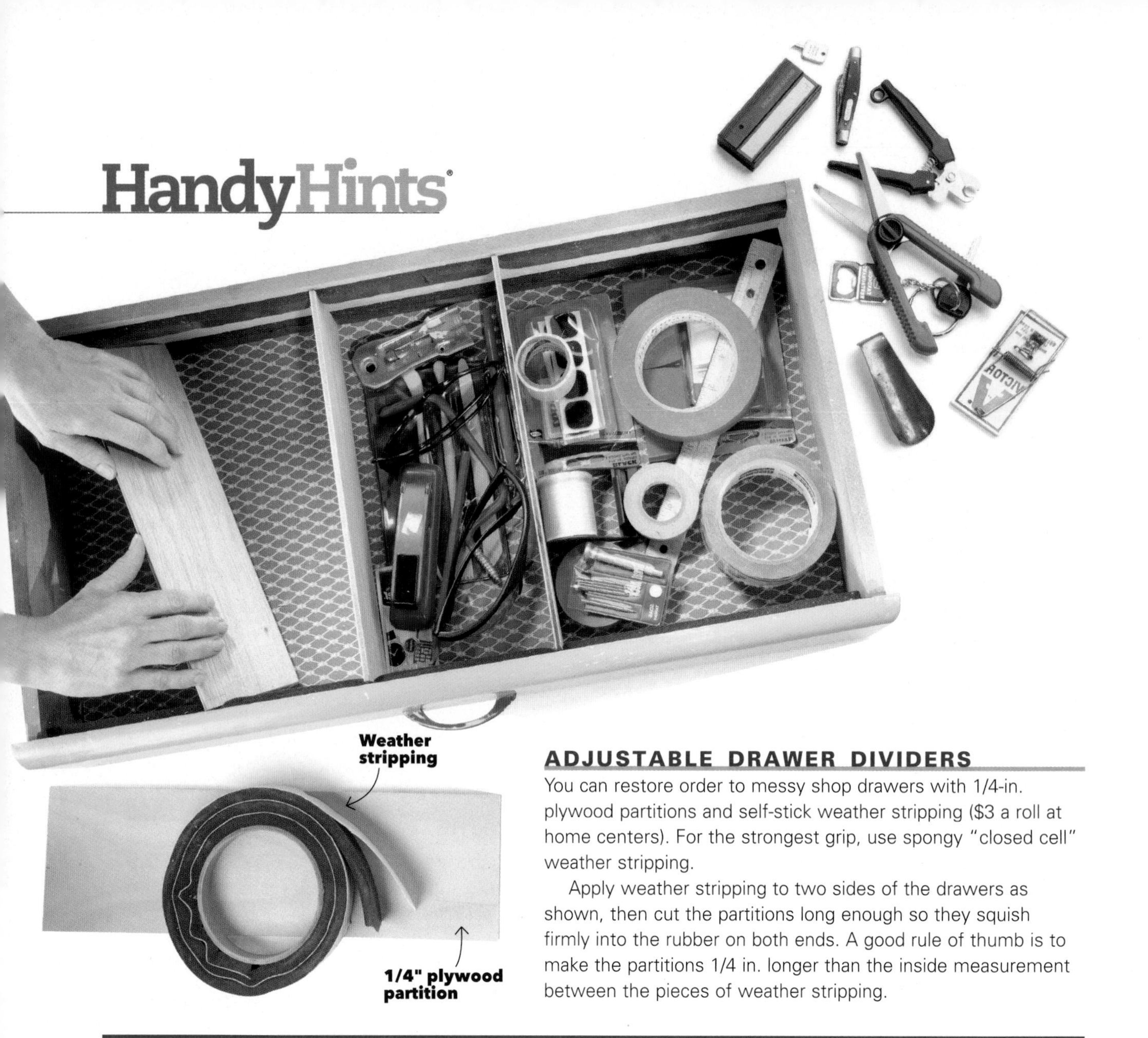

ADJUSTABLE DRAWER DIVIDERS

You can restore order to messy shop drawers with 1/4-in. plywood partitions and self-stick weather stripping ($3 a roll at home centers). For the strongest grip, use spongy "closed cell" weather stripping.

Apply weather stripping to two sides of the drawers as shown, then cut the partitions long enough so they squish firmly into the rubber on both ends. A good rule of thumb is to make the partitions 1/4 in. longer than the inside measurement between the pieces of weather stripping.

PVC PIPE CLAMP RACK

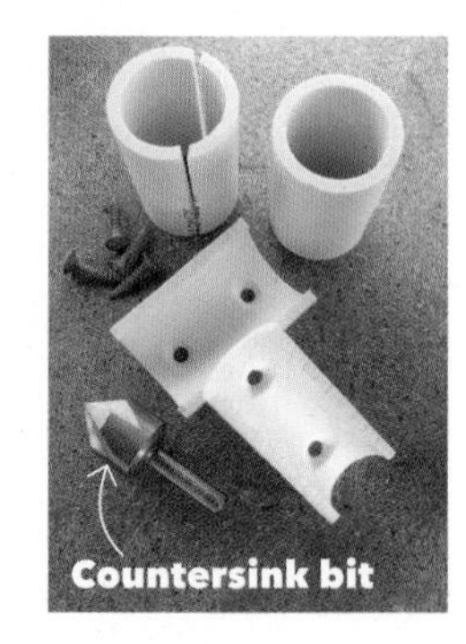

Are your pipe clamps missing in action right when you need them? Build this snap-in, snap-out storage rack from PVC pipe. For 1/2-in.-diameter iron pipe, use 3/4-in. PVC, and for 3/4-in.-diameter pipe, use 1-in. PVC.

To make the rack, cut 2-in. lengths of PVC, and with a hacksaw or band saw, slice them lengthwise about 3/16 in. past the diameter's centerline. This creates the gripping action to firmly hold the heavy iron pipe. Drill and countersink two holes in each PVC piece, then screw them to a pair of boards. Attach the upper board to your shop wall and snap a pipe clamp in each end to position the lower board for screwing to the wall.

STORE SHEET GOODS ON A LADDER

An old extension ladder is just right for holding leftover plywood, drywall, plastic laminate and spare boards. Take the ladder sections apart, lay one on the floor near a wall and then load it up. This handy rack will hold your sheet goods high and dry and make it easier to find what you need.

UP, UP AND AWAY

Put joist spaces to use with this simple storage idea. Fasten eye screws to the joists and cut lengths of chain to keep odd lengths of trim and pipe out of the way but easy to find. Open one side of the eye screw with a pliers to slip the chain into place. Make the chain a bit longer for future expansion.

SPRAY-CAN SIX-PACK

A cardboard six-pack corrals loose spray cans for a neater shop.

HANG-IT-ALL HOOKS

The plastic hooks that plumbers use to support pipes make convenient hangers for just about anything. They're strong and cheap and come in a range of sizes. Find them in the plumbing aisle.

SPECIAL SECTION

Save That Concrete Slab

SAVE THAT SLAB!

If you have an uneven concrete slab, you could replace it or cover it with leveling compound. But consider grinding it instead. Powerful grinding equipment is available at rental centers that cater to contractors. Here are a few of the most common uses:

- Tapering cracks or heaves to reduce tripping hazards.
- Flattening high spots or ridges before you install flooring.
- Grinding down leftover thin-set or other hard coatings.
- Removing a sealed surface to accept adhesive, thin-set or epoxy.

Find a rental store

Call around to find a rental store that carries a few floor-grinding options. Grinding down high spots in concrete requires removing lots of material; be sure to rent a high-speed grinder that rotates about 1,500 rpm or faster. Once you explain your task, the rental store staff should be able to set you up with the right equipment.

Different sizes for different jobs

If you have a large floor that needs to be ground down, plan to rent a walk-behind floor grinder. You'll spend $90 to $150 per day, but a big machine can grind a large space within the rental period. Depending on the store and the machines it carries, a diamond grinding wheel may be included in the rental or you may have to buy diamond grinding inserts for about $150 a set.

For a small job, rent an angle grinder equipped with a diamond grinding wheel ($50 a day or less). It's the perfect tool for taking down just a few high spots or tough-to-reach areas near walls. Be sure the one you rent comes with a means of attaching a vacuum to suck up the dust. If you plan to grind right up to a wall, make sure you rent a grinder with a convertible dust shroud that will flip up to expose the wheel enough to get into the corner.

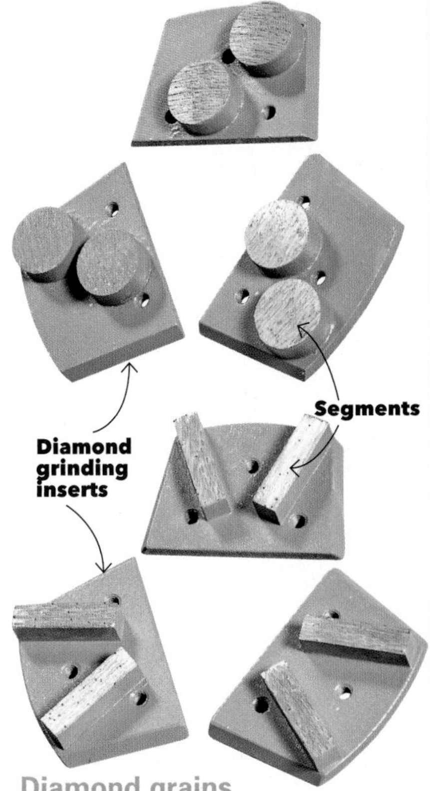

Diamond grains do the cutting

The cutting surfaces of these grinders are diamond grains held by "segments," the raised metal parts of the wheel. An aggressive wheel, which can take down 1/4 in. of concrete or more, grinds away material faster but leaves a rougher surface. A less aggressive wheel removes smaller amounts of concrete and leaves a smoother surface.

Here's the rule of thumb for choosing a wheel: The more surface area it has, the less aggressive the wheel. Choose an aggressive one to remove high, long ridges or large, rough areas of concrete, and a less aggressive one for tasks like cleaning up tile thin-set residue from a wall or prepping for an epoxy coating.

How long will the job take?

If you have a 3/4-in. difference in height between sidewalk slabs, you should be able to knock that down in a few hours, but it depends on how hard the concrete is and the grinding wheel you use.

Save That Concrete Slab

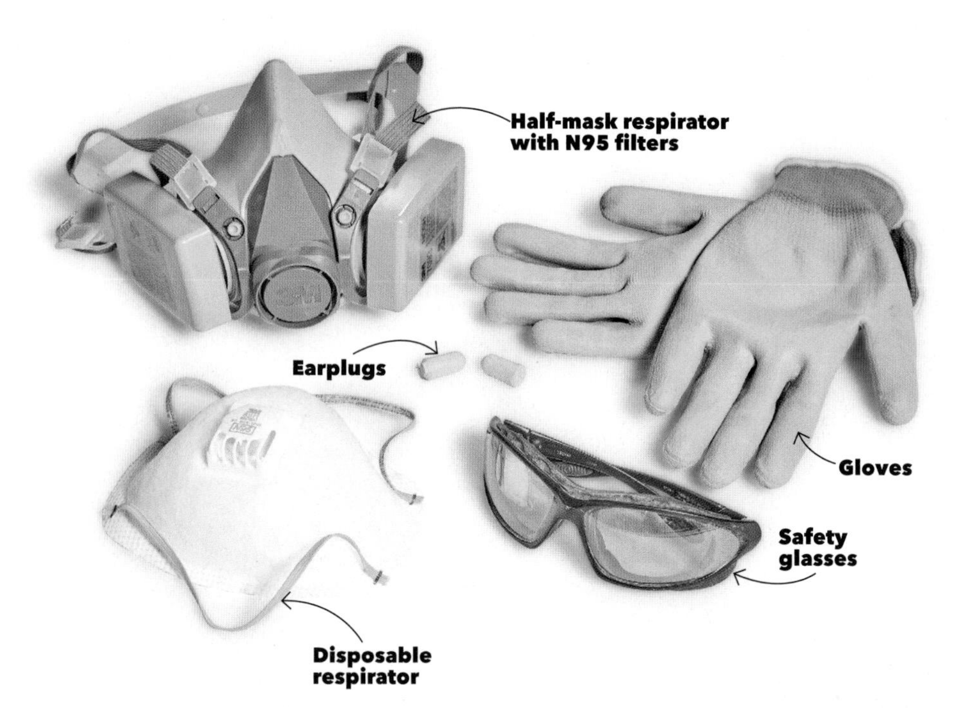

Wear safety gear!

Plan to deck yourself out in safety gear: hearing protection, safety glasses and a respirator. The high-speed machines are loud and can send concrete rubble flying from the grinding wheel. Grinding concrete also releases fine silica dust, which can cause health problems. Always wear a NIOSH-certified N95-rated respirator. Disposable masks cost as little as $2 each, but for $25 you can get a half-mask respirator that will have a better seal. Check the seal with this easy test: If you can exhale and inhale sharply without air escaping, you're good to grind. If you have facial hair, even a bit of stubble will ruin the seal. Go ahead and shave—it will grow back!

Avoid tripped circuit breakers

Both the grinder and the vacuum draw a lot of power, so if possible, plug them into separate circuits and wrap the cord so the connection stays away from moisture. Otherwise you may find yourself flipping tripped circuit switches all day long. And if the grinder is struggling to start up when the cutter head is resting on the ground, lift up the head before starting the grinder. That will reduce resistance during startup.

MEET AN EXPERT

Brian Farmer teaches skills in plaster, concrete floor polishing and floor-coating application. We joined him at the Cement Mason's Union training facility, where he shared tips for dealing with common grinding situations.

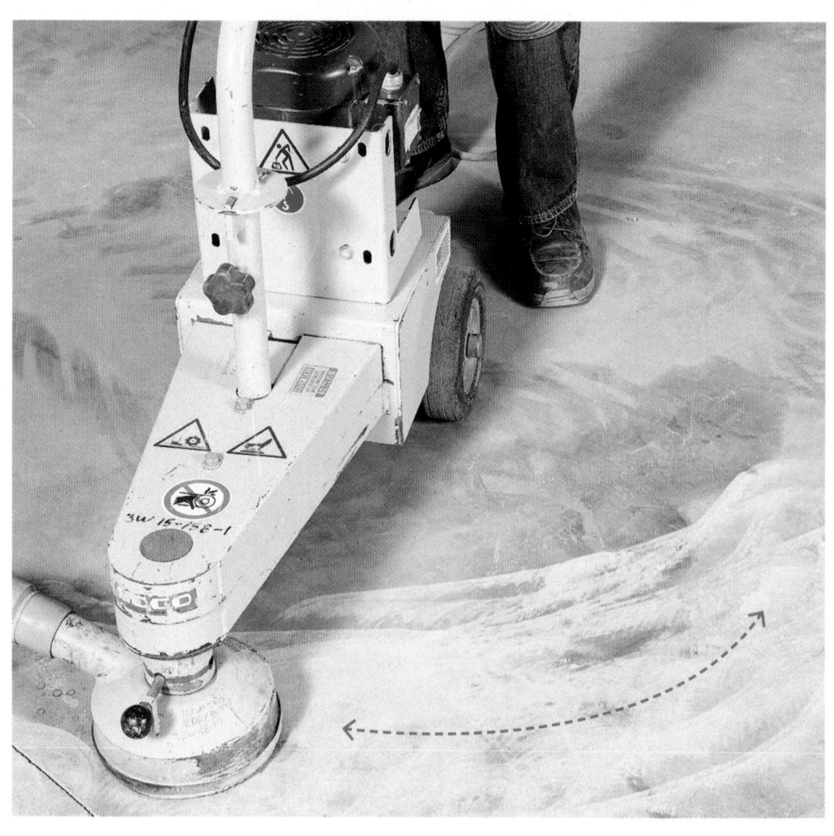

Keep the machine in motion

While you're grinding, keep the cutter head moving, especially with a large floor grinder. Pivot the machine on its wheels, moving the cutter head in an arcing motion. If the cutting surface is riding on only one edge, work the machine in small circles to flatten out the surface.

Choosing dust control

There are two great ways to keep the dust from going wild. You can use a hand-pump sprayer to soak the floor with water as you grind to keep the dust down. But you'll have a messy slurry that will need to be hosed away or sucked up with a wet vacuum.

Or you can rent a heavy-duty vacuum (regular shop vacuums won't be able to keep up) to hook up to the grinder. It will also do a very good job of dust removal, but it will cost $75 and you'll need to put up walls of plastic sheeting and cover nearby vents. The choice is yours, but remember to wear your respirator either way!

Save That Concrete Slab

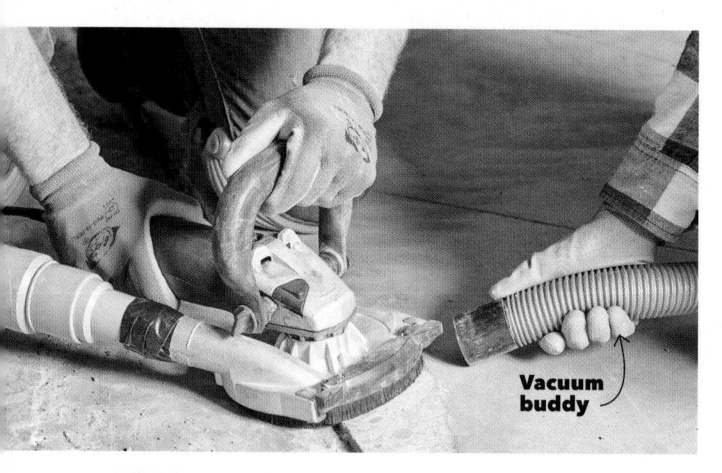

Nibble at a heave

For a heaved sidewalk or cracked slab, tilt the grinder slightly and remove the meat of the concrete and then feather back the high spot. You may never get toe-stubbing heaves completely flat, but you can lessen the hazard. When tilted, the dust shroud can't catch all the dust, so you'll need a second hose and a helper.

Grinding to the edge

Never remove a dust shroud to get close to a wall. You'll increase your exposure to nasty silica and remove a safety barrier. To grind near walls with a convertible dust shroud attached, push the open end of the dust shroud against the wall and make steady, shallow passes. Be sure you don't dig the edge of the wheel into the concrete as you move it back and forth.

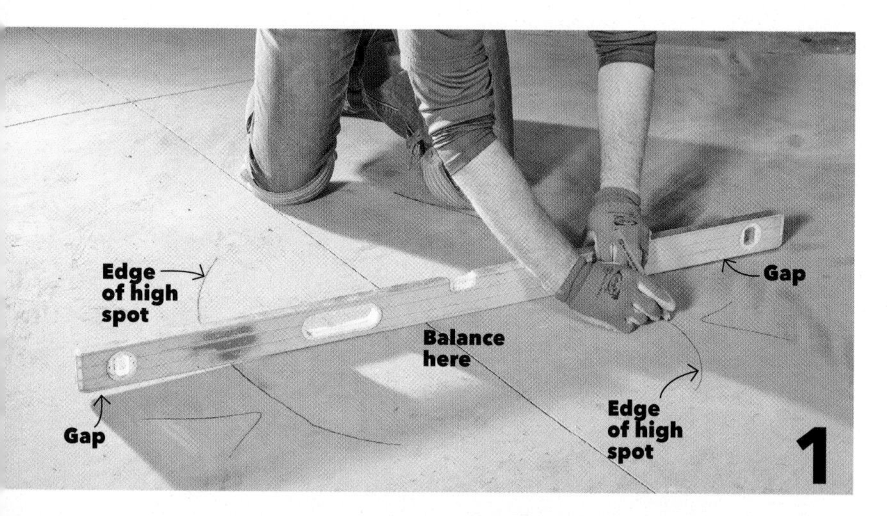

2

Ground area

Mark where to grind

1 Trace the high spots. Outline the space that needs to be ground. Using a level or other straightedge, find where the high spot meets the flat surface. Balance the straightedge on the high spot and mark where the ends of the level are equidistant from the ground and trace around the high spot. This can be done by eye; it won't be perfect, but it will be a good start.

2 Check your progress. Start grinding on the crown of the high spot and work your way toward your marks. When you feel you've made progress, use the straightedge again to check for flatness. Retrace the high spots and grind them down. Repeat this grind-and-check process until the high spot is gone.

Keep grinder flat against concrete

When possible, make sure the entire grinding surface is touching the concrete. Grinding with only one edge of the wheel will wear down the segments unevenly.

5 Exterior Repairs & Improvements

IN THIS CHAPTER

HomeSmarts

KNOWLEDGE YOU NEED TO BE A BETTER HOMEOWNER

INSTALLING DECK **FOOTINGS**

Q I'm replacing my old deck with a new one, complete with new footings and posts. One corner of my old deck would move up several inches in the spring, then move back down as the weather warmed, but it never quite settled to the previous level. What causes this weird seasonal levitation, and can I prevent it when I build my new deck?

—Phillip Morgan
Hayward, WIsconsin

A Your deck has a bad case of frost heave. In the winter, the ground freezes from the top of the soil downward. The depth of frost penetration depends on the soil type, the severity of the winter, the amount of water in the soil and the depth of an insulating blanket of snow.

Frost depth varies by region. In Minnesota, the frost depth is 42 in., whereas a warmer state like Missouri may have a frost depth of only 1 ft. When you contact the local building department to get your building permit, ask what the frost depth requirement is and the required size and shape of the footings. Then dig the footing holes so that the bottoms of the footings are at or below the frost depth.

The mechanics of frost heave are complex, but here's a quick primer. Water in the surrounding soil collects and freezes into thin layers of frost called "ice lenses." When water freezes, it expands about 9 percent—think of how ice cubes

are domed above the original water level in an ice cube tray. Ice exerts a pressure of about 50,000 lbs. per sq. in.—enough force to lift even a large building. A puny little deck on inadequate footings doesn't stand a chance. The reason buildings and decks don't always return to their original height is that surrounding dirt sometimes fills in under the footing while it's lifted. Heavy clay soils don't drain well, so they tend to have more frost heave problems than sandy, well-drained ones. But even if footings are deep enough, ice lenses can latch onto the rough surfaces of wood and concrete and lift footings and posts from the side. That's why concrete piers poured in waxed cardboard tubes and smooth wooden posts work well for below-grade support.

Here's how to get a solid, frost-proof footing:

When you pour concrete footings, hold the cardboard concrete form tube about 12 in. up from the bottom of the footing. Do this by nailing the sides of the tube to the center of a tic-tac-toe grid of 2x4s at the top of the hole. Then dump concrete through the tube into the bottom of the hole. After the wide part at the bottom of the hole has filled, the tube will fill too.

- Flare the sides on concrete footings so the footings will resist heave in harsh winters when frost penetrates especially deep. Greater width at the bottom will also distribute weight over a larger area.
- To direct runoff water away from the posts, mound soil around the posts after the backfill settles.

A concrete postscript:

If you're pouring more than a few footings, order premixed concrete from a ready-mix company. You'd be shocked at how many bags of concrete mix you'd have to mix by hand to fill a form tube. There's typically a chart on the tube indicating how many bags you need. If you want to do the job on your own schedule, rent a portable concrete mixer, or just buy one and sell it when you're done. You can buy a serviceable mixer for as little as $200.

—Travis Larson

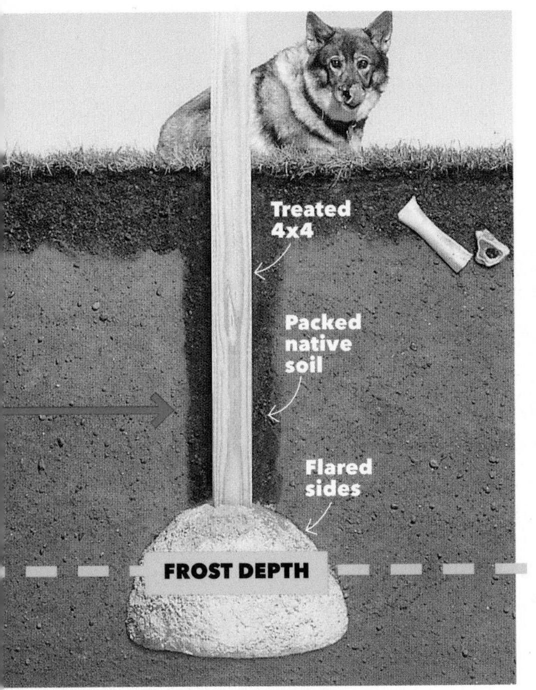

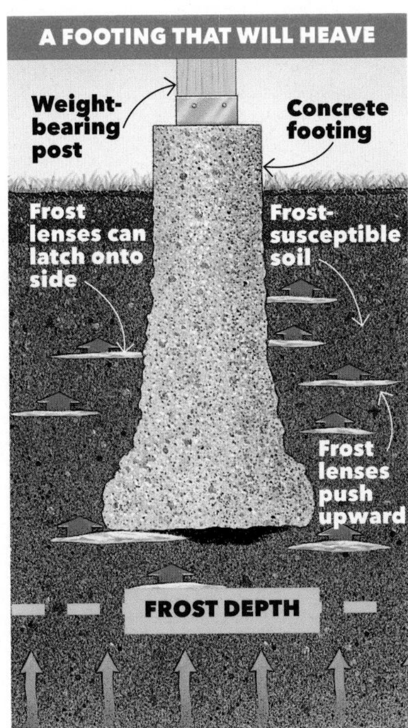

Tips for digging a hole

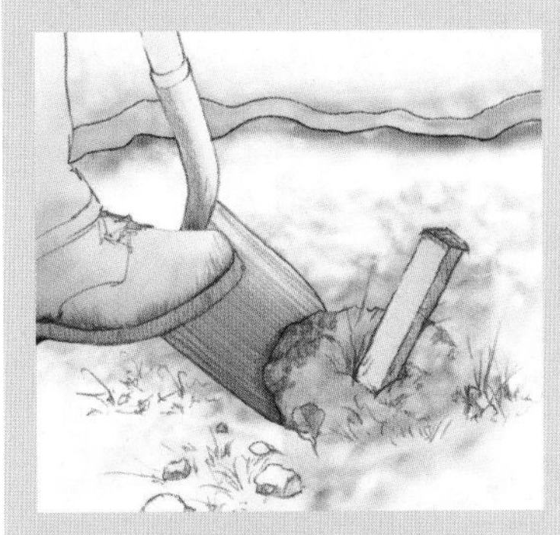

Carve out a soil divot with a spade
Carve out a round plug to outline the posthole. That'll get you started in exactly the right spot. Throw the dirt onto a tarp to protect your lawn.

Loosen earth with a tile shovel
Unless you have very soft soil, you'll work way too hard digging with just a clamshell digger. Loosen the soil and carve away at the sides with a tile spade. It'll easily slice through small roots.

Use a recip saw on large roots
Don't kill yourself chiseling out roots. Just use a recip saw with a long, coarse blade and poke it right into the soil and cut off the roots.

HomeSmarts

THE TROUBLE WITH 4x4s

If you need 4x4s or other large posts, inspect them first. Why? Many of them, especially 8-ft. posts, come from logs used for veneer, which is peeled from the logs like paper towels from a roll, leaving only the very center of the log. The center "pith" is the least stable part of the log and is very prone to twisting, splitting and bowing. This is particularly true of treated 4x4s because the treatment exaggerates the warping. Examine the stack of posts at the home center and reject the posts with end grain that looks like a bull's-eye. Choose the straightest posts you can find, with the least amount of center pith.

—Brad Holden
Associate Editor

Best of the pile
Look for posts without a "bulls-eye" and growth rings from edge to edge. Perfect is rare. Find the best you can.

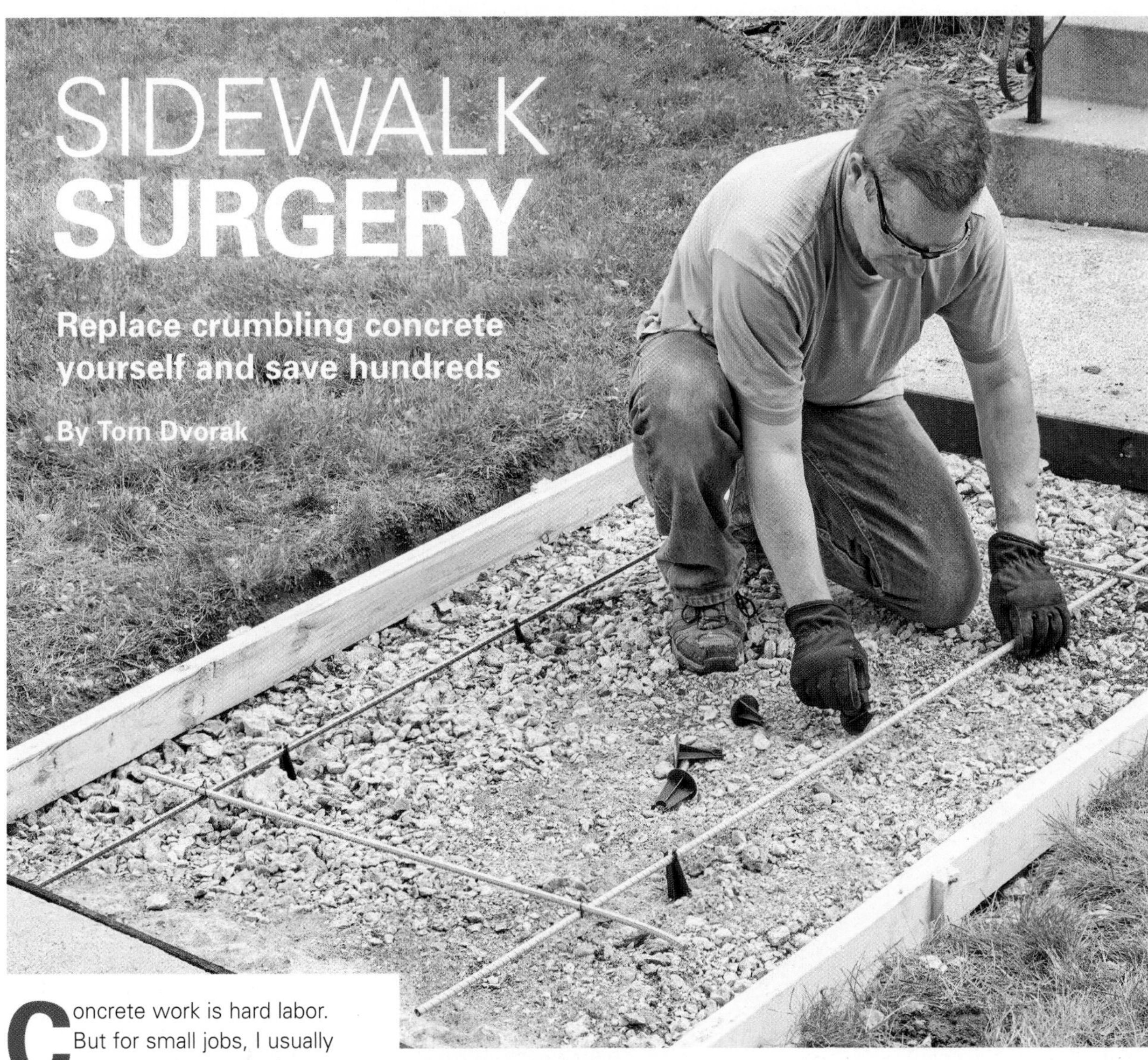

SIDEWALK SURGERY

Replace crumbling concrete yourself and save hundreds

By Tom Dvorak

Concrete work is hard labor. But for small jobs, I usually find I can do it myself—and for about one-third the contractor's bid. This sidewalk is a typical example. The materials and mixer rental cost about $200; a pro would have charged me at least $600. So I saved 400 bucks—not bad! You can do the same. Experience with concrete isn't necessary, but you will need tool know-how and a strong back. You can follow the steps here and find much more info at familyhandyman.com. Just search for "concrete."

MEET AN EXPERT

Tom Dvorak, a civil engineer, has spent 25 years buying bad houses and turning them into good homes.

BEFORE

AFTER

What happened?

This sidewalk is more than 80 years old and still in good shape—mostly. So what went wrong with this section? Most likely, it was excess water: The builders added too much water to the mix or misted the surface to make troweling easier. Or maybe rain came before the concrete cured. Any of these circumstances makes concrete weak, porous and destined to disintegrate.

Expect a mismatch

New concrete looks very different from older concrete. The match improves with time, but that can mean years. One solution is to replace the entire sidewalk. Another approach—much easier—is to coat the whole sidewalk with a resurfacer. For an overview of that job, search for "resurface sidewalk" at familyhandyman.com.

1 Dig ditches. Trench along both sides of the walk at least 6 in. wide and 6 in. deep. These trenches will allow you to set up forms later.

2 Cut a crack stop. When you break up the bad section, a cut that's at least 1-1/4 in. deep will prevent cracks from spreading to the good section. An existing groove in the concrete is usually the best place to cut. Cut with a diamond blade in a circular saw or an angle grinder.

3 Bust up the bad section. A small section of sidewalk usually doesn't require a jackhammer rental; try a sledgehammer first. A mattock is perfect for prying up broken concrete. Remove the chunks. For more concrete-busting tips, search for "concrete demolition" at familyhandyman.com.

4 Place the forms. Select straight 2x4s for the forms and drive stakes every 24 in. Position the forms even with the adjoining sections of sidewalk, then drive screws through the stakes into the forms. The forms should feel rock-solid. If not, add stakes.

5 Trim off the stakes. Cut the stakes flush with the forms with a handsaw or recip saw. Then span the forms with a 2x4 and slide it along the length of the forms. It should slide smoothly without hitting obstructions.

6 Prepare the base. Set a 2x4 across the forms and measure to the soil or gravel below in several spots. Your goal is a 4-in.-deep space for concrete. You may need to add or remove material. Then compact the base with a hand tamper ($30 at home centers).

7 Add expansion joints. Tack expansion joint material to the existing concrete with 1-in. masonry nails. A 50-ft. roll of expansion joint costs about $20 at home centers.

8 Oil the forms. A "release agent" allows for easy form removal after the concrete has cured. Spray lubricant is fast, but you can use a rag to wipe on any oil.

9 Add rebar. Rebar isn't essential for sidewalks, but it adds strength and longevity. The 3/8-in. rebar and support "chairs" shown cost less than $20. "Pin" the new concrete to the old: Drill 3-in.-deep holes into the old concrete, insert 16-in. sections of rebar and tie the rebar frame to the pins (**Photo 10**).

More Concrete Knowledge
Get tips and how-to help for any concrete project at familyhandyman.com. Just search for "concrete."

EXTERIOR REPAIRS & IMPROVEMENTS

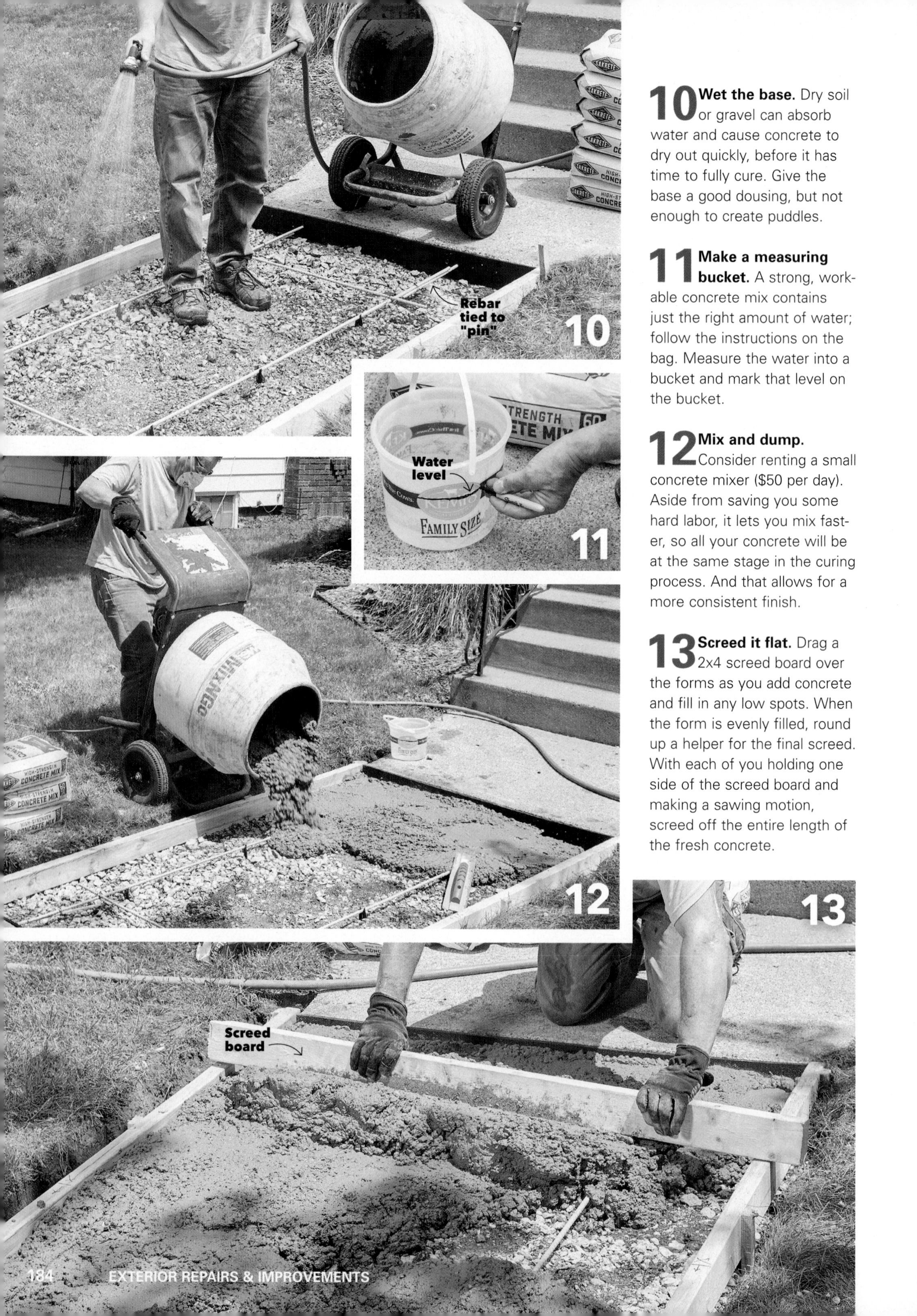

10 Wet the base. Dry soil or gravel can absorb water and cause concrete to dry out quickly, before it has time to fully cure. Give the base a good dousing, but not enough to create puddles.

11 Make a measuring bucket. A strong, workable concrete mix contains just the right amount of water; follow the instructions on the bag. Measure the water into a bucket and mark that level on the bucket.

12 Mix and dump. Consider renting a small concrete mixer ($50 per day). Aside from saving you some hard labor, it lets you mix faster, so all your concrete will be at the same stage in the curing process. And that allows for a more consistent finish.

13 Screed it flat. Drag a 2x4 screed board over the forms as you add concrete and fill in any low spots. When the form is evenly filled, round up a helper for the final screed. With each of you holding one side of the screed board and making a sawing motion, screed off the entire length of the fresh concrete.

14 Float the concrete. Immediately after the final screed, smooth the concrete with a wood or magnesium float. Don't worry about small ridges left by the float; brooming the surface will erase them.

15 Broom the surface. Drag a broom lightly across the concrete to create a nonslip surface. The time to do this is typically 30 minutes after floating, but that will vary a little depending on the temperature and humidity.

16 Edge the perimeter. An edger ($10) forms a rounded edge, which looks good and is less likely to chip off. This can be done before or after you broom the surface.

17 Groove the surface. A groover ($10) cuts a "control joint," which encourages any cracking to occur in the joint, rather than randomly. Typically, control joints are spaced 5 to 8 ft. apart.

Tips for a smooth, successful project

- Once you add water to concrete mix, the clock starts ticking. So the most important step in any concrete work is preparation. Mentally run through the entire job, make a list, and be absolutely certain you have all your tools and materials ready to go.
- To determine how many bags of concrete mix you need, search online for "bagged concrete calculator." Buy a couple extra bags. Running out can lead to disaster.
- Consider renting a mixer or calling in a ready-mix truck. Here's my personal rule: If you need more than 15 bags, rent a mixer. If you need more than 30 bags, order ready-mix.
- Whether you're mixing by hand or using a mixer, it's best to have a helper so you can get the final batch mixed before the first batch becomes too stiff to work with.
- A couple hours after finishing the concrete, cover it with painter's plastic for a few days. Concrete that stays wet longer grows stronger.
- Wait overnight (or longer) before you remove the forms.

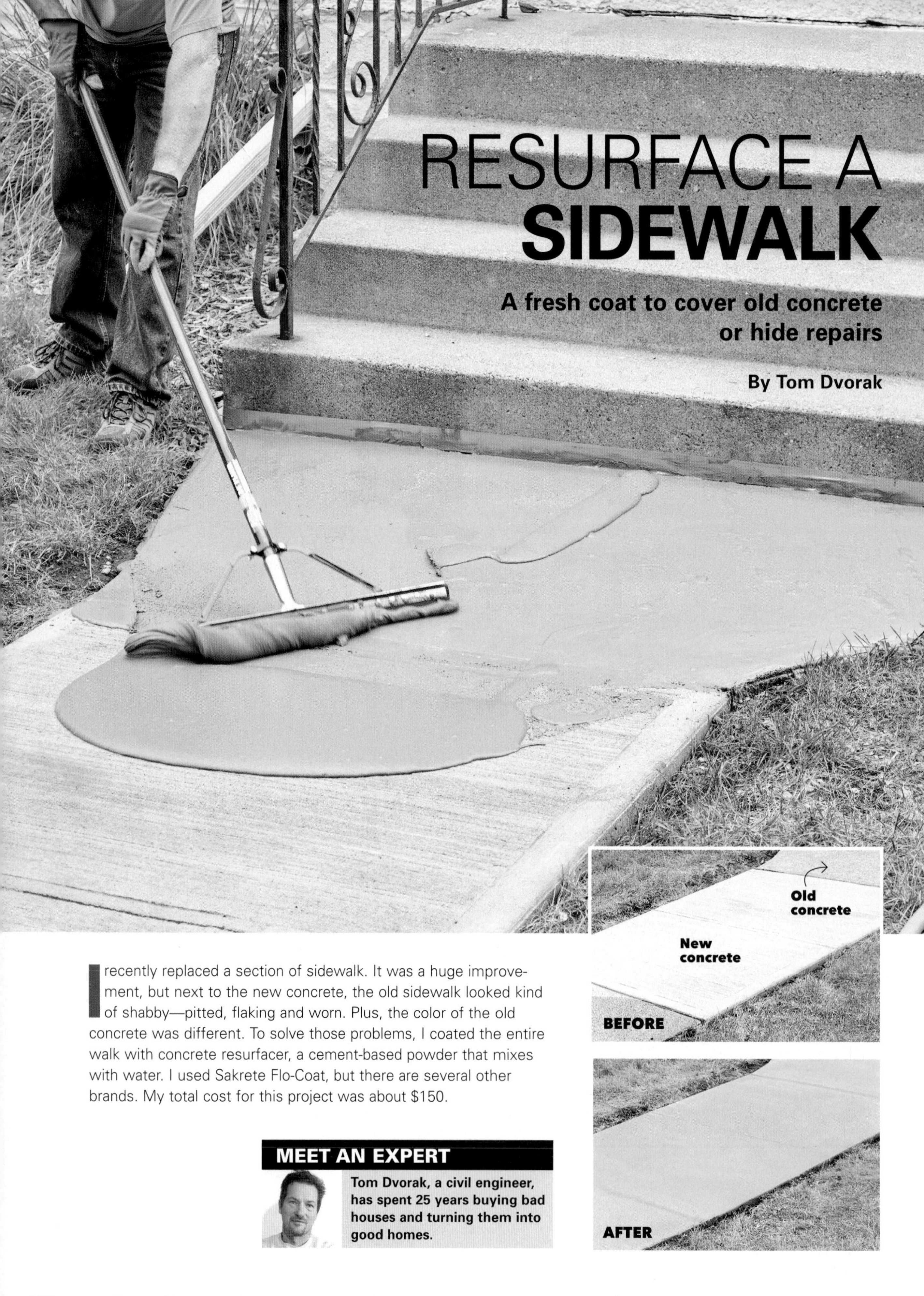

RESURFACE A SIDEWALK

A fresh coat to cover old concrete or hide repairs

By Tom Dvorak

I recently replaced a section of sidewalk. It was a huge improvement, but next to the new concrete, the old sidewalk looked kind of shabby—pitted, flaking and worn. Plus, the color of the old concrete was different. To solve those problems, I coated the entire walk with concrete resurfacer, a cement-based powder that mixes with water. I used Sakrete Flo-Coat, but there are several other brands. My total cost for this project was about $150.

MEET AN EXPERT

Tom Dvorak, a civil engineer, has spent 25 years buying bad houses and turning them into good homes.

1 Trench along the edges. To prep, I power-washed the old concrete and the new, which had cured for a month. The next day, I edged along the sidewalk with a shovel to clear away overhanging grass and create a small trench. A deeper, wider trench would have been much better (see "Lessons Learned," p. 189).

2 Protect against slop-over. To protect areas that I didn't want to coat, I masked the adjoining concrete surfaces with duct tape. Duct tape adheres well to concrete. Masking tape doesn't.

3 Dampen the concrete. Dry surfaces quickly steal water from the mix and inhibit easy spreading. I misted the entire sidewalk to dampen it before I began applying the product. I made sure it was thoroughly damp but not puddling. This is critical.

4 Make a giant measuring cup. I marked a bucket to indicate the exact amount of water recommended per bag of resurfacer. This allowed me to get a consistent mix without wasting time.

5 Mix it up. I poured about three-quarters of the required water into the bucket, poured in a little resurfacer and mixed with a heavy-duty drill. Then I gradually added more resurfacer, mixing each time. Finally, I poured in the last of the water and blended the mix thoroughly. After letting the mix sit for a few minutes, I mixed one last time.

6 Pour it on. I poured resurfacer across the first section, doing my best to distribute it evenly.

7 Spread it out. I used a squeegee to spread the mix across the entire surface to a depth of just over 1/8 in. Although I used the squeegee to push and pull the mix across the section, I always finished by pulling across the sidewalk in the same direction.

8 Hurry up! I continued this process until I'd coated the entire walk. Resurfacer has limited working time. To work fast, I had a helper mix additional buckets while I kept pouring and spreading. Wear a respirator when you mix, pour or cut concrete.

9 Cut a groove. As the coating began to harden, I used a mortar rake to re-form the existing joints in the concrete. If you leave a joint filled, you risk cracks in the future.

More Concrete Knowledge
Get tips and how-to help for any concrete project at familyhandyman.com. Just search for "concrete."

10 Add texture. I applied a broom finish for better traction using a soft-bristle push broom. I found that brooming within 15 minutes of the initial pour worked best, but this depends on temperature and humidity. I watched the surface and broomed when the sheen evaporated. I had to keep moving because once the resurfacer begins to harden, it becomes difficult to broom.

11 Scrape the edges. When the mix had become firm but not hard, I used a trowel to scrape away any excess along the edge of the concrete.

12 Cover up and cordon off. I covered the sidewalk with plastic to keep the resurfacer damp. Slower drying means better bonding and a tougher surface. To keep traffic off the resurfacer, I strung warning tape.

Lessons learned

■ Trench along the edges. My trenches weren't wide enough. I had to spread the resurfacer carefully along the edges to avoid dragging soil in with the squeegee. Make your trenches at least 4 in. wide and a couple inches deep.

■ Good preparation is critical. Resurfacer hardens fast—you have about 10 minutes to spread it. I was well prepared, though, and had a helper mix while I applied the coating.

■ A redo is easy. The first coat took me two hours and wasn't quite perfect. The areas I had troweled were evident and my broom finish was inconsistent. I opted for a second coat, which took just over an hour, and the result was absolute perfection.

First winter, no damage

Freeze/thaw cycles are brutal on cement products, and the winter following this project was especially tough, with endless cold snaps. So I was worried. But my sidewalk emerged from the ice age unscathed—no damage at all!

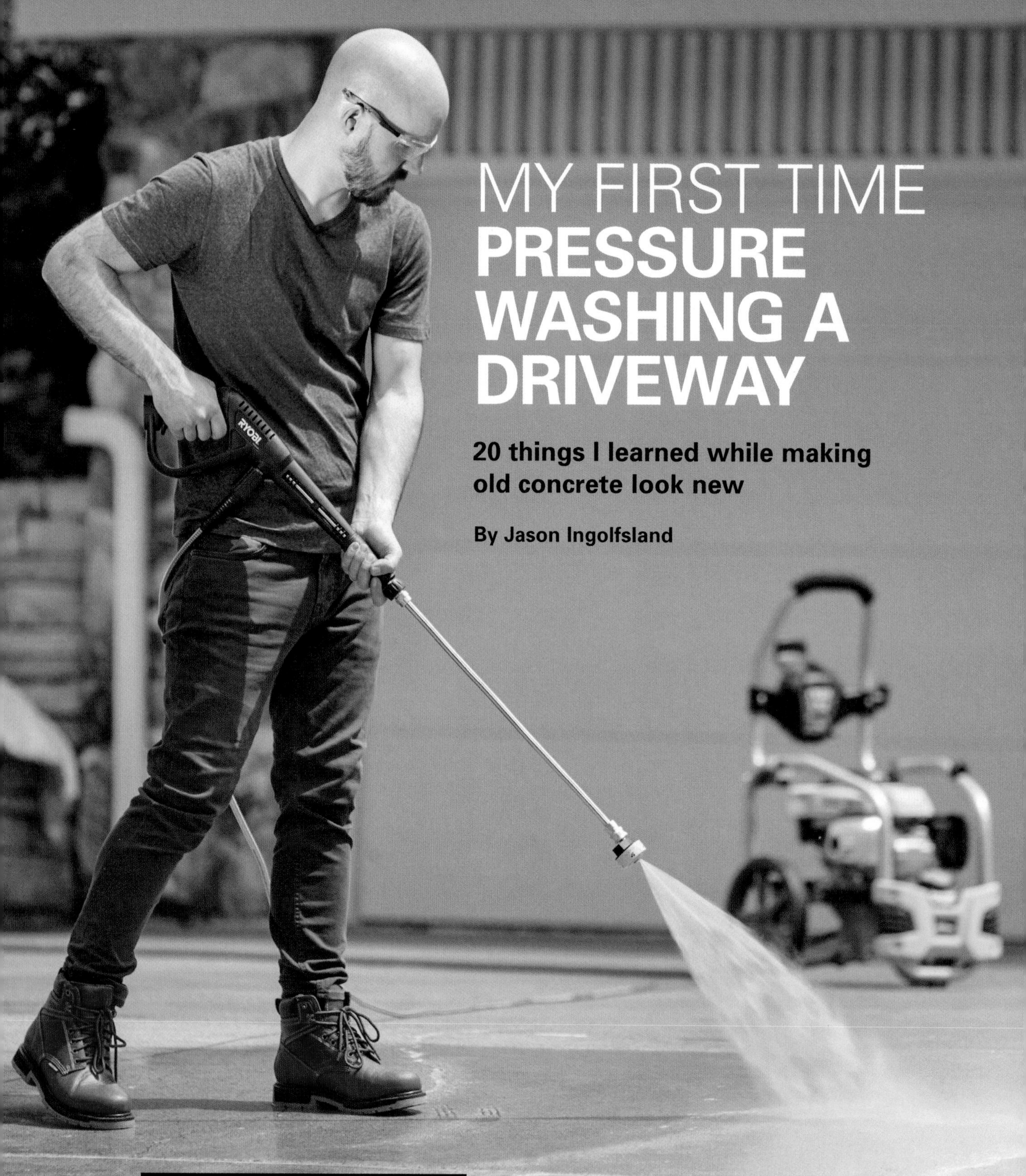

MY FIRST TIME PRESSURE WASHING A DRIVEWAY

20 things I learned while making old concrete look new

By Jason Ingolfsland

MEET AN EXPERT

Vincent R. Christofora Jr. has been a general contractor for 20 years. He's experienced in all kinds of projects, including landscaping, plumbing and wastewater collection systems.

With all the tools, nozzles, psi ratings and equipment, pressure-washing can be intimidating. But it was easier than I thought it would be. With advice from an expert and a little experimenting, I was able to make my driveway look like new in an afternoon. So, whether you want to extend its life or add a little curb appeal, here are some tips to get your driveway clean in no time.

Time it right

Pressure washers use a lot of water. If your water is supplied by a well, it's best to tackle this job when other water use is light. You don't want to deplete your well on laundry day or when you have a house full of guests. And if you're in a drought, you may want to postpone for a few months.

Tarp your plants

Concrete detergent can harm plants; before you begin pressure washing, cover them with tarps. I used canvas drop cloths, but they can be expensive. For a cheap, lightweight option, use a roll of painter's plastic. Remove the tarps as soon as possible to avoid overheating the plants.

Blow away debris

Moving piles of debris with a pressure washer is a waste of time and water. Instead, use a leaf blower to clear away smaller debris like leaves, rocks, sticks and mulch. You can use a broom, but a leaf blower is faster and easier. Don't rush this step, and clear as much as possible.

Wear safety gear

Pressure washers are loud, the water and other debris can splash back in your face, and you'll be stepping around slick, soapy water. Always wear safety glasses, hearing protection and close-toe shoes with good traction. A powerful pressure washer can actually cut skin. Use it with caution, and keep it away from children.

Bigger is faster

The greater the pressure washer's psi rating, the faster the cleaning job. I tested three pressure washers: 1,600, 2,300 and 3,100 psi. There's no doubt that electric pressure washers from 1,300 to 2,300 psi can wash a concrete driveway, but it'll take longer. If you have a large driveway with lots of stains, you'll want more power to do the job faster. I chose the 3,100-psi gas pressure washer and cut the job time in half.

Purge the hose

Once you've connected the garden hose from the spigot to the pressure washer, don't be too eager to turn on the pressure washer. Instead, squeeze the trigger for roughly 30 seconds until a nice, steady stream comes out. This releases the air from the hose and preps the machine for a strong blast.

Choose the right nozzle

Nozzles are calibrated in degrees, and the lower the number, the narrower and more powerful the stream. I experimented with various nozzles and settled on three: For dousing the concrete with detergent, a 65-degree worked well. For the actual cleaning, a 25-degree was fastest. For tough areas, I used a 15-degree nozzle. Pick up a 5-in-1 dial nozzle (about $25 at home centers) to make changes quick and easy.

5-in-1 dial nozzle

Concrete under the gun

You would never use a 0-degree nozzle to wash concrete, but I couldn't resist giving it a try. I used a 3,100-psi gas pressure washer and placed a 0-degree nozzle just a few inches from the concrete. In seconds, I carved a zigzag line with ease. After 45 seconds, the pressure washer left a small crater. Pressure washers can deeply damage concrete, but it'll take some effort. In normal circumstances, all you really need to worry about is light surface etching.

Experiment on a less visible spot

If you hold the nozzle too close to the driveway, the pressure can etch the concrete surface. The distance depends on the power of your pressure washer and the nozzle you're using. Try experimenting on an inconspicuous spot and see how close you can get without damaging the concrete.

Wash other surfaces first

Plan ahead and work from top to bottom. If your roof, siding and retaining walls need to be washed, do them first. Otherwise, dirty water will run off those surfaces and ruin your clean driveway.

Use a detergent

Concrete detergent is incredibly effective. I tried pressure washing without it, and the result didn't come close. It helps remove stubborn oil, paint and dirt stains. I used Zep Driveway & Concrete Pressure Wash detergent, but many great options are available. New pressure washers often include a soap tank to apply the detergent. Wave the wand back and forth roughly 8 in. off the surface to create a nice lather. Let it sit for 10 minutes and then wash. Don't pour bleach or other chemicals into your pressure washer soap tank.

Read the detergent instructions

Concrete detergent is a powerful chemical—if you don't use it correctly, it could ruin your driveway. Used at full strength, it can leave ugly white spots or streaks.

Spot-treat stains

Before you clean the entire surface, spot-treat the oil stains. I saturated these stains with diluted concrete detergent solution from a spray bottle. Let the soap sit for 10 minutes, then rinse with the pressure washer. Some stains are tough to remove—paint stains clean up quickly, but oil and rust stains take longer. If your stain isn't disappearing, treat it a few more times with a less diluted solution.

Start at the top

Start at the high end of your driveway and work your way down. You don't want dirty water running over the places you just cleaned. That might sound obvious, but it's easy to start at the bottom without thinking about it. Also, be sure to park the pressure washer near the high spot so you're dragging the hose behind you, rather than constantly kicking it out of your way.

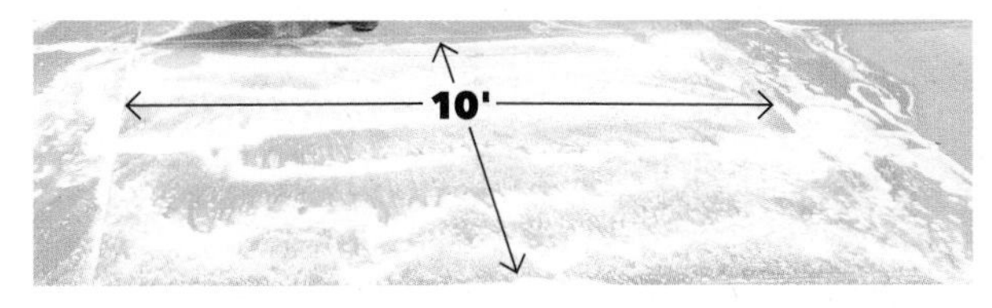

Work in small sections

If you spray your entire driveway with soap all at once, it'll settle and dry before you can wash it off, which could leave white stains and streaks. Instead, soap and wash in 10 x 10-ft. sections. On my driveway, I found the joints in the concrete to be a natural guide.

Move toward the edges

Whether you're applying the soap or washing, start at the center of the driveway and work your way toward the edge. If you're using a nozzle, sweep the water back and forth.

Extend your reach

Pressure washers are no fun to lug around. Do yourself a favor and buy a pressure washer extension hose. They come in 25-ft. and 50-ft. lengths ($45 to $75). I attached a 50-ft. hose to the 25-ft. hose that came with the machine. Be sure the coupler you choose is compatible with your equipment.

Get a surface cleaner

It takes a lot of time and effort to clean a driveway with a nozzle. You can cut both in half by using a pressure washer surface cleaner. And they're affordable, ranging from $20 to $90. The one I used cost $88 online and was worth every penny. As you use it, pull it from side to side rather than pushing it. Also, hold the wand upright to avoid putting pressure on your back.

Wash edges with a nozzle

The surface cleaner doesn't clean the edges along retaining walls, posts or other structures, so you have to clean those with a nozzle. Use a 25-degree nozzle for deep cleaning and a 40-degree nozzle for rinsing away standing water.

Rinse off your plants

Even with a tarp, soap can still find its way onto your plants. The plants also can absorb the soapy runoff at the roots. When you're finished pressure washing, rinse the plants around your driveway with a garden hose.

Protect your driveway with a sealant

After you've done the work to clean your driveway, consider sealing it. A good sealer will protect your driveway, help it last longer and make future cleaning much easier. Be sure the driveway is dry before you begin.

For more information, search for "concrete sealer" at familyhandyman.com.

Best Pro Tips

EXPERT ADVICE FROM THE JOB SITE

ROOF TEAR-OFF

Simplify an ugly job

If you're a roofer, you have your routine perfected already. But for the rest of us—who tear off asphalt shingles only occasionally—here's a primer on how to do it quickly, safely and right.

Roof safety is essential!

Working on a roof is dangerous, so take precautions.

- Set roof jacks ($11 each) and a 2x10 about 3 ft. up from the roof edge (**Photo 1**).
- Wear a safety harness ($150; **Photo 2**), which you can buy at safety equipment stores and at some roofing suppliers and home centers.
- Wear soft rubber-soled shoes for traction, long pants, work gloves and safety glasses.

Prep for the tear-off

Doing a little prep work on the ground will keep nails and other debris out of the grass and flower beds, reduce cleanup time and preserve the landscaping. Place plywood over the air conditioner (be sure the power to it is turned off) and over doors or windows near the spot where you'll be tossing the debris off the roof. Then cover plants, shrubs, grass and other areas around the house with tarps to vastly simplify cleanup.

Rent a trash container (a 20-cu.-yd. size will handle most roofs and costs $200 to $300). If possible, have it dropped next to the house so you can easily throw old shingles directly into it from the roof.

For safety and better footing, nail the roof jacks below the area you intend to strip first (**Photo 1**). Buy the adjustable type designed to hold a 2x10 board. Space the jacks no more than 4 ft. apart. Fasten each with at least three 16d nails driven through the roof sheathing into a rafter.

Strip the roof

Start the tear-off at the section farthest from the trash container. Standing at the peak, use a garden fork or a notched roofing shovel to tear away the ridge caps and the top courses of shingles (**Photo 3**). Forks and roofing shovels are available at roofing and home centers, starting at $26. Some roofers prefer forks because they don't get caught on nails, making it easier and faster to remove the shingles. Others like the shovels because they pull out more nails with the shingles.

Work the fork under the ridge caps, prying them loose. As they come loose, allow them to slide down to the roof jacks. Or, if they don't slide down the roof, carry them to the edge of the roof and throw them into the trash container. Once the ridge caps are gone, slide the fork under the shingles and felt paper and pry the shingles up. Some nails will come up with the shingles. Others won't. Ignore them for now.

Remove shingles in a 2- to 3-ft.-wide section as you work down the roof (**Photo 4**). The shingles will roll up like a ball in front of the fork. Push the shingles down to the roof jacks. Continue tearing off the shingles and underlayment until you reach the roof jacks, then start over at the top of the roof.

Into the trash

As the old roofing material piles up at the roof jacks, carry it to the edge of the roof and toss it into the trash container below (**Photo 5**). If you couldn't get the trash container close to the house, throw the shingles onto a tarp on the ground. Make the pile in a flat area away from flowers and shrubs.

Shingles are heavy. They usually come off in clumps. If you're peeling off two or more layers of shingles, even a small section will be heavy. You may have to pull the shingles apart to make them light enough to carry. Rolling the shingles and underlayment into a ball will also make them easier to handle.

Use care at roof penetrations

Slow down and work carefully near chimneys, skylights, dormers or an exterior wall. While it's usually best to replace metal flashing, sometimes it's better to reuse difficult-to-replace types if they're in good shape. But if you see rust and cracks in the metal, replace it. Damaged metal won't last as long as your new roof.

If you're keeping the old metal flashing, remove nails and bend it upward off the shingles with a pry bar (**Photo 6**). Be careful not to damage the flashing. Once it's out of the way, pull any nails and remove any shingles and underlayment that are underneath. Do the same with step flashing (the flashing interwoven with the shingles) where the roof abuts a wall (**Photo 7**).

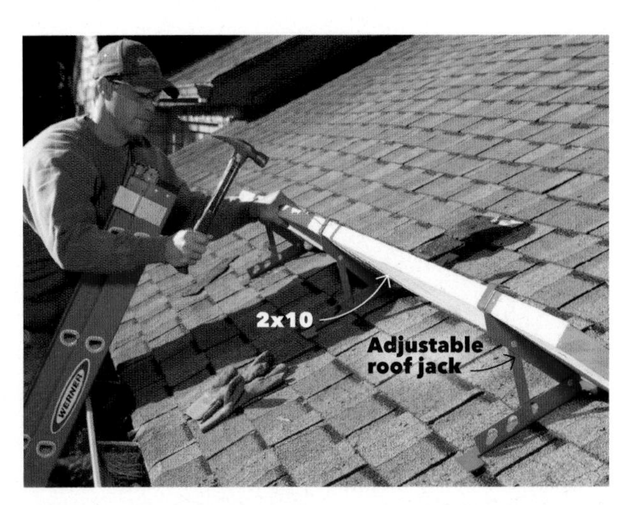

1 Start with roof jacks. Nail roof jacks to the rafters and then nail on a 2x10 to prevent you—and the shingles—from sliding off the roof.

2 Harness up! Use a safety harness system to prevent falls. Wear boots or shoes with soft rubber soles for a good grip and long pants to protect against the skin-scraping shingles.

3 Attack the ridge first. Tear off the ridge caps so you can work the fork under the shingles near the peak.

EXTERIOR REPAIRS & IMPROVEMENTS

BestProTips

4 Roll downhill. Work from the peak down, tearing off shingles in easy-to-carry sections. Tear off a section all the way down to the roof jacks before returning to the peak.

5 Handle them just once. Throw old shingles directly into the trash container as they pile up at the roof jacks. Dispose of the shingles before the pile gets too large and they slide off the roof.

Tear off shingles along the edge

After stripping the shingles down to the roof jacks, remove the jacks. Work the remaining courses loose with a fork or shovel, but don't pry them completely free or they'll slide off the roof (**Photo 8**).

Loosen the shingles all along the eaves. Then pull off the shingles with your hands, carry them across the roof to the trash container location and throw them in.

Some roofs have a self-stick ice and water barrier installed along the edge. This asphalt membrane usually pulls up with a fork or shovel, but it may require some scraping. If it refuses to come loose, simply leave it and install your new underlayment over it.

If you don't have time before dark to clean the roof and apply underlayment, nail down tarps for the night.

Toss old valley and vent flashing

Pry the flashing in valleys and over plumbing vents last. This flashing usually has the same life span as the shingles, so plan to replace it.

Starting at the top of the valley, slip the fork or a flat bar under the flashing and pry the metal edges loose. Continue working down the valley, lifting up the flashing (**Photo 9**). Pry up and toss out old vent flashing as well (**Photo 10**).

Clean the deck

Once a section has been stripped, go back and pull out protruding nails. Then use a large broom to sweep the roof deck clean (**Photo 11**). Walk carefully. The shingle granules make the sheathing slippery.

When the roof is clean and bare, inspect the sheathing for damage. Rotted areas and broken boards are the most common problems. Cut out and replace damaged sections as needed. Use new sheathing that's the same thickness as the old. When you remove a damaged section, center the cuts over the rafters so you can nail the new sheathing to the rafters. Also keep an eye out for loose roof sheathing that needs renailing.

6 Save special flashings. Pull nails carefully around flashings you plan to reuse. Skylight and chimney flashings are often worth saving if they're in good condition.

7 Go gentle on step flashing. Pull nails from any step flashing you want to save, bend it up slightly and pull out the shingles from underneath.

"Buttoning up" the roof

This is the final prep step before shingling. It consists of installing ice and water barrier ($50 a roll) and underlayment. The underlayment acts as a temporary weather barrier to keep rain out. But it won't stop heavy rain and wind, so once you start a section, always try to flash and shingle it by the end of the day.

Ice and water barrier is used at roof edges and other vulnerable areas. To install it, snap a chalk line 36 in. from the edge of the eaves. If you have gutters, you'll want the ice and water barrier to cover all the gutter flashing that's on the roof (**Photo 12**).

Starting at the rake edge of the roof, align the ice and water barrier with the chalk line. Tack it at the top with staples every few feet. Once the entire section is tacked along the chalk line, lift up the bottom part, peel off the backing, then let it fall back into place. The ice and water barrier will immediately stick to the roof.

Flip the top part of the ice and water barrier back over the bottom section (the staples will easily pop out), peel off the backing, then set it back into place on the roof. Work carefully to avoid wrinkles. They're hard to get out. Move on to the next section of roof edge, overlapping the vertical seams of the ice and water barrier by 6 in.

Add a second course above the first, if required, overlapping the first by 4 in. Also lay the ice and water barrier in valleys and around chimneys, skylights and other roof penetrations.

Then unroll and staple down underlayment over the rest of the roof. Use plenty of staples (5/16 in.) to make the underlayment safer to walk on and keep it from blowing off. This is where the hammer-type stapler ($30) pays off. You can drive a dozen staples in seconds.

9 Trash the valley flashing. Pry up the old flashing in the valleys using a fork. Valley flashing is never worth reusing.

8 Finish up the eaves. Remove the roof jacks and work the shingles loose along the roof edge with a fork. Then pull them off by hand.

10 Pop off vent flashing. Pry flashing loose around vent pipes. Use a pry bar rather than a fork to avoid damaging the pipes. Never reuse vent flashing.

Best Pro Tips

Clean up the area

Before climbing off the roof, clean any debris out of the gutters. You don't want nails and shingle granules pouring out of your downspouts the next time it rains.

Run a broom magnet over the yard to pick up stray nails. You can rent one at tool rental stores for about $15. Make several passes in different directions. Even if you were careful, nails have a way of ending up in the lawn.

11 Sweep and inspect. Sweep the roof clean to avoid slips and falls. Watch for any nails you missed earlier and pull them.

12 Button up. Cover the roof right away to protect against rain. Cover the lower end with self-stick ice and water barrier. Then staple down underlayment to protect the rest of the roof.

Handy Hints®

MINIMIZE CONCRETE DUST

If you've ever mixed bagged concrete, you know what a dusty job it is. You end up wearing and inhaling a lot of concrete mix! Now, I have a helper hold a shop vacuum hose close to the top of the bucket. The vacuum catches a lot of the dust before it goes airborne.

—Ricky Jerrett

6 Outdoor Structures, Landscaping & Gardening

IN THIS CHAPTER

HomeSmarts

KNOWLEDGE YOU NEED TO BE A BETTER HOMEOWNER

SNOW BLOWER **SMARTS**

A shear pin is a specially designed bolt that connects the auger assembly to the drive shaft on a snow blower. Its purpose is to break before the auger, drive shaft or gears get damaged when you plow into a rock, stick or other object buried in the snow. Here's how to avoid blowing a shear pin in the first place, and what to do if it happens.

■ Police your driveway: Just before the snow flies, inspect areas where you clear snow. Pick up sticks, rocks, garden hoses and anything that can get drawn into the auger.

■ Pick up your newspapers: Water-soaked frozen newspapers are the No. 1 shear pin killer. Don't let them lie around to become buried in the snow.

■ Beware of frozen slush in car wheel wells: Slush from the road builds up in wheel wells and falls off in big chunks. These frozen chunks are like rocks, and they'll easily take out a shear pin. Shovel them out of the driveway before starting the snow blower.

■ Don't substitute bolts for shear pins; regular steel bolts aren't designed to break. They won't break, leaving the auger and gearbox to take the hit.

■ Buy an extra set: Take a shear pin from your blower to the hardware store and buy a few matching ones. That'll save you a trip in the middle of a blizzard. (Snow blowers can have more than one pin.)

■ Drive out broken pins: Broken pins sometimes get stuck inside the drive shaft. If so, just drive them out with a pin punch.

—Travis Larson
Senior Editor

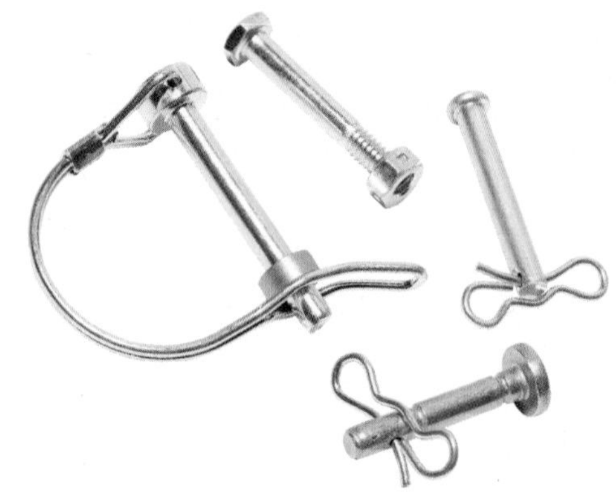

Get more great outdoor and yard advice at lawncare.familyhandyman.com

You can sharpen a mower blade with a file, a rotary tool or a bench grinder, but an angle grinder makes it fast and easy.

First, disconnect the spark plug wire (Photo 1). Next, seal the gas cap vent hole by putting a piece of plastic under the gas cap. Tip the mower with the carburetor facing up.

Clamp a 2x4 block to the mower deck to keep the blade from turning while you loosen it. Mark the "grass side" of the blade so you don't reinstall it upside down. Loosen the blade nut (**Photo 2**). If it's stubborn, use a breaker bar, or soak it with penetrating oil for a half hour and try again.

Clamp the blade securely in a vise or to your workbench. Wear gloves, a face shield, hearing protection and a long-sleeve shirt. Before you start grinding, hold the grinder against the blade and tip it to match the blade's bevel.Maintain this angle as you grind. Keep the grinder moving, using only light pressure so you don't overheat the blade or grind off too much (**Photo 3**). If you overheat the metal, it'll turn dark blue or black and become brittle, and it won't hold an edge. Remove any nicks and dents and create an edge that's about as sharp as a butter knife. A razor-sharp edge dulls quickly and chips easily.

1 Disconnect the spark plug. Pull the wire from the spark plug. Remove the gas cap, put a piece of plastic over the opening and replace the cap. This will help prevent gas spills when you flip the mower to access the blade.

2 Secure the blade. Clamp a block to the lawn mower skirt to stop the blade from spinning while you unscrew the nut. Use the longest wrench you can find to loosen the nut. It's likely to be very tight.

3 Grind the blade. Grind the blade carefully with an angle grinder to remove nicks and dents and restore the edge. Make several light passes to avoid overheating the blade.

4 Check the balance. Hang the blade on a nail after sharpening both edges. If it's unbalanced, mark the heavy side. Grind a little off the heavy side and hang the blade on the nail to recheck it. Repeat until the blade hangs level.

Make several passes across the edge with the grinder, checking your progress frequently. Don't grind off more than necessary. If your blade has a lot of nicks and gouges, start by holding the grinder at a right angle to the blade and grinding the edge of the blade flat to remove the nicks. Use light pressure and move quickly. It's easy to burn the thin edge. After you've removed the nicks, go back to grinding at the correct blade angle.

If your blade has deep nicks or is cracked, bent or worn thin, don't sharpen it; buy a new one. Take the old blade with you to get an exact match.

Be sure to grind away the same amount of metal from both sides so the blade stays balanced. You can buy a blade-balancing cone or just hang the blade on a nail (**Photo 4**). To correct an unbalanced blade, grind a little metal from the blunt end of the heavy side until it balances on the nail. Reinstall the blade with the marked side toward you and tighten the nut securely. Now you're ready to mow.

BACKYARD **SWING**

Easy enough for a beginner, comfortable enough for a long perch

By Gary Wentz

A seat like this is usually called a "porch swing," and a porch certainly is a good location for it. But a hanging seat can go just about anywhere; unlike a chair, it doesn't require a firm, flat surface beneath it. If you don't have a suitable ceiling or tree to support a swing, go to familyhandyman.com and search for "arbor" to see other options.

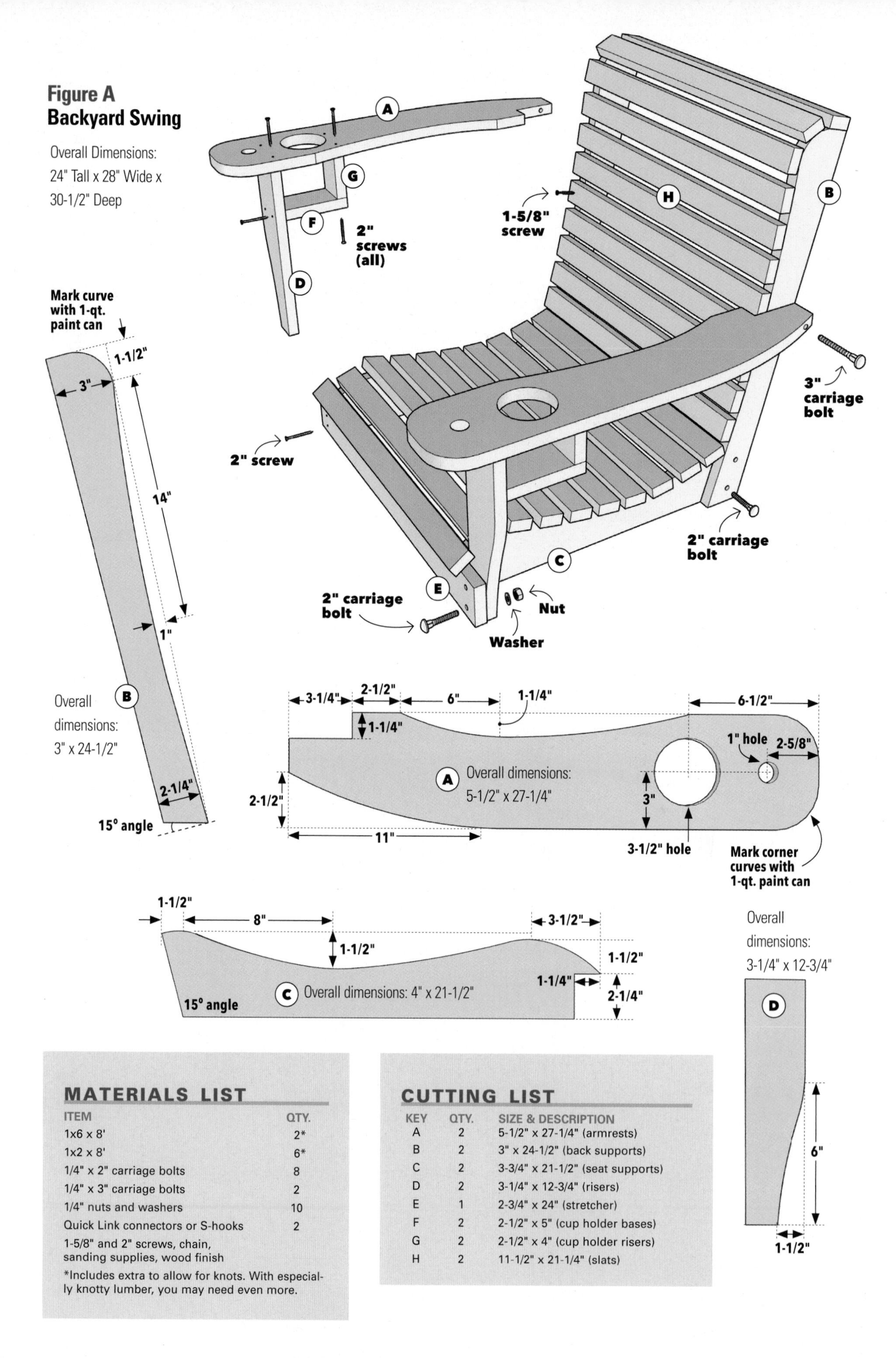

MATERIALS LIST

ITEM	QTY.
1x6 x 8'	2*
1x2 x 8'	6*
1/4" x 2" carriage bolts	8
1/4" x 3" carriage bolts	2
1/4" nuts and washers	10
Quick Link connectors or S-hooks	2
1-5/8" and 2" screws, chain, sanding supplies, wood finish	

*Includes extra to allow for knots. With especially knotty lumber, you may need even more.

CUTTING LIST

KEY	QTY.	SIZE & DESCRIPTION
A	2	5-1/2" x 27-1/4" (armrests)
B	2	3" x 24-1/2" (back supports)
C	2	3-3/4" x 21-1/2" (seat supports)
D	2	3-1/4" x 12-3/4" (risers)
E	1	2-3/4" x 24" (stretcher)
F	2	2-1/2" x 5" (cup holder bases)
G	2	2-1/2" x 4" (cup holder risers)
H	2	11-1/2" x 21-1/4" (slats)

Tools and materials

This swing design is especially forgiving. If your cuts are slightly inaccurate or not quite straight, the swing will still turn out just fine. So, although a table saw, miter saw and band saw are best for this project, you could do it all with only a jigsaw.

The swing shown here is made from cedar, but you could use treated lumber instead. Either material will contain some large knots, which can look bad and create weak spots. Avoid them when cutting parts (**Photo 1**). The Materials List includes 1x2s, but if you have a table saw, you'll get better material by ripping 1x2s from wider boards. Some stores carry cedar that's 7/8 in. thick instead of 3/4 in. If you use 7/8-in. stock, make the stretcher (E) 23-3/4 in. long instead of 24 in.

We chose heavy 5/16-in. yellow zinc-coated chain, but any chain rated for 250 lbs. or more will work. Some stores will cut chain to length for you. Two Quick Link connectors or S-hooks join the front and back chains to the upper chains—they make adjustments and removing the swing easy.

Think ahead when working with cedar

Cedar lumber usually has one smooth side and one rough side. So, when you're making pairs of parts, it's easy to end up with a mismatch: one part with the smooth side visible, the other with the rough.

Watch the video
This swing was originally designed and built by April Wilkerson. To see how she made this swing and others, go to wilkerdos.com and search for "porch swing." April also sells templates ($20) for marking the curved parts—fast, no-fuss and perfect.

DANG! One armrest is smooth and one is rough.

WHAT IT TAKES
TIME: 1 day
COST: $65
SKILL: Beginner
TOOLS: Basic hand tools, drill, jigsaw

How to avoid a mismatch: When using one part to mark its twin, place the smooth sides face to face.

1 **Select the best sections.** Cut the large parts (A through E) from your best-looking wood and avoid large knots, which create weak spots.

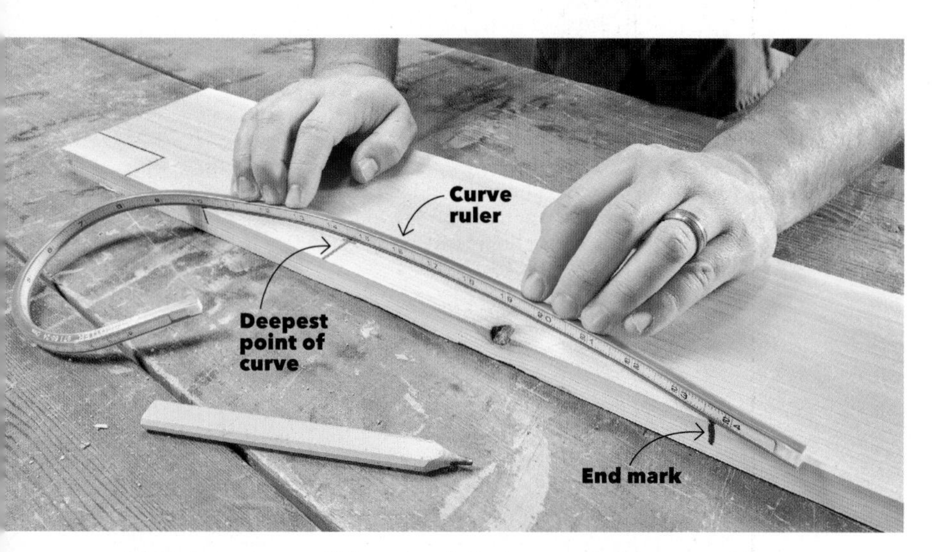

2 **Mark the curves.** Using a bendable "curve ruler" is one good way to mark curves. Just bend the ruler, aligning it with the ends and deepest point of the curve. Cut one of each part, then use those as templates for the twin parts.

3 **Gang-sand the curves.** Cut the curved parts with a jigsaw or band saw, then clamp the pairs together and smooth the edges with a belt sander or random orbital sander. A sanding drum quickly smooths the drink-holder cutout.

Don't sweat the curves

This swing contains eight curved parts (A, B, C, D). Curved parts always make projects a bit harder, but don't be intimidated. The curves don't have to be precise. As long as they're similar to the curves detailed in **Figure A**, you'll get a comfortable, attractive swing.

There are lots of ways to mark out curved cuts. A "curve ruler" ($8 online) is a good option for this project. Mark the ends and height of the curve (see **Figure A**). Bend the ruler so it aligns with the marks and holds that shape (**Photo 2**). After marking and cutting the curved parts, clamp them together for sanding (**Photo 3**). This ensures the parts will be identical.

Sand and assemble

Ease the sharp edges of the parts by sanding or by using a router. A 1/4-in. round-over bit is one good option. Then sand all the parts before assembly; that's a lot easier than sanding afterward. You can prefinish all the parts or apply a finish after assembly. Deck stain or spar urethane is a good choice for exterior wood.

Begin assembly by bolting the risers (D) to the stretcher (E). Drill 1/4-in. holes, tap the lower carriage bolts into place and secure them with washers and nuts. Install the upper carriage bolts in the same way, but run the bolt through the chain. Next, bolt the back supports (B) to the seat supports (C). Join the three assemblies by driving screws through the stretcher and into the seat supports.

Now that the frame of the swing is complete, add the slats (H). Starting at the front of the seat, screw the first slat into place. Drill pilot holes to avoid splitting the wood. Then install a slat at the back of the seat. To fill in the remaining space, continue from back to front, positioning slats with a 3/8-in.-thick spacer (**Photo 4**).

Before fastening the last four slats, lay them out and check the spacing. You'll have to cut one slat to fit between the risers. You may need to increase or decrease the spacing slightly for a consistent look. Add the back slats, working up from the bottom and again adjusting the spacing of the last few slats. To complete the swing, screw the armrests (A) to the risers (D). Then, with the swing on a level surface, level and bolt on the armrests and chain (**Photo 5**).

Hang it up!

If you want the seat to swing easily from side to side—not just back and forth—fasten the tops of the upper chains about 22 in. apart. If you want to reduce side-to-side movement, space the upper chains 28 in. apart or more. Be sure to leave the upper chains a little long so you can lower the swing if desired. You'll also want to adjust the tilt of the swing for comfort; that's as easy as moving the Quick Link connectors or S-hooks to raise or lower the back of the swing.

4 Assemble the seat. Assemble the seat frame as shown in **Figure A**. Add the seat slats, using blocks to position them. Space the back slats in the same way.

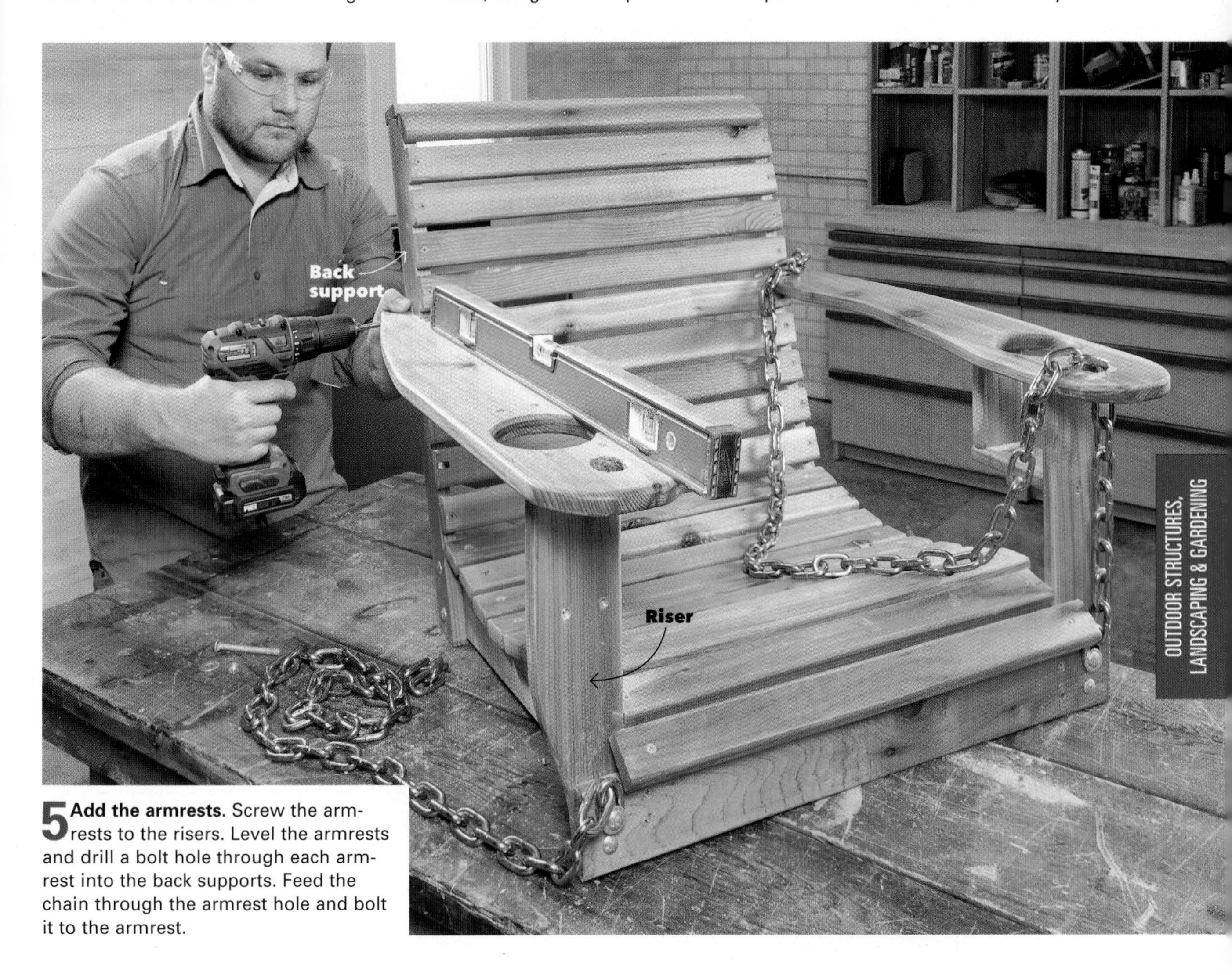

5 Add the armrests. Screw the armrests to the risers. Level the armrests and drill a bolt hole through each armrest into the back supports. Feed the chain through the armrest hole and bolt it to the armrest.

OUTDOOR LIVING

A platform deck is the easiest way to add space

By Mike Berner

If you want to expand your outdoor living space, a platform deck might be your best option. Since it's not connected to a house, it can go anywhere in your yard and doesn't require deep footings. Because it rises just inches above ground, it doesn't need stairs or railings. All together, these factors make it a cost-cutting, labor-saving alternative to standard decks and patios. It's simple, too. If you have a little building experience, you can do it in a weekend!

MIKE BERNER IS AN EDITOR AT *FAMILY HANDYMAN,* A CARPENTER AND A WOODWORKER.

JAKE AND JENNA PROVIDED THE BACKYARD, HARD WORK AND WARM HOSPITALITY FOR THIS PROJECT.

From barren space to favorite place

Four years ago, Jenna and Jake bought a small house and got busy turning it into a home. So far, they've built a garage and a chicken coop from the ground up and fixed up the front porch after Hurricane Irma toppled a tree onto the house. Like a lot of homeowners, they wanted more living space, but weren't ready to build an addition. The solution was in a neglected corner of their backyard—the perfect spot for an outdoor living room based on a simple platform deck. I hopped a plane to Florida to help them build it. Three days later we were sitting on this finished deck, happily complaining about our sore muscles.

Mike Berner

Start with a plan

You can follow our plan (see p. 215) or create your own. Here are some things to keep in mind:

- A platform deck can be any shape, but basic rectangles are easiest. The fireplace notch in the corner of our deck made the whole structure a bit more complicated.
- Your deck can be any size. But if you're using 2x6 framing material as we did, place footings no more than 5 ft. 11 in. apart, and limit joist length to no more than 6 ft. 8 in.
- This deck is "picture framed" (see **Photo 11**). The frame hides the cut ends of the decking but also adds some labor, such as miter cuts and blocking to support the decking. A simpler approach is to raise the fascia so it covers the ends of the decking.
- The decking makes up most of the cost. The total materials bill for this deck was about $5,000. We chose Fiberon's Horizon decking (fiberondecking.com) because it's super tough, beautiful and will stay beautiful with just occasional cleaning. Inexpensive options such as pressure-treated decking could cut the total cost in half, but they will require refinishing every few years.

A simplified layout method

The standard way to position deck footings involves a maze of stakes and strings, endless measurements and lots of head-scratching. Instead, Jake and I assembled the perimeter (or "rim") of the deck, squared and braced it (**Photo 1**). Then we used it as a template to mark the footing locations (**Photo 2**). No strings, no guessing, and we had everything laid out and ready for digging in less than an hour.

Then we moved the (heavy!) rim aside and got to work digging the footing holes (**Photo 3**). I was anticipating lots of roots in the sandy Florida soil, but the digging was easy. We made sure the holes were deep enough to hide our footings and wide enough for us to be able to shift them to catch the frame when we moved it back into place.

PHOTOS: TINA SARGEANT

1 Build and square the rim. Assemble the rim joists, which form the perimeter of the deck, and add the beam. Take diagonal measurements to square the rim, then brace it with 2x4s. We added an extra 2x4 to act as a handle for moving the rim later.

2 Mark the footing locations. Position the rim and then mark for the footing holes with spray paint. We placed footings about 5 ft. apart and positioned them so they wouldn't interfere with joist installation later.

Easy, adjustable footings

You may be able to buy precast footings, but we were unable to find any in the area. Being DIYers, we made our own by pouring concrete into 12 x 12-in. cardboard boxes ($2 at home centers). Later, we drilled holes in the concrete to accept the adjustable post bases (**Photo 4**).

Once it's in place, the post base is adjustable with the turn of a nut. This allows you to speed through setting the footings instead of leveling them all. Before setting the rim onto the post bases, we lined up the brackets and made sure the beam and opposite rim joist were parallel (**Photo 5**). We moved the rim back into place and shifted the blocks to fit the frame into the post bases (**Photo 6**).

3 Dig the footing holes. Make the holes about 10 in. deep and a couple inches oversized so you can adjust the location of the footing. Add 2 in. of gravel and set the footing in the hole.

4 Insert the post bases. Place the post bases in the hole in the footings. Start with bases adjusted to their lowest height. Later, you'll turn the nut to raise or lower the bracket.

5 Line up the footings. Pick out straight boards to line up the brackets. Make sure the footings form straight lines and that the rows of footings are parallel to one another.

6 Set the rim onto the footings. With a few strong helpers, move the rim back into place. Lift the frame and move the footings so the framing falls into the brackets.

7 Double up the rim. Nail on the outer rim joists. Doubling up the rim will make the deck very sturdy. You may need to shift the footing slightly to fit.

Complete the rim

With the tricky parts of the job done, Jake, Jenna and I doubled up the rim by adding an outer rim joist that overlaps the joints of the inner rim joists (**Photo 7**). A cutting list is helpful, but in this situation, I always measure and cut each piece to fit. We fastened the outer rim to the inner rim with three nails every 12 in. It was Jake's first time using a framing nailer, and the first few squeezes of the trigger sent two or three nails in at once. After I showed him how to avoid doing this, he made sure Jenna had a turn. As all my experience teaching women and girls would have predicted, Jenna outdid Jake and nailed off the rest of the outer rim in perfect rows with no misfires. They both learned that a framing nailer isn't as intimidating as it looks.

Level the rim

You can level a deck with a standard level or a high-tech laser level. But I went low-tech with a water level, which is fast, simple and super accurate. We used a store-bought version that connects to a garden hose ($12 online), but any type of clear tubing will work. To check for level, set the water line at one corner of the rim and tack the tube into place. Then move the other end of the tube from point to point, raising or lowering the post bases (**Photo 8**).

8 Level the rim. Be sure the framing is level before adding the joists. We used a "water level," which is clear tubing connected to the ends of a garden hose. Mount one end on a corner of the rim, then check the height of the water to level the other corners. Once it's level, nail the brackets to the rim joists.

9 Tack the joists into place. Fasten each joist end with a screw driven at an angle. The screw will hold the joist in position so you can install joist hangers, which provide the real support.

10 Add joist hangers. Make sure the joist hangers hug the joists and that all nail holes are filled. A "positive placement" nail gun makes quick work of this job and saves your elbow.

11 Picture-frame the deck. Install a perimeter frame to hide the cut ends of the decking. Miter these deck boards and fasten them with screws. You'll have to leave gaps for expansion; check the decking manufacturer's instructions.

12 Attach the decking. We went with hidden fasteners for our decking. These clips fit into grooves and are screwed to the joists.

Hang the joists

Composite decking isn't as rigid as wood, so we placed joists every 12 in. instead of the standard 16 in. Jenna lined up the joists while I toe-screwed them from the top (**Photo 9**). It's easiest to start the screws into the joists before you hold the joists in place. Then I attached the joist hangers with a positive placement nailer (**Photo 10**). To support the picture-frame decking, we added an extra joist about 3 in. inside the rim joist and blocking every 16 in. in between.

Deck it!

To mark the picture frame, we snapped chalk lines 3-1/2 in. from the outer edge of the rim. This accounts for 3/4-in.-thick fascia and allows the decking to overhang the fascia by 1-1/4 in. Taking measurements from the intersections of the chalk lines, we mitered the boards and placed them around the perimeter (**Photo 11**).

When the picture frame is in place, you can start filling in the deck boards. We used hidden fasteners (**Photo 12**). During my planning, I had carefully calculated the widths and spacing of the deck boards so they would fit perfectly inside the picture frame. But when Jake and I got to the last few boards, I realized we were going to end up about 1/2 in. past our picture frame. After I got over the shame, we fired up the table saw and cut 1/2 in. off the width of the board.

Finish up with fascia

Before we could enjoy the deck, we needed to install the fascia board to cover the rim joists. Fascia is installed with mitered corners with a slight gap in between and fastened with the same type of composite screws we used on the picture-frame boards (**Photo 13**). With an extra hand, installing these was a snap.

When everything was put together, we relaxed and celebrated a job well done. In true DIY fashion, Jake wouldn't let me throw anything away—he plans to use some decking cutoffs to build a tabletop.

Figure A
Platform Deck

Overall Dimensions:
16' Long x 12' Wide

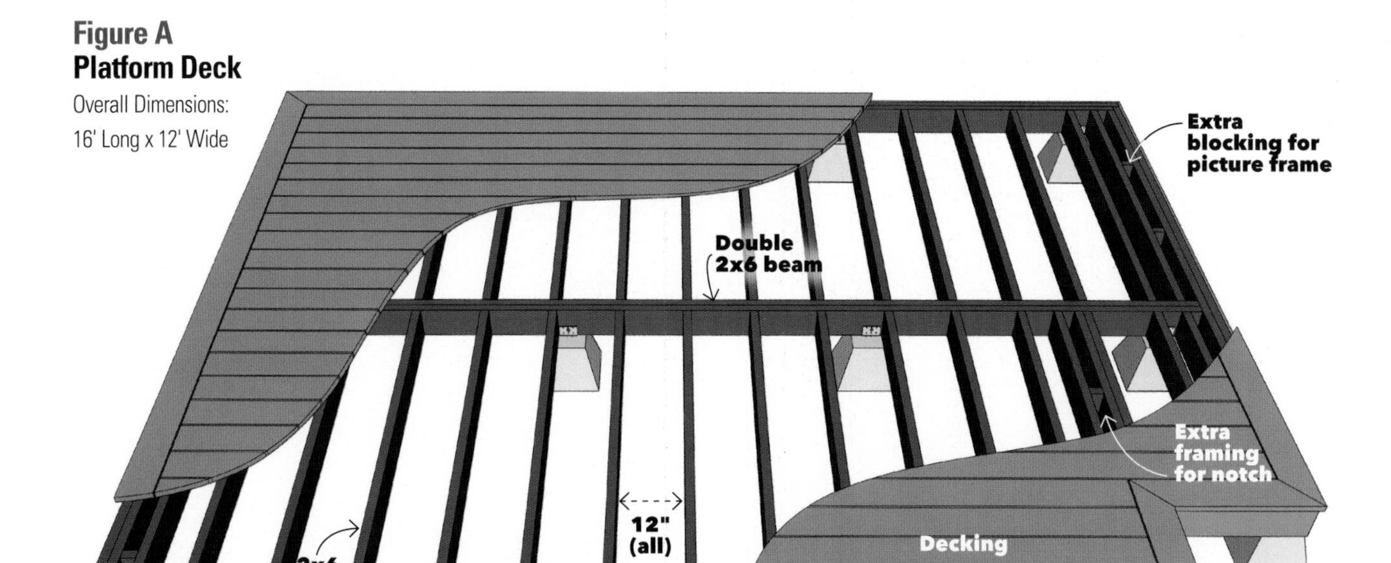

MATERIALS LIST

ITEM	QTY.
DIY FOOTINGS	
60-lb. bags of concrete mix	20
12" x 12" cardboard boxes	20
Adjustable post bases (Simpson EPB44PHDG)	13
FRAMING	
2x6 x 16' pressure-treated lumber	6
2x6 x 12' pressure-treated lumber	21
DECKING	
1x6 x 16' grooved deck boards	23
1x6 x 20' solid deck boards	4
3/4" x 12" x 12' fascia boards	5
HARDWARE	
2x6 joist hangers	64
2x6 double joist hangers	3
3x3 inside corner plates	5
3-1/8" ACQ framing nails	1 box
1-1/2" positive placement nails	1 box
3-1/8" construction screws	1 box
Hidden fasteners system	

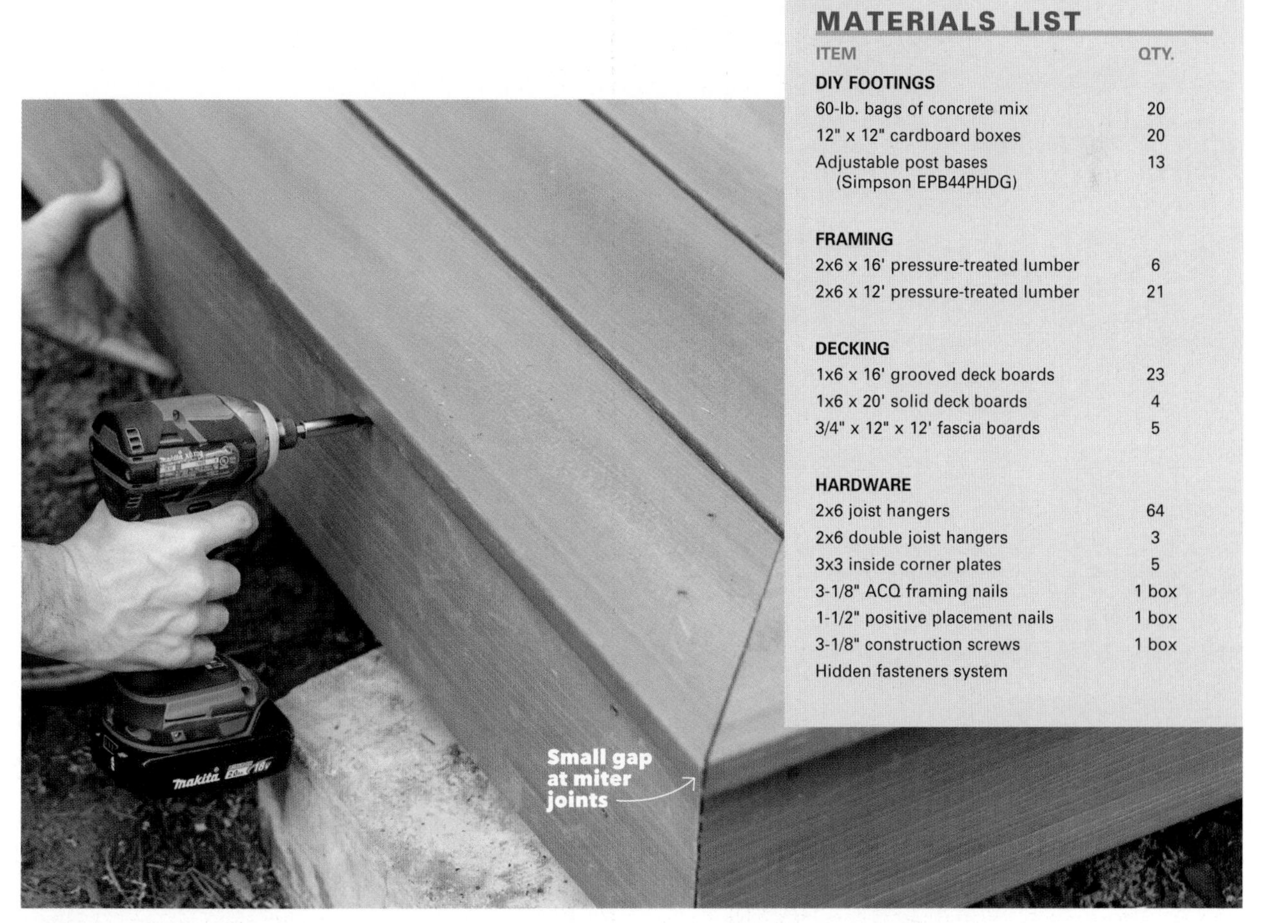

13 Finish with the fascia. Cover the rim joists with a fascia that matches the decking. Ours was 12 in. wide, so we had to cut each board to fit between the decking and the ground.

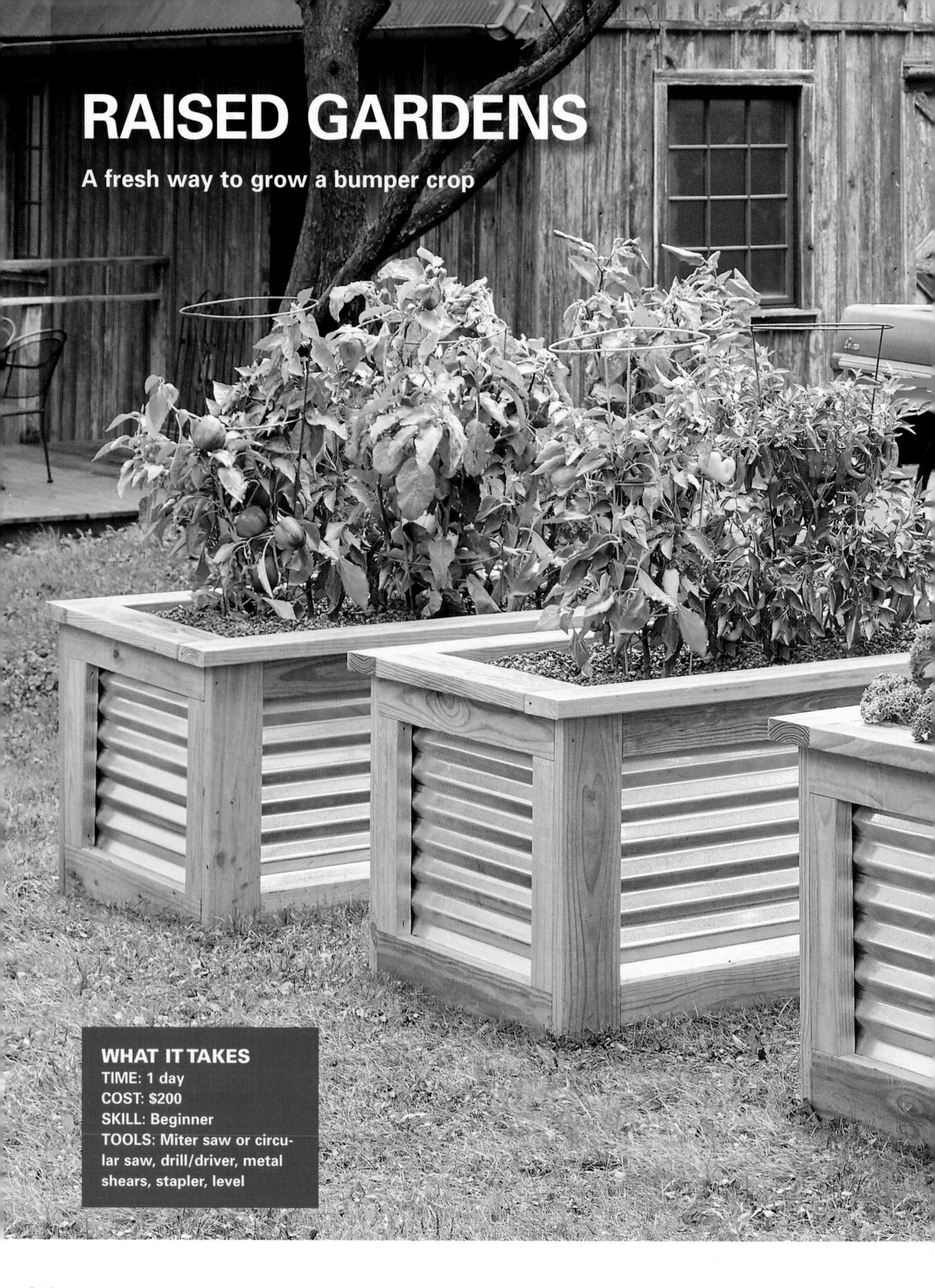

RAISED GARDENS

A fresh way to grow a bumper crop

WHAT IT TAKES

TIME: 1 day

COST: $200

SKILL: Beginner

TOOLS: Miter saw or circular saw, drill/driver, metal shears, stapler, level

FORD

Accessorize it! Easy add-on options:

1 Screen out critters. Simple arched ribs made from CPVC pipe let you protect your crop from hungry birds and beasts, especially deer!

2 Extend the season. Those same ribs can support plastic sheathing. This creates a "cold frame," allowing you to start plants earlier in spring and protect them against frost in autumn.

3 Water once a month. Fill a buried reservoir that keeps soil moist for weeks. For details on how to add this feature to any raised planter, search for "self watering" at familyhandyman.com.

Some gardeners prefer traditional ground-level gardening, but not the ones we've been hearing from in recent years. Those who've made the switch love raised garden planters and won't go back.

The list of reasons is long, but these are the main advantages:

- Tending raised plants is a lot easier on the back and knees.
- You can fill planters with top-quality soil for more productivity in a smaller space.
- Raised beds curtail creeping weeds and drifting seeds.
- The height discourages pests, especially rabbits.

To build on these advantages, we designed our own raised planter. On the outside, it looks a lot like others. But we engineered ours for longevity and simple construction. And we added some optional improvements to make an even better home for your vegetables.

Gathering materials

Everything you need is available at home centers for about $200 per planter. We chose pressure-treated lumber that's cedar tone rather than green. Take the time to select straight, good-looking lumber. When you get it home, cover it with plastic to slow its drying. Pressure-treated lumber tends to warp badly as it dries; much better to let it dry after assembly when the parts are fastened together.

MEET AN EXPERT

Tom Dvorak is an engineer and carpenter who is also a contributor to *Family Handyman*.

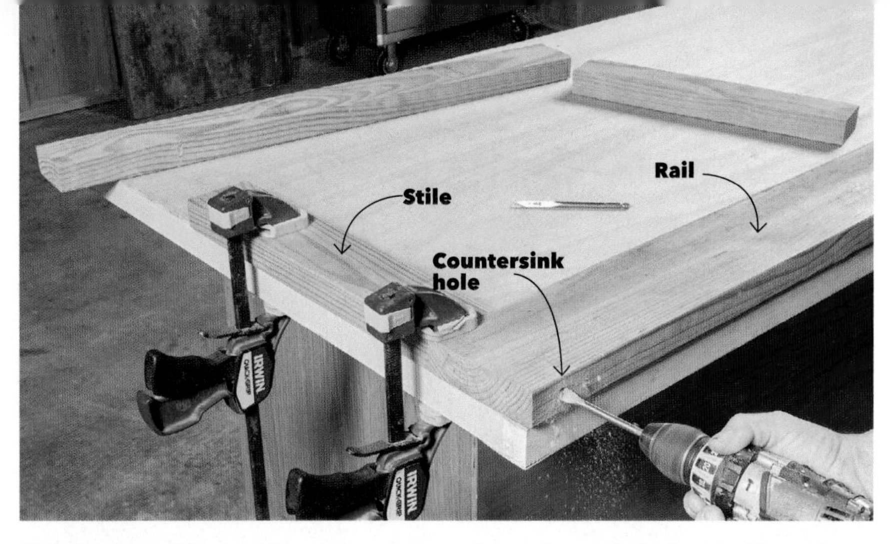

1 Build the end frames. Clamp the parts to a flat surface with the best-looking sides face up. Join the parts with screws as detailed in **Figure A**. The bottom rails (C) require a 2-in.-deep countersink hole drilled with a 5/8-in. spade bit.

2 Build the side frames. Fasten the side frame parts with "toe screws" (screws driven at an angle). If any of the screw heads don't sink into the wood, drill a shallow countersink hole sized to match the screw head. See **Figure A** for details.

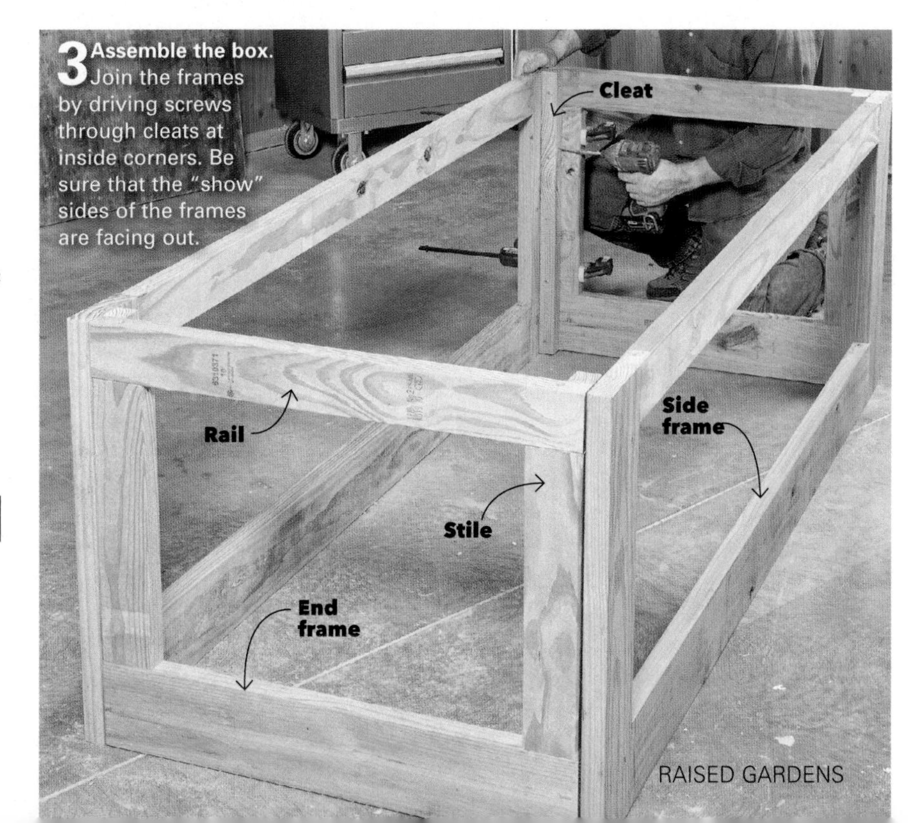

3 Assemble the box. Join the frames by driving screws through cleats at inside corners. Be sure that the "show" sides of the frames are facing out.

4 Cut the metal. First, slip on gloves—those metal edges are sharp! Then cut the panels to length with metal shears. Standard 26-in.-wide metal panels don't require cutting to width.

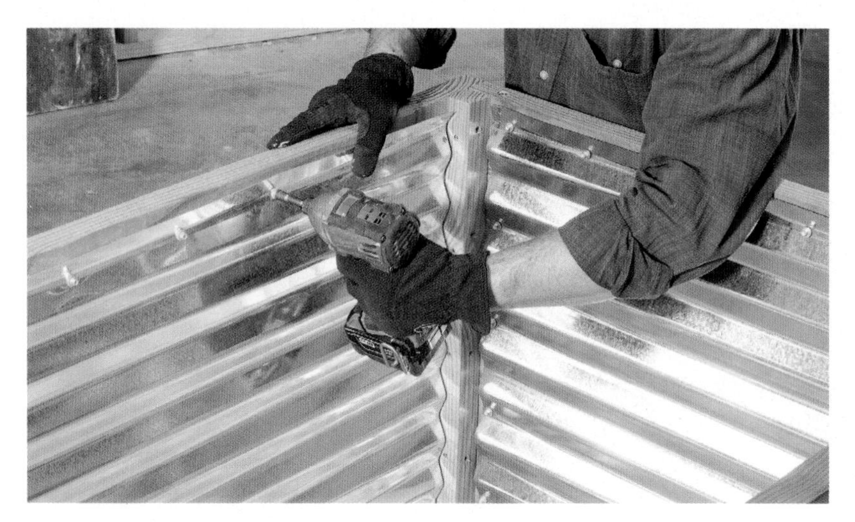

5 Install the metal. Screw the panels to the frames, placing screws every 8 in. along the top and bottom edges. Along the side edges, drive a screw at every second rib.

6 Add plywood backing. Reinforce light-gauge corrugated metal by screwing plywood over the metal. Set the plywood on 2x4 blocks to help position it.

Home centers typically carry light-gauge corrugated metal, which is fine for this project as long as you reinforce it with plywood (see **Photo 6**). Our metal is 30 gauge. When looking at gauges of metal, remember that a higher number means thinner material. Also, make sure all the screws you choose are rated for use with treated lumber.

Building tips

- Start by cutting the parts according to the Cutting List. Cut shorter parts from your imperfect boards and save your straightest material for the long parts (E, G, M).
- To avoid assembly mix-ups, note that the rails fit between the stiles on the side frames. On the end frames, the stiles fit between the rails.
- We didn't use a finish on our planters. If you do, note that it will be much easier to apply before you install the metal panels.
- If you're tempted to miter the corners of the rim, reconsider. Outdoor miters look better than square-cut butt joints at first, but they inevitably develop ugly gaps as the wood absorbs and releases moisture.
- Here's how to install the planter: Set it into position, then slice into the soil around it, marking its footprint. Move the planter aside and dig a shallow perimeter trench, just a couple inches deep. Set the planter in place again and check it for level in both directions. Add soil or deepen the trench to level the planter.
- When the planter is in place, cut a couple large slits in the bottom of the plastic liner so excess water can drain into the soil below—unless you plan to install a self-watering system. That requires a watertight liner.
- Filling this planter requires a lot of soil, almost a cubic yard. But there are ways to fill the lower half of the planter with less effort and expense. One common filler is plastic milk jugs (with caps screwed on tight). Another trick is to set plastic buckets in place upside down.

Figure A
Raised Garden Planter

Overall Dimensions: 84" Long x 36" Wide x 28-1/4" Tall

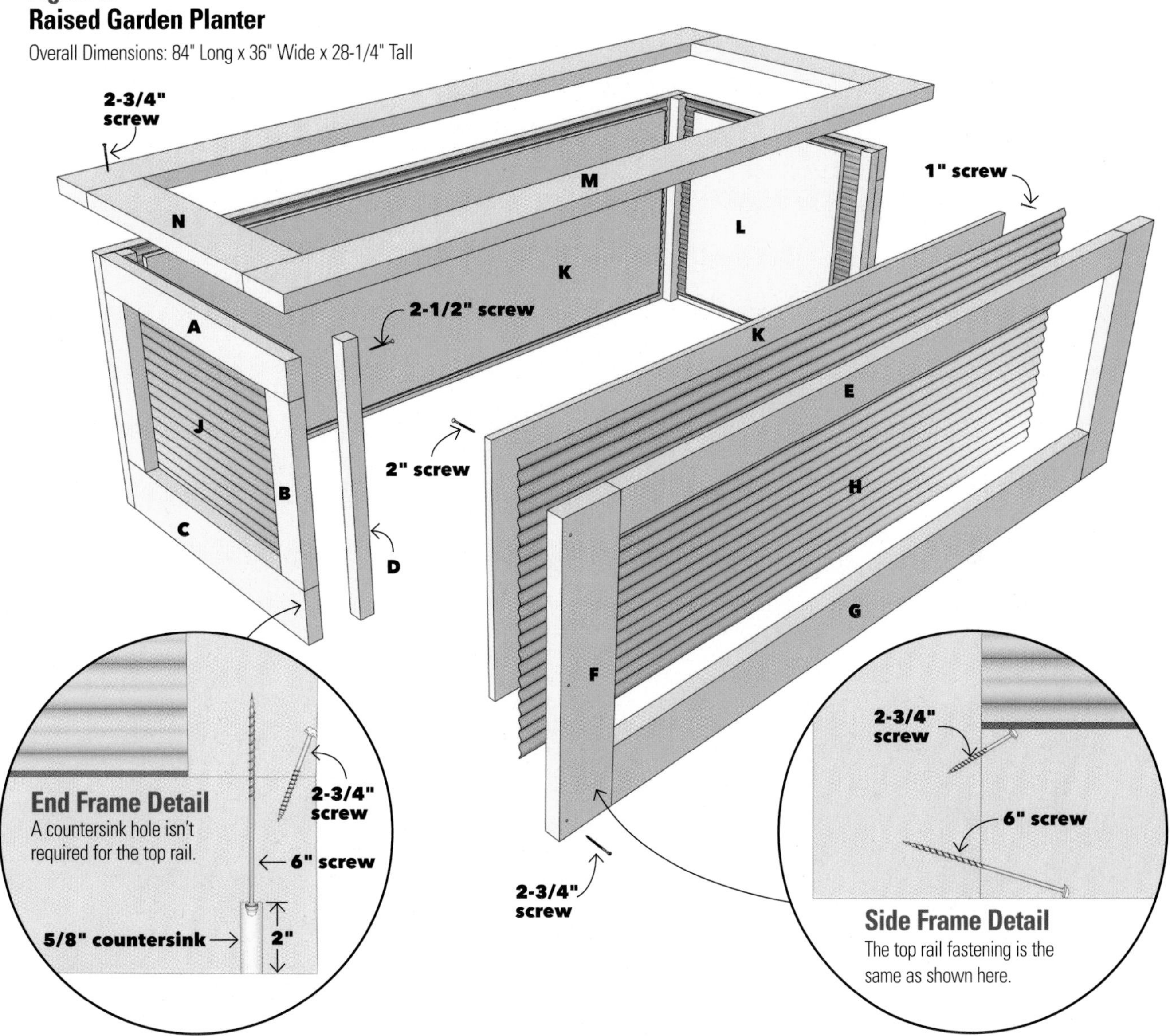

CUTTING LIST

KEY	QTY.	DIMENSIONS	NAME
A	2	2x4 x 31"	End frame top rails*
B	4	2x4 x 17-3/4"	End frame stiles*
C	2	2x6 x 31"	End frame bottom rails
D	4	1-1/2" x 1-1/2" x 26-3/4"	Cleats
E	2	2x4 x 71"	Side frame top rails
F	4	2x6 x 26-3/4"	Side frame stiles
G	2	2x6 x 71"	Side frame bottom rails
H	2	26" x 75-1/2"	Metal side panels
J	2	26" x 27-3/4"	Metal end panels
K	2	3/4" x 24" x 73-1/4"	Plywood side panels
L	2	3/4" x 24" x 22-3/4"	Plywood end panels
M	2	2x6 x 84"	Top side rims
N	2	2x6 x 25"	Top end rims

MATERIALS LIST

ITEM	QTY.
2x6 x 10' treated lumber	5
2x4 x 8' treated lumber	4
2x2 x 8' treated lumber	2
3/4" x 4' x 8' treated plywood	1
26" x 10' corrugated metal panel	2
1/4" x 6" coated construction screws	1 lb.
1" sheet metal screws with washers	1 lb.
2" coated deck screws	1 lb.
2-1/2" coated deck screws	1 lb.
2-3/4" small-head deck screws	1 lb.
6-mil plastic, 9' x 12'	1
1/4" stainless steel staples	1 pkg.

*Stiles are the vertical parts of a frame.
*Rails are the horizontal parts. These terms are most often applied to cabinet doors and face frames.

7 Line the box. Staple plastic sheeting to the inside of the box, then trim off the excess with a utility knife. A plastic liner helps to keep the wood dry and the soil moist.

8 Trim the box. Top off the planter with a 2x6 rim. If necessary, add toe screws to the joints to hold parts flush.

Easy arches for pest or frost protection

Arches can support screen or mesh to stop pests, or poly sheeting to keep plants frost-free overnight. The three arches are simply 5-ft. sections of 1/2-in. CPVC pipe that you can bend and slip into 12-in. sleeves made from 1-in. PVC pipe. A 4-ft. x 25-ft. roll of fiberglass window screen costs about $20.

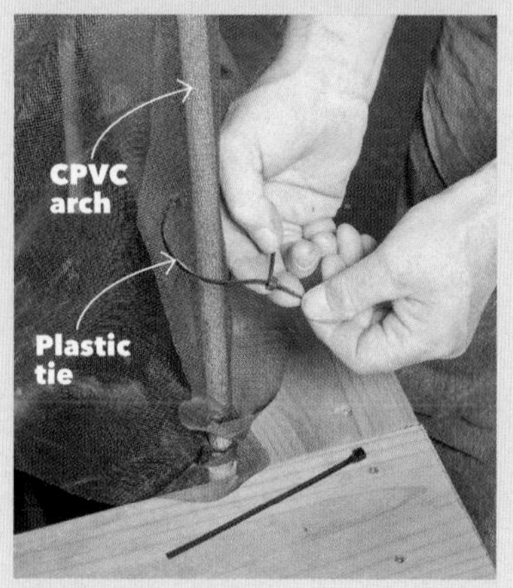

VIKING BENCH

Stylish seating, made from construction lumber!

By Spike Carlsen

MEET AN EXPERT

Spike Carlsen is a former editor at *Family Handyman* and a builder of "Viking furnture." This bench is a companion to his Viking table, which appeared in our April '18 issue.

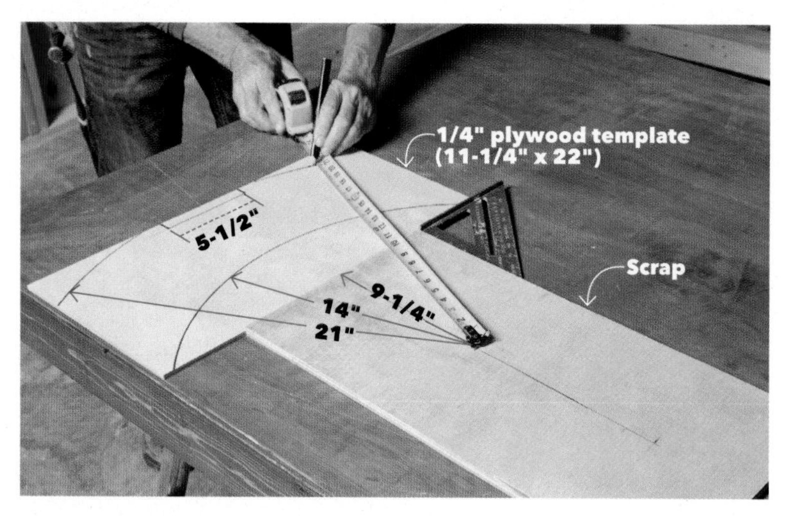

1 **Make the leg template.** Set a scrap of plywood against the template. Drive a screw 9-1/4 in. from the end of the scrap and use that screw as a pivot point for your tape measure. Then swing the two arcs to create the leg shape.

2 **Make a glue sandwich.** Trace the leg shape onto two leg sections at a time, lightly dampen the bottom piece, then apply polyurethane glue. Use a plastic putty knife to spread glue slightly beyond the edges of the layout lines and across the main body of the leg.

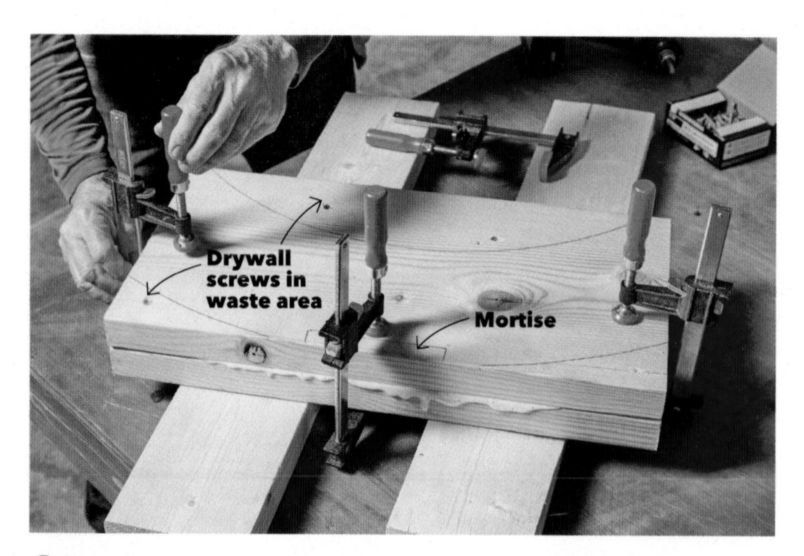

3 **Clamp the leg blanks together.** Line up the mortise edges of the boards, then drive a few drywall screws into the waste wood to keep the boards aligned. Fasten clamps around the perimeter to force the boards tight together.

If you think this bench looks sturdy, you're right; it's brawny enough to withstand decades of hard use. But if you think it's complicated, take a close look at the following pages. You'll see how simple it is to turn inexpensive framing lumber into graceful curves.

Create the legs

Start with flat, straight boards—free of splits, twists, cupping and loose knots—and you'll spare yourself a lot of head scratching and extra work down the road. I chose Douglas fir lumber, but any 1-1/2-in.-thick stock will do. If you have trouble finding perfect 2x12s for leg material, purchase extra lumber so you can cut around the defects.

To create a single bench, cut the four 22-in. leg blanks (A) to length; the ends need to be square, so cut carefully. Pair up your boards so when one is laid atop the other, there is little or no gap along the ends and edges. If you flip or rotate the boards, you might find the perfect fit. Try to have any defects fall in the areas of the wood you'll be cutting away as you form the legs.

Build the legs

Mark out your leg template on 1/4-in. plywood as shown in **Photo 1**. Cut just outside the line with a fine-tooth jigsaw blade, then use a belt sander to sand right up to the line.

Use your template to mark the leg shape on all four leg parts (A). With the marks facing up, lightly dampen one board—polyurethane glue needs moisture to work—then apply the glue in squiggles across the main body of the leg. Use a putty knife to spread it

WHAT IT TAKES

TIME: 15 to 20 hours
COST: $90
SKILL: Intermediate to advanced
TOOLS: Circular saw, jigsaw, router, belt sander, drill, clamps and basic hand tools

4 Cut the leg blanks. Make a series of relief cuts along the concave side of the leg, then use a jigsaw with a coarse blade (or a band saw) to cut the curves. Make a series of relief cuts for the stretcher mortise, and then use a jigsaw and chisel to make the opening.

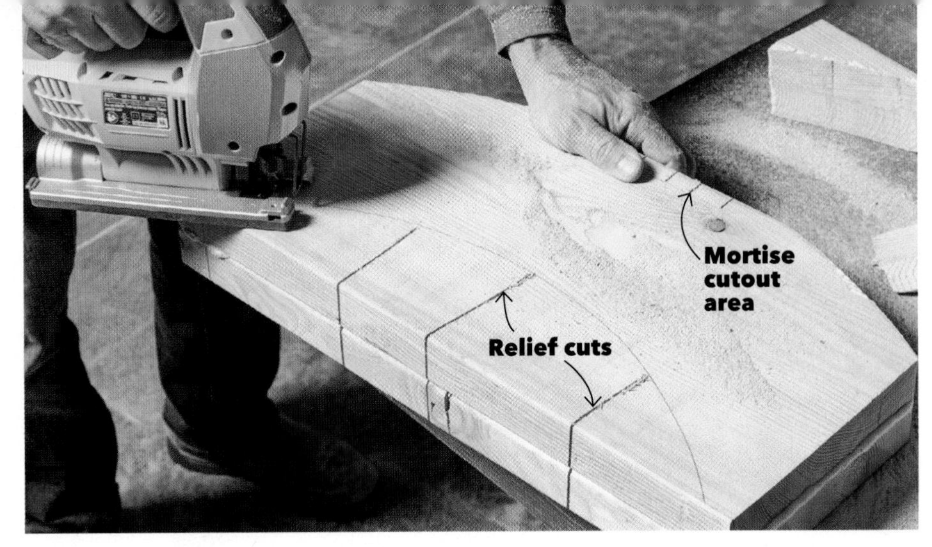

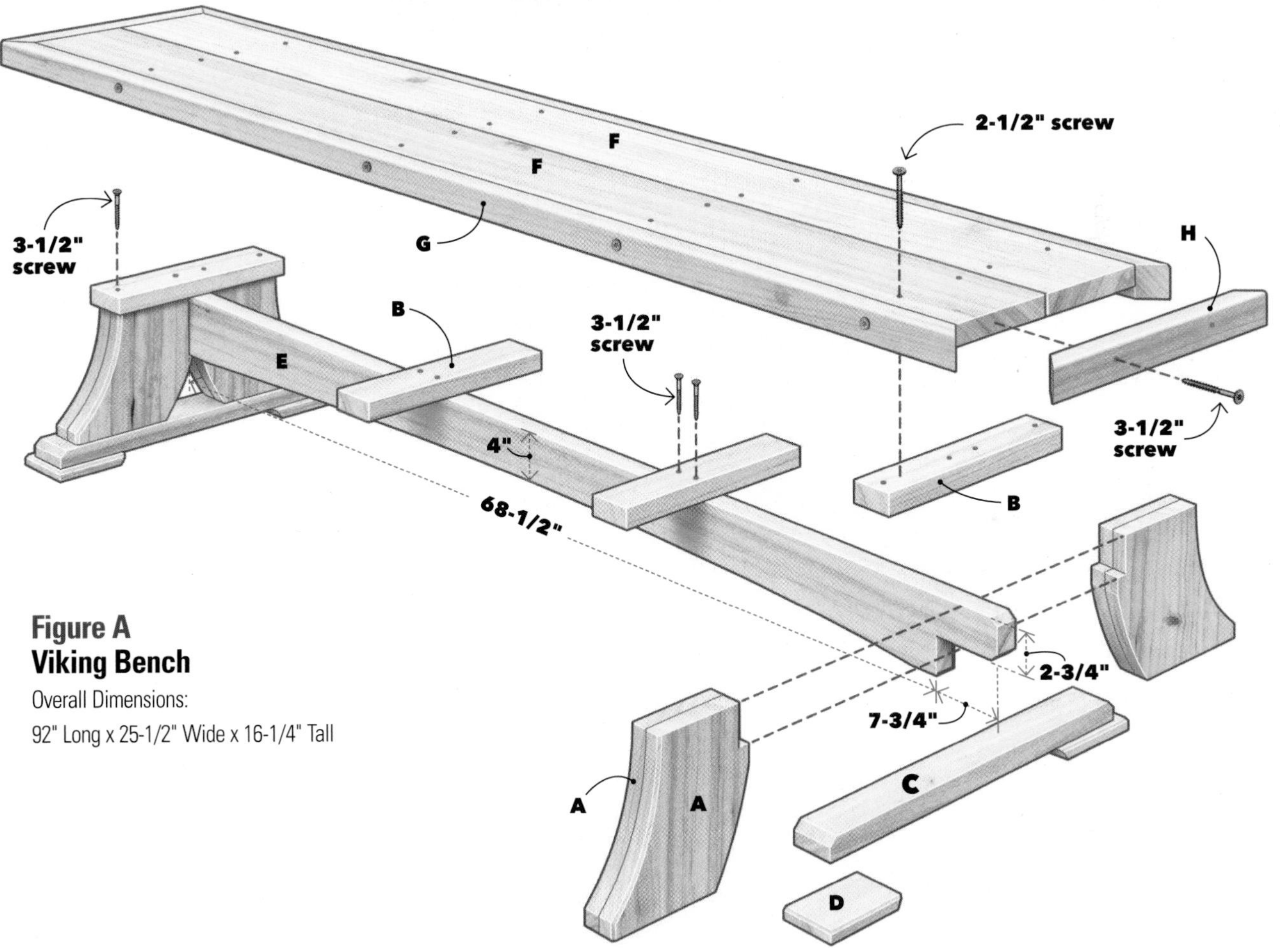

Figure A
Viking Bench
Overall Dimensions:
92" Long x 25-1/2" Wide x 16-1/4" Tall

MATERIALS LIST

ITEM	QTY
2x12 x 8' Douglas fir	1
2x8 x 8' Douglas fir	2
2x6 x 8' Douglas fir	3
2x4 x 10' Douglas fir	1
3/4" x 4" x 3' white oak	1
2-1/2" washer-head screws	1 lb.
3-1/2" washer-head screws	1 lb.
Polyurethane glue	6 oz.
Construction adhesive	1 tube

CUTTING LIST

KEY	QTY.	SIZE	PART
A	4	1-1/2" x 11-1/4" x 22"	Legs
B	4	1-1/2" x 3-1/2" x 14"	Seat braces
C	2	1-1/2" x 3-1/2" x 25"	Bottom leg plates
D	4	3/4" x 4" x 6"	Feet (white oak)
E	1	1-1/2" x 5-1/2" x 84"	Stretcher
F	2	1-1/2" x 7-1/4" x 89"	Top boards
G	2	1-1/2" x 2-1/4" x 92"	Long edge boards (mitered)
H	2	1-1/2" x 2-1/4" x 17-3/4"	Short edge boards (mitered)

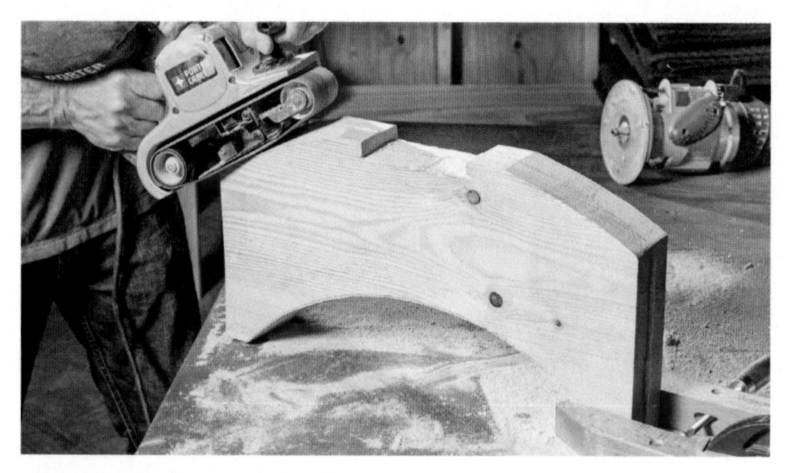

5 Sand the leg blanks and rout the edges. Smooth the curves and eliminate blade marks with a belt sander. Use a router with a 1/2-in. round-over bit to soften the curved edges, but leave the top, bottom and stretcher areas square.

6 Cut the leg blanks in half. Mark the exact center of the leg blanks and use a circular saw—cutting from both sides—to cut them in half. Use a belt sander to smooth out any ridges or unevenness on the ends.

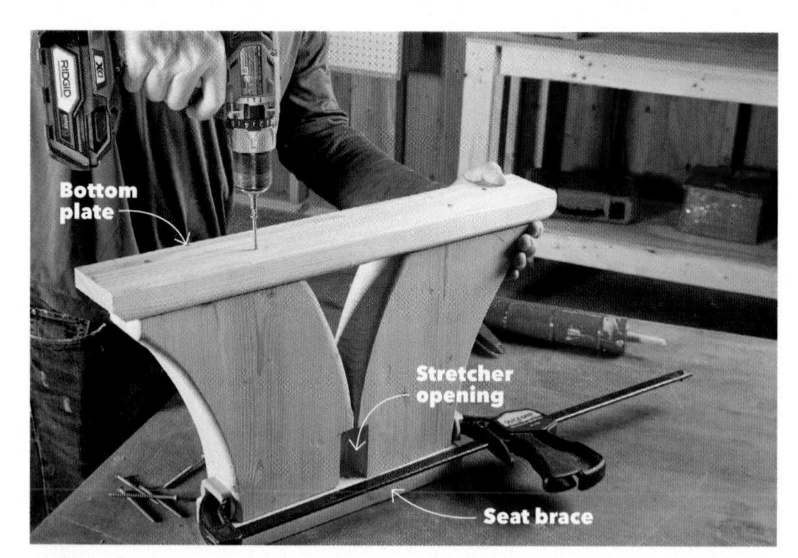

7 Screw the leg assemblies together. Clamp the leg halves together and check the size of the stretcher opening. Adjust if needed. Apply adhesive to the leg ends and attach the seat brace and bottom plates with screws.

slightly beyond the edges of your template marks. Polyurethane glue is waterproof, and with tightly glued seams there's less chance of moisture working its way between the boards.

Place a second board—marked side up—over your glued board (**Photo 2**) and align the edges. Install two or three screws in the waste material area, and then apply clamps—the more, the better—around the perimeter (**Photo 3**). Add more screws as needed. The glue will foam as it goes to work. Keep your boards clamped together for at least two hours; I left mine overnight for good measure. Repeat this procedure for the other leg blank.

Cut the legs to shape. A jigsaw with a long, coarse blade (**Photo 4**) works fine, but a band saw means less sanding. Whichever tool you use, make a series of relief cuts as shown. These allow you to remove waste material as you cut. They also allow your blade to get back on track if it wanders and begins making angled cuts. If you have a jigsaw with reciprocating action, set it at zero; it will cut slower, but your blade will wander less.

Build the leg assemblies

Next, use a belt sander to smooth and true up the curved sides (**Photo 5**). Begin with a coarse belt, then progress to finer grits. If you have access to a benchtop sander of some sort, use it; you'll get better results.

Figure B Leg

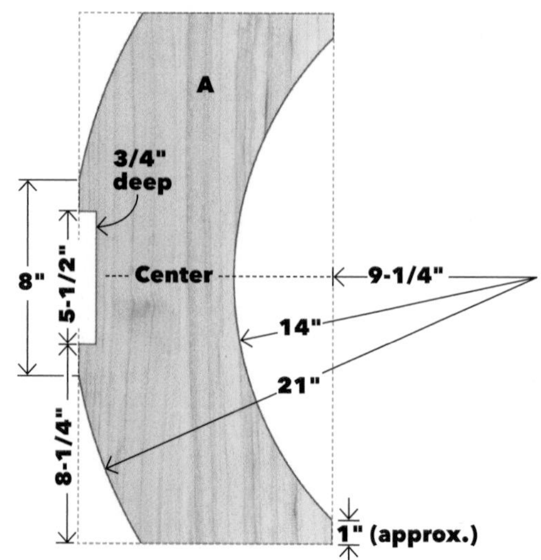

Use a router with a 1/2-in. round-over bit to soften the edges of the curved parts. DON'T rout the tops and bottoms of the legs or the flat area where the mortise cutout will be.

Cut the leg blanks in half as shown in **Photo 6**. They're 3 in. thick, so you'll need to cut from both sides. Dry-fit the pieces to be sure the parts fit tightly together. Butt the tops of the legs together, then place the seat brace (B) and bottom leg plate (C) in their respective positions. Make sure the stretcher fits into the opening between the legs. Also, be sure the ends of the legs sit flat against the seat brace and bottom plate; you may need to do a little sanding or trimming until the pieces fit tight. Once all systems are a go, apply construction adhesive to the ends of the legs, cinch the tops together with a clamp, position the seat brace and bottom leg plate (B and C) and then secure them with 3-1/2-in. exterior screws (**Photo 7**). Repeat for the other leg assembly.

Build the bench

Having built the leg assemblies, you've done the hardest part. Cut, shape and install the bench stretcher (E) as shown in **Figure A** and **Photo 8**.

Fasten the seat braces (B) to the stretcher, then position the two 2x8 top boards (F); they should run past the outer seat braces by about 6 in. Fasten the top boards with 2-1/2-in. washer-head screws. Install the 2-1/4-in. edge boards (**Photo 9**).

Apply two coats of exterior finish; I used a semitransparent deck stain. Finally, screw on the feet (D). I recommend using white oak for the feet because it's rot resistant. To keep your benches in tiptop shape, set them up on 2x4 blocks and cover them with a tarp before winter strikes.

More online!
To find the article and plans for the matching table, search for "viking long table" at familyhandyman.com.

8 Secure the stretcher to the legs. Use clamps to pull the stretcher shoulders tight against the legs, and drive in wedges or shims to snug the tenon tight against the seat brace. Drive screws through the seat brace into the tenon.

9 Complete the seat braces. Add the two top boards, then install the edge boards along the four edges of the bench. Drill pilot holes to avoid splitting the edge boards.

EASY GARDEN ARBOR

A small project that makes a big impression!

By Jeff Timm

This arch would make a beautiful portal to your yard or garden, and it's easier to build than most. Made from just six parts, it can be built in less than a day—even if you're a rookie carpenter. The design is versatile, too: It can support climbing plants, serve as a gateway in a fence, frame a walkway through a hedge, or stand alone as a striking wooden structure. You can stain it for a rustic look or paint it for a more formal one.

OUTDOOR STRUCTURES, LANDSCAPING & GARDENING

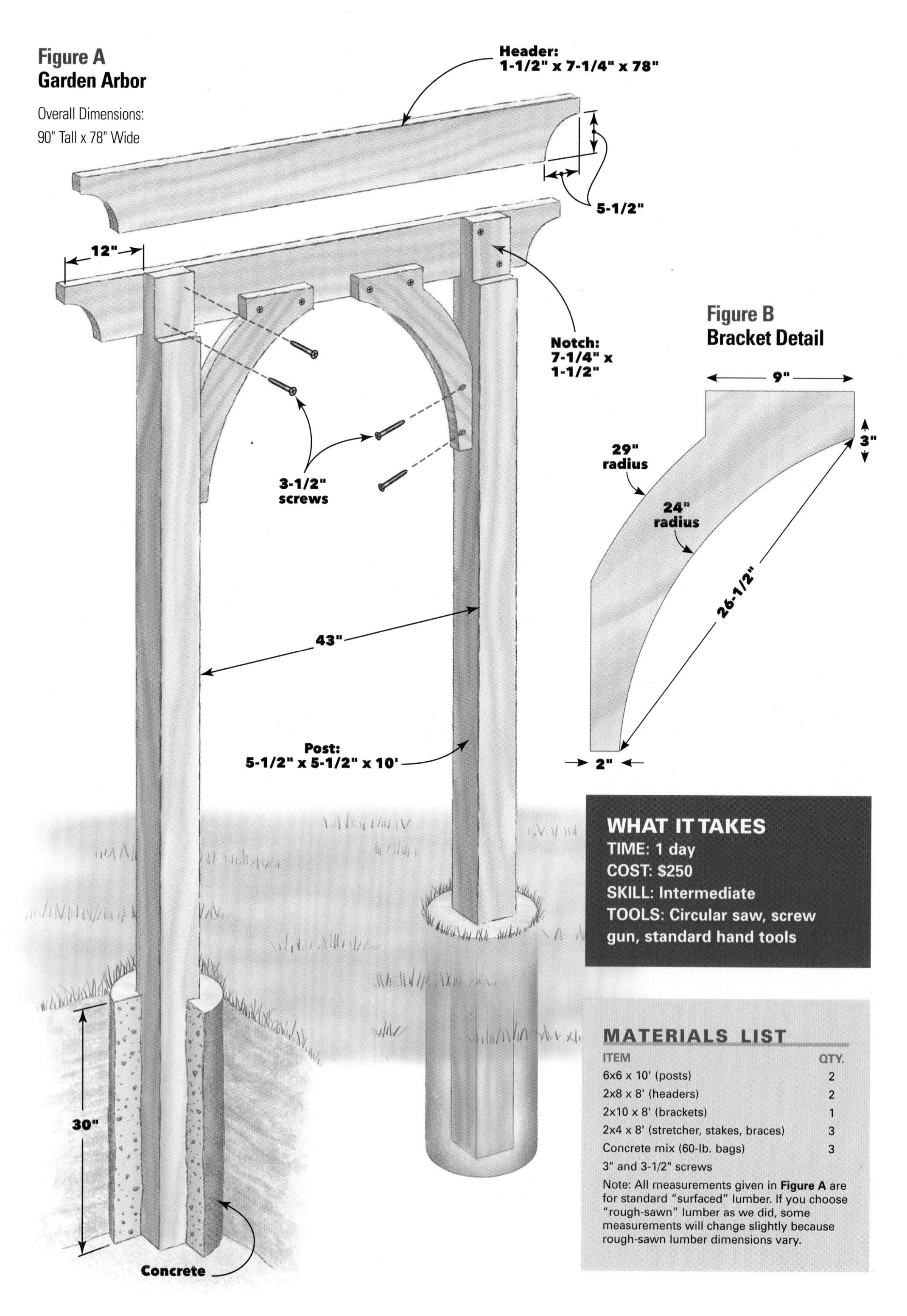

WHAT IT TAKES

TIME: 1 day
COST: $250
SKILL: Intermediate
TOOLS: Circular saw, screw gun, standard hand tools

MATERIALS LIST

ITEM	QTY.
6x6 x 10' (posts)	2
2x8 x 8' (headers)	2
2x10 x 8' (brackets)	1
2x4 x 8' (stretcher, stakes, braces)	3
Concrete mix (60-lb. bags)	3
3" and 3-1/2" screws	

Note: All measurements given in **Figure A** are for standard "surfaced" lumber. If you choose "rough-sawn" lumber as we did, some measurements will change slightly because rough-sawn lumber dimensions vary.

Money and materials

The total materials bill for our cedar arbor was about $250. Depending on where you live, you may have other varieties of rot-resistant lumber available, such as cypress or redwood. If you choose treated lumber, you'll find everything you need for this project at home centers.

For tools, you'll need only standard ones like a drill, a circular saw and a jigsaw. Make sure your framing square is a standard model (16 x 24 in., with a longer leg that's 2 in. wide). If yours is an oddball, buy a standard version ($10) so you can easily mark out the brackets (see **Photo 2**). A few days before you dig the postholes, call 811 to have underground utility lines marked.

Cut the parts

Begin by cutting notches in the tops of the posts (**Photo 1**). If you're using "rough-sawn" lumber as we did, you may have to change the length and depth of these notches to suit your 2x8 headers. (The dimensions of rough-sawn lumber vary.) Set the cutting depth of your circular saw to 1-1/2 in. to make the crosscuts for the notches. Then set your saw to full depth to make the other cuts.

Next, cut the 2x8 headers to length and mark arcs at the ends as shown in **Figure B**. To mark the curves, use the bottom of a 5-gallon bucket or any circle that's 10 to 11 in. in diameter. Cut the curves with a jigsaw.

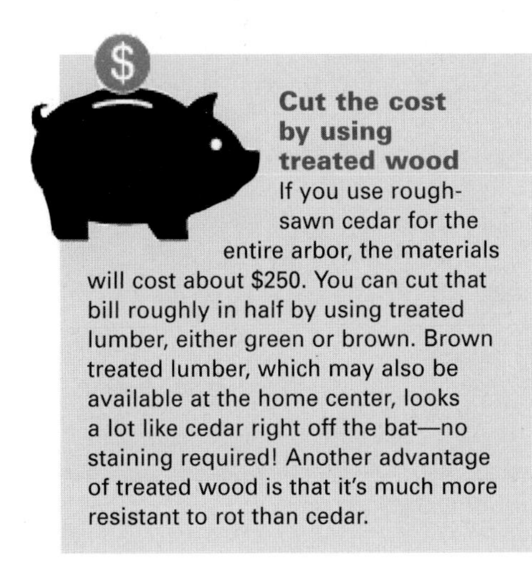

Cut the cost by using treated wood

If you use rough-sawn cedar for the entire arbor, the materials will cost about $250. You can cut that bill roughly in half by using treated lumber, either green or brown. Brown treated lumber, which may also be available at the home center, looks a lot like cedar right off the bat—no staining required! Another advantage of treated wood is that it's much more resistant to rot than cedar.

1 Cut the notches. Notch the tops of the posts. Cut as deep as you can from both sides with a circular saw. Finish the cuts with a handsaw.

2 Draw the bracket angles. Mark out the brackets without fussy measurements or geometry—just align the tips of the framing square with the edges of a 2x10 and draw the straight cuts on the bracket. (See **Figure B**, p. 230.)

3 Draw the curves. Draw perfect curves fast using a tape measure to guide your pencil. Cut out the bracket and use it as a pattern for the other bracket.

4 Assemble the parts. Screw through the posts and brackets into the header. That way, one header will have no visible screws. Screw through the second header into the posts.

5 Stand, plumb and brace. Set the arbor level and plumb before you pour concrete into the postholes. Wedge shims under the stretcher until the header is level, then plumb and brace the posts.

The curved brackets may look complicated, but they're easy to mark out since they're based on a standard framing square. After marking with the square (**Photo 2**), set a nail in your sawhorse 20 in. from the edge of the board. Carefully adjust the position of the board until both corner marks of the bracket are 24 in. from the nail. Then, holding your pencil at the 24-in. mark on the tape, draw an arc. To draw the second arc, move your pencil to the 29-in. mark on the tape (**Photo 3**). Cut the straight edges of the brackets with a circular saw and the arcs with a jigsaw. If the curves turn out a bit wavy, smooth them with an orbital or a belt sander. Don't be too fussy, though. Nobody will notice small imperfections.

Put it all together

Mark one header 12 in. from both ends and lay out the posts, aligned with the marks. Take measurements at the other end to make sure the posts are perfectly parallel. Drive 3-1/2-in. screws through the posts and into the header. At the tops of the brackets, drive 3-in. screws at a slight angle so they won't poke through the face of the header (**Photo 4**). Set 1-1/2-in.-thick blocks under the other ends of the brackets. Then drive screws at an angle through the sides of the brackets and into the posts, drilling 1/8-in. pilot holes so you don't split the brackets. Set the second header in place and screw it to the posts. Note: The brackets aren't centered on the posts; there's a 1-in. gap between the second header and the brackets.

Set it up

You'll set the arbor posts into 10-in.-diameter holes 30 in. deep. But before you move the arbor into place, screw on a temporary 2x4 "stretcher" 30 in. from the post bottoms. Then round up a helper or two and set the posts into the holes. Patiently level and plumb the arbor, bracing it with stakes and 2x4s (**Photo 5**). Be careful not to nudge the posts out of position as you fill the holes with concrete. Let the concrete harden for at least four hours before you apply finish to the wood. We brushed on two coats of clear penetrating wood finish to deepen the color of the wood and repel moisture.

Best Pro Tips

EXPERT ADVICE FROM THE JOB SITE

PREP A DECK **FOR STAIN**

Preparing an old deck for stain is easy; chemicals do most of the work. But it's not a job that allows for shortcuts. If you break a few basic rules, your finish will fail fast and you'll be back for a redo. Here's how to do it right.

MEET AN EXPERT

Rick Bautista, a senior product manager at Behr Process Corp. for the past eight years, specializes in wood stains and finishes.

Best Pro Tips

Pick up a deck stripper and a cleaner

To prepare your wooden deck for restaining, you'll need to pick up these two types of products from a hardware store or home center:

Deck stripper removes the old stain. An average-size deck will require about 2 gallons at $20 each.

Deck cleaner gets rid of stripping residue, refreshes the surface of the wood and opens the wood pores to better receive the new stain.

Caution:
The two types of products used to prep a deck contain hazardous chemicals. Deck cleaner is actually an acid, and the stripper contains a caustic chemical that will burn your skin. Wear long pants, eye protection and rubber gloves. Above all, avoid skin and eye contact.

1 Test the existing stain. Water-based (acrylic) stains must be stripped off before you apply a new finish, while oil-based stains can be recoated after you use a deck cleaner. So, your first step is to determine which type of stain is on the deck. Apply a small amount of deck stripper to an inconspicuous spot. Let it sit for about 15 minutes, then wipe it off. If the stain comes off, the stain is a water-based product and you'll have to strip it off. If the stain doesn't come off, it's an oil-based product that can be recoated with an oil-based deck stain once properly cleaned. If you have a deck that's never been stained, just go right to the steps shown in **Photos 8** and **9**.

2 Protect plants and siding. Deck stripper and cleaner can kill grass and plants. Protect vegetation with a fabric drop cloth or light-colored tarp. (Clear plastic sheeting will trap heat from the sun and fry your plants.) Then wet down the siding near the deck using your garden hose. Wet surfaces are less likely to be damaged by splashes of stripper. Clean off all loose deck debris with a push broom or leaf blower.

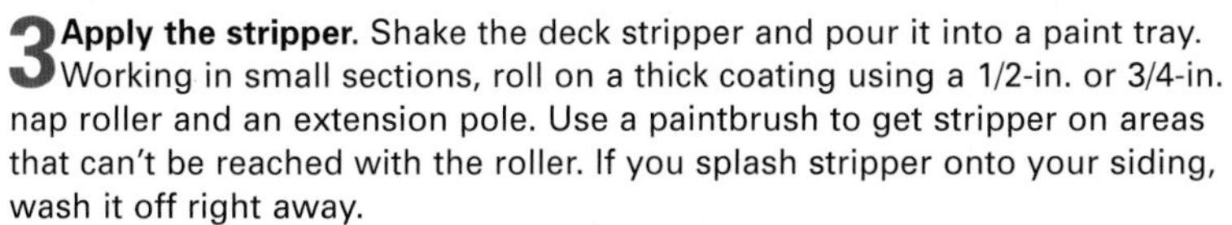

3 Apply the stripper. Shake the deck stripper and pour it into a paint tray. Working in small sections, roll on a thick coating using a 1/2-in. or 3/4-in. nap roller and an extension pole. Use a paintbrush to get stripper on areas that can't be reached with the roller. If you splash stripper onto your siding, wash it off right away.

4 Keep the stripper damp. Let the stripper work its magic for 15 minutes. If the stripper starts to dry during this period, keep it damp with water from a pump-up sprayer.

5 Scrub away the dissolved stain. Scrub with a stiff-bristle broom. If you have thick layers of stain, you may need to scrape off the residue with a floor scraper first. If that's the case, you'll likely have to reapply more stripper for the scrubbing step.

6 Power-wash the stripper. Rinse off the stripper and dissolved stain using a stiff stream from a garden hose nozzle, or a pressure washer on the lowest setting. A pressure washer makes the job much easier. If you only have a garden hose, you'll have to scrub more as you rinse.

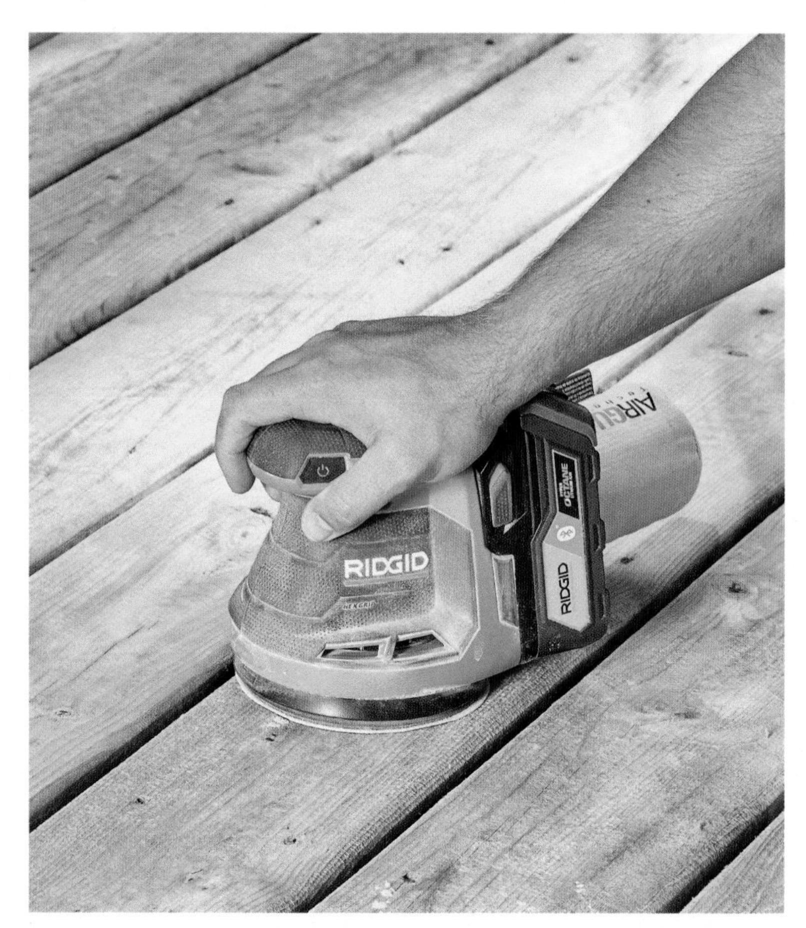

7 Sand the stubborn spots. Let the deck dry. Areas that need additional treatment will be obvious. Repeat the stripping/scrubbing routine on those spots. If there's no improvement after a few rounds, sand those areas with a random orbital sander.

8 Clean and neutralize the deck. Clean the deck with a deck cleaner. Mix a 50/50 solution of water and cleaner if your wood is reasonably clean. For extremely weathered boards, try the cleaner at full strength. Experiment with a small area to determine which is better. Wet the wood with your garden hose and apply a liberal coating of the cleaner using a pump sprayer. Let the cleaner sit for 10 to 15 minutes and keep it damp before scrubbing with a stiff-bristle broom. Then rinse the entire deck and let it dry.

9 Sand away the burrs. The cleaning step will raise lots of small fibers. After the deck dries to the touch, lightly sand the deck with a drywall sanding pad and 100-grit sanding screen. That'll knock down any raised wood fibers and give your deck a much smoother finish. Blow the sanding dust off with a leaf blower, and after a couple days of dry weather, you'll be ready to stain.

10 Make the stain last! Follow the directions on the can. Typically, the surface of the wood should be completely dry, and the stain should be applied in temperatures between 40 and 90 degrees F. Check the forecast and don't apply stain if rain is expected within 24 hours.

Sanding down the deck may be the best option

If you have a tired-looking deck with an oil-based finish, your best option may be to sand. That's a slow job if you use belt sanders and orbital sanders. Most pros use a large electric drum floor sander instead, and edge sanders for areas the drum sander won't reach.

You can rent a drum floor sander for about $35 for four hours and an edge sander for about $20. However, it takes practice to run a drum sander without gouging the wood. If you've never run one before, we recommend hiring a deck refinishing pro to do the sanding for you.

HandyHints®

FROM OUR READERS

FERTILIZING DENSE PLANTS

To get fertilizer to the base of bushes and other dense plants, use a length of 2-in. PVC. Slide one end down to the plant base and pour the fertilizer into the pipe. Cut the top of the pipe at 45 degrees to give yourself a larger opening for pouring in the fertilizer.

—Gordon R. Watson

CUT TRIMMING TIME

To cut my string trimmer work in half, I ran a rope through my mower's grass chute and tied a knot. I tied the other end of the rope to the tractor so it can't get caught in the blades. This way, I can pull up the grass chute and get closer to trees and other obstacles from the comfort of my tractor seat.

—Travis Larson

DOUBLE POTTING

Ever wish you could reorganize your garden in the middle of the growing season? Here's a clever way to do it. You'll need a bunch of pots of similar sizes. Put your plants in doubled pots, and then bury them up to their rims. Whenever you want a change, lift out the top pot and put in a different one. This method is also really slick for bringing plants indoors over the winter.

—Maria Klakegg

VINE SUPPORT

To get the vines to climb my trellis instead of just flopping over at the base, I use zip ties to attach the stalks where I'd like them to go. If you do this, keep the ties loose enough for the vine to move and grow.

—Craig Sullivan

FILLER FOR BIG PLANTERS

Add empty cans and broken clay pots to a deep planter to cut down on the amount of soil you'll need to fill it. The cans and pots also improve drainage and aeration.

—Claire Batassa

WATERING JUG

When my trusty old metal watering can rusted through, I decided to reuse and recycle instead of buying a new one. I rinsed out a milk jug and drilled a few holes in the cap. It's a good size, lighter weight and easy to carry.

—Matt Boley

HOLD YOUR HOSTAS!

Our hostas were always spreading and taking over entire flower beds. So I divided them with a spade and removed the excess plants, roots and all. Then I stuck 12-in. lengths of 8-in.-diameter duct around each plant. Works like a charm!

—Tom Dvorak

GARDEN STRAIGHTEDGE

If you need to pull up sod for a new garden or flower bed, one good way to cut straight lines is to use an edger and a 2x6.

—Marcia Willis

GreatGoofs®

LAUGHS & LESSONS FROM OUR READERS

HOT TUB DASH

My wife and I had installed a new hot tub in our yard and were eager to use it. On a very dark night, we decided to go for an inaugural skinny dip. We got halfway to the tub when the motion sensor fixture flooded the area with bright, show-you-in-all-your-glory light. We ran back toward the house, falling in a heap on the ground in our hurry to get there. We don't forget that light anymore—or our towels!

—John McCarthy

JUST ADD CONCENTRATE

I serve on our homeowners' association board and oversee the landscaping. Last spring, I decided to spot-spray the dandelions with weed killer. I poured 10 oz. of concentrate into a measuring cup, using up the last of the weed killer. I rinsed the bottle and put it in the recycling bin, then grabbed my 4-gallon backpack sprayer and spent the rest of the morning treating dandelions in a four-block stretch.

When I got back to my garage with my empty sprayer, I saw the measuring cup with the 10 oz. of weed killer concentrate still sitting on the workbench. So I got to spend my afternoon spraying the same weeds—this time with weed killer, not just water.

—Joe Albaugh

STUCK ON HIMSELF

I built a tree fort for my son and made the roof out of fiberglass panels. The problem was that bees loved to use the openings along the underside of the roof for nests. After my son got stung, I bought expanding foam to fill the holes. It was a great idea—until I decided to smooth the foam with my bare fingers (I ignored the disposable gloves that came with the can). When my fingers got stuck together, I tried wiping off the foam on my pants. My hands stuck to my pants. Well, after two hours in the emergency room with the doctor and the nurse trying everything, I had to have my fingers separated by a knife. Then I wore rubber gloves for a couple days until most of the foam wore off. My wife asked simply, "Didn't you read the warning label?" Oh, please. Did she really need to ask?

—Richard W. Alcorn

SPECIAL SECTION

Car & Garage

5 THINGS TO CHECK BEFORE A **ROAD TRIP**

Prevent travel disasters

Whether you're headed south for a beach vacation or to Grandma's for the holidays, you'd better do a quick check of your car's health first. Some discoveries can help you prevent "towable" events; others are safety issues. It would be best to run through this five-minute checklist a week before departure so you'll have time to get the car repaired if a mechanic is needed.

MEET AN EXPERT

Rick Muscoplat has decades of automotive repair experience and a great website: ricksfreeautorepairadvice.com.

S_PHOTO/SHUTTERSTOCK

1 Check for fluid leaks. Small leaks can turn into gushers once you leave town, and that can be costly. The most common sources: the radiator, engine oil pan, transmission oil pan and hoses, power steering hoses, steering rack, and heater and radiator hoses. Use a flashlight to check for leaks. Note the color of the fluid and trace the fluid trails back to their source.

2 Check and top off all fluids. With the engine off, check power steering fluid, brake fluid, coolant, windshield washer fluid and engine oil. Most automatic transmissions must be checked with the engine hot and running and the gearshift in "park." Check your owner's manual to confirm. Look for the power steering fluid level to reach the "cold" mark on the dipstick. If it's low, check your owner's manual and buy the right fluid for your vehicle.

3 Check the condition of all belts. Broken belts are one of the most common reasons for roadside assistance calls. Replacement belts are easy to locate and replace in a city. But the belt for your car may be tough to find in rural areas if you break down. Twist the belt slightly to expose cracks or glazing. Replace any belt that is cracked, worn or delaminating.

4 Check all exterior lights. They're easy to check and inexpensive to replace. Bulb numbers and replacement procedures are listed in your owner's manual. Turn the key to the "accessories" position (there's no need to start the engine). Operate the turn signals, brake lights and backup lights, and check for reflections in your rearview mirror. Perform the same checks on the front turn signal lights, headlights, high beams and running lights.

5 Check the tire pressure. Low air pressure causes tires to use more gas, wear faster and run hotter. Hot tires are more prone to blowout during extended highway drives. Check them all (including the spare) before you leave town. Look for the correct air pressure on the decal located on either the driver's door or the door pillar. If the decal is missing, check your owner's manual. Always make sure the tires are cold when you check tire pressure.

Expert advice: Six-point vs. 12-point sockets

Six-point socket

12-point socket

Q My gearhead neighbor keeps telling me I should quit using my 12-point sockets and buy a set of six-points. Is this really necessary?

—Jeff Albright, Columbia, MO

A It's true that 12-point sockets are fine for most lightweight repairs, but heavy wrenching calls for a six-point socket. A six-point socket is much less likely to slip off a stubborn fastener or round over the corners.

Here's why: (1) Six-point sockets have thicker walls, so they're less likely to flex. (2) A six-point socket is designed to contact the head of a fastener well away from the corners so contact is made on the thickest part of the socket and the flattest part of the fastener. This dramatically reduces the likelihood of slippage and rounding over of the corners. And (3), the edges of a socket are angled back a few degrees to allow the socket to slide easily over a fastener. The angle on a six-point socket is less than on its 12-point counterpart, again providing more contact area inside the socket.

One last point. Most high-quality sockets are chrome plated to prevent rusting and make cleanup easy. However, after years of use, the chrome finish can flake off. Don't use a socket if the chrome is peeling. The chrome will be as sharp as a razor blade. Any reputable tool company will replace one of its tools that has peeling chrome.

YOUR VERY OWN DUMP TRUCK FOR $40

If weekend landscaping projects are your thing, think about getting your hands on this Haul-Master 1/2-Ton Truck Bed Cargo Unloader. It's ingenious even though it's nothing more than a sheet of polypropylene mesh that wraps around a shaft turned by a hand crank. Just hook it on the end of your lowered tailgate, pull the mesh sheet across the length of the bed and load your cargo right on top.

When you're ready to unload, just spin the crank and watch your precious cargo spill right out the back; no more tiresome trips up into the bed with a shovel. If you need to spread gravel or topsoil, you could drive slowly and have a buddy dump the load as you go.

The Haul-Master Truck Bed Cargo Unloader can handle a load up to 2,000 lbs. and takes less than 10 minutes to install—no tools required. It won't work well on an antislip bed surface, and it may not fit on the thicker tailgates on some new trucks. You can pick up the Haul-Master for $40 at Harbor Freight, or find out more at harborfreight.com.

GET A LEG UP!

FORD

Newer pickups often feature built-in steps so you can easily access your pickup bed. Some steps are built into the bumper; others are part of the tailgate like the one on the Ford F-150 shown above. The steps are handy for pros and DIYers alike, especially if you have an elevated 4WD pickup.

If you have an older truck, there's no need to cry in your beer—you'll find many aftermarket truck steps to choose from. Some bolt onto the bumper and fold up or slide out of the way under the bed; others slip into the receiver hitch and telescope or swing out when needed. You'll find styles to help you access both the rear and the side of the bed. Just search online for "truck steps"—you'll find something to suit your needs and the size of your wallet.

LUND

This retractable Lund BedStep is just one aftermarket option. It's rated for 300 lbs. and costs $220 at realtruck.com.

EASY **OFF-LOADING**

A dump trailer can save you tons of labor (literally) on a job, but the cost of owning one is steep: Most sell for $8,000 or more, though small models cost as little as $3,000. If those costs don't make sense for you, this might: We checked rental costs in a few U.S. locations and found you can rent one for $100 to $200 per day, depending on the size. Be sure you call the rental center to make sure your truck can handle the load. Large dump trailers require large trucks and maybe a trailer brake controller. Lift systems are powered by a battery mounted on the trailer, and operation is as simple as pushing "up" and "down" buttons. Sure beats a shovel!

A side gate is handy
Some dump trailers have a side gate in addition to the standard rear gate, which allows for easier access and leveling of the trailer load if needed.

Recharging options
This trailer has a solar panel to charge the battery, but most are charged by your truck or by plugging into a standard electric outlet.

Unload with your thumb
Most trailers have a wired controller, but some new models have a wireless remote just like the key fob for your truck.

Car & Garage

THE WELL-PREPARED TRUCK

Gotta-have items our editors carry everywhere

Easy bed liner

Know about Bagster bags? You can buy one for about $30 at a home center or Amazon. Fill it with demolition or other debris, then schedule a pickup by Waste Management, which costs about $135. I buy the bag, skip the pickup and use it over and over as a truck bed liner for hauling demo and lawn and garden debris. It makes unloading at the dump or compost site super easy, and my pickup bed stays immaculate. Refolded carefully, it fits under the seat.

—Mike Berner, Associate Editor

Moving blanket

A cheap moving blanket is a nice thing to have in your truck. A few uses:

- Put it on the ground to keep yourself clean and prevent losing nuts and bolts.
- Use it to cover your carpeting when you're slogging through mud at job sites.
- Shield your seat covers when you're filthy or your dog is with you on the job. (It works under children and ice cream cones too.)
- Protect delicate furniture and appliances that are tied down in the bed.
- Keep it on hand for an emergency blanket.

—Brad Holden
Associate Editor

Home center cutting kit

When I buy long materials at the home center that I don't need full length, I often cut them down to size in the parking lot for easier hauling. A small saw works great for slicing trim, plastic pipe or conduit; snips easily handle metal items like drip cap or roof edge.

—Gary Wentz
Editor-in-Chief

DIY fix-a-flat kit

My flat-tire kit includes: plugger, reamer, needle-nose pliers, plugs, valve stem tool, extra valve stem caps, air chuck and tire pressure gauge. A kit like this will likely pay for itself the first time you use it. And yes, we know the tire experts say you're not supposed to plug a tire from the outside, and you definitely shouldn't plug sidewalls. But I've personally plugged at least 20 tires (lots of nails and screws on construction sites) without any failures, safety issues or reduction in the overall life of the tires.

—Mark Petersen
Senior Editor

Handy tie-down gear

I keep this container under my front seat at all times to hold my ratchet straps and a red flag for when I haul long material in the back of my truck. My ratchet straps stay together and untangled, and the flag is easy to wrap around the load because I punched a hole in it for use with a bungee cord.

—Travis Larson
Senior Editor

TRICK OUT YOUR TRUCK

Our editors give these four accessories a big thumbs-up

Roll it out!

A few years ago, I bought this giant roll-out drawer. I absolutely love this thing. It fully extends over the tailgate, so I can access everything in the bed without crawling up there or reaching over the sides of the truck. The one I bought isn't available anymore, but many other models can be found online; search for "truck bed drawer system." There are versions with multiple drawers, simple trays like mine and ones with higher sides. Prices start at about $800. Most have a load capacity of 750 to 1,000 lbs. If you have a pickup, I urge you to get one.

—Rune Eriksen
Contributing Editor

Bulletproof floor mats

Over 10 years ago, I replaced the mats in my truck with WeatherTech FloorLiners. They fit like a glove and hold a gazillion gallons of water/melted snow. What I love most is the way the mats extend up the sides. The fabric on the side of my gas pedal doesn't get dirty and worn from my work boots. I'm pretty sure these mats will outlast my truck. A new set of four costs about $180.

—Mark Petersen
Senior Editor

Easy-load bike rack

I take several dirt bike camping trips every year. That used to mean loading my Husky in the bed of the truck, which didn't leave much room for my camping gear. Then I went online and found theVersaHaul carrier. It slides into the receiver hitch, making bike loading a super-simple operation. Now the bed is available for all my gear, and I can keep everything secure under my weather-tight, locking tonneau cover. The end of the rig has another receiver hitch opening, so I can even pull a trailer or boat while hauling the bike. I bought the VersaHaul VH-55 RO at discountramps.com for about $500 with free shipping.

—Vern Johnson
Associate Creative Director

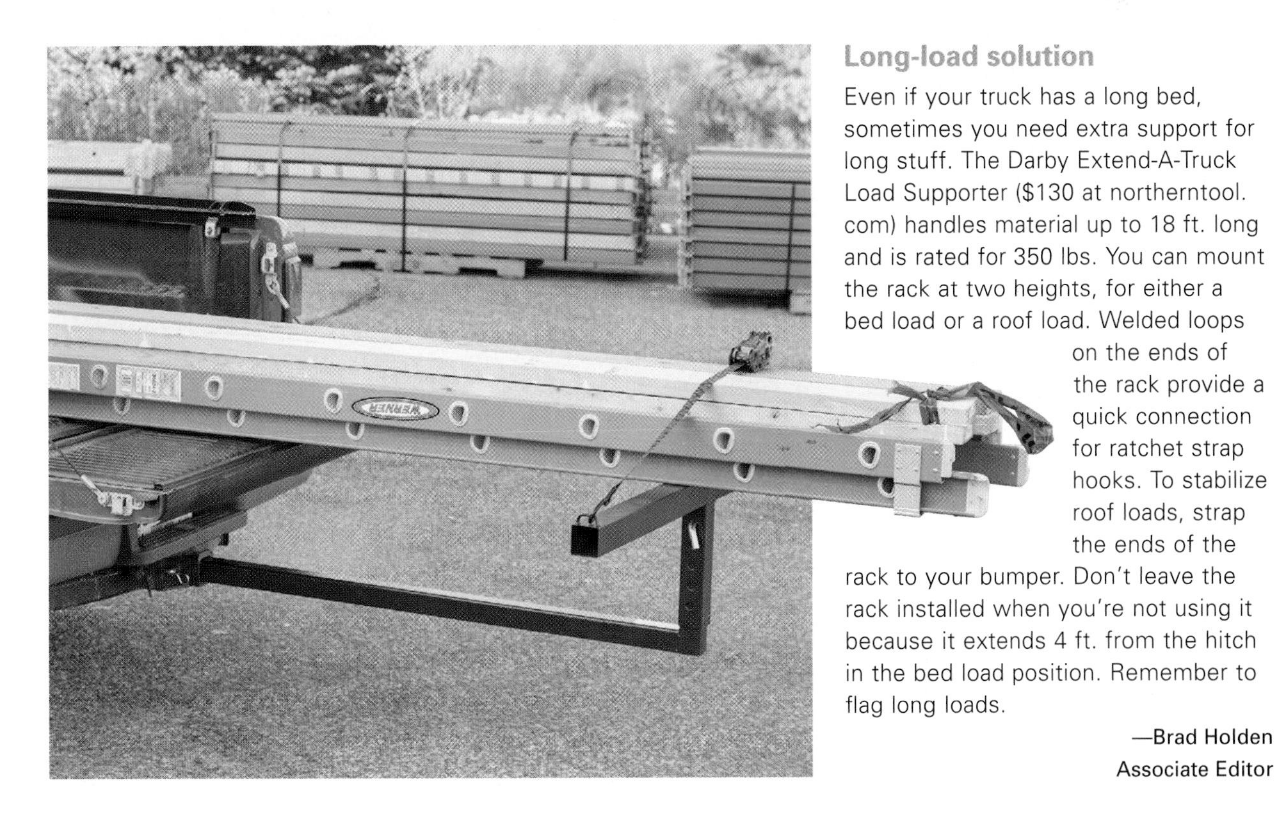

Long-load solution

Even if your truck has a long bed, sometimes you need extra support for long stuff. The Darby Extend-A-Truck Load Supporter ($130 at northerntool.com) handles material up to 18 ft. long and is rated for 350 lbs. You can mount the rack at two heights, for either a bed load or a roof load. Welded loops on the ends of the rack provide a quick connection for ratchet strap hooks. To stabilize roof loads, strap the ends of the rack to your bumper. Don't leave the rack installed when you're not using it because it extends 4 ft. from the hitch in the bed load position. Remember to flag long loads.

—Brad Holden
Associate Editor

Mounting bracket

The box swings out to make it easy to access your tools. It makes a nice cooler, too!

SWING-OUT STORAGE

I needed more tool storage space in the bed of my truck. I wasn't willing to give up my tonneau cover, and I couldn't stand the idea of losing valuable hauling capacity. The solution was this UnderCover SwingCase, which rests over the wheel well and sits below the top edge of the bed. Unlike other wheel well boxes, it swings out so you can get at it from the back of the truck instead of having to reach over the side of the bed. And you can lift it right out to free up space or to use it as a portable toolbox.

The SwingCase has a locking lid, and the whole unit can be secured with a padlock. It has a capacity of 75 lbs. and costs about $200. It took me only about 30 minutes to install two boxes using the vehicle-specific mounting brackets. You can find a model selector as well as a dealer at undercoverinfo.com.

GARAGE **UPGRADES GALORE!**

To cut clutter, consider installing an electric attic lift. That makes moving out-of-season gear into the attic safe and effortless—and opens up lots of floor space. Aside from careful positioning and adjustments, the installation is quick and simple.

For year-round comfort, add ductless mini-split heating/cooling. If you're intimidated by this HVAC project, don't be. Supplying the power can take creative planning, but the rest is amazingly easy.

Turning a garage into a home theater could be as simple as hanging a TV on the wall. But if you want to protect all the electronics from sawdust and stray basketballs, build our giant cabinet. Don't be fooled by the size; it's big, but construction is basic.

Concrete floors are bland and hard to keep clean. One solution is an epoxy floor coating. More than any other project, this stunning floor can transform the garage into an inviting living space.

Car & Garage

WANT A FRIDGE IN **YOUR GARAGE?**

Cold facts you need to know

No one needs to be convinced of the convenience of a garage refrigerator. Whether you have one already or are thinking about getting one, here's how to help it perform its best.

Understand the basics

In a non-climate-controlled garage, refrigerators struggle. Excessive heat forces them to work extra hard, resulting in high electric bills and early failure. Freezing temperatures make your refrigerator think it doesn't need to work, letting frozen things thaw and refrigerated items freeze. Humidity is also an issue, as it can cause rust on the coils. The ideal way to keep your garage refrigerator running at peak performance is to condition the garage air. However, this gets expensive and involves insulating the garage. You could frame up, insulate and condition a small space within the garage, but that's not very practical and there are easier options.

Garage-ready refrigerators
Standard new refrigerators, because of their efficiency, often struggle in a garage more than old refrigerators. But you can buy a "garage-ready" refrigerator. These are designed to take extreme temperatures and humidity. However, some units are built for heat but not cold, and vice versa.

Keep things cool

If your garage gets too hot (over 100 degrees F), set up a fan to increase airflow over your fridge's cooling coils. Just make sure the air is moving across and around the back of the fridge. If humidity is an issue, set up a dehumidifier. If your garage is also your workshop, clean up sawdust daily and make sure it doesn't build up on your refrigerator's coils.

Fridge heaters

In cold climates, you need to heat the air around the fridge's thermostat. One way to do this is to install a heating coil around the thermostat. Many manufacturers make heating coils for their refrigerators and freezers, or you can buy a generic heater. These units cost less than $50. Another option is to put a metal clamp-on work lamp near the fridge with an incandescent lightbulb aimed at the thermostat.

Stock smart

Every time you open and close the fridge door, the air is sucked out and replaced. Keep your garage refrigerator well stocked. The cooled items inside help cool the new air, preventing the fridge from working too hard. But don't fill it too full. This can block the blower, preventing cold air from circulating efficiently.

7 Using DIY Tools & Materials

IN THIS CHAPTER

HomeSmarts

KNOWLEDGE YOU NEED TO BE A BETTER HOMEOWNER

STAND-UP TOOL **CADDY**

When you need to carry your tools to the task at hand, you could use a toolbox. But unlike a toolbox, this slick tool caddy puts all your necessary tools in plain sight. With a little imagination, it can be configured to hold whatever tools or fasteners you like. The caddy stands up on its own when in use and hangs flat on the wall between projects.

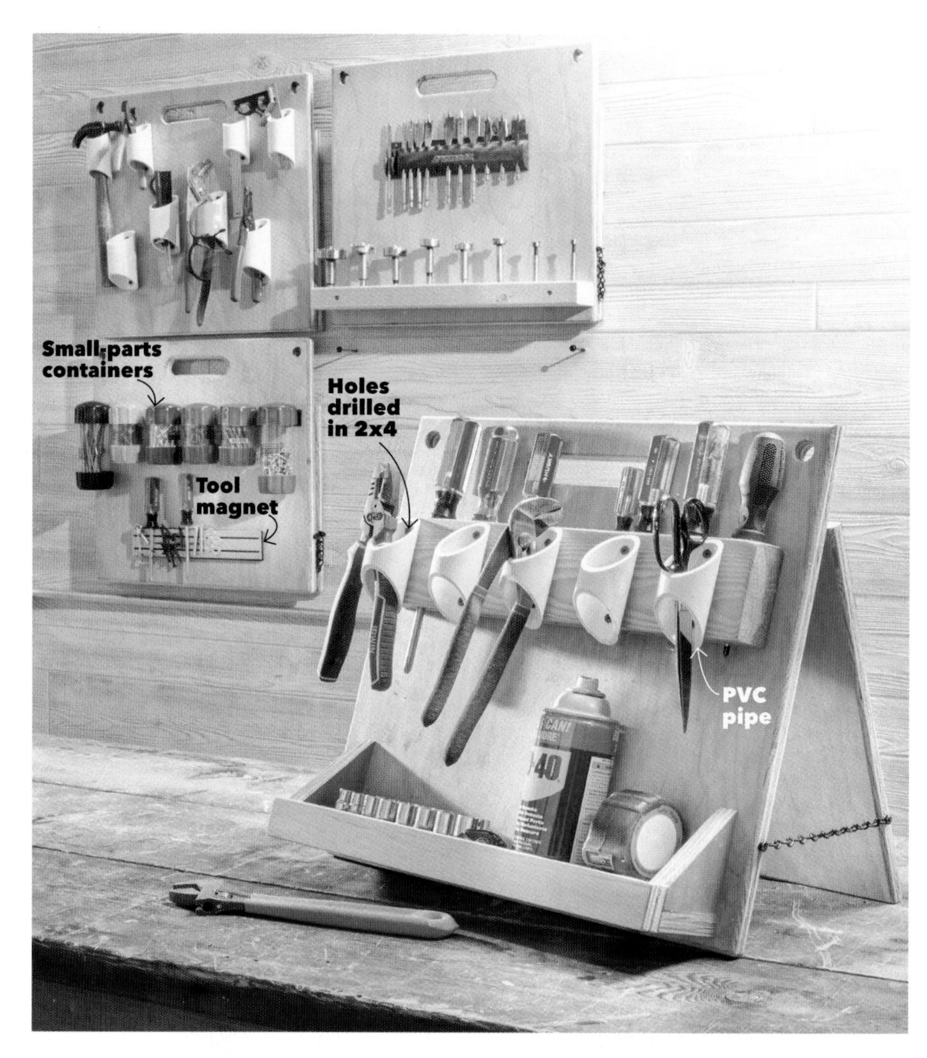

- A generous handle makes carrying easy. Drill a starter hole and then cut out the rest with a jigsaw.
- You can make them any size you'd like, but 18 x 18 in. holds lots of stuff and is a nice carrying size.
- Hanger holes are centered 16 in. apart, so you can hang the caddies on lag screws driven into studs.
- You can install whatever tool-holding system suits your needs.
- Cut PVC at an angle so you have space to drive the mounting screws.
- Two-inch butt hinges connect the prop to the tool panel.
- The chain stabilizes the open caddy.

—Brad Holden
Associate Editor

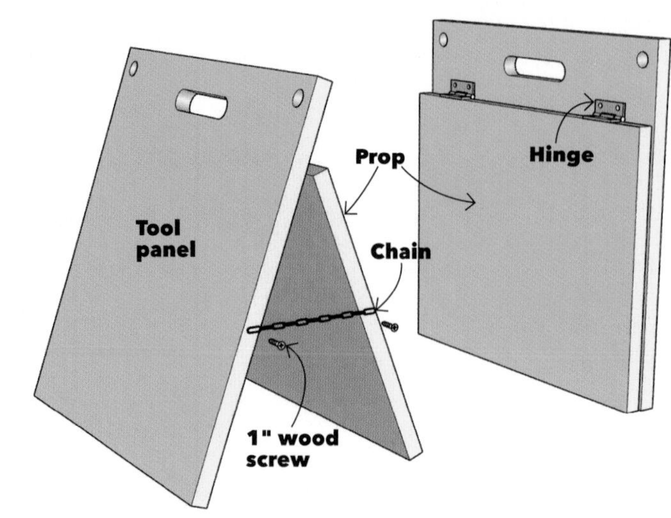

THE DIRT ON **DUST MASKS**

Much DIY work produces dust and/or fumes. It's essential to protect your lungs from both; there's no amount of dust or vapor that's good for your lungs. And the harm is cumulative. The more work you do without protection, the more damage you're doing. So if you're producing dust or using finishes or solvents, use the proper mask.

Certified Filter Ratings

A mask's certification denotes its filtering efficiency and what it's capable of filtering. There are three letter ratings—N, R and P—pertaining to a mask's effectiveness at removing airborne oils or vapors found in solvents and finishes.

N = Not resistant to oils
R = Somewhat resistant to oils
P = Strongly resistant to oils

The number following the letter indicates the percentage of particles that the mask is capable of filtering out. An N95-rated mask, for example, filters out 95 percent of airborne particles, but it offers no protection against airborne oil-based particles found in solvents and finishes.

Bargain Masks

Don't buy a mask with a rating of less than N95 or one that shows no rating at all. These cheap masks may keep you from inhaling insects or small birds, but they offer no protection against airborne particles.

The Bottom Line

Consider the level of protection you need for the job and choose your mask accordingly. If you're just doing dusty work, such as sanding wood or drywall, a disposable N95 mask is a fine choice. If you're working with paint, finishes, adhesives, mold or lead paint removal, go for a reusable cloth or cartridge mask with activated charcoal as part of the filter. A note of caution: If you have a beard, no mask will perform as advertised.

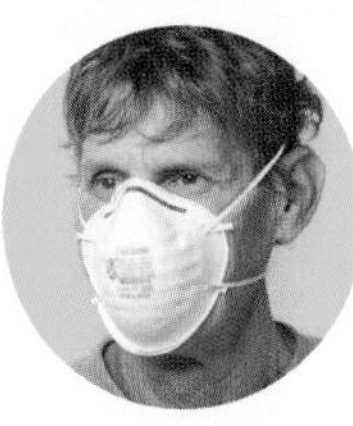

Standard Disposable Mask
If you're sanding wood, drywall or doing some demolition work, this disposable mask will serve the purpose. They're about $2 each. Make sure the ones you buy have a rating of at least N95.

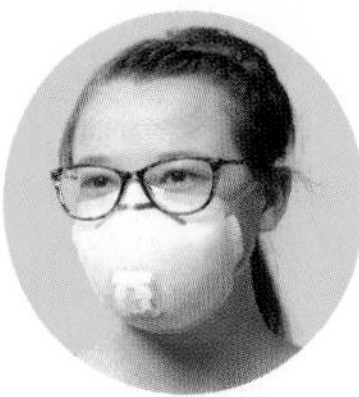

Disposable Mask with Exhalation Valve
This one covers the same types of dust as the standard disposable mask. But if you'll be wearing your mask all day or doing physically demanding work, spring for a mask with an exhalation valve ($3 each). The valve makes breathing a lot easier. It's well worth the extra cost.

Reusable Dust Mask with Replaceable Filters
If you're doing lots of work that requires a mask, consider a reusable mask. These reusable fabric masks are far more comfortable than the disposable type. This model M2 mask from RZ has an N99 rating and costs about $35.

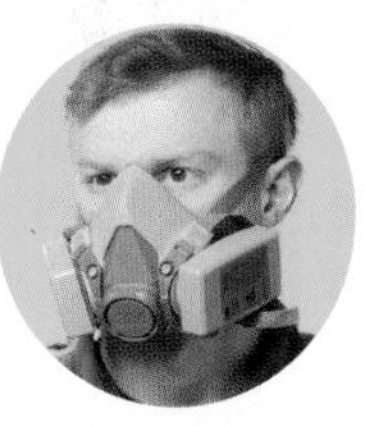

Reusable Cartridge Filter Mask
These are the most versatile masks. The replaceable filters are available for different things: HEPA for dust, or a chemical filter for VOCs (volatile organic compounds). If you're applying finishes or working with solvents, get a mask with replaceable activated charcoal cartridge filters. A cartridge filter mask costs about $30. This mask has a P100 rating.

5 THINGS YOU MUST KNOW ABOUT VERMICULITE

1. What is it? Vermiculite is a mineral that was used for insulation. If your home was built before 1990, you might have vermiculite insulation in your walls or attic. Up to 85 percent of all vermiculite insulation in the U.S. came from a mine in Libby, Montana, sold under the name Zonolite.

2. Why is it bad? Nearly all vermiculite contains asbestos, which can cause lung cancer when inhaled. While it's true that undisturbed, encapsulated asbestos doesn't pose a health risk, the asbestos in vermiculite insulation isn't encapsulated and can easily become airborne during cleaning, maintenance or remodeling. And, the type of asbestos found in vermiculite—called amphibole—is even more hazardous than the chrysotile asbestos that was more commonly used in the U.S.

3. Federal guidelines are weak. The EPA (Environmental Protection Agency) recommends that if you have vermiculite, it's best to assume it contains asbestos and leave it alone. You can have it tested for asbestos, but here's the rub. The EPA defines an asbestos-containing material (ACM) as having greater than 1 percent asbestos. If it's found to contain less than 1 percent asbestos, it's not considered an ACM. That's misleading, as it seems to imply that the product is safe. But, as part of a major class-action lawsuit, a study determined that exposure to vermiculite with less than 1 percent asbestos is still a potential health hazard and the product should be considered an ACM.

4. What to do. Contact an insulation contractor. In Minnesota, where I live, an insulation contractor's first step is having the insulation tested for asbestos. The vast majority of tests come back having less than 1 percent asbestos. That means no asbestos abatement contractors get involved, and removal of the vermiculite insulation is done with essentially a giant vacuum. The risk of airborne particles in this method is high. And according to the Zonolite attic Insulation Trust (see No. 5), the presence of vermiculite is tantamount to the presence of asbestos. For this reason, I recommend having this work done by asbestos abatement professionals regardless of the test results.

5. The good news. The Zonolite Attic Insulation Trust was established in 2014 to help homeowners with the cost of removing Zonolite Attic Insulation from their homes. The trust reimburses homeowners for 55 percent of their removal and reinsulation costs, with a maximum payout per owner of $4,125. So, if you have vermiculite insulation, look into this. In the meantime, leave it alone, even if you had it tested and the test came back "clean." For more information, visit zonoliteatticinsulation.com.

—Reuben Saltzman
Home Inspector

MEET AN EXPERT

Reuben Saltzman has been a home inspector since 1997 and is the president of Structure Tech, a home inspection company in St. Louis Park, MN.

DIY & YOUR **HEARING**

3 Things You Must Know

1. Most power tools do damage

OSHA requires hearing protection for extended exposure to noise at 85 decibels or above, and most power tools, lawn mowers and chain saws are louder than that.

Vickie Tuten, a member of the American Speech-Language-Hearing Association and an audiologist with the U.S. Army, offers a rule of thumb—if someone walked up to you and started talking while you were working, would you have to turn the tool off to hear them? If so, there's a good chance it's hazardous and you should be wearing hearing protection.

2. Plugs and muffs don't work as labeled

How much hearing protection you need depends on two factors—how loud your equipment is and how long you're exposed to the noise. Tuten says both earmuffs and earplugs work as long as you wear them properly. With earmuffs, make sure the temple of your protective goggles (or anything else) doesn't break their seal. And with earplugs, be sure to insert them according to the instructions on the package.

When you purchase earmuffs or earplugs, they'll have a noise reduction rating (NRR) on the package. But you can't simply subtract that number from the decibels you're exposed to. "That's a number derived under lab specifications with an expert fitter," Tuten says. NIOSH (the National Institute for Occupational Safety and Health) recommends that the labeled NRRs (Noise Reduction Ratings) be adjusted for real-world use as follows:

Earmuffs: Subtract 25 percent from the manufacturer's labeled NRR.

Formable earplugs: Subtract 50 percent from the manufacturer's labeled NRR.

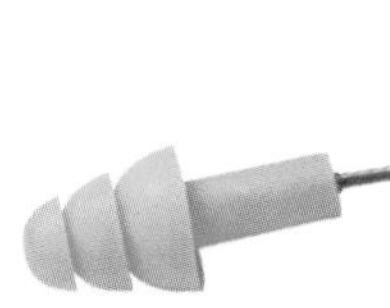

All other earplugs: Subtract 70 percent from the manufacturer's labeled NRR.

To increase your protection, you can wear earplugs and earmuffs together. Results vary depending on the products you choose, but expect four to eight dB of additional protection.

3. Every exposure does some damage

Tuten says a lot of people believe that a one-time exposure to loud noise doesn't matter. "That's a false sense of security," she says. "Damage actually does often occur. It's a cumulative kind of damage." Even if you've already lost some hearing, with protection you can preserve the hearing you have left. "If you can keep the loss at a mild level, that's a win," Tuten says.

Fast Fact

The decibel scale is logarithmic, so, for example, 85 dB is 15 times louder than 70 dB. Many power tools are loud enough to damage your hearing. Here are a few examples from the University of Florida's Hearing Conservation Program:

DECIBEL SCALE

TOOL	DECIBELS	NEEDED NOISE REDUCTION
Chain saw	110	32
Miter saw	109	31
Band saw	104	26
Hedge trimmer	103	25
Pressure washer	100	22
Table saw	93	15
Air compressor	92	14

THE EXPANDING **UNIVERSE OF FOAM**

Expanding foam is magical stuff for sealing gaps and insulating hard-to-reach areas. But it has unexpected uses too—it can protect fragile items and even replace concrete for setting posts. Here's a rundown of various products and what they can do.

By Matthew Knopp

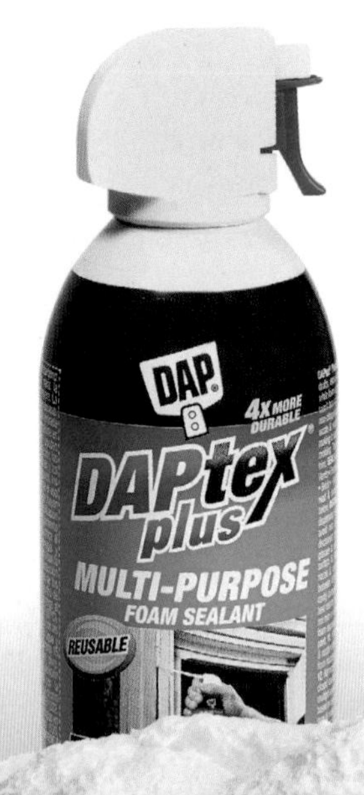

All-purpose
This is the go-to foam for most jobs. Labeled to seal cracks and gaps 1 in. wide or less, it will fill larger gaps if you slow down and waggle the nozzle a bit. Or you can apply the foam in stages after each application cures. It sticks to just about anything and is suitable for interior and exterior use.

Like any other foam, it can be trimmed with a serrated knife after it cures. If it will be exposed to the elements, protect it with a coat of paint. A 16-oz. can of the cream-colored version costs about $4. In black it costs about $8.

Latex
DAPtex Plus is a minimally expanding latex foam that seals, insulates and waterproofs. Unlike polyurethane foams, it cleans up with water, which simplifies the job and lets you reuse the applicator. It doesn't expand as much as polyurethane foams and takes longer to cure, and after curing, it remains flexible. It's for interior and exterior use and costs about $7 for a 12-oz. can.

Large gaps
This formula expands three times as much as conventional all-purpose foam, making it easier to fill gaps wider than 1 in. in a single pass. Monster-size gaps may still require several applications. $6 for a 12-oz. can.

Diy-friendly foam Shown here is the most popular type of foam: single-component (mostly polyurethane) foam that you apply with a straw-type dispenser. These can be messy, but they work well and are easy to use. Just shake the can, insert the straw in the gap and pull the trigger. Several formulas are available, including a latex. It's available in 12- to 26.5-oz. cans.

Fire barrier
Colored bright orange to increase visibility for code inspections, this formula sometimes includes a flame retardant. Otherwise, it performs just like standard foams, sealing gaps where pipes and wires penetrate the structure. In this way, it blocks airflow that can feed flames. $8 for a 16-oz. can.

Windows and doors

You can seal a window or door with all-purpose foam, but it's a little risky. The expansive pressure may push the jamb inward, making the window or door hard to operate. This foam's low-pressure expansion prevents that. Although minimally expansive, it performs just as well as conventional foams in preventing air and moisture leaks. $7 for a 12-oz. can.

Anti-pest

These formulas are designed to keep out mice, birds, insects and other undesirables. Some versions are for interior use only, while others can also be used outside. $7 for a 12-oz. can.

What else can you do with foam?
To see some creative uses for expanding foam, search for "spray foam" at familyhandyman.com.

Landscape and pond

This filler/adhesive bonds to stone blocks, wood and most pond materials, including rocks, but they must be dry when it's applied. It's safe around fish, and because it's black, it's less visible in the gaps between stones. And it stays black even when exposed to sunlight, unlike all-purpose foams that turn rusty orange and become crumbly unless they are painted. Manufacturer-suggested applications include filling gaps in rock walls and plugging holes and cracks in trees. $10 for a 12-oz. can.

Adhesives

All polyurethane foams have adhesive properties, but some are intended to bond materials such as subfloors, drywall or roofing, even in cold weather or when materials are wet. Dispensing adhesive foam from a can is faster than applying adhesive with a caulking gun. It also provides more coverage: One 12-oz. can yields the same as eight 10-oz. tubes of construction adhesive. This adhesive collapses into a sticky gel instead of expanding, and compresses as you bond materials. $20 for a 12-oz. can.

TOUCH 'N SEAL

For larger jobs

In most cases, it takes no more than a few cans of foam to insulate and seal problem areas around a home. For big jobs and specialized projects, consider using the larger "pro" cans. It could save you money in the long run, but be sure to factor in the cost of the gun-type dispenser, which is sold separately. Additionally, the pro-size cans give you access to products not available in cans that use straw-type dispensers.

Single-component cylinders

These kits include a 10- or 16-lb. cylinder of one-component foam, a 10-ft. length of hose and an applicator wand. This single-component, Quick Cure foam from Touch 'n Seal is tack-free in 15 minutes, has an R-value of 4.9 and is certified as residential fire block sealant.

High-yield and reduced-expansion foams are available. Prices range from $100 to $190.

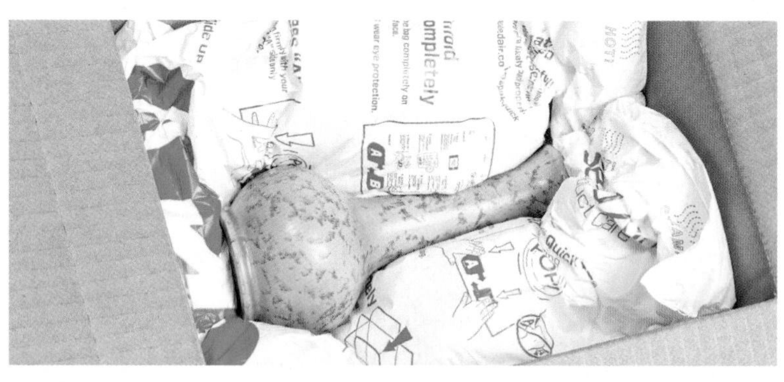

Packaging

Two-component foams can protect fragile objects for shipment and storage. Instapak Foam Packing Kits are bags that you massage to combine the ingredients, activating the foam. After activating, nest the object on the bottom bag, and then activate a second bag to cover the object. The bags come in a variety of sizes. A 15 x 18-in. bag costs $9 online.

SIKA

Posts

It costs more to set posts in foam than in concrete. But if you want to save your back, it's a bargain. You just combine the two components in a bag or bucket and pour the liquid into the hole around the post. The foam sets in minutes and reaches full strength in an hour or two.

Foam might seem like a wimpy substitute for concrete, but we've heard good reports from people who have used it for fence, mailbox and sign posts. It's not for use with structural components like decking posts. A 33-oz. pouch of Sika Fence Post Mix ($20) does the job of two 50-lb. bags of concrete mix. For $80, you can get a Secure Set kit with a gallon of each component, enough to set 10 posts.

Two-component spray foams

Most foams in cans are for filling gaps, while two-component spray foams are mainly for insulating. They come in bags or pouches that need mixing and are commonly applied in attics, crawl spaces and at rim joists. They're also used to dampen sound, set posts, protect fragile items, increase buoyancy and do crafts.

CHESAPEAKE LIGHT BOATS

Flotation and hobby

Like the post-setting foams, these products are mixed in a container and poured into a cavity. Flotation Foam from TotalBoat comes in 2- to 6-lb. densities. The lowest-density product is for adding buoyancy to watercraft and floating docks. The others are for buoys and art projects, such as statues, which require more compressive strength. They cost the same—about $110 gets you a gallon of each component—and yield anywhere from 8 to 30 cu. ft. of foam.

Gun dispensers

The guns screw to the top of cans and let you control the flow of foam better than straw-type dispensers. They also stop the flow of foam quickly at the tip, so it won't ooze out when you let go of the trigger. Because of the sealed tip, gun dispensers keep the foam usable up to 30 days after the first use, as long as the gun stays attached to the can. There are disposable guns, guns for water-based polyurethanes and guns with extended barrels for sealing difficult-to-reach areas. Brand-name guns cost $40 to $100; aftermarket versions cost about half that. Designs differ among the manufacturers, so make sure the gun you buy works with the brand of foam you plan to apply.

Some products sold in the pro format for use with gun dispensers also come packaged in the smaller cans, but others are only available in the pro format. They include adhesives, all-season foams and gasket foams.

Replacement straw nozzles

Even nozzles made for reuse can get clogged. If you don't want to clean them, keep a pack of replacement nozzles on hand (shown at right). A pack of 10 costs $7 online.

Gun cleaners

Cleaning products flush the gun dispenser barrel and remove uncured foam from tools and other surfaces. Available in VOC-free formulas. $8 for a 12-oz. can.

Better dispenser straws!

The Smart Dispenser included with Great Stuff foams makes applying spray foams cleaner and more precise. It functions more like a gun-type dispenser: Pull the yellow tip at the end of the straw to dispense foam. When you're done, push the tip to close the straw, keeping the remaining foam for future use.

Closing the straw at the tip prevents oozing, makes it easier to control the bead size and lets you apply foam from the can up to 30 days after its first use. The nozzle also eliminates the need to invert the can during application. It dispenses however the can is oriented.

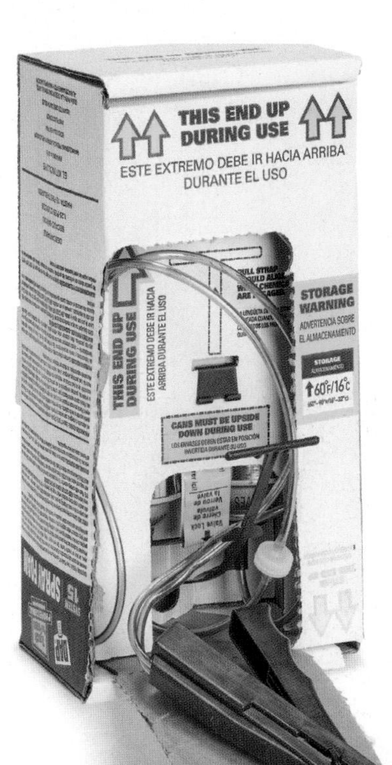

Insulation kit

DAP Touch 'n Foam spray kits cost anywhere from $40 to $800. Before you buy a kit, get a bid from an insulation contractor. For large jobs, hiring a pro might be cheaper than a kit.

SEE IT IN ACTION!
For a video of the gun dispenser and gun cleaner, go to tfhmag.com/expandingfoam

LEAF BLOWERS TO THE **RESCUE!**

They can do many tedious tasks—fast

By Travis Larson

My wife and I live in the middle of a mature hardwood forest, which puts us knee deep in leaves much of the year. In October and April, I spend hours with a commercial-grade backpack blower strapped to my back. But the other 10 months, I depend on my battery-powered blowers—and I'm not kidding. Let me show you what I use them for.

Cleaning shop vacuum filters

I used to hold shop vacuum filters at arm's length and blow them out with my air hose nozzle—ideally when there was a breeze so the dust would blow downwind of me. But I still ended up covered in dust every time I did it. Now I just hold the filter down with my foot and blow it out with the leaf blower. I stay a lot cleaner with this method.

Wood shop

A few times a year, I give my dust-covered shop a blowing-out. First I open the doors and put a couple of box fans in the doorways, blowing air outside. Then I open all the blast gates on the power tools and switch on the dust collector.

I put on my dust mask, safety glasses and hearing protection, and then I go nuts with the leaf blower, starting at the back of the shop and working my way toward the doors. Under and over benches, shelving, air collection ducts and overhead lights—everything gets blasted. The dust that isn't blown outside gets sucked into the dust collector, which I leave running for about 20 minutes after blowing.

Grass-free mower decks
Grass that collects on top of the mower deck gets under the pulleys and wrapped around the drive shafts. Blow it off before it becomes a problem.

Soffit blasting
When you're blasting your soffits to get rid of all the cobwebs, do one more thing. Diligently blow out all the dust from the perforations in your aluminum soffits (or rectangular screens if you have plywood soffits). Dust can block some of the airflow into your attic, and that airflow is important for keeping the attic cooler in summer and for preventing ice dams in winter.

After the rain...
Want to dine alfresco on the deck tonight? Blow the water off the chairs and table so you can enjoy the evening with friends and family without worrying about wet seats.

Electric fire bellows
Need to get that fire started in a hurry? Give it a massive shot of oxygen. Just don't get so close that you melt the plastic nozzle—and be sure to wear safety glasses.

Spot-free car washing
Whether you go to a self-service car wash or swab your car down at home, blow-dry it after rinsing and your car will be spot-free. Start at the roof and work your way down. By the way, if you use car-wash detergent from an auto parts store, you'll get far better results than you would using dishwashing soap or other household cleaners.

Light snow
If my car is covered with light snow, I just blow it off with the leaf blower. I do the same with my deck.

Blowing out the cars
I haul around a lot of construction tools—and therefore debris—in my cars (two long years now without a pickup). So I use my leaf blower to do a big overall cleaning. I blow out the back, the floors, the dash—everything. I even take out the rugs and blow them off. It isn't exactly "detailing" a car, but if you're like me and you'd rather be watching golf, you've got to get creative once in a while.

MEET AN EXPERT

Travis Larson has been an editor at Family Handyman magazine for a couple of decades now. When he's not creating stories for the magazine or producing videos for familyhandyman.com, he's at home doing woodworking projects and playing with his leaf blowers.

GIVING UP GAS

Battery-powered chain saws can handle big jobs

By Michael Springer

MEET AN EXPERT

Michael Springer is a former editor of tool and construction magazines and a longtime tool tester.

PHOTO: EGO BOTTOM: TIM BENKO

I do tree service work as a side job, and back in 2011 I made the switch to battery-powered saws for almost all of that work. After eight years of real-world experience, I can tell you that battery power will handle almost any job you'd need a chain saw for. I rely on compact saws with 12- and 14-in. bars for most of my trimming work, and I turn to larger battery saws with a 16-in. bar. for felling and bucking bigger wood. I still fire up my gas saws occasionally, but only for really big jobs.

Battery-powered saws are much quieter than gas models. That's good for your ears—and your neighbors'.

DEWALT

Brushless is better
A brushless motor is a desirable feature in any power tool because it's more efficient than a traditional motor and typically offers greater power and run-time.

Battery benefits

The advantages of battery power over gas are overwhelming: no mixing and storing of fuel, no using up or emptying the tank before the gas goes bad, no starting problems or annual maintenance. Then there are the noise and exhaust benefits: With a gas saw, you can never get more than an arm's length away from one of the loudest tools ever made. And you can't escape breathing in exhaust at that distance either. In striking contrast, a battery chain saw whirs along more like a blender than a dirt bike, and without any toxic fumes.

TIP: Choosing a saw that can run on batteries you already own will typically save you $50 to $100.

Battery power isn't cheap

Battery chain saws typically cost anywhere from $130 to $550, so a good battery-powered saw might cost you more than a gas saw of similar capacity. But as a clever salesperson first told me years ago, just think of the extra initial cost as paying up front for all the gas and oil you would otherwise need to buy.

Battery included?

When you're shopping—especially online—be sure to check whether a battery and a charger are included. Most saws are available as all-inclusive kits or as "bare tools." But pro-line models usually aren't available in kits with a charger and battery; they only come à la carte.

TIM BENKO

Run-time

Run-time—the work you can get from one battery charge—is the main limitation of battery saws. But it's not a disqualifier. I've tested some battery saws that can make 100 or more cuts through wood 6 to 7 in. in diameter on one charge. That's probably a full day's work for most homeowners. And, of course, you can buy spare batteries, which cost from $30 to $275, depending on the size and brand.

Voltage doesn't mean much

Voltage alone isn't the best indicator of power. Computer chips in brushless motors manage the voltage drawn to optimize a tool's output. This means that there are very powerful saws in every voltage class. The size of the battery pack matters a lot, regardless of the voltage on the label. A larger battery contains more cells, so the tool can draw current from more cells simultaneously.

Look at watt-hours

A watt-hour (WH) is the best measure of a battery pack's energy capacity, regardless of voltage. To get the watt-hour rating, multiply the voltage by the battery's amp-hour (AH) rating. For example, an 18-volt, 4-amp-hour battery has a watt-hour rating of 72. The amp-hour rating indicates the energy density of assembled battery cells within a pack, so it's useful only for comparing batteries of equal voltage.

Use the batteries you already have

If you've already bought into a cordless tool system, you can add a chain saw as a tool-only purchase. Keep in mind, however, that chain saws are power hungry, so the bigger the battery, the better. If you only have compact battery packs with low amp-hour ratings, they might not be enough.

Get a brake

I think all chain saws should have an active chain brake to stop the chain instantly in the event of a kickback and to use as a "parking brake" in between cuts. Some less expensive saws omit this safety feature to cut the cost. It's probably true that small saws that omit brakes aren't likely to overpower you and lack the chain speed to cause a violent kickback, but I still prefer saws with brakes.

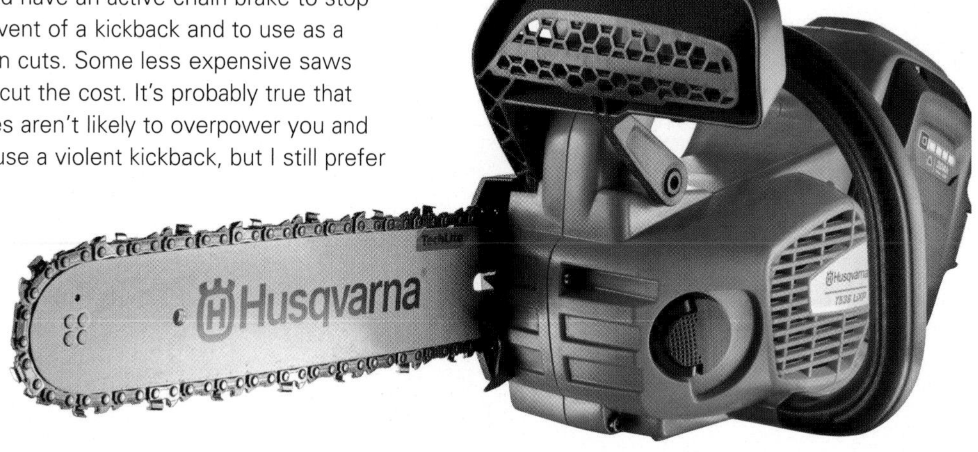

"Top-handle" saws like this one allow for better reach, but most homeowners should stick with a rear-handle model.

Saw shopping?
Michael is constantly field-testing chain saws and has specific recommendations at familyhandyman.com/bestchainsaws.

This Oregon saw even includes a self-sharpener.

Power comparison

I estimate that the mightiest battery- powered saws can do the work of gas saws in the 40 to 50cc range, while good compact models can easily keep up with 25 to 35cc gas saws. No redwood slayers here, but certainly enough muscle for the work I typically do. I never bother with a gas model below 60cc—a battery saw can handle the same jobs without the drawbacks of gas.

Don't forget about corded saws

For much less money than a battery-powered saw kit, you can buy a corded electric saw (some less than $100). Corded models have at least as much power as the largest battery saws, unlimited run-time and the same benefits as battery saws. However, their main drawback is that you're tethered to a power cord. Cutting up firewood in a fixed location in your yard or sectioning up thick wood pieces for projects—inside the shop or out—are great tasks for a corded electric saw. Tending trees at the farthest reaches of your property or pruning in dense, cord-tangling branches—not so great.

Where gas still rules

I can't totally give up gas chain saws. On some jobs, I need to run bars from 20 in. up to 32 in. long. Those require the power of a 70cc or 80cc gas saw. I also need the all-day run-time of a gas saw for clearing jobs where the amount of wood I cut in a day is measured by the trailer load.

Bar length: longer isn't better

Bar length doesn't indicate a chain saw's power. Saws can typically be used with a range of bar lengths as specified by the manufacturer, and a shorter bar on a saw will actually cut faster because there's less friction between the bar and the chain. A longer bar will provide larger cutting capacity, but only if the saw can power it effectively. Bottom line: Don't get a longer bar than you really need. For battery saws, I generally don't use bars longer than 16 in.

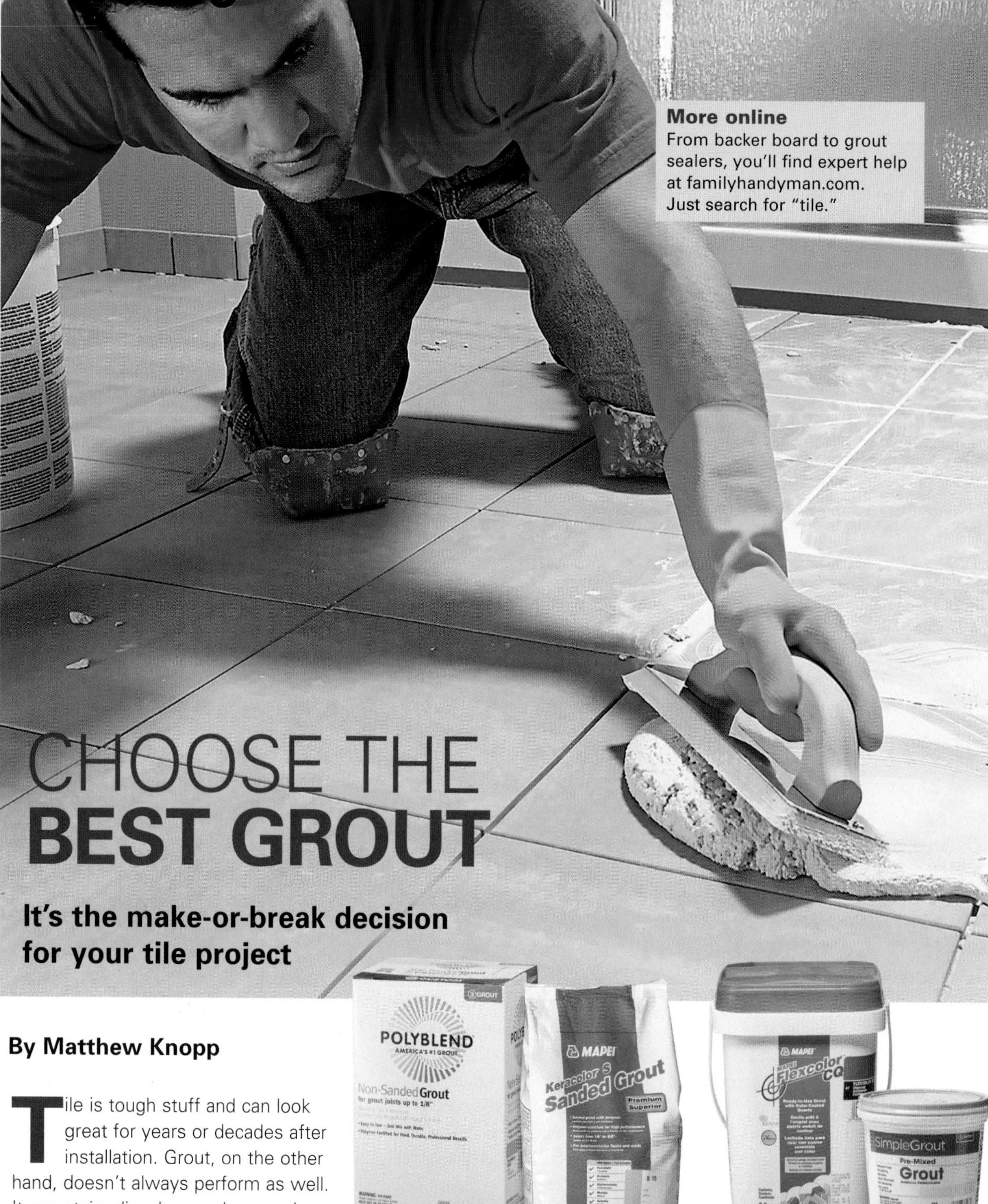

More online
From backer board to grout sealers, you'll find expert help at familyhandyman.com. Just search for "tile."

CHOOSE THE BEST GROUT

It's the make-or-break decision for your tile project

By Matthew Knopp

Tile is tough stuff and can look great for years or decades after installation. Grout, on the other hand, doesn't always perform as well. It can stain, discolor, crack or erode. In the worst cases, it allows water to enter walls or floors, which leads to much bigger problems. Bottom line: Your choice of grout is at least as important as your tile selection.

Home centers carry high-quality grout, but they don't make choosing it easy. Luckily, Dean Sorem, our tile expert, has tried all the options and offers clear recommendations based on decades of experience.

Here's what you'll find at home centers and flooring suppliers:

Standard cement grout

Like concrete or mortar, these grouts begin as a powdery mix that contains Portland cement. Then, when mixed with water, they gradually harden. While some of these products are superior to others, none of them is a bad choice. But you can find much better options that cost just a few bucks more.

Ready-to-use grout

All the formulas in this category let you skip the messy mixing process, and some offer excellent durability and stain resistance. But they can be tricky to use. Some harden very fast; you need to work quickly so they don't harden on the tile before you can wipe them off. And Dean has found that they can stain porcelain tile that has a matte finish.

Best choice: Top-quality cement grout

The three products shown here are superior formulations of traditional cement grout. Dean considers them the best choice for DIY projects and for most of his own jobs. Here's what makes them stand out:

- The particles, or "aggregate," in the powder are much smaller. That makes the grout less porous and more stain resistant. Dean has tried to stain these products and found that every stain—even red wine—disappeared with a little detergent and light scrubbing.
- There's no need to seal the grout. Stain resistance is essentially built in.
- Unlike standard cement grout, there aren't "sanded" and "unsanded" versions. The same product can be used on walls and floors, with narrow and wide grout joints.
- This type of grout achieves better color consistency, with very little blotchiness, even with dark-colored grouts.

Dean has one warning about these grouts: They harden fast—not as quick as epoxy or some of the premixed products, but faster than standard grout. To avoid hardened residue on the tile, mix up smaller batches, have your sponges and water buckets ready to go and don't delay the wipe-off phase of the job.

The cost? Who cares!

The best grout might cost you twice as much as the cheapest option. But after spending all that time, energy and money installing the tile, do you really want to risk the whole project just to save 20 bucks?

What about epoxy?

You may have heard that epoxy is the best grout available—incredibly durable and stain resistant. That's probably true, but Dean doesn't think DIYers should even consider epoxy. It's difficult to use and hardens fast, and any residue that hardens on the face of tile is a nightmare to remove. With other great options available, epoxy just doesn't make sense.

MEET AN EXPERT

Dean Sorem has been installing tile and teaching others how to get the best results for more than 40 years.

HandyHints®

HOLE-SAW DEPTH MARKER

The best way to avoid tear-out with a hole saw is to drill halfway through the wood and flip it over to complete the hole. But how do you know when you've cut halfway? I mark my saw with a line that's slightly more than halfway. With 3/4-in. stock, mark the saw at just past 3/8 in. Use a pencil so you can easily wipe off the line and mark a different depth as needed. This tip also makes it easier to remove the plug; more of it extends past the saw teeth so you can grab it to pull it free.

—Christopher James

BOBBY PIN NAIL HOLDER

When you're hammering small nails or nails in tight quarters, keep your fingers out of the line of fire with a bobby pin. It will grip even the smallest nails.

—Ed Barros

SHOP VACUUM PRESCREEN

I use my shop vacuum for many woodworking chores, including dust collection from every power tool that features a dust port. But the filter quickly plugs with coarse dust from the table saw and finer dust from sanding. I solved part of the problem by placing window screen over the filter. Now the coarse particles are filtered out and stay at the bottom of the tank, and the filter doesn't plug as fast.

—Bill Wells

DOUBLE-DUTY SANDPAPER

For some jobs, a single sheet of sandpaper is too flimsy; the paper backing wears out before the grit. My solution is to glue two pieces back to back with spray adhesive. Sometimes I use two different grits for versatility.

—Brad Holden

Great Goofs®

LAUGHS & LESSONS FROM OUR READERS

I'VE STRUCK OIL!

I moved to a rural area where power outages are common, so I bought a portable generator. When I woke up one morning to find my entire neighborhood without power, I started it up.

Having once ruined a lawn mower because it didn't have enough oil, I wanted to make sure my generator wouldn't suffer the same fate. The ingenious design engineers put the oil compartment at the very bottom of the machine—without a dipstick. The generator was humming along beautifully, but I couldn't stop thinking about the oil. I just had to check it.

Here's what I learned the hard way: Never, ever remove the oil cap while the machine is running. It's amazing how fast and how far oil can shoot out of an engine. I was covered from head to toe with dripping oil. I guess the generator was full of oil after all.

—Grace W. Glowacki

ASHES, ASHES— THEY ALL DRIFT AROUND

When we put our house on the market, one of my jobs was to clean out the fireplace. Armed with my trusty shop vacuum, I went to work sucking up the ashes. Everything was going fine until my wife ran into the room yelling, "Stop!"

I pulled my head out of the firebox to see a huge cloud of ash dust floating across the room. My face turned whiter than the ash as I realized that I'd forgotten to put the filter in the vacuum, and the exhaust vents were blowing the fine particles all over the room. The upside: We were already planning to replace the carpet, and we learned that ash doesn't stick to walls. Now if we can just find a home buyer...

—Eric Nelson

SAFE, BUT SORRY

I decided to buy a floor safe to protect my wife's jewelry. The locksmith wanted $200 to install it in my concrete floor—which was more than the safe cost! To do the job myself, I rented the biggest jackhammer known to humankind and bought some concrete mix for the patchwork. I fired up the jackhammer and it broke through the basement slab just fine. Then it hammered through the main water line, sending water shooting up like a geyser.

The project took some extra time and an emergency visit from my plumber, but you know what? That $200 locksmith would have caused the same disaster!

—Patrick Findley

SPECIAL SECTION

Hacks!

DOG FOOD SCOOP

It's true that the tops of plastic jugs make good funnels. But if you keep the cap on and angle the cut, they also make handy scoops for everything from potting soil to pet food. I used a half-gallon jug for this scoop.

—Ray Dean

DRYER-LINT FIRE STARTER

To build a fire properly, you need to have tinder (easy-lighting material), kindling (finger-size sticks) and fuel (logs). We all have a ready supply of tinder: dryer lint. To make fire starters, I stuff empty toilet paper tubes with dryer lint. My lint "logs" light quickly and burn long enough to ignite the kindling. And I don't have to resort to lighter fluid!

—Ryan Franza

INSTANT HARDWARE PATINA

I've found that gun bluing ($10 for 3 oz. at sporting goods stores) gives off-the-shelf hardware an attractive, aged patina. Simply dip nuts, bolts, washers or other hardware into a cup of gun bluing. When the hardware turns black, rinse it with water and dry it with a paper towel. Be sure to wear rubber gloves and eye protection.

—Brad Holden
Associate Editor

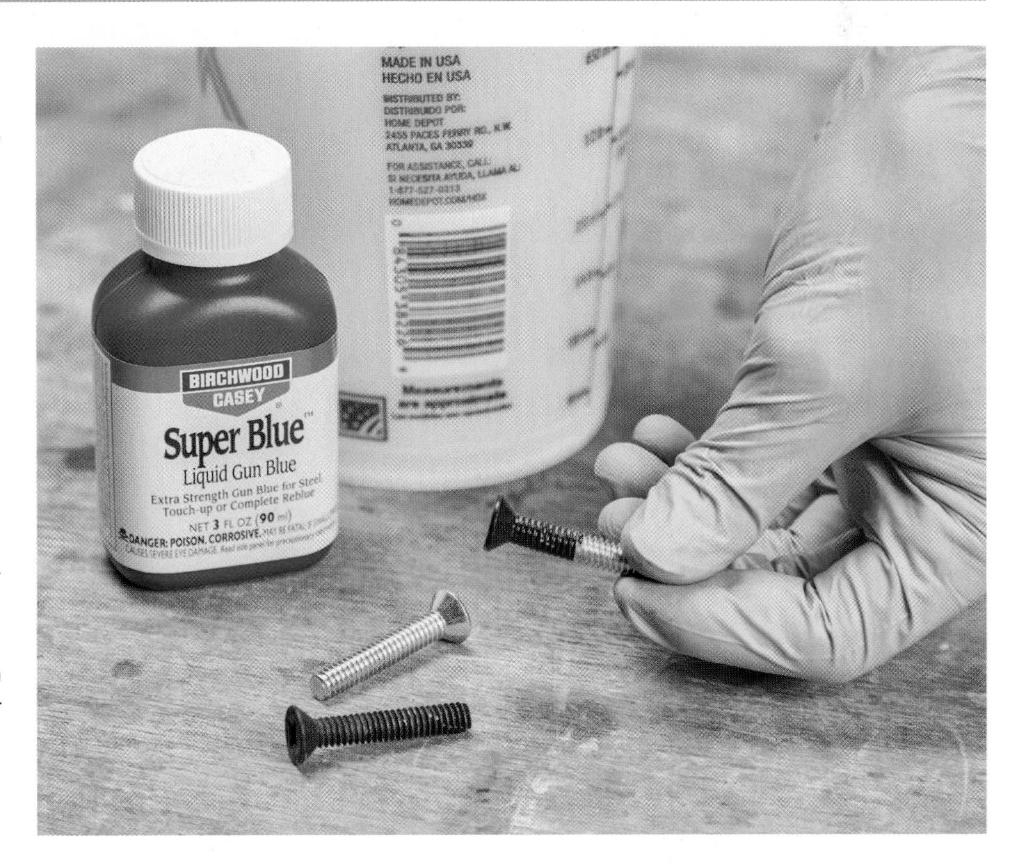

Hacks!

SAFE BLADE DISPOSAL

While removing a bunch of old caulking on my boat, I burned through a lot of utility knife blades. To safely dispose of the used blades, I put them in a soda can and pushed the pop top back over the opening to contain them.

—Justin Zack

KITCHEN TRAY IN THE BATHROOM

A silverware drawer insert works just as well in the bathroom as it does in the kitchen. The various compartments are perfect for organizing toothbrushes, toothpaste, razors, clippers, lip balm and more.

—Carrie Breinik

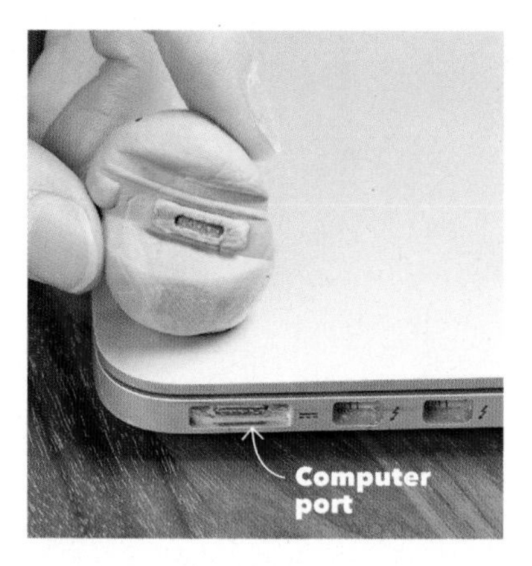

POSTER-PUTTY PORT CLEANER

I use my computer a lot in my shop. Once, the magnetic charging port collected a bunch of metal filings. I tried blowing out the filings with compressed air, but that didn't work; the magnet wouldn't let go of them. What finally did the trick was a ball of poster putty. It removes debris without leaving any residue.

—Travis Larson
Senior Editor

WINE CORK FIRE STARTERS

Fill a mason jar with wine corks and rubbing alcohol and let the corks soak. The corks will burn fairly well in a few days, but for the best results, soak them for a week. Be sure the corks are natural, not synthetic.

—Laurie Aamoth

BOTTLE GNAT TRAP

Want to get rid of gnats or fruit flies? Wash a soda bottle, cut off the top and make a line at about the one-third mark. Dissolve 3 tablespoons of sugar in 1/4 cup of vinegar, pour it in and add water up to the line. Set the top upside down in the bottle. The pests can easily get in, but it's hard for them to get out. Place the trap wherever the bugs gather.

—Kelly Dahlin

GREAT GROUT HAZE CLEANER

When I tile a backsplash or floor, I like to use a scrap of carpet to clean off the grout haze and buff the tiles to a shine in one easy step. The carpet fibers are slightly more abrasive than a sponge or cotton rag but not abrasive enough to scratch the tiles. They just remove the grout haze quickly with minimal elbow grease. If you don't have a clean carpet scrap handy, check at a home center—most have small samples available for free.

—Matthew Farmer

COFFEE-CAN SALT SHAKER

I buy ice-melt compound in 20-lb. bags, which aren't handy for dispensing. So I pour the granules into an empty coffee can and punch holes in the lid.

—Mike Magnussen

Hacks!

DON'T FILL THE RIM

Pouring paint from a can always results in paint in the rim. When you tap the lid back on, paint splatters everywhere. To prevent this, just put a strip of painter's tape across the rim of the can before you pour.

—Richard Monda

FLOWER-POT FILLER

Water settling at the bottom of pots can lead to root rot from poor aeration. To combat this, toss a few old sponges in the bottom of the pot. The sponges retain moisture and create necessary air space. They also help prevent water from running out the bottom.

—Angie White

HANDY BROOM CLEANER

Every time you sweep, clumps of dust and hair collect at the ends of the broom bristles. To get rid of them neatly, hot-glue a wide-tooth comb to the top of the dustpan. Just run the bristles through it to remove the debris.

—Jaren Lemanczik

FEWER FINGERPRINTS

The next time you clean your stainless-steel kitchen appliances, follow up with a coat of car wax. It not only makes wiping off grime after cooking easier but also inhibits fingerprints. Simply apply a light coat of wax, let it dry and buff with a soft cloth. Apply wax only to the area around the controls, not the cooking surface.

—Carol Lloyd

TOILET BRUSH FRESHENER

To keep your toilet brush as fresh as possible, put a splash of pine-scented cleaner in the bottom of the brush holder. This will disinfect the brush and keep your bathroom smelling clean.

—Bri Aitchison

Hacks!

CARDBOARD DROP CLOTH

Most of our cardboard boxes end up in our recycling bin, but I always make sure to save a couple of the larger ones. They're perfect for keeping my clothes clean when I crawl under the car. Stored flat, they don't take up much room.

—Mike McNamara

FASTER FILING WITH LESS CLOGGING

When you use metal files on soft, nonferrous metals such as aluminum or brass, the teeth clog quickly. This means frequent cleaning with a file card. To keep the teeth from getting clogged, try this old trick: Rub a piece of chalk along the teeth before using the file on the workpiece.

—Connor Wright

POWER SCRUBBER

You can buy scrub brushes for your drill, but I decided to make my own rather than spend $15. Once you gather the materials—which you may already have—it takes about five minutes. You'll need a 4-in. carriage bolt, a washer, a nut and a scrub brush.

Start by cutting the handle off your brush. Drill a hole through the brush and slide the carriage bolt through. Slip on the washer, thread on the nut and you're set. Chuck the carriage bolt into your drill and clean with power!

—Tom Heaphy

FISHING ROD SAVER

When I go on fishing trips, I'm notorious for being careless with my rods, just tossing them into the truck bed. But lately I've started covering my rods with pool noodles to avoid breakage. I cut a slot down the length of the noodle and slip it over the rod. No more damaged or broken rods, thanks to a $2 pool noodle.

—Tim Wurmlinger

CORRAL THOSE CONTAINER LIDS

To keep storage container lids organized, pop a tension rod into a drawer and stand them up along the side.

—Terri Schultz

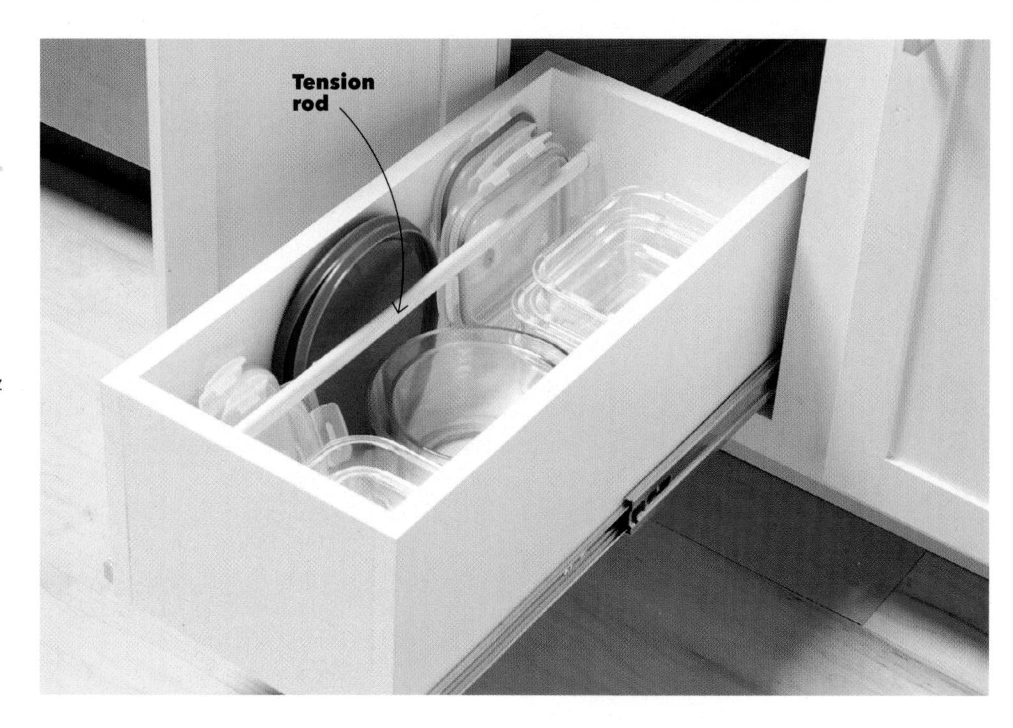

INDEX

Visit ***familyhandyman.com*** *for hundreds of home improvement articles.*

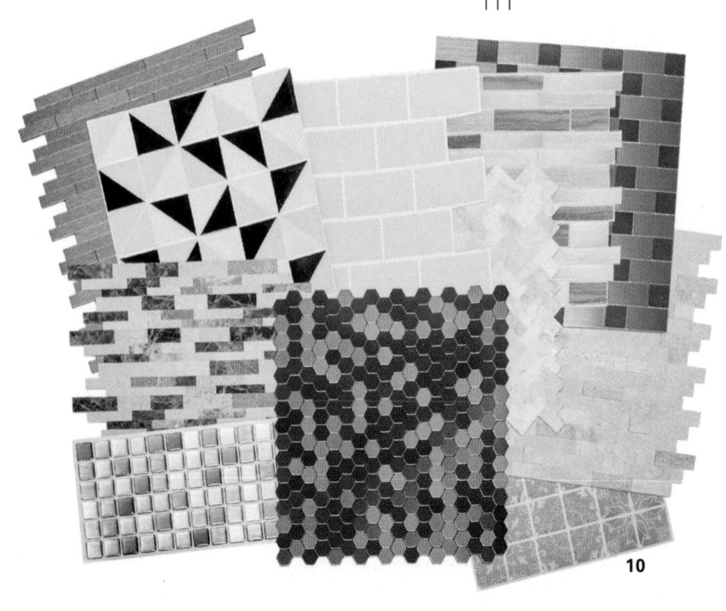
10

213

261

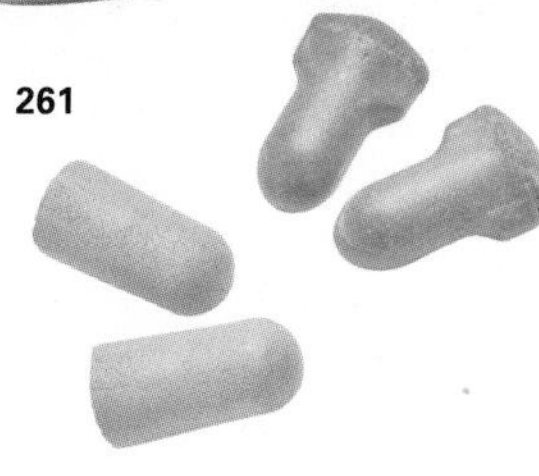

155

E

F

G

H

I

J

K

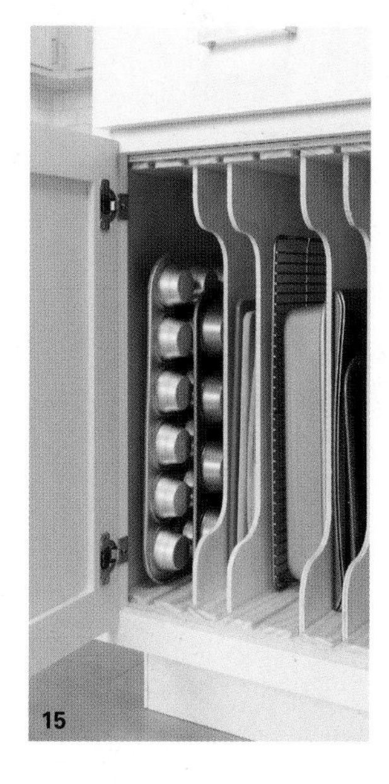

15

L

59

M

O

P

R

169

S

T

U

V

W

Z

ACKNOWLEDGMENTS

FAMILY HANDYMAN

Chief Content Officer	Nick Grzechowiak
Editor-in-Chief	Gary Wentz
Assigning Editor	Berit Thorkelson
Associate Assigning Editor	Mary Flanagan
Associate and Contributing Editors	Bill Bergmann
	Mike Berner
	Jay Cork
	Brad Holden
	Jason Ingolfsland
	Rick Muscoplat
Associate Creative Director	Vern Johnson
Senior Designer	Marcia Roepke
Junior Art DIrectors	Mariah Cates
	Jenny Mahoney
Graphic Designer	Andrea Sorensen
Photographer	Tom Fenenga
Managing Editor	Donna Bierbach
Production Artist	Mary Schwender
Lead Carpenter	Josh Risberg
Editorial Services Associate	Peggy McDermott
Production Manager	Leslie Kogan

ILLUSTRATORS

Steve Björkman
Matt Boley
Jeff Gorton
Brad Holden
Frank Rohrbach III

OTHER CONSULTANTS

Al Hildenbrand, electrical
Rune Eriksen, electrical
Tim Johnson, electrical
John Williamson, electrical
Les Zell, plumbing

For information about advertising in *Family Handyman* magazine, call (646) 518-4215

To subscribe to *Family Handyman* magazine:

- By Internet: familyhandyman.com/customercare
- By email: customercare@familyhandyman.com
- By mail: The Family Handyman
  Customer Care
  P.O. Box 6099
  Harlan, IA 51593-1599

We welcome your ideas and opinions.
Write: The Editor, Family Handyman
2915 Commers Drive, Suite 700
Eagan, MN 55121
Fax: (651) 994-2250
E-mail: feedback@familyhandyman.com